BUILDING UP AND TEARING DOWN
REFLECTIONS ON THE AGE OF ARCHITECTURE

BUILDING UP AND TEARING DOWN
REFLECTIONS ON THE AGE OF ARCHITECTURE

PAUL GOLDBERGER

The Monacelli Press

All of the essays in this book were originally published in *The New Yorker*,
with the exception of "New York Becomes Like America," "Glass Is the New
White Brick," and "Disconnected Urbanism," which originally appeared
in *Metropolis*, and "The Sameness of Things," which originally appeared in
The New York Times.

Library of Congress Cataloging-in-Publication Data
Goldberger, Paul.
Building up and tearing down : reflections on the age of architecture /
Paul Goldberger.
p. cm.
Articles originally published 1997–2009 in the New Yorker, the New York
Times, and Metropolis magazine.
Includes index.
ISBN 978-1-58093-264-6
1. Architecture. I. Title.
NA27.G58   2009
720—dc22
2009028451

Printed in the United States of America

www.monacellipress.com

10 9 8 7 6 5 4 3 2 1
First edition

Designed by Pentagram Design

Cover: © Richard Cummins/CORBIS
Page 2: Courtesy Robert Polidori

CONTENTS

Introduction 8

Buildings that Matter
Good Vibrations 16
High-Tech Bibliophilia 20
Unconventional 24
Seductive Skins 28
Spiraling Upward 33
Situation Terminal 38
Out of the Blocks 42

Places and People
Bringing Back Havana 50
Casino Royale 60
Forbidden Cities 64
Many Mansions 69
The Eames Team 75
House Proud 84
Eminent Dominion 91
Toddlin' Town 97

New York
A Helluva Town 104
Dior's New House 111
Busy Buildings 116
High-Tech Emporiums 122
Miami Vice 127
West Side Fixer-Upper 132

Center Stage 140
The Incredible Hulk 144
Triangulation 148
Home 152
Towers of Babble 156
Gehry-Rigged 160
New York Becomes Like America 164
A New Beginning 170

Present and Past
Shanghai Surprise 178
Why Washington Slept Here 182
Athens on the Interstate 188
A Royal Defeat 193
Down at the Mall 202
Requiem 207

Museums
The Politics of Building 214
The People's Getty 219
When in Rome 223
Beaubourg Grows Up 227
The Supreme Court 232
Art Houses 237
A Delicate Balance 242
Artistic License 246
Outside the Box 251
Molto Piano 256
Mile High 260
Lenses on the Lawn 264
Bowery Dreams 268
Hello Columbus 272

Ways of Living
A Touch of Crass 278
Past Perfect 283
Glass Is the New White Brick 287
Some Assembly Required 291
Homes of the Stars 296
Green Monster 301
Disconnected Urbanism 305
The Sameness of Things 308

Index 314

To the memory of my father,
who taught me the value
of a few well-chosen words,
and to Adam, Ben, and Alex,
who learned his lessons, too

INTRODUCTION

Architecture always connects to something; it is never a thing unto itself. That is one reason it is such a good subject for *The New Yorker,* where almost all of these essays were originally published. *The New Yorker* is a magazine that tends to look at most things, including the arts, in terms of their relationship to the wider world and, hence, their potential to make an engaging narrative. Architecture is politics, it is sociology, it is money; it is housing and cities and old buildings both crumbling and revived. Maybe more to the point, architecture is created out of a curious mix of good intentions and hubris. Perhaps that can be said of all kinds of art, but no other art makes the claims of social responsibility that architecture does, and no other art has the arrogance to think it will remake the world. An architect can sometimes be like an emperor, commanding vast resources to carry out what are often, when you get right down to it, just a designer's dreams. But he or she is more likely to be a struggling artist, grateful for the chance to redo someone's kitchen, or a functionary stationed at a computer, producing designs for a doorknob in a skyscraper.

Buildings do not just happen: they are the products of a peculiar combination of artistic vision, money, political wherewithal, and engineering skill. To the extent to which it is possible to take note of the process by which buildings happen, I do, not to excuse the results—no critic should ever do that—but to place the building within a context that enhances its meaning. You understand Palladio a lot better if you know that the villas he designed around Vicenza in the sixteenth century were not just expressions of classical grandeur but attempts to enhance the image of his aristocratic clients, whose houses were as often as not working farms. You understand Herzog and de Meuron's "Bird's Nest" stadium and Norman Foster's airport, both in Beijing, better if you see them as having been made possible by the mix of high aesthetic ambition and cheap mass labor that existed in China in the years leading up to the 2008 Olympics, and that may never come again. While you do not absolutely need to know that the Basques, in northern Spain, were eager to remake the old, industrial city of Bilbao when they turned to Frank Gehry and the Guggenheim Museum to give them a new symbol of their region—and that they wanted the building both to stand out and to reflect the city—you will surely understand Gehry's remarkable building better if you know something of its origins.

I say this not to diminish the aesthetics of architecture or to deny that, when we strip away the layers of real-estate finance and zoning and construction and politics, and get beyond the arguments about what kind of environment is best for educating people, or healing people, or housing people, we are left with the reality that a building is an object. That is what buildings are: physical objects with walls, floors, ceilings, roofs, doors, and windows, which look a particular way and function a particular way. Evaluating how a building looks and how it works as a physical object will always be the core of the architecture critic's obligation. My point is only to say that if the critic's responsibility begins with considering the building as an object, it doesn't end there.

Matthew Arnold defined criticism as "a disinterested endeavor to learn and propagate the best that is known and thought in the world"; implicit within that is the obligation to share your judgments as well as your enthusiasms. Both judgment and enthusiasm are ways of expressing love, and a critic who does not love his field cannot last long in it. To love the thing—whether we call it architecture, design, planning, whatever—and also to love what it means in other people's lives, and not only your own, is, I think it is fair to say, a further prerequisite to functioning well as a journalistic critic. This is not inconsistent with exercising judgment; judgment and education go hand in hand and are parts of a critic's role as a kind of interpreter, to communicate his love of things and, in so doing, instill love in others.

Now, I realize that all of this can sound more than a little touchy-feely and distant from the notion that the point of this realm of journalism ought to be to expose the wretchedness of 99 percent of what gets built in the United States, not to mention elsewhere in the world; or to reveal the rampant inequities in redevelopment schemes, or the horrendous lack of a housing policy in this country, or the failure of planners to create a viable public realm in cities today. Well, yes, and the critic who is only an enthusiast risks being seen, like Browning's duchess, as "too soon made glad, too easily impressed." As I look back at what I have done in *The New Yorker*, I think several of the negative pieces I've written—such as the one on the Westin Hotel in Times Square by Arquitectonica (on which the editors plunked the headline "Is This the Ugliest Building in New York?"), or the Astor Place condominium by Gwathmey Siegel, or the Prada store in Soho by Rem Koolhaas (which I compared unfavorably to the Toys 'R' Us store in Times Square)—have had at least as much impact as the positive pieces. Because *The New Yorker* does not as a matter of policy try to cover everything—because the magazine is selective, for reasons of both limited space and editorial judgment—the decision to write a negative piece has a special weight. There has to be something important enough to say to justify giving a building some of the few precious column inches the magazine allocates to architecture. After all, we can always simply ignore a building—we ignore most of them anyway.

But it is important that criticism not follow what we might call the Kindly Grandmother's Rule—in other words, if you don't have something nice to say, don't say anything at all. At *The New Yorker,* because we are so limited in what we write about, I am always a little worried that people may think we are operating on this rule of criticism since there are so many buildings we never discuss at all. Often we pass on them merely because they do not present significant issues that can inspire an interesting and provocative short essay, not because I don't like them and don't want to say anything negative. Then again, sometimes I pass on a building that I don't like because there isn't anything negative to say that feels enlightening enough, or meaningful enough.

In 2005, I wrote about a high-profile condominium building by the architect Charles Gwathmey not to be critical of Gwathmey, an architect I very much admired, but to make a point about the way in which real-estate developers during the condo boom managed to conscript some of our most gifted architects into the process of marketing and in so doing led many of them to compromise their work. All architecture involves some degree of compromise with the demands of the real world; if it didn't, it would be art, not architecture. But sometimes there is such a thing as too much compromise, and it is one of the critic's jobs to say so. The Westin Hotel piece was written to inquire into what constitutes vulgarity today, but underlying it was the same point, which is to take note of a situation in which commercial demands become so extreme that serious design intentions are all but invisible.

A key difference between an architect and a critic, or a theoretician and a critic, is that in both cases the former has a right, even an obligation, to proceed from a theoretical viewpoint, while no such obligation exists for a critic. Indeed, the opposite is true—a critic should not believe that there is just one right way to do things. The belief that there is only a single solution to a problem can strengthen the work of the architect, and enable the thinking of the theorist. You do not want an architect who sees too many ways to go, who does not feel a passionate drive toward one of them. But that worldview weakens the work of the critic, who needs to proceed from a pluralist position, at least nominally; if not, he forfeits his ability to interpret, explain, and judge the work that is before him.

But a critic has to stand for something, obviously. He cannot proceed from the view that anything is acceptable so long as it is well done. So how do you combine an absence of rigid ideology with some guiding principles that are necessary for criticism? The answer, I think, lies in the difference between what we might call social or moral or ethical issues and aesthetic ones, between issues of social and political responsibility and those of aesthetic choice. A critic can and should establish a set of social and political principles that define his judgment and act as a foundation for his criticism. The challenge is to hold onto these principles and at the same time to remain open to a broader range of aesthetic responses to these principles than any one architect might have, and then to be able to judge these different aesthetic responses on their own terms. To say it one more time: I believe architecture exists in a social and political context and almost always needs to be judged within that context.

For a long time critics yearned for an age when people paid attention to architecture, when society cared about it. Beware of what you wish for, as they say, for we have now gotten that wish, and it is a mixed bag. If we once expected too little of architecture, I fear that today we may expect too much of it. Architecture does not cure cancer, and it does not put bread on the table. It is not justice in the courtroom, or peace on the battlefield. If there is anything the critic needs to be mindful of today, it is that architecture does not solve all of our problems. It does not sustain life. But it can make the already sustained life much more meaningful, much more pleasurable, and it is the critic's job, in a way, to observe and encourage and support that process.

I have had the privilege of writing the "Sky Line" column for *The New Yorker*—created by Donald Chappell, writing as T-Square, in the 1920s, and continued by Lewis Mumford and Brendan Gill—since 1997, when I left the *New York Times*. For years I had said, half in jest, that the only place that would ever tempt me away from the *Times* was *The New Yorker*, but when Tina Brown invited me to join the magazine, I had a moment of pause. Was I really prepared to move on from the place where I had spent my entire career? I said yes, of course, in part because I so admired the magazine, in part because Tina is nothing if not persuasive, and in part because I decided it was time to figure out whether anyone would return my calls if the message didn't have "from the *New York Times*" at the end of it.

Now, looking back on more than a decade of writing for the magazine, it is hard to imagine being anywhere else. When I joined *The New Yorker*, Tina Brown's reinvention of the magazine was already in its fifth year, and it was clear that reinvigorating its cultural coverage was a high priority. Tina was eager for the kinds of stories that other publications were not doing, and soon I was flying to Havana to write on the plight of the city and its historic architecture, or to London to write about the war on modern architecture launched by Prince Charles, which, for all the royal prestige and publicity he brought to it, had all but collapsed in failure. I felt energized, just like the magazine. Although Tina remained at the magazine for only a year after my arrival, my debt to her for bringing me to *The New Yorker* is ongoing.

My debt to David Remnick, the current editor, is at least as great, and is in every way more ongoing. David has presided over what has to be called a golden age for the magazine, and I am grateful to him not merely for allowing me to be a part of it but for affirming that architecture as a subject is a vital part of the continuing dialogue about politics and culture that the magazine conducts with its readers. I know that, in David's view, the distinguished legacy of architecture criticism that *The New Yorker* has in the extraordinary work of Lewis Mumford is not in itself enough to justify devoting precious space to this subject. Architecture criticism needs to add some meaning to the life of this moment.

There are many others who work alongside David who provide critical support to me and to so many other writers. First among them are the remarkable editors who deal directly with writers: my current editor, Leo Carey, and before him Daniel Zalewski, Sharon DeLano, and Susan Morrison. Dorothy Wickenden, Henry Finder, Pam McCarthy, Ann Goldstein, Elisabeth Biondi, and Peter Canby are not only valued colleagues but also essential parts of the process of creating pieces that are right for *The New Yorker*. So, too, are the relentless fact checkers whose rigor benefits us all. Rhonda Sherman, Bruce Diones, Kilian Schalk, Tanya Erlach, Perri Dorset, Alexa Cassanos, Risa Leibowitz, Jillian Kosminoff, and Stanley Ledbetter have provided other kinds of essential help. In the magazine's Critics section, Alex Ross, Peter Schjeldahl, Nancy Franklin, Hilton Als, John Lahr, David Denby, Anthony Lane, Sasha Frere-Jones, and Joan Acocella provide through their regular columns what amounts to an ongoing seminar in the art of critical writing, and if readers learn from them, so do colleagues, and I express deep appreciation to all of them.

Natalie Matutschovsky has handled photo research with intelligence, grace, and her usual fine eye. When it comes to the photographs, however, I owe a special debt to Robert Polidori, whom I met in 1997 when we traveled together to Havana, and who to my great fortune has been assigned to photograph many of my pieces ever since. An architecture critic cannot ask for a more talented photographer, or one more sympathetic to the issues I hope to illuminate through these pieces. I am deeply grateful to Robert for his extraordinary generosity in making so many of the images he took originally for *The New Yorker* available for reproduction in this book.

It bears mentioning that I have not included in this book the long pieces I wrote in *The New Yorker* about the rebuilding process in Lower Manhattan following the terrorist attacks on the World Trade Center, since they formed the basis of an earlier book, *Up From Zero,* published in 2004. (A later piece on Ground Zero, from 2005, is included here.) A handful of the pieces in this book—three, to be exact—come from *Metropolis* magazine, where I once wrote a column on design called Object Lessons. Martin Pedersen, the magazine's executive editor, helped to make these pieces and so many others possible, and I am grateful to Martin for his knowledge, his ideas, and his commitment to writers. The final piece in this book, "The Sameness of Things," comes from the *New York Times*. It is among the last things I wrote for the paper, in 1997, and its message—that the good news that quality design has become a part of the common culture also has a downside—is as relevant today as it was then.

I have had the pleasure of working with Gianfranco Monacelli, founder of The Monacelli Press, on a wide range of projects over many years. It is he who first proposed collecting my work into this book, and I am grateful to him not only for initiating this project but also for assuring that his gifted lieutenant, the brilliant Andrea Monfried, serve as its editor. Elizabeth White and Rebecca McNamara at The Monacelli Press have also played essential roles in bringing this book to publication. A critical decision early in this project was the Press's invitation to Michael Bierut of Pentagram, one of the most distinguished graphic designers of our time, to design this book. It is a privilege to have a book designed by Michael and his colleague, Yve Ludwig.

Every writer owes a debt to his readers, both the real ones who comment on what he writes and the imaginary ones whose reactions are always somewhere in his head as he is trying to turn his ideas into words. First among my real readers are my wife, Susan Solomon; my sons, Adam Hirsh, Ben Goldberger, and Alex Goldberger; and my daughter-in-law, Delphine Hirsh. Each of them has been an astute reader who has helped me more times than I can count.

The title of this book, *Building Up and Tearing Down*, comes from a talk I gave a few years ago that was something of a memoir of life as an architecture critic. It seemed particularly appropriate to use it here—journalists are the original recyclers—since the essays in this book, collectively, are also a review of a career. But the title alludes as well to an oft-quoted comment made by that greatest of all amateur architects, Thomas Jefferson, who described his love of tinkering with architecture by explaining how he liked to pass his time at Monticello: "Putting up and tearing down," Jefferson said, "is my chief occupation."

And so, I suppose, is it mine.

Paul Goldberger
New York, July 2009

BUILDINGS THAT MATTER

Frank Gehry, Walt Disney Concert Hall, Los Angeles

GOOD VIBRATIONS

Frank Gehry is one of the most famous architects in the world, and the Walt Disney Concert Hall is the most important thing he has built in his home city of Los Angeles—or anywhere else in the United States, for that matter—so of course people are complaining about it. It looks like Gehry's other buildings. It's too showy.

It doesn't contribute enough to the downtown L.A. environment and doesn't justify the $274 million (much of it from private funds) that it cost. These are inevitable, although probably not very significant, views. The building, which opens on October 23 with a concert by the Los Angeles Philharmonic, has already received the kind of adulatory advance press usually reserved for blockbuster movies. In early September, however, a reporter for the *Los Angeles Times*, Scott Timberg, observed—in a piece that consisted of negative comments about the building—that "a distinct rumble of Disney Hall disenchantment has become audible." A few days later, another writer in the *Times* remarked that the hall looked like "half-torn-up cardboard boxes left out in the rain, spray-painted silver."

There are those who will never respond to Gehry's work—who feel that his intensely romantic, emotional forms are self-indulgent—and those people are missing an architectural experience of immense power and subtlety. There are also people who admire Gehry's Guggenheim Museum in Bilbao, with its swirling mass of titanium cladding, but who think that the Disney building looks too much like Bilbao's second cousin, and like Gehry's performing-arts center at Bard College, and his new business school in Cleveland. These are superficial comparisons. The facade of Disney Hall is more refined than that of the Guggenheim, and more sumptuous, even though it is made of stainless steel, a cheaper material than titanium. Gehry has not repeated himself here so much as he has expanded his architectural vocabulary. Most of Gehry's recent buildings have swooping metal forms, but their shapes are different, their proportions are different, and their relationship to their surroundings is different. Disney and Bilbao are no more similar than buildings designed a few years apart by Mies van der Rohe or Le Corbusier.

It is ironic that Gehry is being criticized for not producing a building that will transform a dreary, lifeless downtown area, since that is what he did more successfully than any other living architect when he designed the Guggenheim in Bilbao. (The phenomenon is even referred to generally as "the Bilbao effect.") He made the first truly popular piece of avant-garde architecture in our time, and suddenly everybody else wanted one, including his own city, where he had not received a major commission until 1988, when he won a competition to design the new hall for the Los Angeles Philharmonic. Construction began a few years later but was stalled because of fund-raising problems and issues of design control, and the project ground to a halt in 1994. When the museum in Bilbao opened, in 1997, and Gehry became a household word, the largely unbuilt concert hall (it hadn't got past the foundation and the underground garage) became a major source of embarrassment: Gehry, who is now seventy-four, had lived in Los Angeles since the 1940s, and the city still couldn't get a big Gehry project going. Several civic leaders joined together to resuscitate the building, Gehry updated his designs, and construction resumed in 1999.

Downtown Los Angeles has only a handful of singular pieces of architecture—Bertram Grosvenor Goodhue's Central Library of 1926, Arata Isozaki's Museum of Contemporary Art of 1986, and Rafael Moneo's Cathedral of Our Lady of the

Angels, finished last year—and Disney Hall is now surely the most distinguished building in the area. It is, indeed, monumental, but it isn't fair to say that it doesn't respond to its urban context, which is, more or less, like the downtowns of many other major American cities—a lot of glass skyscrapers surrounded by a lot of freeways. Disney Hall is set on Grand Avenue, a boulevard almost as wide as a freeway, and the site has a steep grade, making it even more unfriendly to pedestrians. Still, the building has a large public garden, and the gracious, flowing staircase at the formal entrance on the corner of Grand Avenue and First Street is far more inviting than any entry to the tired old Dorothy Chandler Pavilion—the Philharmonic's former home—across the street. Gehry has placed the exhilarating stainless-steel sails that define the exterior atop a limestone base, but on the Grand Avenue facade, the limestone disappears in favor of hinged glass panels that will open the building up to the street before concerts.

The outside of Disney Hall lifts the spirits of those who see it from the sidewalk or, this being Los Angeles, from the windows of their cars, and the inside is equally inspiring. The auditorium is the finest interior Gehry has ever made. It is constructed of warm Douglas fir and is relatively intimate, with only about twenty-two hundred seats, spread over terraces, balconies, and mezzanines on all sides of the stage. The hall is set within a two-layered plaster box that forms an acoustical shell and soundproofing. Gehry developed its shape with Yasuhisa Toyota, a partner in Nagata Acoustics of Tokyo, who was also his partner at Bard. The focal point, above the stage, is an enormous pipe organ whose wooden pipe enclosures create a sculpture that looks like a stack of lumber that has just exploded. The ceiling seems to be made of fabric rather than of wood, a gargantuan version of the canopy on a four-poster bed. It billows over the hall. The curved wooden walls do not meet the ceiling, and in the space between them, one can glimpse white plaster walls behind the wooden forms, washed with light from hidden skylights. The hall appears to float in the larger space.

The shape of the hall and its warm, rich wood suggest a musical instrument, although I doubt that Gehry thinks in such literal terms. He is an expressionist—a romantic expressionist—who has always designed by instinct (even though he could not produce his astonishingly complex buildings without the aid of the most sophisticated computer software, a program called CATIA, used for the construction of aircraft), and what he did here was create a space that is not only acoustically suitable for listening to music but emotionally right for it.

Gehry has, clearly, studied the Berlin Philharmonic Hall, which was designed in the 1950s by the German Expressionist architect Hans Scharoun. Scharoun created the first modern symphony hall in the round, an asymmetrical space with dozens of jutting terraces. It is an exciting place in which to hear an orchestra—and, until now, the only convincing new model for a concert hall—but it appears almost crude in comparison to Disney Hall. One of the best things about Scharoun's building, besides its intense, kinetic energy, is how democratic it is, and Gehry has picked up on this. There are no fancy boxes in the Disney auditorium. I moved around from the front of the orchestra to the side terraces, the mezzanines, and the balconies while listening to a rehearsal of a Mahler symphony, and I could not decide where I would rather sit. There is no obvious hierarchy, and, indeed, the upper-level seats offer a benefit that the seats closest to the musicians do not—the special pleasure of being able to take in the whole of Gehry's space.

The hall was endowed with a $50 million gift from Lillian Disney, Walt Disney's widow. Mrs. Disney, who died in 1997, was not, initially, much of a fan of Gehry's architecture, but she was an unusual philanthropist. She didn't insist that her checkbook buy her veto power, although she did tell Gehry that she loved gardens, and he designed the bright carpet and the fabric on the seats in the hall in an intense, abstract version of a floral pattern in tribute to her. Mrs. Disney collected Delft china, and Gehry also designed a witty fountain for the outdoor plaza, a mosaic of pieces of smashed Delft.

Culture can be a potent redevelopment tool. We saw that long ago at Lincoln Center, and it is why great hopes have been placed on the role of cultural facilities at Ground Zero. But the Los Angeles Music Center has sat across the street from the site of Disney Hall for nearly forty years with almost no noticeable effect on the nearby area. It may be that restaurants, stores, and housing will rise up around Disney Hall and transform the neighborhood into the urban mecca that so many people seek, but I wouldn't bet on it, and it doesn't matter. Disney Hall is something rarer than a great urban street. It is a serene, ennobling building that will give people in this city of private places a new sense of the pleasures of public space.

The New Yorker, September 29, 2003

Rem Koolhaas/Office for Metropolitan Architecture, Seattle Public Library

HIGH-TECH BIBLIOPHILIA

If you wanted to build a new library downtown somewhere, Rem Koolhaas is probably the last architect you would think to hire. For years Koolhaas has been ranting about how traditional cities don't matter anymore, and how the rise of new technologies has made public space obsolete, and how when people leave their houses, the only thing they want to do is shop. His firm, the Office for Metropolitan Architecture, which is based in Rotterdam, wasn't on the original list of architects being considered for a new library in Seattle, but one day in 1999, Koolhaas's partner, Joshua Ramus, who comes from Seattle, got a phone call from his mother saying she had read in the local newspaper that any architect who wanted to be considered should show up the next day for a briefing. Ramus rushed to the airport, flew to Seattle, and eventually the firm got the job.

The result is the most important new library to be built in a generation, and the most exhilarating. Koolhaas has always been a better architect than social critic, and the building conveys a sense of the possibility, even the urgency, of public space in the center of a city. The design is not so much a rejection of traditional monumentality as a reinterpretation of it, and it celebrates the culture of the book as passionately, in its way, as does the New York Public Library on Fifth Avenue. The Seattle building is thrilling from top to bottom. Koolhaas and Ramus started out by investigating how libraries actually work and how they are likely to change. They went with Deborah Jacobs, Seattle's chief librarian, and several trustees and staff members to look at libraries around the country, and then they held a series of seminars about the future of the book with scholars and representatives of Microsoft, Amazon, MIT's Media Lab, and other organizations. They concluded, not surprisingly, that people are not ready to give up on books and that they are not ready to give up on libraries, but that they find most libraries stuffy, confusing, and uninviting. Patrons wanted a more user-friendly institution, and librarians wanted one that was more flexible and would not require constant rearrangement as collections expanded.

The architects saw that in most older libraries, where books are stored on rows of shelves on separate floors, collections are arbitrarily broken apart, depending on the amount of space available on each floor. But since the Dewey decimal system is a continuous series of numbers, they reasoned, why couldn't books be stored on a continuous series of shelves? And what if the shelves wound up and up, in a spiral? They saw that it was possible to design stacks in the manner of a parking garage, with slanted floors joined in a series of zigzagging ramps. The stacks, which the architects named the Spiral, take up the equivalent of four floors in the middle of the eleven-story building. They are open, which means that you can browse. You get to the Spiral via a chartreuse-colored escalator and stairway that slices through the middle of the ramped floors. (All vertical circulation in the building, including the elevator cabs, is chartreuse.)

Above the stacks area, on the tenth floor, is a spectacular reading room, with slanted glass walls. The room has an unusual perspective on the Seattle skyline, since the library building is surrounded by skyscrapers, and the waters of Elliott Bay are visible only between the towers. The soaring glass shed is as spectacular, in its way, as the Rose Main Reading Room in the Fifth Avenue library. Just below the stacks is a room full of computers. Koolhaas calls it the Mixing Chamber, which sounds more high-tech and radical than it really is. The Mixing Chamber is simply a reinterpretation of the traditional library reference room. People who visit it are directed to the books they need. Koolhaas's verbiage is always a little annoying. He calls an expansive, atrium-style lobby the Living Room. The Living Room is a splendid vestibule that anoints the act of reading with grandeur and civic pride, and Seattle is lucky to have it. But what Koolhaas has done here is not so different, in its way, from what Carrère & Hastings were trying to achieve when they put Astor Hall at the entrance to the New York Public Library.

I thought of the Carrère & Hastings building often as I walked through the Seattle library. Two buildings could not possibly look less alike, but both were born of a marriage of earnestness and opulence. When the library on Fifth Avenue was finished, in 1911, a grand library that was free to the public was still a fresh, almost radical notion, and the architecture was intended to give it gravitas. In the same way that McKim, Mead & White designed the original Pennsylvania Station to confer a kind of nobility on the act of entering and leaving the city, Carrère & Hastings expected the public library not only to house books but to dignify the act of seeking them out.

Koolhaas and Ramus did not pretend that the world is unchanged since 1911—a view that held sway in Chicago a few years ago when a huge new central library designed by the architect Thomas Beeby went up. It looks vaguely like a nineteenth-century train station and is overbearing and bombastic. The complex polygonal form of the Seattle library, which is sheathed almost entirely in glass set in a diamond-shaped grid, has a dazzling energy; it's the most alluring architectural object to arrive in this city's downtown since the Space Needle. The building manages the neat trick of seeming exotic but not bizarre. Once you have walked around the block a couple of times, it seems almost conventional. In a few years, the great glass tent will connote the appeal of reading as much as New York's marble lions do. It's significant that the building was put up in the land of Microsoft (and with some of the company's money), since it is such a powerful testament to architecture as a container for the delivery of information. We don't need big library buildings the way we once did, but if you surf the Internet at home, you are just a click away from a video game. When you do it here, you feel that you are engaged in a serious pursuit. A building like this emphasizes the value a culture places on literacy. (It cost $165 million, most of which was paid by voter-approved city bonds.)

The library, for which the Seattle firm of LMN Architects served as associate designer, is clearly organized and will be easy to use. When Koolhaas and Ramus designed the building, they did what architects often do—they made a diagram. It was, essentially, five boxes: the book stacks were one box, the administrative offices were another, and there were boxes for staff work areas, meeting rooms, and below-ground parking. Then they did something remarkable. For all intents and purposes, they built the diagram. They sketched the boxes floating in space and placed the large public areas—the Living Room, the Mixing Chamber, and the Reading Room—above and below them, surrounded by glass. Turning a diagram into an actual architectural form seems like something of a parlor trick, not to mention being crudely indifferent to aesthetics. In fact, it was neither of these things. The building has a logic to it: functional sections are the starting point, but they are placed so that the spaces between them are large enough and spectacular enough to produce powerful architectural effects. The glass skin is thrown over the entire structure, like a blanket. The diamond pattern in the skin is actually seismic bracing, engineered to protect the building in the event of an earthquake or strong winds.

Deborah Jacobs seems to have been about as close to an ideal client as could be imagined, and she protected the architects from some of their worst instincts. She rejected the green-colored, unfinished sheetrock that they had used in other recent projects, including the Prada store in New York, on the ground that it was trite and cheap-looking. "I thought it was important that you have a sense of awe when you come into a public building, especially a library," she said. But she had no interest in a traditional building: "This is the first library of the twenty-first century." Jacobs analyzed every aspect of the library's operations, and insisted that there be no compromise in accommodating them. When the library's trustees saw Koolhaas and Ramus's first design, they were relieved to find that the building fulfilled all the practical demands that had been set. The architects presented the building as a reinvention of the idea of the public library, which in many ways it is. Their greatest achievement, though, is not in reinventing the library but in reaffirming it.

The New Yorker, May 24, 2004

Massimiliano Fuksas, Fiera Milano

UNCONVENTIONAL

Convention centers are supposed to revive cities by bringing in revenue from out-of-town visitors and creating local jobs. But the more gargantuan they become, the less happily they fit into the places they are intended to benefit. In terms of architectural beauty, the convention center these days ranks somewhere close to the aircraft hangar, and for some of the same reasons: both must provide acres of space for a continually shifting configuration of objects, and cater to a temporary crowd of people whose minds are on other things. Putting one of these megaliths into the heart of a city is like trying to dock the Queen Mary in the local marina.

Architects have tried various solutions to the problem of enclosing a huge volume of space and making it look palatable, generally without success. San Francisco originally put its Moscone Center underground, but the park on top feels unnatural—like a landscaped roof on a parking garage. Seattle's convention center sits above a freeway, which makes a little more sense, since one urban intrusion is used to mask another. In Washington, D.C., the architecture firm Thompson, Ventulett, Stainback wanted to minimize the new Washington Convention Center's impact on the city, but the only design scheme that seemed feasible was to break up the exhibition space into two separate levels, one of which bridges two city streets. New York, it would seem, gave up altogether: the Javits Center, designed by James Ingo Freed, just sprawls along five blocks of the far West Side, a reflective glass wall between the city and the Hudson River. In Pittsburgh, Rafael Viñoly tried a little harder, topping his building with a big, swooping roof intended to evoke the city's bridges. But generally people seem to want their convention centers to attract a crowd and to disappear at the same time.

Not so the Italians. They know better than to plant something in the heart of a city which doesn't fit there. The most exciting convention center in the world currently isn't anywhere near the center of a city. It is the Milan Trade Fair, known as Fiera Milano, which was built on the site of an old gas refinery at the intersection of a couple of highways not far from the Milan airport. Conceived on a scale that makes the Javits Center look like a dinky cottage, the Fiera stretches for almost a mile, and its various sections provide nearly three and a half million square feet of exhibition space. When you first approach the Fiera, it looks like an endless modern factory, the epitome of every bad planning idea in the book. But, once you find your way in, you realize that the architect, Massimiliano Fuksas, has taken the blandness of convention centers as a challenge, a spur to create the kind of architectural flourish that dispels all thoughts of dull functionality.

The underlying scheme is brilliant in its simplicity. Dividing the exhibition space into eight halls, each as large as a medium-sized American convention center, Fuksas has placed them on either side of a central axis, an elevated street a mile long. This gives the site the kind of strongly defined core that most convention centers lack. To enliven the space, and to give it a human scale, Fuksas has designed the Fiera's centerpiece—a swirling glass canopy that is as arresting as anything built anywhere in the past five years.

This is a canopy that dances. Its undulating glass-and-steel swoops and swells as if it were not a solid mass but a billowing length of fabric. Supported on a nest of white steel columns, the structure forms a voluptuous counterpoint to the pristine boxes of the exhibition halls. Fuksas sculpts with glass as unself-consciously as a children's entertainer sculpts with balloons, and with the same sense of delight. The glass is set in a pattern of diamonds and triangles, which play off the rhythm of the curves. At a couple of points, Fuksas brings the glass down to the ground in a vortex construction that recalls a whirlpool; elsewhere he bends it skyward in a sudden surge of monumentality. From the top of the canopy, it is possible to see the peaks of the Italian Alps to the west, and the resemblance between the two is unmistakable.

The street beneath the canopy is punctuated by twenty cafés and restaurants, and by a series of freestanding structures containing meeting rooms and offices. Each of these building types is expressed by a particular architectural form: all the office buildings, for instance, are simple boxes of glass and steel, almost Miesian (although some of them are raised on very un-Miesian angled pillars, like crossed legs); all the meeting rooms are stainless-steel-clad pods, and they, too, sit atop columns. Such rational patterning insures that you never get that feeling, so typical of the convention-center experience, of being lost in a wilderness designed by Kafka. At ground level, there are reflecting pools and gardens, creating a constantly changing series of landscapes. The exhibition halls, of necessity unadorned inside, are clad in red-orange metal panels, which I take as Fuksas's acknowledgment that, since the halls are too big to disappear, you may as well have some fun with them. The orange facades also go some way toward lightening these leviathans, so that they don't overwhelm the rest of the place. As in a city, the public space connecting the buildings is more important than the buildings themselves.

Massimiliano Fuksas is based in Rome, and, like almost every other contemporary Italian architect not named Renzo Piano, he is all but unknown in the United States, despite having designed major projects in Europe for Ferrari, Armani, and the French government. "It was my idea to make it like a piazza for the suburbs—there are a hundred thousand people around it, and they have nothing," Fuksas told me recently, when I visited him in the Renaissance palazzo that houses his practice. By focusing his design around his invented street rather than around the exhibition space itself, Fuksas departed from the model that most architects have used in designing convention centers.

Almost every convention center has owed something to the Crystal Palace, the great exhibition hall outside London, completed in 1854, whose architect, Joseph Paxton, created an interior space more than eighteen hundred feet long, the biggest room anyone had ever built. Fuksas seems to have taken as his inspiration not the Crystal Palace but, rather, the Galleria Vittorio Emanuele, the glass-covered arcade of shops begun a few years later opposite Milan's cathedral. This is Milan's most important public space, and arguably the greatest covered street in the world. Keeping his exhibition spaces in the background, Fuksas has reserved the glitter for the connecting spaces between them.

The Fiera cannot replicate the serendipity that makes Italian cities so beloved, and which can be created only over centuries. But Fuksas doesn't pretend to. Convention-goers are expected to stay in Milan, and most of them travel to and from the city center via a new underground rail link. The Fiera is only a convention center—not one of those "edge city" nodes, like Tysons Corner outside Washington or the Galleria section of Houston, which try to provide all the elements of a traditional city amid suburban sprawl and end up draining the metropolis to which they are attached. The Fiera has no shopping, no cineplexes, and, for now, no hotels—nothing to fulfill the current mantra of "mixed use" as the obligation of all large-scale urban-development projects. Like other recent large-scale projects in Europe, such as La Défense, outside

Paris, and Canary Wharf, to the east of the City of London, it has been pushed to the outskirts in order to keep the historic core intact.

In some ways, the Fiera is an example of history repeating itself. The old Fiera di Milano, a few minutes from the historic center of the city, was erected in the 1920s. At that time, it was on the outskirts of Milan, but the city grew up around it. In recent years, the old Fiera had become a jumble of disconnected buildings in the middle of a fashionable residential neighborhood. It had neither the exhilarating disorder of a great agora nor the efficiency of a new convention center; it also had absolutely no room to expand. This site has now been sold to developers, who, predictably, have plans for large condominium towers to be built by superstar architects, including Zaha Hadid and Daniel Libeskind. But Milan will be lucky if this fashionable vertical architecture envisioned for its center manages to equal Fuksas's horizontal masterwork on the periphery.

The New Yorker, July 31, 2006

**Herzog and de Meuron, Allianz Arena, Munich (above);
de Young Museum, San Francisco**

SEDUCTIVE SKINS

Most sports stadiums that have been built
in recent decades are hulking concrete
monoliths or cute exercises in nostalgia,
and they give the impression of having been
crafted either by highway engineers or
by theme-park designers. Jacques Herzog
and Pierre de Meuron, whose firm won
the Pritzker Prize in 2001, appear quite
determined to be architects, and that is
why it is remarkable that the Swiss team

was invited to create two of the most conspicuous sports venues in the world: the recently completed Allianz Arena, in Munich, which will house this year's World Cup of soccer; and the Olympic Stadium in Beijing, which is now under construction and will be the centerpiece of the 2008 Summer Games. Both designs suggest that a sports arena, for all the blood and sweat on the field, can be an exalted space of otherworldly beauty.

The Allianz Arena has a delightfully surreal appearance. The exterior is covered in tufted, translucent material; viewed from afar, the stadium resembles a giant, quilted doughnut. At night, it becomes positively radiant: the facade is lit from within, which means that the entire arena glows. (The windows of 106 luxury boxes can be partially discerned behind the curved scrim.) On most evenings, the building emits a soft white light, reflecting the silvery tone of the synthetic skin, but on nights when one of the two Munich soccer clubs has a home game—the teams share the stadium—it changes its skin color: red for Bayern Munich, blue for the Munich Lions. The shifting lighting schemes atop the Empire State Building seem timid compared with this chameleon.

The arena retains its allure during the day. The unusual material—ETFE, or ethylene tetrafluoroethylene—gives the stadium a cushiony texture, as if it were an oversized, permanently moored blimp; you want to climb up and touch it. And its subtle white hue eerily duplicates the Munich sky on a cloudy winter afternoon—the stadium practically disappears. In the sun, it brightens. The 2,760 tufts—made of two sheets of ETFE, each 0.2 millimeters thick, which are sewn together and filled with air—are arranged in a strict diamond pattern, giving the facade a subtle sleekness. There are obvious jokes to be made about the Allianz Arena—one could say that it resembles the Michelin Man, or even a soccer ball—but Herzog and de Meuron are too good to play trite visual games, and the building easily transcends such literal-minded comparisons.

The Allianz Arena also serves its function superbly. The membranelike roof, which is retractable, permits ultraviolet light to filter through, allowing the natural turf on the playing field to thrive. Nineteen of the exterior tufts tilt open on days when a breeze is welcome. The stands, arrayed on three tiers, are unusually steep, creating nearly flawless sight lines; the elegant gray seats, curved and comfortable, look like miniature versions of the famous egg chairs by Arne Jacobsen. Like a great opera house, the stadium seems more intimate than it is, and you feel connected to the field even if you are in the upper tier.

The Allianz Arena is on Munich's northern fringe, near the intersection of two Autobahns, and it is designed to be as exciting when you zip past it in your BMW as it is when you approach it on foot. It has the magnetic pull of a true icon: I was glad I wasn't behind the wheel when I rode in a car to the arena at night, since I couldn't take my eyes off its luminous form and unsettling monumentality. Buildings aren't supposed to be so huge and so soft. These days, we tend to associate softness with spinelessness, as if worthy architectural ideas had to be expressed in terms of crisp, hard form. (Think of the brutal angularities of Rem Koolhaas or Zaha Hadid.) With this gently radical stadium, Herzog and de Meuron prove that softness is not for sissies.

Unlike most American stadiums, the Allianz Arena is not surrounded by acres of parking lots, and the visual approach to the arena is as meticulously designed as anything within the building itself. Parking space is embedded in a partially sunken multilayered structure, atop which is the main pedestrian entry path to the arena. The path is lined with enormous lamps that look like hot-air balloons—whimsical echoes of the facade—and it begins at a train-and-bus station, so that people who arrive by car and those who take public transportation merge together as they walk along the elevated boulevard.

When you enter the arena, you go up one of several monumental staircases tucked between the pillowy exterior and the concrete inner structure of the stadium. The staircases curve as they rise, reflecting the rounded shape of the stadium. The stairs are one of the best things in the building. You get enticing glimpses of the angular metal framework that supports the facade as you walk up, and, at night, the colored lights create a lurid atmosphere that bears a beguiling resemblance to German Expressionism: *The Cabinet of Dr. Caligari* transported to the realm of sport.

Oddly, one of the few significant precedents for this building is also in Munich: Frei Otto and Günter Behnisch's great Olympic Stadium of 1972, with its lyrical Plexiglas roof. Compared with the Allianz Arena, the Olympic Stadium is just a jaunty tent stretched over a conventional stadium, but it was quite something in its time, and it still looks good. Herzog and de Meuron, however, have made a more profound statement about the potential of sensual form to achieve epic grandeur, and there are no self-indulgent gestures: every aspect of their design amplifies the experience of attending a soccer game.

The supple exterior of the Allianz Arena would seem to overwhelm everything else about the building, until you go inside and discover how well it works, and how much else there is in Herzog and de Meuron's repertoire. The same thing can be said about their design for the de Young Museum, in San Francisco's Golden Gate Park, which opened this past fall. The museum's facade—made up of intricately textured sheets of embossed and perforated copper—is so dazzling that you expect the building to be an empty showpiece; yet its interior is useful and intelligent. The museum is as dark as the Munich stadium is light, and as hard-edged as Munich is rounded, but in both cases Herzog and de Meuron have managed to invent a wholly new kind of exterior, and marry it to a fully realized building. They use these seductive skins to lure us into their architecture, but they don't leave their imaginations at the door.

The original de Young Museum, a grandiose Spanish Colonial structure, was so badly damaged in the Loma Prieta earthquake, in 1989, that it couldn't be repaired. In 1998 the museum's trustees decided to erect a new building and to hold a competition to find an architect. Herzog and de Meuron, who are based in Basel, had designed the Tate Modern, in London, but they were primarily known for small, minimalist spaces—such as the exquisite Goetz Collection, a private museum in Munich—and they hadn't completed any major commissions in the United States. They had, however, been among the three finalists for the expansion of the Museum of Modern Art, in New York, and although their scheme was deemed too experimental for the conservative Modern, being on its short list raised Herzog and de Meuron's status. In 1999 they won the de Young competition.

The museum consists of two sections: a long, horizontal wing, containing the galleries and several internal garden courts; and an unusual tower, a kind of twisting parallelogram, containing the museum's education and study centers. The tower rises 144 feet, and it has an observatory room at the top. Its odd form seems willful, and it is based on an unnecessary conceit: the top section is perfectly aligned with the street grid of San Francisco, which can be seen from the observatory's windows. No matter; it's a well-wrought piece of sculpture, and the tower and the three-level main wing form a strong composition, a modern version of a cathedral and its campanile.

The remarkable pointillist facade covers both the main wing and the tower, further unifying them. It is actually a computer-generated pattern of dots, a gargantuan version of the pixels that make up a digital photograph. Such an effect could seem slick, but the building feels dignified and compellingly strange. It is smooth, like so many modern buildings, yet it is as textured as a rococo church. And do those dots make a picture of something, or are they simply ornament? They are both things at once—strictly speaking, the dots form a picture of dappled light filtering through a canopy of trees, but it comes across as a tantalizing abstraction, a color-field painting without the color.

The ambiguity of the copper facade entices you into an entry court, and, from there, into a high central lobby. The layout is irregular but clear and easy to grasp. The galleries are gracious and accommodating, with varying ceiling heights, natural light, and, in some cases, lovely views of Golden Gate Park. The twentieth-century galleries, on the main floor, have stone floors, skylights, and white walls; the upstairs galleries, which contain smaller and earlier works, have wood floors, colored walls, and, in several rooms, wooden ceilings. The tight, triangular garden courts bring the expansive landscape of the park inside, with a special intensity. Throughout the museum, the flow through space is as logically programmed as in any classical building. The art—in particular, a spectacular triptych by Ed Ruscha, commissioned for the lobby—looks superb in the variety of settings that Herzog and de Meuron have crafted for it. Walking through the de Young, you begin to wonder why we tend to think of new museums as being either potent works of architecture or sensitive environments for art, when this museum so deftly manages to be both.

Last year, Herzog and de Meuron also completed work on an expansion of the Walker Art Center, in Minneapolis. The addition is clad in aluminum mesh that has been delicately crinkled, softening the most hard-edged of materials. Both museums have a kind of painstaking sensuousness. They are somber and inviting at the same time. Can there be such a thing as Swiss passion? Herzog and de Meuron seem determined to prove that this is not an oxymoron—that utter precision need not come at the cost of emotional engagement with architecture.

Herzog and de Meuron's office in Basel, once tiny, now has 170 employees, and they are getting all kinds of work. Ian Schrager just hired them to design a condominium project on Bond Street, in Lower Manhattan, for which the architects have devised a facade that will have large plate-glass windows separated by heavy, rounded glass columns—a shimmery, twenty-first-century version of Soho's cast-iron facades. It is a brilliant scheme, and Schrager and his partner, Aby Rosen, are building it pretty much as the architects designed it.

Herzog, who is the firm's spokesman, has positioned himself less as an architectural theorist than as an acute observer of culture who happens to design serious buildings. The point of his practice, he told me recently, is "not just to make a beautiful object." Ambiguity, he said, lies at the heart of his designs. He wants his architecture to make a point about the human psyche. "Architecture must deal with doubt—it is not just about style, or 'I like this' or 'I don't like that,'" he said. Herzog is known for making delphic pronouncements, and his words tend to be more pensive than the sweeping absolutes that architects like Koolhaas adopt. Life is a complicated, painful business, he seems to be saying, and architecture should be neither an escape from stress nor a literal representation of it but, rather, a means of achieving complex insight. Herzog rejects the idea that architecture should provide either simple physical comfort or intellectual challenge—to him, these two things are not mutually exclusive.

I asked him about his firm's turn from the austere visual vocabulary that defines his early work. "The really interesting thing about ornamentation is the strong psychological side inherent in it," Herzog said. Ornament, as he sees it, is a reflection of the intricacies of the human mind. The Beijing Olympic Stadium, for example, will look like a vast mesh of concrete sticks, crossing one another in every direction—a network that is both literally and symbolically a web. It will be impossible to tell where structure ends and decoration begins, for they are one and the same. The result should be disconcertingly gorgeous.

"I am more interested in the dark side—the dark side inside comfort, the comfort inside the dark side," Herzog said. "It is like the films of Hitchcock— that's how life is. The dark moment, the criminal moment, the sexual moment, sits within everything else. Perhaps it is strange to hear this from someone who became known as a minimalist. But minimalism is just another guise, another form of dress."

The New Yorker, March 20, 2006

Santiago Calatrava, Turning Torso Tower, Malmö, Sweden

SPIRALING UPWARD

Eero Saarinen's swooping concrete TWA terminal, at Kennedy Airport, has often been compared to a bird with outstretched wings. When Saarinen, who died in 1961, was asked if that was what he meant his building to look like, he responded that people could say whatever they wanted, but he had far more serious things on his mind than birds. The Spanish architect Santiago Calatrava, who has been greatly influenced by Saarinen's forms, takes the opposite tack—he embraces analogies between his buildings and living creatures. If Calatrava had designed the TWA terminal, he would have named it the Soaring Eagle.

And so Calatrava's first high-rise apartment tower, in Malmö, Sweden, has been christened the Turning Torso. The title is a reference to a white marble sculpture, by Calatrava, of a human form in motion; in 1999, the five-foot-high work so captivated the building's developer that he hired Calatrava to stretch the piece into a skyscraper—even though the architect had not yet designed one. The fifty-four-story structure, which has views of Copenhagen from across the Øresund Strait, opens in November. There are 147 apartments—each of which has slanting windows, curving walls, and oddly shaped rooms—and all of them have been rented.

Calatrava is the most crowd-pleasing architect since Frank Gehry. His work, too, is dazzling and emotionally engaging. And, just as Gehry exploited the trend of museum building in the 1990s, Calatrava has aligned himself with the latest architectural fashion: bespoke luxury-apartment towers. In 2003 he designed a striking apartment complex for Lower Manhattan consisting of twelve four-story cubes stacked in a tall, open frame. And this spring a Chicago developer, Christopher T. Carley, announced that Calatrava will design a corkscrew-shaped, 115-story tower, along Lake Michigan, which will contain condominiums and a hotel; the building, when completed, will be the tallest in the United States.

At the press conference for the Chicago building, Calatrava, who speaks English with a heavy accent, began with an awkward description of the design. He called the shape of his building "helicoidal," which is as arcane a term for "spiral" as there is. He then turned to his secret weapon: an easel-size pad. He drew a human body, torqued like a tennis player in mid-swing. He then sketched a tree trunk. Finally, he drew a lovely spiral, and explained that what he had in mind was a tall tower that rose organically, in a way that echoed natural forms.

Calatrava's slick salesmanship helps to explain his success with real-estate developers, especially considering how little commercial work he has built. For years, he was best known for a series of magnificent bridges, including one in Seville, Spain, that resembles a giant harp. A Calatrava form tends to appear both delicate and powerful, like a futuristic version of a Gothic cathedral. It is almost invariably white, which emphasizes its lightness and modernity. His first American project, an expansion of the Milwaukee Art Museum, completed in 2001, has a lacy, curving facade—a spectacular homage to Saarinen.

The museum addition, for all its allure, is not particularly practical: it's basically a soaring entry hall, with little exhibit space. Still, when Christopher Carley went to see it shortly after it opened, he was smitten. "I said, 'My God, even the parking garage is beautiful,'" Carley told me. "I stumbled out in total awe. I thought, Chicago ought to have this, I have to get Calatrava down here." Carley attended a lecture that Calatrava gave at the Art Institute of Chicago, and introduced himself afterward. Calatrava took out his pad, sketched a dove, and handed it to Carley as a gift. A few months later, Carley flew to Zurich, where Calatrava has his headquarters, to plead with the architect to design an apartment building for him. Calatrava rejected the sites that Carley proposed until the developer came up with some prominent waterfront land, opposite Navy Pier. Architects have long fantasized about being approached with such deference by real-estate developers; usually, they are treated like hired hands and ordered to cut the frills. Calatrava is one of the few architects living the dream.

Calatrava has had similar good luck in Sweden. The Turning Torso's developer, HSB, generally builds co-ops aimed at middle-class tenants. But Johnny Örbäck, the company's former managing director, let Calatrava create the kind of opulent tower that, until now, had been unheard of in Sweden, a country generally suspicious of concierges and wine cellars. And Calatrava was offered a prominent open site along Malmö's developing waterfront, assuring that his building will stand out. As you drive from Denmark on the Øresund Bridge, one building fully pierces the horizon: the Turning Torso.

Calatrava designs are ordered up as icons, and the architect proudly delivers. The Malmö tower has no relationship with the buildings around it. Whereas Gehry takes care to play his whorled-metal shapes off the older architecture nearby, Calatrava attempts to transcend his surroundings. His designs are abstractions, and strangely otherworldly. (As a Calatrava retrospective at the Metropolitan Museum of Art reveals, his building models are virtually indistinguishable from his sculptures.) A Calatrava building has none of the hard edges of many modern structures, but it isn't lush, either. You feel as if you were looking at a mystical vision—something that might evaporate in the mist. Indeed, his buildings often look best from afar, when they appear most apparitional. Calatrava buildings don't sit on the ground; they dance above it.

Dancing is not what skyscrapers are expected to do, and Calatrava's Turning Torso takes some getting used to. Unlike most skyscrapers, which are designed to look immobile no matter how much they may sway in the wind, this tower looks strangely kinetic—as if it were poised to move horizontally. Usually, the thrust of skyscrapers is vertical: capped with fancy tops, they resemble castles or rocket ships. Most architects who design skyscrapers focus on two aesthetic problems: how to meet the ground, and how to meet the sky—the bottom and the top, in other words. Calatrava is interested solely in the middle. For him, the skyscraper isn't a classical column, with a base, a shaft, and a capital. It's all shaft—which he has made an object of propulsion and energy.

Calatrava is an engineer as well as an architect and a sculptor, and his work is undergirded by a strong structural logic, separating it from, say, the work of Daniel Libeskind, whose ill-fated initial concept for the Freedom Tower at Ground Zero had an off-center spire intended to echo the outstretched arm of the Statue of Liberty. Libeskind's idea was pure imagery, a picture that the architect expected engineers to translate into reality. Calatrava's Malmö design begins with a structural motif—the human spine—and builds from there.

The Turning Torso literally has a spine, since Calatrava has designed the building with an external steel frame running up one side of it. Although from a distance the sleek white tower looks simple, its shape is anything but straightforward. Calatrava likes to describe the tower as a stack of nine white aluminum-clad "cubes," each of which is five floors high; the cubes are separated by recessed intermediate floors, so that the boxes appear to float atop each other. In truth, Calatrava's cubes are imperfect: in order to make the form appear to spiral upward, the floor plan on each level looks something like a square with a small triangle affixed to one corner. And the entire east side of the tower consists of a triangular glass projection that is supported by the external steel spine.

Calatrava's dancer, then, is more like a marionette—controlled by visible means of support. But this doesn't detract from the design: the steel bracing is one of the handsomest things about this building. The frame curves right up the full height of the tower, highlighting the fluid, flowing form in a way that Calatrava's pseudocubes don't fully manage to do. This exoskeleton also connects the Turning Torso to a long tradition of skyscrapers whose form illuminates their structure. Louis Kahn once referred to the Seagram Building as a beautiful lady with hidden corsets, because its bracing was tucked behind Mies van der Rohe's exquisite facade; Calatrava's lady has confidently removed her dress. For all its surface delicacy, the Malmö tower is closer kin to a building like the hulking John Hancock Center, in Chicago, whose hundred stories are wrapped in huge X-braces.

Inside, the Malmö apartments are generally what you would expect— sunny living spaces with sleek, refined European kitchens. The rooms are small, the fittings are handsome, and the views are wonderful. What makes the apartments special—but also more difficult, depending on your standpoint—is that there are almost no rectangular rooms. Living rooms are shaped like pie wedges, or have the zigzag outline of a W. Some wall-height windows are raked nearly at the angle of a car windshield. Unlike in most apartments, a person inside the Turning Torso is always aware of the building's exterior.

The Malmö tower is somewhat cluttered conceptually: the audacious stacked-box idea competes with the even more powerful notion of a twisting skyscraper. In Calatrava's design for Lower Manhattan, the concept of stacked cubes is expressed more cleanly and successfully. A vertical street of ten private houses, the four-story boxes are delicately offset from one another, so that each town house will have a garden and a terrace on the roof of the unit below. (Two cubes at the bottom will contain commercial venues.) The result is not at all anthropomorphic: it is pure geometry.

Whether ten people will want to pay between $30 and $45 million to live in a large box suspended in the skyline of Lower Manhattan, however, is an open question. It's not certain that the design will be built—although the developer, Frank J. Sciame, says that he expects to begin construction next spring, his financing is not yet complete. What is clear is that Calatrava—along with Richard Meier, whose glass towers in the far West Village went up in 2002—has helped create a more ambitious climate for apartment design in New York. Sleek glass condominium towers, once a rarity in white brick Manhattan, are going up even in Hell's Kitchen.

Calatrava has had a similar inspirational effect in Chicago. Although the glass tower he has produced for Christopher Carley looks nothing like the New York project—Calatrava has essentially proposed the world's largest and most beautiful drill bit—it's a similar attempt by a developer to elevate a project above the real-estate fray. (Far above: the planned height is two thousand feet.) The building would add an elegant and memorable shape to Chicago's skyline, but, as in Malmö, Calatrava has shown little interest in connecting to street life. The tower's base is bulky and unwelcoming.

If the tower is built—and Carley doesn't yet have all his financing, either—its status as the country's tallest skyscraper will mark the first time that an apartment building has held this title. It would become a symbol of the evolution of the American city from being a center of commerce to a center of culture and entertainment. Nobody is clamoring to work in high-rises anymore, but plenty of people are willing to live in them, and the fact that the biggest and most interesting towers are being built to contain apartments is a significant shift. It means, among other things, that we will finally see very tall buildings that are slender rather than chunky. (Calatrava's design will look like a needle in comparison to the Sears Tower.) Thin towers have more light inside, and, collectively, they would create a skyline less dominated by hulking masses—perhaps inspiring a renewed willingness to view the skyscraper in romantic terms. Calatrava is both a romantic and a rationalist, and his gift lies in his ability to find an equilibrium between these two poles.

The Chicago tower's official name is a pedestrian one: the Fordham Spire. But it may well acquire a more glamorous title. Carley originally proposed naming the building for his famous architect. The offer was declined, Carley said. But, he went on, Tina Calatrava, the architect's wife, said that it didn't matter: "Everyone is going to call it the Calatrava anyway."

The New Yorker, October 31, 2005

Norman Foster, Terminal 3, Beijing Capital International Airport (above);
Richard Rogers, Terminal 4, Madrid Barajas International Airport

SITUATION TERMINAL

Airports are essentially machines for processing people, airplanes, automobiles, cargo, and luggage—all of which move in different ways, and which need to be connected at certain points and separated by rigid security at others. Just getting all the parts to work together seems overwhelming—indeed, it did overwhelm British Airways last month at Heathrow, outside London, when Terminal 5, an $8 billion structure that was supposed to transform Heathrow from a congested tangle into a place that would thrill passengers with the joy of air travel, all but shut down on its opening day, when a computerized baggage system malfunctioned.

Airports, in short, are a logistical nightmare, and this is surely the reason that most of them today are such depersonalized wastelands. With all those moving parts to organize, the last thing that cash-starved airlines and airport authorities want to think about is aesthetic appeal. Most airports built in the last generation, at least in the United States, have followed a simple, established pattern, along the lines of the huge ones in Atlanta and Denver. Gates, arranged in long, boxy concourses set way out in the field, are linked to central terminals by underground trains. Driverless trains enhance the sense that the whole thing is less a piece of architecture than one big machine. Within the concourse, you walk, sometimes as much as a half mile, or ten city blocks, between gates. It is an efficient layout for airport operations, as long as you don't consider passenger pleasure to be a part of airport operations.

Architects trying to reinvent the airport have done so at their peril. Paul Andreu designed the first terminal at Charles de Gaulle, north of Paris, as a doughnut-shaped structure with glass tubes crossing through the middle, but when it came time to expand the airport, in the 1980s, only a few years after the first part was finished, his futuristic form seemed more like a cartoon than like a functional building, and more conventional terminals were ordered up. Eero Saarinen tried twice. His TWA terminal, in New York, whose soaring concrete shell became an instant modernist emblem in the early 1960s, turned out, in the age of jumbo jets and security walls, to be about as futuristic as a log cabin, and no more adaptable. At Dulles, outside Washington, D.C., Saarinen tried to protect his glass-and-concrete terminal from the ugliness of conventional jetways; he came up with a scheme that kept the planes parked out on the field, where they were reached by custom-built trailers that rose up to the airplane doors like hydraulic elevators. It was all very dramatic, but it didn't work, either, and, when the airport expanded, conventional concourses were built out on the field.

Since then, airport authorities have been wary of letting any architect have a say on what should go where. Now most architects don't get to do much more than give the main concourse a big, swooping space with natural light—like the one in the new American Airlines terminal at Kennedy airport—which acts as little more than a distraction from the banality of the rest of the terminal.

But recently Asian countries, and some European ones, have been approaching the problem with a bit more imagination. The best new airports in the world right now are in Beijing, where Norman Foster's Terminal 3 has just opened, and on the outskirts of Madrid, where Terminal 4 at Barajas, designed by Richard Rogers Partnership, has been in operation since 2006. Foster has achieved what no other architect has been able to: he has rethought the airport from scratch and made it work. Foster has done for airports what the architects Reed & Stem did for train stations with their design for Grand Central, a building whose greatest achievement is not its sumptuous main concourse but its orchestration of an intricate web of people, trains, taxis, and passing automobiles into a system that feels straightforward and logical, as if the building itself were guiding you from the entrance to your train. Foster, likewise, has established a pattern so clear that your natural instinct to walk straight ahead from the front door takes you where you need to go. The sheer legibility of the place would be achievement enough, given its size. Foster's office claims it is the largest building in the world: it has 126 aircraft stands, and it had to include separate sections, with their own security stations and travel-document-control areas, for domestic and international travel; a train station for a new rapid-transit line to downtown Beijing; an array of luxury shops; and even a Burger King. Even more remarkable than this organizational feat, however, is the fact that Terminal 3 is also an aesthetically exhilarating place to be.

In layout, the airport is roughly like a pair of triangles whose points face each other and are connected by a long line. Foster has likened its shape to that of a dragon. I suppose you could consider either of the triangles, whose sides curve inward and whose roofs swell upward in a generous swoop, to be a dragon's head, and the long, straight section connecting them to be its tail, but the comparison is silly. Had Foster built the airport in Mexico City, would he have said that it looked like an iguana? Besides, one of the main strengths of the building is that you're not really aware of its layout, even as it subtly directs you. But you are aware of the structure's sensuous curves, which all but embrace you as you approach on an entry road. It makes you think of movement, while still appearing serene. Its long, low shape appears to rise gradually, as if its roof touched the ground at each end. Inside, the terminal, with its high, vaulted ceiling and walls of glass facing the airfield, loosely recalls Saarinen's TWA terminal. But this room is big enough to contain that entire building.

Foster placed the gates for domestic travel along two sides of the front triangle, which means that some of the planes, instead of being on a faraway concourse, nestle right up to the building. That's one part of his reinvention. The other is in the kind of aesthetic experience that Foster gives international travelers as they disembark. In most airports, you are hustled off the plane and up stairs, down escalators, around corners, and along endless low-ceilinged, interior corridors before you have the privilege of standing in a line to show your passport. At Beijing, Foster has put all the international flights in the rear three-sided building, which is similar to the front one and almost as grand, and you walk off the plane right into his vast space, a celebration of arrival awash with natural light. Nothing could be further from the windowless basements of Kennedy airport.

The Beijing terminal cost $3.65 billion to build, which in China bought a structure bigger than all five terminals at Heathrow put together, for less than half the cost of the new Terminal 5. The project was conceived, designed, constructed, and opened in four years, whereas the Heathrow terminal, from conception to completion, took twenty years. (That building, by Richard Rogers, is a somewhat compromised version of his original design—far better than the rest of Heathrow, but much less interesting than Rogers meant it to be.)

These widely divergent timetables are not a matter of Chinese efficiency versus British dallying: the British, like the Americans, pay the price of democracy. The Chinese government does not have to contend with environmentalists, financing problems, or recalcitrant airlines; the public hearings over the Heathrow terminal took the same amount of time as the entire construction of the Beijing one. China simply decrees what it will build, and floods the construction zone with migrant workers whose daily pay probably wouldn't buy a British construction worker's lunch.

Toward the end of the project, the Beijing Capital Airport Authority must have had some misgivings that Foster's cool modernity did not seem sufficiently Chinese, because it filled the elegant halls with oversized reproductions of traditional Chinese sculpture and enough potted plants to stock a nursery. At Barajas, the Spanish felt no such need for the crutch of kitsch. Then again, Richard Rogers designs warmer, more playful buildings than Foster does. There's no question that Foster's solution to the airport problem is more fundamentally inventive than Rogers's, but Rogers has another kind of inventiveness, which shows you how good an airport can be, even when the architect doesn't rethink things from scratch. The aircraft gates are organized around the kind of long, straight gate concourse you see everywhere, but Rogers's version is more breathtakingly beautiful than any airport I have ever seen. The ceiling is lined with bamboo slats and supported on a series of enormous Y-shaped steel trusses running down the center which are painted in the colors of the spectrum. When I emerged from my plane at one end of the concourse, I saw red columns in front of me, and it was only as I walked down the concourse that I saw that the columns were becoming orange, then yellow, then green and blue and violet. Rogers puts you inside a rainbow that stretches for half a mile. The colors make the space exuberant, the bamboo makes it warm, and together they make the building as much an exercise in sensuous comfort as in structural bravado—although the swaggering structure is there, too, replete with glass and natural light and a sense of grand space everywhere. Before I went to Madrid, I would have said that an airport architect's most important task was to reduce the distance you have to walk to and from the planes. But, at Barajas, you want to keep going.

The New Yorker, April 21, 2008

Olympic Architecture: Herzog and de Meuron, National Stadium (above); PTW Architects, National Aquatics Center; Studio Pei Zhu, Digital Beijing

OUT OF THE BLOCKS

To understand just how important the Beijing Olympics are to China, you have only to look at where the Olympic Green has been built. During Beijing's first building boom—six hundred years before the current one—the city was laid out symmetrically on either side of a north-south axis. As in Paris—where the Louvre lines up with the Tuileries, the Arc de Triomphe, and the Champs-Élysées—

Beijing's most symbolically important structures have fallen along the main axis. In the center is the former imperial residence of the Forbidden City. North of this is the Jingshan, a park surrounding an artificial hill where the last Ming emperor is said to have hanged himself, and, beyond that, the Drum Tower and the Bell Tower, which for centuries helped Beijing's inhabitants tell the time. In 1958, when the Communists expanded Tiananmen Square, at the southern gate of the Forbidden City, they placed the Monument to the People's Heroes on the same axis, in the center of the square. Mao Zedong's mausoleum, also in the square, is on the axis, too. And now, spread over twenty-eight hundred acres at the opposite end of the axis, is Beijing's Olympic Green. If Tiananmen Square is a monument to the Maoist policy of self-sufficiency, the Olympic Green, ten miles and fifty years away, is an architectural statement of intent every bit as clear—a testament to the global ambitions of the world's fastest-growing major economy.

At least two of the buildings on the Olympic Green—the National Stadium, by the Swiss architects Jacques Herzog and Pierre de Meuron, and the National Aquatics Center, by the Australian firm PTW Architects—are as innovative as any architecture on the planet, marvels of imagination and engineering that few countries would have the nerve or the money to attempt. The Chinese, right now, have plenty of both. These buildings, some of the most advanced in the world, are made possible partly by the presence of huge numbers of low-paid migrant workers. When I visited the stadium with Linxi Dong, the architect who heads Herzog and de Meuron's Beijing office, he told me that the construction crew for his project numbered nine thousand at its peak.

The National Stadium is already widely known by an apt nickname, the Bird's Nest. The concrete wall of the arena is wrapped with a latticework exterior of crisscrossing columns and beams, a tangle of twisting steel twigs. The lattice arcs upward and inward over the stadium's seats (there are ninety-one thousand), supporting a translucent roof and forming an oculus around the track. The center of the roof, over the field, has been left open. The engineering required to keep all this metal in the air is highly sophisticated: the building may look like a huge steel sculpture, but most of the beams are structural, not decorative. The drama of the Bird's Nest is even more arresting than that of the Allianz Arena, the Munich soccer stadium, which Herzog and de Meuron sheathed entirely in billows of translucent plastic, in 2005. Much of the spectacle derives from the interplay of the steel lattice and the concrete shell underneath. The outer wall of the concrete structure is painted bright red—one of the building's few overtly nationalistic touches—and when lit up at night, it shines through the latticework, an enormous red egg glowing inside its nest. On leaving, you experience the excitement of the knotted metal in a new way, looking out over Beijing through the wacky frame of the slanting columns.

Next door to the Bird's Nest is the Aquatics Center, known as the Water Cube, a rectilinear building with a blue-gray exterior of translucent plastic pillows set in an irregular pattern intended to evoke bubbles. John Pauline, who is the head of the Beijing office of PTW Architects, told me that the design emerged from a desire to find a way of expressing the feeling of water. "We started out with ripples and waves and steam," he said. "We basically looked at every state of water we could imagine. And then we hit on the idea of foam." Working with the engineering firm Arup, which also collaborated on the Bird's Nest, PTW developed cladding made of variously sized cells of ETFE, or ethylene tetrafluoroethylene, a translucent plastic somewhat similar to Teflon. Among architects, ETFE is the material of the moment—Herzog and de Meuron used it for the facade of their Munich stadium and for the roof of the Bird's Nest—and it has many practical virtues. It weighs only 1 percent as much as glass, transmits light more effectively, and is a better insulator, resulting in a 30 percent saving in energy costs. Furthermore, the pillows don't just evoke bubbles; they *are* bubbles, twin films of ETFE, .008 of an inch thick, placed together to form a cell, which is then inflated.

The real achievement of the Water Cube is less its technical wizardry than the transformation of the faintly trite idea of a bubble building into a piece of elegant, enigmatic architecture. The architects decided that, to play off the oval shape of the Bird's Nest, the Aquatics Center would have to be square, and the constraint of straight lines seems to have insured that the bubble metaphor didn't get out of hand. The Water Cube's walls suggest the soap foam on a shower door—or perhaps, since some of the bubbles are as much as twenty-four feet across, on the slide of a microscope. From the outside, the almost random arrangement of cells establishes a kind of correspondence with the irregular struts of the Bird's Nest. When you are inside the main hall of the Water Cube, the pattern of cells above and the green-blue tinge of the pool give you the feeling of being underwater yourself and looking up toward the surface.

Although China's burgeoning wealth owes much to its export industries, for the Olympics the country has been content to play the reverse role, buying the most futuristic architecture that the rest of the world has to offer, rather than showcasing native talent. The work of Chinese architects has largely been relegated to a jumble of functional but uninspiring buildings. (There are thirty-one Olympic venues in all.) An important exception is Digital Beijing, a control center on the Olympic Green, designed by a Chinese firm, Studio Pei Zhu. Like the Water Cube, Digital Beijing steers dangerously close to a kitschy conceit. It consists of four narrow slabs set close together in parallel to resemble a row of microchips or, perhaps, hard drives. Some of the walls have glass cutouts in a linear pattern clearly designed to evoke a circuit board—they light up green at night. Yet the finished building has a dignity that is surprising. This is due in part to Pei Zhu's choice of materials—the walls are clad in a sober grayish stone—and in part to the proportions of the four slabs, whose narrowness and lack of adornment give the building an austerity that is the opposite of kitsch.

Pei Zhu may be Chinese, but his building is thoroughly international in style. (He was educated at the University of California and has worked both in China and abroad.) Indeed, apart from the red of the Bird's Nest, there is little that is traditionally Chinese in any of the Olympic developments. The scale and ambition of the project is an unmistakable statement of national pride, yet China, strangely, has been content to make this statement using the vocabulary of the kind of international luxury-modernism that you might just as easily see in Dubai or Soho or Stuttgart—dizzyingly complex computer-generated designs, gorgeously realized in fashionable materials. The message seems clear: anything you can do, we can do better.

The first Olympic Games of the modern era, in 1896, were held in an ancient stadium in Athens that the Greeks refurbished for the occasion. The swimming events took place in the Aegean Sea. The next Olympics, in Paris in 1900, had no stadium at all. The track-and-field competitions were held on the streets of the city and on the grass of the Bois de Boulogne, which the French did not want to disfigure with a proper track. Swimmers were left to cope with the currents of the Seine.

The idea that cities could attract the Olympics by promising lavish facilities probably began after 1906, when the eruption of Mt. Vesuvius put an end to a plan to have the 1908 Games in Rome. The British saw Italy's misfortune as an opportunity and offered to build a stadium big enough to hold a hundred and fifty thousand people, in Shepherd's Bush, London. The White City Stadium, as it was called, was the first stadium to be erected specifically for the Olympics. Soon, countries were openly vying with one another to host the Games. (What is the Olympic ideal, after all, but national rivalry dressed up as global amity?) The apogee of triumphalism was reached, notoriously, in Berlin, in 1936, when Hitler, who wasn't yet in power when the Games were awarded to the city, embraced the Olympics as the way to show off the might of the Nazi regime. Architecture was as much a part of his vision as the gold medals, though his taste ran to the turgid and overblown. He tore down a perfectly good, barely used stadium, replaced it with the largest stadium in the world, and then built a 130-acre Olympic Village, with 140 buildings laid out in the shape of a map of Germany.

Since World War II, host countries have avoided such bombastic excess, but they have usually seen the Olympics as an opportunity to pin a gold medal on one or more of their leading architects. There was Pier Luigi Nervi's innovative, seemingly floating concrete dome on his stadium for the Rome Olympics, in 1960; Kenzo Tange's swooping, sculptural gymnasium for Tokyo, in 1964; Günter Behnisch and Frei Otto's canopied stadium for Munich, in 1972. For the Barcelona Olympics, in 1992, the Spanish architect Santiago Calatrava was enlisted to build a communications tower that would serve as an Olympic symbol. Calatrava's angular, precarious-looking design, inspired by an arm holding the Olympic torch, established his worldwide reputation and remains one of the city's most visible structures. But the Barcelona Olympics also marked a new approach to Olympic architecture, one that placed as much emphasis on the relationship between the city and its facilities as on the sports venues themselves. Barcelona used the Games as an occasion to redevelop its waterfront and design a series of new parks, fountains, and works of public art to attract tourists after the Games were over. Since then, cities have been keen to use the Olympics to leverage other civic improvements, on the premise that if you're spending billions to refurbish a city you should at least invest in buildings that have long-term utility. That's why the legacy of the 1996 Olympics, in Atlanta, isn't any of the athletic buildings but a major new park and housing for athletes that became new dormitories for Georgia Tech.

The plan for the 2012 Olympics, in London, takes this idea a step further. Although there is one flashy commission for a British architect (an aquatics center, designed by Zaha Hadid, in the form of a giant wave), the London Olympics are distinctly short on architectural extravaganzas. The main stadium, to be designed by a large American firm that has had a lock on football and baseball stadiums for years, will be dull compared to the Bird's Nest. When I talked to Ricky Burdett, a professor of architecture and urbanism at the London School of Economics, who is an adviser to the London Olympics, he told me that London did not feel the need to prove itself through spectacular works of Olympic architecture. "We had a big debate over whether we should build a new stadium at all," he said. "We were much more interested in how an intervention on this scale will affect a city socially and culturally." The British government plans to invest roughly $19 billion in an Olympic site, in the East End of London. When the Olympics end, much of the area will become a park, and sales of private development sites around it are expected to enable the government to recoup much of its investment. Burdett said, "London has always been poor in the east and rich in the west. The London Olympics can rebalance London."

Beijing, evidently, has other priorities. For all the sleek modernity of much of the construction, there's no mistaking the old-fashioned monumentalist approach behind it. This is an Olympics driven by image, not by sensitive urban planning. It's true that there has been a much needed and well-executed expansion of Beijing's subway system, but most of the impact of the Olympics has been cosmetic—the trees planted along the expressway to the airport, for example, or the cleanup of some of the roadways leading to the Olympic Green. Bordering one stretch of congested elevated ring road, stone walls, like the ones surrounding the old Beijing *hutongs*, or alleyway neighborhoods, have been erected. But, with not much behind them, they are little more than a stage set—Potemkin *hutongs* designed to distract visitors from the fact that so many real *hutongs* are being demolished for high-rise construction. In today's Beijing, forcible eviction is common, and hundreds of thousands of people have been displaced to make way for the Olympics. The brightness of the Olympic halo gives Beijing's relentless expansion a surface sheen, but it's only a distraction from the city's deeper planning problems, such as air and water pollution and overcrowding.

In general, the Chinese authorities have been less interested in solving these problems than in keeping the construction engine going at full throttle. Still, the Olympic site did require some planning and, in 2002, a competition was held to create a master plan. It attracted entries from ninety-six architects around the world and was won by a Boston firm, Sasaki Associates. Despite its straight-line connection to the Forbidden City, the Olympic Green lies in a district that, in recent years, has become a forest of undistinguished high-rise apartment buildings and commercial towers. (The site also includes a mundane athletic compound erected for the 1985 Asian Games, and these leftover structures are all being refurbished for the Olympics.) Dennis Pieprz, the president of Sasaki, who was in charge of the scheme, explained to me that the firm struggled for a long time with the question of how to treat Beijing's axis. The Chinese tradition of aligning important public buildings created "a huge temptation to put the stadium right on the axis," he said. "But we decided that in the twenty-first century we were beyond that, and that we should, instead, symbolize infinity, and the idea of the people in the center, not a building." So Sasaki placed the stadium just to the east of the axis and the Water Cube just to the west; the space directly on the axis was left open.

Pieprz told me that he felt that considering the long-term use of the site was essential. "We needed a plan that could accept other civic, cultural, recreational, and commercial uses, so the place would become a major destination," he said. Sasaki envisions the Olympic site as becoming a large park, with each of the major buildings taking on a public function. The Bird's Nest will remain as the national stadium, its capacity reduced to a more practical eighty thousand by the removal of several tiers of seats; the Water Cube will lose almost two-thirds of its seventeen thousand seats, the upper tiers to be replaced by multipurpose rooms. "You are making a city, not a spatial extravaganza that will be interesting just for sixteen days," Pieprz said.

But, whatever the architects feel, it's not clear that the Chinese are really that interested in long-term uses. The focus is on August, and on confirming before the world Beijing's status as a modern, global city. However well the buildings are refitted afterward, it's hard to see how the Olympic park will relate to the rest of the city, beyond being a welcome piece of green space in an increasingly built-up, sprawling metropolis. The success of what China has built for the Olympics will ultimately be measured not by how these buildings look during the Games but by the kind of change they bring about in the city. The billions of dollars spent on the Olympic site, after all, are only a fraction of the money that has been invested in construction in Beijing since the Games were awarded to the city, in 2001. The city, however, has yet to build a public space as inventive as that of post-Olympics Barcelona, or to think of the impact of the Olympics in terms as sophisticated as pre-Olympics London. In both conception and execution, the best of Beijing's Olympic architecture is unimpeachably brilliant. But the development also exemplifies traits—the reckless embrace of the fashionable and the global, the authoritarian planning heedless of human cost—that are elsewhere denaturing, even destroying, the fabric of the city.

The New Yorker, June 2, 2008

PLACES AND PEOPLE

Preservation in Cuba

BRINGING BACK HAVANA

In Havana, perhaps even more than in Los Angeles, you are what you drive. Samuel González, a taxi driver, has a red-and-white 1953 Chevrolet, which by the standards of this city, where American cars from the 1950s are among the chief ornaments of the cityscape, qualifies as a coveted vehicle, almost chic. For a long time, Mario Coyula, an architect who travels in more sophisticated circles than Samuel González, had one of Cuba's only Porsches. Now, conscious of his role as vice-director of a group overseeing architectural planning for the Havana region, he drives one of the colorless Russian-made Ladas that were the cars preferred for years by the Cuban government. Ambassadors from other countries, restricted neither by the ideology of the revolution nor by the need to choose their cars from what happens to be around, ride in Mercedes-Benzes, but then so does Fidel Castro. And Eduardo Luis Rodríguez, an architectural historian, has no car at all.

Rodríguez, who is one of the most highly respected scholars of twentieth-century Cuban architecture, has no telephone, either. He lives, with his wife and two sons, in a small apartment beneath the parish house of a church in Havana's Vedado section, and he moves around the city by bicycle. To reach him, you go to his house, walk across a tiny patio, on which sits the empty frame of a 1950s sling chair, and rap on a sliding-glass door. If there is no answer, you leave a note telling Rodríguez when and where you hope to meet him. If he is not already committed, he will show up.

At thirty-eight, Rodríguez is more worldly than most Cubans: he has traveled to Europe and the United States to lecture on the architecture of his homeland. A stocky, bearded man, he has an amiable bearing, and his manner bespeaks graceful discretion more than scholarly hauteur; like many Cubans, he wears his erudition lightly. Despite his reputation abroad, he has not had an easy time as a scholar, because he does not always hew to the official line about architecture and preservation in Havana, which is, in effect, that the city is fine and that it will become even finer thanks to the work now being done by the official city historian, a man named Eusebio Leal, whose genteel title belies the fact that he has become something like the Robert Moses of Havana.

There is some disagreement about whether Havana is, in fact, so fine. The city is one of the richest and most eclectic urban environments anywhere, overflowing with architecture that is extravagant in its ambition and spectacular in its execution. But Havana is largely crumbling. Its buildings are falling down, its sewers are a mess, and its telephone system resembles that of an Eastern European city c. 1975. The Calzada del Cerro, the main street of the once prosperous El Cerro neighborhood, is one of the most remarkable streets in the world: three unbroken kilometers of nineteenth-century neoclassical villas, with columned arcades making an urban vista of heartbreaking beauty—linear monumentality of a sort that exists nowhere else, except, perhaps, in Bologna. It is now deteriorating so dangerously that when I stopped for a moment in front of one building, a passerby grabbed my arm and pulled me away; the cornice, he said, looked as if it was about to collapse.

In Cuba now, the only buildings that get taken care of are the ones that bring in tourist dollars, and this situation makes local preservationists like Rodríguez fear for the city's future. While Old Havana is protected as a UNESCO World Heritage site and is being restored as a quaint tourist attraction—this is Eusebio Leal's project—the rest of the city seems to be viewed less as an irreplaceable artifact than as turf on which Cuba can play out its romance with capitalism.

A glimpse of the Havana that Rodríguez fears appeared two years ago in the form of the Hotel Meliá Cohiba, a shrill, twenty-two-story tower of brown marble and reflective glass erected by a Spanish hotel chain in the hope of attracting tourists and businesspeople. It sits next to the Riviera, the flashy hotel erected by Meyer Lansky just before Castro came to power, which is a prize relic of 1950s architecture. Beside the Cohiba, the Riviera looks as venerable as a Renaissance palazzo. And last November the Carlos III Mall, four stories of shops and fast-food outlets around a central atrium, opened up in the center of Havana, providing a taste of Paramus, New Jersey, within blocks of the Plaza of the Revolution and its three-story-high bas-relief of the face of Che Guevara.

Carlos III is hardly the Mall of America: it is tiny, and full of little stores selling, for the most part, ordinary goods. But in a city that for the last four decades has compensated for the grimness of socialist deprivation with an exceptionally vibrant street life, the very idea of an enclosed mall goes against the grain in two ways. It does not just reek of capitalism, but of American suburban capitalism. In a city that, despite the deprivations of socialism, has always been known for its vibrant street life, the mall is an ominous symbol: it represents not just capitalism, but suburban American capitalism.

No one believes that Havana will remain as it is for much longer. That American investment is forbidden has not prevented Havana from becoming ever more American in its way of doing business. The question, however, is what American model the city will embrace—sprawl and high-rises in the manner of south Florida, or more sanitized renovations of its older buildings designed to attract tourists.

Eduardo Luis Rodríguez rejects both scenarios and wants to see, instead, a Havana in which Art Deco palaces from the 1930s and good modernist architecture from the 1950s are as carefully restored as the city's nineteenth-century colonial buildings. "The government, the potential investors, they do not have any consciousness of the breadth of twentieth-century architecture in Havana, where we received every style in a very short period," he said. "But unlike the colonial buildings, none of it is protected." Rodríguez's passionate feelings about preservation in Havana have occasionally put him in disfavor. In a speech in 1995, in Washington, D.C., he said that he thought the Castro government should establish strong regulations for foreign investors to insure that new projects would not jeopardize Havana's architectural heritage. "I said something that was not politically correct, and I was told that what I was saying would discourage foreign investors," Rodríguez recalled.

Rodríguez's counterparts abroad are concerned about Havana's future, too. In the United States, where businesspeople watch and wait for the day when the American embargo ends, architects, many of them Cuban born, are looking forward to the day when they can return and begin to plan the city.

Some of them are not waiting. Andrés Duany, the Miami-based architect celebrated for the traditional villages he has designed, like Seaside, Florida, and his brother Douglas, a landscape architect, visited Havana two years ago. Their goal was to devise building codes that would protect the city's eclectic old architecture and prevent Cuba from turning into a landscape of malls and Wal-Marts—another Miami. "If they convert Havana into Hialeah, it would be the greatest failure of all," Nicolás Quintana, a Cuban-born architect who left Havana in 1960 and has lived in Miami since 1986, told me. "The moment investments come from the outside, they will rip apart the urban fabric," Douglas Duany said. "This is a very poor country. It will do anything for dollars, and its codes are not geared to protect Havana against large-scale investment. People in Cuba are sick of leaky roofs, which is what they associate old architecture with." The Duanys are part of an increasingly large and vocal group of Miami architects and planners who are studying Havana in the hope of protecting it, in a sense, from the Cuban government, which they do not trust to treat the city with the care it deserves. Among the others are Quintana, who is helping to found a program in Cuban studies at the architecture school of Florida International University, and Raúl Rodríguez, a successful Cuban-born architect in Coral Gables who maintains close relations with a full range of architects and planners in Cuba, from Leal, the most powerful government official, to Eduardo Luis Rodríguez, who might be called the loyal opposition.

Unlike the political Cuban-Americans who united under Jorge Mas Canosa to pressure the American government to keep the economic embargo alive, the architectural lobby is not skittish about dealing with the present government of Cuba: it is much more realistic, is politically more centrist, and, in some cases, even left of center. There is an absurdist paradox underlying this effort: a group of American architects in a capitalist country, trying to persuade a Communist system that it has to be less indiscriminate in its embrace of the marketplace.

"In order to save this incredible architectural inventory from destruction, you need an infusion of capital that is impossible under the present system," Raúl Rodríguez said. "But too strong an infusion of unregulated capital will bring it down. Isn't it significant that it is those of us who live under a capitalist system who are now preaching abstinence?"

"I can't think of a single Miami firm that doesn't have an eye on Cuba right now," Michael Smith, who heads the operations of the Turner Construction Company in the southeast United States, says. "Castro won't be there forever, and we see a terrific opportunity."

The Castro government, in contrast to many regimes whose power is absolute, has shown almost no interest in architecture. It constructs relatively little and—what is stranger still for a Communist government—it ascribes little symbolic power to buildings. The government has not built great monuments to itself, and it has not torn down the monuments built by its predecessors. It tends to adapt them instead. The Havana Hilton, finished just a year before Castro came to power, in 1959, was renamed the Habana Libre and for some time housed the revolutionary government's offices. A modern bank tower that was begun just before the revolution was stopped in midconstruction, but, instead of being torn down as a capitalist symbol, it was finished and turned into a hospital. Even the monument built to memorialize American lives lost in the explosion of the battleship Maine in Havana Harbor in 1898 remains, except that it has been shorn of the bronze eagle that once crowned its summit, because the Castro government considered the eagle too overt an American emblem. Fidel Castro works in a Mussolini-modern building that his predecessor, the dictator Fulgencio Batista, erected as the Palace of Justice. Castro changed its name to the Palace of the Revolution and moved right in.

It isn't so surprising, then, that Havana's stunning range of architecture remains virtually intact, if in dire condition. For nearly four decades, the Cuban government has dealt with Havana by ignoring it. Improving living conditions in the provinces took priority over building in Havana, and the city was largely left alone, preserved by default. "Fidel hated Havana. He thought it represented the work of the bourgeoisie," Nicolás Quintana says. "He abandoned it, and now the city is going to pieces."

Havana nevertheless still looks less like a Caribbean city than like a European or a South American one—Barcelona, perhaps, or Buenos Aires. It is easy now to forget that when Cuba's elite began to flee Havana for Miami after Castro came to power, they were leaving a city that was one of the world's most cosmopolitan, for what was, by comparison, a swampy backwater. In the thirty-nine years since then, Miami has been transformed into an international city, and Havana has all but stopped. It is wrong, however, to say that the city is frozen in time. Time is very visible in Havana; it just shows itself by decay.

Havana possesses as varied a mixture of twentieth-century architecture as New York: there are Art Nouveau palaces to rival those of Barcelona, Art Deco houses to equal those of Paris, Spanish Colonial mansions in the style of Beverly Hills, and as much first-rate International Style modernism as in Berlin. Most of the grand residences had been occupied by sugar barons and industrialists who fled after the revolution, and only a handful are in decent condition. Some, like an ornate house with a grand marble staircase a block away from my hotel, which was abandoned by a pharmaceuticals-maker, have become *ciudadelas*—literally, "little cities." That is, they are home to more than a dozen families. Laundry hangs from an elaborate stone-carved veranda, and one of the occupants of the house sells souvenirs from a cart amid weeds that were once a front lawn. Part communes and part squatter communities, *ciudadelas* have taken over some of the city's greatest houses. At the rate they are decaying, it is hard to imagine that many of them will still be standing ten years from now. "It is a pity, to know that there is no possibility of saving this," Eduardo Luis Rodríguez says. "You can maybe save a hundred great buildings, but here there are a thousand of them."

The streets of the suburbanized Vedado neighborhood are haunting. At night, they are completely dark—Cuba cannot afford many streetlights— and much of the light within the houses is fluorescent, creating an eerie shrill-ness amid the soft features of the sculptured cornices and columns. This is aristocratic architecture taken over by another class, and while that is not in itself a process unique to Havana (it has also happened in Bedford-Stuyvesant and parts of Harlem), its impact here is staggering. These houses still possess a majestic presence, and the streetscape, though marred by empty lots and jangly

Streetscape, Havana

new buildings put up in the 1950s, continues to have a sense of coherence. It resembles the Garden District of New Orleans: there is the same mixture of great mansions, multiple dwellings, slight decay, and, here and there, well-tended preservation, all softened by lavish foliage. But nowhere in New Orleans is there a house like the stone mansion at the corner of Havana's Twenty-seventh and K Streets, where a broken-down 1958 Cadillac Fleetwood sits rusting in the front yard like a piece of sculpture, with families of cats and dogs turning its inside into an animal *ciudadela*, and where a woman watches over them from a balcony grand enough to review an army battalion.

In the formerly posh neighborhood called Miramar, there is something even spookier: a sprawling stucco palace with a round turret, huge gables, and a roof of green tiles which has holes large enough to drop a breadbox through. What had been the glass on the front door is entirely broken, leaving only open ironwork between the outside and the marble vestibule. The place is so dilapidated that I assume it to have been entirely abandoned, but it turns out to be occupied by a Spanish-born woman named Luisa Faxas, who, with her mother, bought it in 1942 and has never left. After the revolution, the Cuban government seized commercial assets but not residences, and a few members of the upper classes remained in them. Señora Faxas, a thin, chain-smoking woman of seventy-five who was dressed in pink pedal-pushers, has three children in the United States, but she refuses to leave the house to join them. The house has been badly damaged by water, with the exquisite plaster detail in the living room half destroyed, the master-bedroom ceiling crumbling, and most of the furniture gone.

I imagined that Señora Faxas was so devoted to her sumptuous home that she remained, like a Cuban Miss Havisham, oblivious of the realities of the world around her and determined to hold on to her castle and protect it from a government that is more comfortable with the idea of twelve people living in one room than one person living in twelve rooms. I assumed she wanted only to die amid the remnants of the splendor she once loved. That turned out not to be true at all. "When I'm in another country, all I want to do is come back," she said, puffing on a cigarette and shooing away her dog. "But I don't love this house. I never did. The government keeps trying to persuade me to leave, so it can take the house, but all it keeps offering me is small apartments. And if the deal is not going to be fair, I stay here."

Eduardo Luis Rodríguez's drafting table hangs a framed black-and-white photograph of a strange, voluptuous modern building. It turns out to be his private passion: the Castro government's first, and last, foray into serious architecture, a Cuban national arts institute built on the former golf course of the Havana Country Club, not far from Miramar. The country club, a place where Luisa Faxas might well have spent her afternoons playing tennis, was seized shortly after the revolution by the government, which intended to convert it to a more populist use. The regime commissioned Ricardo Porro, a prominent Cuban architect, to design an extraordinary campus of Expressionist modern buildings, each one housing a different artistic discipline, and while not all the institute was built, the first stages, which included a fine-arts complex and a modern-dance complex by Porro and a ballet complex by Vittorio Garatti, were enough to establish the school as a project of stunning ambition.

And then, almost as quickly as the government commissioned the project, it withdrew its support. A set of buildings which brings to mind such architects as Eero Saarinen, Philip Johnson, José Luis Sert, and Louis Kahn, the school had an earnest, determined aestheticism that did not sit well with a regime increasingly influenced by the harsh Leninism of the Soviet Union. The college continues to operate, although its buildings have never been properly maintained. A huge, Soviet-style concrete bunker of a dormitory was put up in front of several of Porro's buildings, making a mockery of their careful relationship to the landscape, and the most beautiful section of all, Garatti's ballet school, was never even opened. Its monumental brick vaults, its long, serpentine brick gallery, and its extraordinary brick dome are now virtual ruins, with the tropical jungle closing in on their lyrical, floating planes.

Ricardo Porro, after being cast aside by the revolution to which he had hoped to give an architectural identity, abandoned Cuba altogether and now lives in Paris. His school, however, is a masterwork, and it has been more thoroughly rejected by the government than the grandiose classical buildings put up by Castro's predecessors. The current regime, it seems, cannot bear to accept its own parentage of an architectural treasure. I had never heard of the school until Eduardo Luis Rodríguez directed me to it, for it has been written out of architectural history as definitively as certain government figures who fall out of favor are written out of political history. Rodríguez knows it's unlikely that the buildings will ever be fully put back together, but he sees restoring the institute's good name as a duty. "For young architects, this school is the flag in our war to recover architecture," he says, walking across the former golf course. He insists that I see every nook and cranny of the school: swirling, sensual curving passageways; arcades that seem like a cross between Gaudí and Le Corbusier; and domed studios littered with broken glass. "Porro wanted to make a statement about disorder against order, tranquility against tension," Rodríguez said. "This complex started as a symbol of what the revolution could do in architecture, and then it became the opposite—a symbol of what the revolution didn't want."

What the revolution does want, apparently, is Eusebio Leal. A scholar and politician—he is a member of the National Assembly, and functions within the highest reaches of the Castro government—and a relentless, if subtle, self-promoter, Leal has awakened the government's interest in the city. Almost single-handed, he has revived Old Havana, the once decaying colonial core near the waterfront, making it safe for tourists. Leal made restoration into a vehicle for development, just as it might be in an American city. The Old Havana he has made has a pristine, slightly too-perfect air about it: Old Havanaland. But the government knows that theme parks are profitable. So the new tourist route in Old Havana includes craft markets on the plaza in front of the cathedral; a church restored as a concert hall; and a Benetton boutique in the Plaza San Francisco. The tourist route doesn't include the main art museum, which has been closed since last summer for renovation, or the Granma, the boat in which Fidel Castro returned to Cuba in 1956, which has been displayed for years behind the old Presidential Palace in a glass enclosure that looks like an auto showroom. The boat is still there; it is just that it has been reduced to a kitschy curiosity, barely relevant to the new form of tourism, in which Old Havana feels every day more like Old San Juan.

Leal alone decides what will be restored in Old Havana. In addition to running the city agency that oversees old buildings and cultural facilities, he controls a state-owned company called Habaguanex, which develops and runs hotels, restaurants, shops, and offices in Old Havana, and another company, called Fénix, which is a real-estate-management company. You do not do business in Old Havana without running into Leal, whose mini-capitalist empire will bring in around $43 million this year, $21 million of which his agency plans on reinvesting in its projects. (The rest goes to the state.)

"Leal does whatever he wants, and no one can say no," a young architect in Havana says. "He treats Old Havana as his private fiefdom." But Leal has largely ignored the rest of the city, which is off the tourist route and crumbling fast. Leal, unlike many high officials of the Cuban government, is extremely visible: he has his own television show, and he can sometimes be seen on the streets of Old Havana, surveying his dominion. Early one evening, Eduardo Luis Rodríguez and I ran into him as we were heading toward the Plaza Vieja, the most active restoration site right now in Old Havana. A man of medium height with wavy steel-gray hair, Leal dresses in guayabera shirts. His manner is unfailingly courteous, but it is a courtesy that, like his traditional Cuban dress, is designed to create the illusion of accessibility. His demeanor is formal and cool, and he greets Rodríguez kindly but somewhat warily, with the tone of a person who is not accustomed to participating in conversations he cannot control.

Leal's restorations are stunning to look at, and they are technically superb: a staff of sophisticated, mostly young architects has remade such landmark hotels as the Ambos Mundos and the Santa Isabel with elegance and finesse. They consider their work to be important in holding back the onrush of sprawl development in Havana and in asserting the importance of traditional urbanism. Their goals, in this sense at least, are identical to those of the Miami architects' lobby. It is just that Leal's people draw the line at Old Havana; and the lobby (and Rodríguez) are far more concerned about the rest of the city.

"I am against malls, and we give a lot of value to traditional neighborhoods. What we are doing is insuring that at least in Old Havana, the wrong things will not happen," says Patricia Rodríguez, one of the architects in Leal's office. But these restorations, exquisite though many of them are, constitute a kind of Potemkin village: luxury hotels face picturesque squares, while a block or two away are deteriorating houses with entire families living in single rooms, often open to the street. Leal's office operates with so resolutely capitalist an attitude that it has produced an elegant forty-three-page book, much like a corporate annual report, that celebrates the achievements of its restoration projects. When Patricia Rodríguez hands me a copy at the end of our meeting and I express thanks, she says that it will be fifteen dollars, please, in American currency. Leal has from time to time asked journalists for thousand-dollar contributions to his restoration funds in exchange for interviews.

"Eusebio Leal is a very compulsive person, and very forceful," Eduardo Luis Rodríguez told me, choosing his words with care. "He managed to convince people that the colonial buildings had value and should be restored. The problem was that he forgot about twentieth-century architecture." Colonial architecture is easy to like, not only because it is pretty, charming, and relatively unchallenging but also because it is ideologically safe. Putting money into fixing it up doesn't make the Castro regime nervous, since Old Havana was created neither by the capitalist sugar barons, who made the city's great mansions in the first three decades of this century, nor by the hated Batista regime, which made the city's early-modern buildings in the 1950s. Colonial architecture was made by settlers who lived in the nineteenth century—long enough ago so that to the current regime, they are quaint rather than threatening.

If Eusebio Leal is the New Age Cuban bureaucrat, turning capitalism to the benefit of socialism, and Eduardo Luis Rodríguez the independent scholar, pleading the case for the city as an artifact, Mario Coyula is something in between. An architect, scholar, planner, and urbanist who has been a central figure in the development of Havana since just after the revolution, he has managed, more successfully than anyone, to operate on all sides of the table. He does not have anything like the power of Eusebio Leal, however, and seems increasingly to function as a philosopher on the city. He has close ties both to the international architectural community and to the Cuban government; he travels often in and out of Cuba discussing the development of Havana at academic conferences. He believes that the dangers of overdevelopment in Havana posed by the architects in Miami are exaggerated. But he nonetheless looks at Havana today with a certain amount of despair, because he feels that the country's economic problems will make it impossible for it to repair its older buildings, or to plan wisely for its future development.

Coyula is best known in Havana as the master of "the model"—a spectacular, sprawling miniature of the city, 116 meters square, which fills a two-story hall in his organization's Miramar offices. The main purpose of the model is to allow planners to evaluate the effects of new projects on the cityscape, and Coyula points with pride to the fact that a new high-rise hotel proposed for the Malecón, Havana's waterfront boulevard, was rejected after its insertion into the model suggested that it would have a far more deleterious effect on the skyline than the investors behind it had indicated.

The model is color-coded, with colonial buildings in red, twentieth-century buildings in beige, and brand-new or unbuilt ones in pure white. As soon as you see it, you realize that Havana is primarily a twentieth-century city, that most of its growth occurred after the end of the Spanish occupation in 1898. A modernist by training, Coyula is exceptionally proud of the city's heritage of modernist architecture from the 1950s.

Coyula is that oddest of creatures—a Communist elitist. "I remember before the revolution people tended to show their best facades to the street— the facades of their buildings as well as of their characters," he says. "I despised that at the time, because I thought it was hypocritical. But at least it provided a friendly streetscape. Now the situation has been reversed, and people are not giving the proper value to good manners at all." Coyula is in a bind. He loves Havana, deeply and passionately ("thanks to my Havana, graceful and crumbling/waiting for this body, already fulfilled" are two lines of a poem he wrote as a dedication for his new book on the city), and yet he is, technically at least, part of a government that seems increasingly willing to allow large corporate enterprises from abroad to dictate the city's future form.

The dilemma for Havana is not just that there seem to be two alternative scenarios for its future—another south Florida, full of sprawl and high-rises, or more Leal-style restorations of historic buildings creating a kind of cordon sanitaire for the benefit of tourists—but that, in the end, the two are not really so different. They are both American models, and neither embraces the richness and the scope of the Havana that exists now. The question is whether Havana will be taken over by the world outside the theme-park gates or by the one inside it.

"For thirty-five years we haven't been thinking about money," Mario Coyula said. "But now we are learning very quickly."

The New Yorker, January 26, 1998

Las Vegas Urbanism

CASINO ROYALE

Las Vegas was built on the premise that the degree to which people loosen their wallets is in direct proportion to the amount of fantasy that is offered to them. In other words, the less the city looks like home, the more money visitors will spend. This notion depends on ignoring one of the essential qualities of most successful cities. Continuity, usually a source of joy and comfort, is counterproductive in Las Vegas, where this year's bedazzlement is next year's snooze. Keeping the city going takes ever-increasing doses of invention.

Once, years ago, neon was enough to do the job. As Robert Venturi, Denise Scott Brown, and Steven Izenour observed

View from McCarran Airport: Mandalay Bay, Luxor, Excalibur, New York-New York (above)

in 1972, when they wrote *Learning from Las Vegas*, the signs were more important than any of the buildings. But the city that Venturi, Scott Brown, and Izenour studied—and, to a certain extent, romanticized—hasn't existed for years. It was a victim of its own success. Now the buildings are more important than the signs, although they aren't nearly as sexy. The new measure of success is size. Several hotels nearing completion in Las Vegas are so big that three thousand rooms constitutes a medium-sized establishment. The MGM Grand, which is currently the biggest place in town, has five thousand rooms and is expanding. When the latest wave of construction is finished, the Strip will look less like the Las Vegas of old than like Wilshire Boulevard on steroids.

The creators of the new hotels are high on ersatz versions of European culture. The imagery of choice is no longer the Wild West, gambling, and naughtiness. The Sands is gone, and so is the Aladdin. The coming months will bring the Paris, the Venetian, and the Bellagio, which has a $295 million art collection containing works by Van Gogh, Renoir, and Picasso. The Venetian's owner, Sheldon Adelson, says that he chose the theme for his six-thousand-room hotel because his wife found Venice "enchanting." That's a long way from what Bugsy Siegel was thinking about when he named the Flamingo. The Paris will have a fifty-story-high replica of the Eiffel Tower in its front yard, and the Venetian will be enhanced by replicas of the Doges' Palace and St. Mark's tower, and Las Vegas's very own Rialto Bridge, which crosses a six-lane automobile entrance. (It is not entirely clear how this fits in with Adelson's claim that he is "not going to build a 'faux' Venice. We're going to build what is essentially the real Venice.")

Every one of the new hotels has become an attraction for visitors on its own terms, and not just a mecca for gamblers who detest the sun. The popularity of the buildings has created what is surely the most bizarre and wonderful thing about Las Vegas right now: the way in which it has begun, almost inadvertently, to function like a real city. The urbanism of Las Vegas is perverse, for it blossoms most where it should not exist at all, on the Strip, an eight-lane boulevard that shoots southward from the edge of the city's old downtown and is filled with casino hotels all the way to the airport, a distance of more than four miles. The Strip emerged in the postwar years, but its buildings weren't much more than glorified motels until the 1970s, when the first of the megahotels, the original MGM Grand, went up.

While the big hotels would seem to be entirely oriented to the automobile—and most of them are brilliantly designed to swallow and disgorge hundreds of cars an hour—each of them has also become a kind of node in the new urban experience of Las Vegas, one of the stations along the Via Striperosa. The Strip is full of people walking. They throng the sidewalks at all hours, marching from hotel to hotel, having figured out that if you want to see the MGM Grand and the Tropicana and the Luxor and the Monte Carlo, then there is no reason to get in your car each time just to move it one location down the Monopoly board. It is much smarter to use your feet. There are pedestrian bridges over the Strip to accommodate the huge crowds, complete with elevators to assure that the disabled are not excluded from the total urban experience.

Unlike the experience of Disneyland, to which it is sometimes compared, the new urbanism of Las Vegas is free. It is right out there, on the street, for all to partake in. Every night, huge crowds gather to see the pirate ships in front of the Treasure Island hotel and casino engage in battle, and the volcano in front of the Mirage, next-door, erupt, and after that the crowds surge back and forth, seeking entertainment wherever they can find it. In all likelihood, most of the people who come to Las Vegas are unaccustomed to thinking of cities as a source of entertainment, and the notion that walking along a crowded street can be exciting in itself is probably new to them. Urban activity for most people in this country occurs in private, enclosed places, like malls and atriums, and, while in one sense Las Vegas represents the absolute triumph of the private realm—these casino hotels aren't exactly efforts at public enterprise—it ends up staking an odd claim for the public realm.

It is only on the Strip that Las Vegas's weird and powerful urbanism exists fully. The city's rapidly growing suburban residential areas, with acre upon acre of Mediterranean-Deco-Baroque villas crammed one next to the other, are indistinguishable from Orange County. (A lot of Las Vegas, once you get away from the casinos, is indistinguishable from Orange County.) The old downtown, where locals and less-well-heeled tourists mix, struggles along, its seedy motels and wedding chapels still dominating the landscape. A handful of people walk along the sidewalks, their number only slightly increased by the completion, nearly three years ago, of something called the Fremont Street Experience, a metal vault that has turned the main drag into a pedestrian mall with a light show. But on the Strip, which Venturi, Scott Brown, and Izenour said existed only to be viewed from a moving automobile, one can see how much has changed since the 1970s. The buildings are hardly cheek by jowl, as in a conventional city, but the scourge of suburban sprawl, those vast, oppressive seas of parked cars, does not exist, since all the large hotels provide parking garages and limit grade-level parking to a tiny number of cars. Now even shopping malls are integrated into the quasi-urban casino-hotel complex. The best of them, the spectacular Forum at Caesars Palace, with its plethora of outrageous, overdone Roman detailing, is the most striking architectural solution to the vexing problem of the shopping mall anywhere in America. (It's amazing what a few columns, some statuary, some fountains, and some audio-animatronic figures can do for the shopping experience—not to mention a few slot machines.)

Las Vegas has always embraced the new with more passion than any other city; it also rejects its past more decisively. Obsolete hotels in Las Vegas don't get restored, they get blown up—"imploded," in the local jargon. Architecture, like cash, is easy come, easy go. Old signs may be preserved in a junkyard at the edge of town, but buildings just disappear. The local landmarks commission doesn't have much to do on the Strip.

The new architecture, for all its aspirations to grandeur, has little of the panache of the old. It is bigger but also thinner, and less sure of itself. Most of the new buildings are not much more than prettied-up Y-shaped skyscraper slabs, and collectively they can look disturbingly like the skyline of Bucharest. The new Las Vegas is less the Emerald City than Co-Op City with a mansard roof. The theme-park appliqué on these huge places—the Eiffel Tower in front of the Paris, the reference to Monegasque grandeur at the Monte Carlo—represents something of a toning down. A few years ago, when the city began its evolution into a so-called family resort, the most striking new hotels were the ones in which not just a few details but the whole building became a kind of play object. There was the Excalibur, a medieval castle; the Luxor, a pyramid of black glass with a massive sphinx as a porte-cochere; and New York-New York, a knockoff of the whole Big Apple skyline that seemed designed to serve as the backdrop for a production of *On the Town* for a cast of giants. But New York-New York is almost two years old, and the new generation of architecture is influenced by a municipal craving for respectability that you cannot get from make-believe Chrysler Buildings and fake sphinxes. The citizens of Las Vegas brought in Antoine Predock, the New Mexico architect, to design a library and children's museum, and Clark County just celebrated the completion of a county office building of red sandstone by the Denver architect Curt W. Fentress that is one of the most serious government buildings constructed anywhere in the last few years. Not long ago, it would have looked ridiculous next to all the neon signs and funny-shaped buildings on the Strip, but today, as the hotels become more conventional themselves, or at least more representative of a kind of bourgeois yearning, the county building's earnest, desert-style modernism is a natural emblem of the city.

Las Vegas is striving to go mainstream, but it is still addicted to fantasy, and these conflicting impulses have to be resolved. The city plunders the past with an exquisite combination of naïveté and cynicism; its buildings are the architectural equivalent of the sentimental gangster, yearning for respectability. One is tempted to say that the mixture of desires is no different from what Henry Clay Frick felt when he built a French Renaissance mansion on Fifth Avenue. But, of course, it is different, because Las Vegas represents culture for the masses; unlike Frick or the Vanderbilts, who built their castles to proclaim their distance from everyone else, Las Vegas aspires to push democracy farther. The only reason the new hotels exist is to have crowds swarming through them. The aristocracy here, such as it is, lives far from the center of town, behind locked gates. The heart of Las Vegas belongs to the new skyline—brash, glib, strangely banal, and urban in spite of itself.

The New Yorker, September 14, 1998

Iwan Baan

New Architecture in Beijing

FORBIDDEN CITIES

The city planner Edmund Bacon once described Beijing as "possibly the greatest single work of man on the face of the earth." When he was there, in the 1930s, you could still see that the city, from the walls surrounding it to the emperor's Forbidden City at its heart, was conceived as a totality—a work of monumental geometry, symmetrical and precise. Even the *hutongs,* the warrenlike neighborhoods of small courtyard houses set along alleyways, which made up the bulk of the

Rem Koolhaas/Office for Metropolitan Architecture, CCTV Headquarters, Beijing (above)

city's urban fabric, were as essential to Beijing as the temples and the imperial compound, which has the same intricate mixture of courtyards and lanes. Beijing was all of a piece.

It couldn't last forever, and it didn't. Mao Zedong tried to change Beijing into an industrial and governmental center, putting up factories and ponderous administrative buildings. But now Mao's Beijing is nearly as much a part of the past as the Forbidden City. The factories are being pushed to the outskirts, and in their place the city has developed a skyline. It isn't like the height-obsessed skyline of Shanghai, or the tight, congested skyline of Hong Kong. In Beijing, the towers are sprinkled all over the place. Most of them are mediocre, and some are ridiculous—a few have pagodalike crowns, to satisfy a former mayor who insisted that new buildings appear Chinese—but a handful are among the most compelling buildings going up anywhere in the world. In Beijing, the latest trend is architecture that will force the world to pay attention, and the result is a striking, unmistakably twenty-first-century city, combining explosive, relentless development with a fondness for the avant-garde. Beijing is as ruthlessly unsentimental today as it was in Mao's time, with little patience for history if it gets in the way of development, and yet the city doesn't feel as if it were defined solely by growth, like Shanghai, or like the kind of entirely manufactured environment that you see in Dubai. When I visited Beijing recently, the architect Ole Scheeren said to me, "I think Beijing is incredibly strong in its ability to completely override its own history and yet not surrender its identity."

Scheeren is the coarchitect, with Rem Koolhaas, of the most eagerly awaited building in Beijing, the headquarters of the Chinese television network CCTV, a monumental construction that has become world-famous long in advance of its completion, scheduled for late this year. A vast structure of steel and glass, it is a dazzling reinvention of the skyscraper, using size not to dominate but to embrace the viewer. The building will contain more office space than any other building in China and nearly as much as the Pentagon, but, as skyscrapers go, it is on the short side, with just fifty-one floors. Looking from a distance like a gigantic arch, it is a continuous loop, a kind of square doughnut. Two vertical sections, which contain offices, lean precariously inward, connected by two horizontal sections containing production facilities, one running along the ground, the other a kind of bridge in the sky. When you get closer, you see that each horizontal section is made up of two pieces that converge in a right angle. The top section, thirteen stories deep, is dramatically cantilevered out over open space, 530 feet in the air, and it seems to reach over you like a benign robot. The novelty of the form—some Beijingers have taken to calling it Big Shorts—takes time to comprehend; the building seems to change as you pass it. "It comes across sometimes as big and sometimes as small, and from some angles it is strong and from others weak," Scheeren said. "It no longer portrays a single image."

You might think that, like a good deal of Koolhaas's work, the building is as much showmanship as architecture, but it evinces a quiet, monumental grandeur. Some of that is due to the color of the glass, which is a soft gray, almost perfectly echoing the overcast Beijing sky. Around the glass, the diagonal grid of the building's steel framework is visible, the lines getting denser in the cantilever, where the structural stresses are more extreme. Scheeren told me, "I had the fantasy that the facade would disappear against the gray sky, and you would be left with only the black grid."

Like the CCTV building, a new development designed by the New York architect Steven Holl—a cluster of linked apartment buildings—displays a boldness that would be unlikely to escape compromise in a Western city. And, like the CCTV building, its most notable feature is a bridge—or, rather, bridges—high in the air. Holl has built eight squarish towers and one round one (which will contain a hotel), each about twenty stories tall. The residential towers have identical aluminum facades in a grid pattern, with square windows set back and edged in bright colors that Holl says he took from Buddhist temples. Holl placed the towers in a ring around the property, connecting them with glass-enclosed bridges at various heights—a kind of public, or semipublic, street in the sky running all the way around the complex. Some bridges start on one floor and end on another, so that you walk up or down a ramp—a hill in the sky. Each bridge contains some facility that the tenants share—a gym, a café, a bookstore. The most eye-catching has a swimming pool, which feels as if it were floating in the air, seventeen stories above Beijing.

The idea of the street high above the city is intended to counteract the sense of isolation that high-rise living usually brings, and to create an incentive for residents to walk around the complex. "In Beijing, to go anywhere means taxis and traffic jams and pollution," Hideki Hirahara, the project architect in Holl's Beijing office, told me as we walked around the site, where construction crews were just beginning to enclose the steel bridges. "We wanted to create all city functions inside the project."

The bridges are spectacular, inside and out, and one can imagine that there will be an allure to walking in the air from tower to tower that having a cup of coffee on the ground can't match. But there's a hitch. This clever prototype for a city without streets is also an admission that the traditional street-based city doesn't have much of a future here. As an attempt to bring avant-garde ideas to high-rise housing, the development is impressive, but at another level it's not unlike the gated apartment compounds that now fill much of Beijing's rapidly developing outskirts. The twenty-first-century equivalent of the ancient *hutongs* is a kind of skyscraper suburbia. You drive there, and then you get back in your car every time you go outside—exactly the model that planners in the United States have been trying to get away from in recent decades.

In this context, it's not surprising that another example of big-ticket Western architecture in Beijing—the National Center for the Performing Arts, by the French architect Paul Andreu—is about as disconnected from the street as possible. It's an ovoid of reflective glass set in an artificial lake and designed to look as if it were floating on water; there isn't even a door, lest the purity of its shape be disturbed. You descend to a sunken plaza beside the pool, walk through a tunnel under the water, and ride up an escalator to find yourself inside the ovoid. There's excitement in being under a huge, curving roof that shelters three different halls, but, in general, the entrance, striving for high drama, comes off as silly and cumbersome. The Chinese refer to the building as the Egg.

Locals call Beijing Tan Da Bing, which means Spreading Pancake. Since 1991, it has gained, on average, nearly three hundred thousand people a year, and by the end of last year, it had a population of around seventeen million. Old Beijing—designed for pedestrians and imperial processions but not much in between—has turned out to be a bad framework on which to construct a modern city. It has too few conventional streets, and they are spaced far apart. There aren't many traditional city blocks. In the days when Beijing was famous for swarms of cyclists, its unsuitability for automobiles didn't matter; now that the Chinese have cars, Beijing has gone in one generation from emanating an ancient spirit to feeling like Houston. When I visited three years ago, I thought that its problem was a compulsion to repeat the mistakes of American cities. Now the picture is much less clear. Crowding, pollution, and sprawl still define the city, but the new architecture, far from replicating an American mistake, surpasses what most American cities would be willing, or able, to do. This has an effect on the city's mood: people talk about the new buildings and, whether they approve or not, recognize that such daring constructions would not get built anywhere else.

Beijing is also beginning, slowly, to talk about historic preservation. Wang Jun, a thirty-nine-year-old journalist who was born in southwest China, has become Beijing's Jane Jacobs, an outspoken advocate of old neighborhoods and traditional streets. "When I started to work, it was the period of Beijing's most intensive dismantling," he told me. "I did a lot of investigating, and the city officials were very unhappy, which drove me to more investigating, which made the city officials even more unhappy." Now, Wang says, city officials invite him to meetings they once refused to let him attend, and the city has begun to put money into renovating some *hutongs* that would have been demolished a few years ago.

There are urbanists who think that Wang Jun's position smacks of nostalgia, and that the challenge facing Beijing is to develop a new urban form. "In China, bigness has become the only tool to keep pace with the fast developments," Neville Mars, a Dutch architect in Beijing, said to me. "The European model of urbanization is outdated, and China proves it. Beijing is a scattered city—how can we patch it back together? The Chinese appear to be in control, but it is really moving too fast for anyone."

Still, developers have lately begun to grasp the appeal that older buildings have, at least for the rapidly growing professional class. SOHO China, a marketing company that established itself with huge modern residential and commercial complexes in Beijing, is now at work on a retail complex, at Qianmen, just south of Tiananmen Square, that will be built around preserved and reconstructed sections of a *hutong*—a kind of Beijing version of Boston's

Fanueil Hall. Zhang Xin, who, with her husband, Pan Shiyi, controls SOHO, told me, "So much has been destroyed. Now what excites me is keeping what is left." But often what's left isn't much, and most of the new complex will have to be built from scratch. Zhang said, "Chinese people don't like anything old— they want everything new. If someone came from the moon, they would think this is a newer country than America." She paused. "Maybe that is what Mao wanted," she said.

The New Yorker, June 30, 2008

Louis Kahn

MANY MANSIONS

When Louis Kahn collapsed and died of a heart attack in a men's room in Penn Station on a Sunday evening in March 1974, he was the most celebrated architect in the United States. He had recently finished the Kimbell Art Museum in Fort Worth. The Yale Center for British Art was under construction in New Haven. A business school he had designed in Ahmedabad, India, was nearly complete, and in Dacca, Bangladesh, he was overseeing the largest project of his life, a series of government buildings that would eventually become the national capital.

Kahn was a seventy-three-year-old man with messy white hair and a badly scarred face. He wore rumpled suits, and on the day he died, he had spent nearly twenty-four hours traveling from India to New York.

He looked exhausted and unkempt, and the authorities who dealt with his body didn't recognize his name. He was sent to the city morgue. His passport said that he lived at 1501 Walnut Street in Philadelphia, but the police who went to that address found that it was an office building. Since it was Sunday and nobody was there, they let the matter drop for the time being.

It wasn't until late on Tuesday that word got out that Kahn had died two days earlier. I was then a young architecture critic at the *New York Times*, and I wrote an obituary that said that Kahn was considered by most scholars to have been the nation's foremost living architect, that his somber, poetic buildings of stone and concrete led a generation of younger architects away from glass boxes, and that he was survived by his wife, Esther, and a daughter, Sue Ann.

Several years later, I learned that there was more to Kahn's personal story. He had another daughter, Alexandra Tyng, who was twenty when her father died, and a son, Nathaniel, who was eleven. Kahn, it turned out, had three families. Alexandra was the daughter of Kahn and Anne Tyng, an architect who had worked closely with him. Nathaniel's mother was Harriet Pattison, a landscape architect who followed Tyng in Kahn's extramarital affections. Kahn did not flaunt his habit of forming liaisons with colleagues and keeping the relationships going on parallel tracks with his marriage. In fact, he said so little about his private life that Vincent Scully, the architectural historian who wrote the first book on Kahn's work, in 1962, hadn't known that Kahn was married. "For a while, I didn't know he had even one family—that was part of his mystery," Scully said.

Nathaniel Kahn, who is now thirty-eight, told me recently that once a week for several years, his father would take the train to Chestnut Hill, a suburban part of Philadelphia, have dinner with Nathaniel and his mother at their house, and put the boy to bed. Nathaniel would be awakened at one or two o'clock in the morning and bundled into the backseat of his mother's car, in his pajamas. Then they would all drive downtown, stopping half a block short of Kahn's house on Clinton Street, where he lived with his wife. Nathaniel remembers his father waking him up, kissing him, and walking down the street in the darkness.

Kahn's professional life seemed to be in a kind of vague disarray that paralleled his personal situation. His office was above a cigar store in downtown Philadelphia. Old coffee cans were plunked on top of drafting tables and used as ashtrays. Just before Jacqueline Onassis came by to talk to him about designing the Kennedy Library, Kahn ran out to buy real ashtrays, but they didn't do much to offset his shabby surroundings. Not necessarily because she cared about this sort of thing, Onassis hired the more corporate I. M. Pei instead. Kahn attracted clients whose high ambitions were matched by their patience and their disdain for conventional symbols of architectural fashion. His work is brooding and deep, like a Rothko painting. He combined materials in an unusual manner—for instance, wood panels are set into concrete frames in the symmetrical laboratory wings of the Salk Institute overlooking the Pacific in La Jolla—and he could use natural light to profoundly moving effect, as with the lightwells that bring indirect natural light into the sanctuary of the Unitarian Church in Rochester, which is made of concrete block.

Kahn used the basic tools of architecture—space, proportion, light, texture—sparely and with an almost religious reverence. He didn't want his buildings to appear to be so light that they could float off the earth, like Mies van der Rohe's, and he didn't want them to have swooping, eye-catching shapes, like Eero Saarinen's, or to be full of decoration, like the work Philip Johnson and Edward Durell Stone were doing in the 1960s. Kahn's buildings are tough.

Kahn had the manner of a slightly distracted academic. He tended to ramble on in a poetic, quasi-mystical way about light and space and stone, but this could be something of an act. He would say, "I asked the brick what it wanted to be, and it said, 'I want to make an arch.'" Or, "The sun never knew how great it was until it hit the side of a building." If you were his kind of client, you ate this up. Jonas Salk told Kahn that he wanted to build the sort of building he might bring Picasso to. He didn't talk to Kahn about how many square feet his scientists needed. It was pretty clear from the beginning that Kahn and Salk would get along.

Esther Kahn was a medical researcher. Her daughter, Sue Ann, remembers her mother listening to one of Kahn's discourses on architecture and observing that she understood barely a word. But Esther was protective of Kahn, and loyal. "She told me my father was an artist, that he wasn't like the other fathers," Sue Ann says. From time to time, Esther used her earnings to keep Kahn's office afloat financially, and when Sue Ann was growing up, the family lived with Esther's mother to save money.

Esther sent word through friends that neither her husband's other children nor their mothers were welcome at Kahn's funeral. They showed up anyway and were given seats at the rear of the funeral parlor. Four years ago, Nathaniel, who is a filmmaker, began work on a documentary about his father and his unusual family. He interviewed me about the night I wrote Kahn's obituary, and last spring he called to say that he had just been filming his father's work in Bangladesh and wanted to show me what he had come up with. There are interviews in the film with people who were close to Kahn, encomiums from Frank Gehry and Philip Johnson, a conversation with the owner of a music barge Kahn designed in the early 1960s who remembered Nathaniel as a child. The material is only partly edited, and I sensed that Nathaniel still hasn't quite figured out what he thinks of his father, whom he views with a mix of anger, exasperation, and awe.

The Bangladesh segment of the film is remarkable. It is the story of a Jewish architect who is hired to design the capital of a Muslim country, nearly goes broke while doing so, and is posthumously revered by the people he worked for. "He was no ordinary person," Shamsul Wares, a professor of architecture in Dacca, says in an interview. "He wanted to be Moses here. It was nothing, only paddy fields, and you are going to build something that is going to be the best building in the world?" Kahn spent the last twelve years of his life on the Bangladesh project, which was started when the country was still part of

Pakistan. When Bangladesh declared independence, in 1971, Kahn's contract was terminated and construction halted, but he kept working away on his designs. The government of Bangladesh hired Kahn back the next year to start the project up again, but it was not finished until 1983, nine years after he died.

At Dacca, Kahn achieved a commission adequate to his yearnings for monumentality. The heart of the complex is a sprawling set of geometric forms in concrete, framed by strips of marble that make the concrete sections look like enormous blocks. The central building is a composition of boxes and cylinders arranged around an assembly hall. Huge triangular, square, and circular openings are cut into the facade. The buildings in the complex are harsh, like so much of Kahn's work, but they have a primal quality and are serene rather than cold.

Curiously, there are no biographies of Louis Kahn, although there have been many books about his work. He would have been a hundred this year. He was born in Estonia in 1901 and came to Philadelphia when he was five. The biographical section of the books about him usually mention that his face was burned by coals when he was a small boy, and that he grew up in poverty and walked across Philadelphia every day to attend first art school and then the University of Pennsylvania on a scholarship. He started his career as a fairly conventional modern architect, designing public housing in Philadelphia, much of it in partnership with the architect Oscar Stonorov. Most architectural historians accept the premise, put forth by Scully, that he didn't really find his way until he went to the American Academy in Rome in the early 1950s. He discovered the power and beauty of Roman ruins, and when he came back to the United States, his architecture had less glass and more masonry, and instead of being light and airy, it was solid and heavy and full of simple geometric shapes, not unlike ruins.

Kahn's first important commission was for an addition to the Yale Art Gallery, which was finished in 1953, when he was fifty-two years old. He had been teaching part-time at Yale, and the president of the university, A. Whitney Griswold, asked him to design the first of a series of modern buildings for Yale's largely neo-Gothic campus. Kahn was followed by Eero Saarinen, Paul Rudolph, Philip Johnson, and Gordon Bunshaft, but his art gallery was more influential than anything the others designed. From the street, the building looks nearly blank, with a brick facade decorated with thin lines of limestone. But inside there is an innovative concrete ceiling of tetrahedrons for the galleries and a remarkable triangular stairway set inside a cylinder of concrete.

As part of his film project, Nathaniel, along with his producer, Susan Behr, visited the neighborhood Kahn grew up in, an area just north of downtown Philadelphia called Northern Liberties, which has diagonal streets, narrow alleys, freestanding houses, and, most striking of all, a number of red brick factory buildings. When Nathaniel and Susan walked through the streets of Northern Liberties, it became clear that the roots of Kahn's style are not in Rome but much closer to home. The big factories are remarkably like many of Kahn's buildings. One of them has large square windows and a sliced-off corner, and it looks for all the world like the exterior of the library Kahn designed for Phillips Exeter Academy. The most unusual industrial structure in Northern Liberties has a kind of zigzagging facade of brick and a series of open loggias, like brick-enclosed balconies, set into the facade, with solid brick walls behind them. The brick window openings are topped by concrete lintels. It is a composition of light and shadow, solid and void, with a solemn grace.

The similarities between the factory buildings in Northern Liberties and the architecture Kahn designed, not only at Exeter but also in India and Bangladesh and elsewhere, are too great to be accidental. The impression the old buildings made on Kahn could have been unconscious, or perhaps he carried it around with him knowingly, afraid for years to make much of it. Nathaniel, who went to Northern Liberties in search of a personal connection to his father, seems to have come back with a scholarly insight.

Louis Kahn designed with more self-assurance than almost any other architect of his time, but he had great difficulty making up his mind. He was excruciatingly slow. Architects like Frank Gehry look to him as the model of what it means to pursue an artistic vision with little compromise. Kahn was not practical; he was passionate. He ran his office so casually that he died hundreds of thousands of dollars in debt, and, while some of his financial problems surely came from his unusual domestic arrangements, he also tended to agonize over his work, designing and redesigning. A Kahn building was a work of art, and if the first version of the design turned out to cost two or three times as much as the budget, which often happened, Kahn would cut it back. He seemed to see the need to edit not as an affront but as a chance to keep on designing. He liked to talk about permanence and to place his buildings in the continuum of architectural history, but when a building was done, it meant that all the alternative ways he could think of to make it were no longer possible.

In the late 1960s, Kahn designed a house for Norman and Doris Fisher in Hatboro, a suburb of Philadelphia. It cost $45,000. Kahn charged them a $5,000 fee, and Norman Fisher told me that he is sure the architect lost money on it, because he redesigned the house nine times. Kahn was not a great architect of houses, but the Fisher house, a set of tall boxes of cypress, stone, and glass built at angles to one another, is warm and modest. While there are details, like the built-in wooden bench and the fireplace set within a stone half cylinder, that hint at aspects of Kahn's public architecture to come, the place doesn't seem like a public building in miniature, the way some of Kahn's houses do.

One day a few months ago, Nathaniel Kahn filmed a meeting with his two half sisters at the Fisher house. Sue Ann Kahn is a flutist and an administrator at Mannes College of Music. Alexandra Tyng is a painter. Sue Ann, through her mother, was Kahn's primary heir. He did not include his younger children or their mothers in his will, which may have been just as well for them, given that his office was so deeply in debt when he died. Kahn was an unusually gifted draftsman, and his most valuable assets were his exquisite pen-and-ink drawings, pastel sketches, and pencil renderings on tracing paper. Two years after Kahn died, the state of Pennsylvania appropriated $450,000 to purchase the drawings in his office, and they were deposited in a Kahn archive. Sue Ann ended up with the drawings that had been Esther's, along with most of her father's personal property. In the early 1990s, Sue Ann led a successful campaign to stop renovations on the Kimbell Art Museum in Fort Worth, one of Kahn's greatest buildings. The director of the Kimbell wanted to expand it by lengthening the travertine-and-concrete vaults, which would have made the building the architectural equivalent of a stretch limousine. Alexandra and Esther joined in the protest, and also in an unsuccessful effort to dissuade Jonas Salk from putting a new building awkwardly close to the one Kahn had designed for the Salk Institute.

On the day of the filming, the Kahn children walked through the Fisher house, making genteel comments. Then they sat down before a huge stone fireplace in the living room and talked about their father. Sue Ann said that when she was growing up, she asked him many times why he didn't build a house for her and her mother. "He told me about this vision he had of a window with many mullions," she said. "Like an old house at dusk, with a light on inside, where a woman is preparing a meal." But Kahn couldn't afford to build a house for himself, and if he had been able to, he wouldn't have designed one with an old-fashioned window and mullions. When an architect designs his own house, he presents his aesthetic aspirations as they conform to his private life. The private realm becomes a public statement. It can be no accident that Kahn's least successful buildings were his houses. He liked orchestrating public life in grand buildings.

At the end of his life, Kahn was almost willfully eccentric. His words were self-conscious in a way that his buildings never were, and he seemed to like being seen as a guru. It makes sense that he enjoyed going to India and Bangladesh. In Philadelphia he had to cope with debts and three families clamoring for his attention, but on the subcontinent he was a prophet. He was a difficult, self-absorbed artist devoted to his work. He would go to his office at night and on holidays, perhaps not so much to escape domesticity but simply because his greatest passion was drawing buildings and thinking about what architecture means. His earnestness put him somewhat out of fashion for a while after his death, and even now it dates him more than anything else. "Did the world need the Fifth Symphony before it was written? Did Beethoven need it?" he asked. "He designed it, he wrote it, and the world needed it. Desire is the creation of a new need." Kahn believed in designing for the ages, and he pretty much did. Only a few buildings in our time can be called sublime. Many of them—the Salk Institute, the Kimbell, Dacca—are Kahn's.

The New Yorker, November 12, 2001

Timothy Street-Porter © 2009 Eames Office

Charles and Ray Eames

THE EAMES TEAM

In 1976 the publisher and philanthropist
Walter Annenberg offered the Metropolitan
Museum of Art $40 million to construct
a new wing of the museum that would be
devoted not to art itself but to explaining
art through film, video, and computer
images. The wing, which was to be called
the Fine Arts Center of the Annenberg
School of Communications, was never
built. Some critics of the project objected

to Annenberg himself, whose father, Moses Annenberg, was a somewhat shady character; others were suspicious of Thomas Hoving, the flamboyant art historian who was the director of the Metropolitan and who had hoped to use the center as a means of maintaining power when he left office. Several members of the City Council questioned the propriety of yet another extension of the museum into Central Park, while many of the city's most prominent art critics feared that the center's emphasis on technology would cheapen the museum experience. In 1977, when Annenberg withdrew his gift in a fit of pique and the project collapsed, the general feeling in the city's cultural community was of relief. In fact, what had just occurred was one of the biggest fiascos in the museum's history.

While Hoving and city officials traded brickbats—so acrimoniously that Annenberg took out an advertisement in the *New York Times* to defend the project—nobody was paying much attention to what the Annenberg Center would actually contain. In a dozen articles on the proposed wing, including a column by Hilton Kramer, who sneered that it "overturns the very idea of a museum, and effectively destroys its reason for existence," the *Times* never once mentioned where the idea for the center had come from, the name of its designer, or any specifics about the proposed program.

The idea for the center had emerged following discussions between Hoving and the designer Charles Eames, who with his wife and partner, Ray, had been exploring the connections between art, science, technology, and education for years. In 1975 Eames produced a nine-minute film, called *Metropolitan Overview*, that laid out his vision for a new wing of the museum very much like the one Annenberg offered to underwrite the following year. The film took viewers on a simulated tour of the facility, which he foresaw as containing an exhibition on the history of the museum itself; several orientation areas to give visitors an overview of the museum's collections; and what would have been among the first—perhaps the first—computer-operated catalog of works of art. Eames's idea was that people would go to a computer terminal and punch up a reproduction of an artist's work, and then use the computer to bring up images of other work by that artist, or other works from a particular period or a particular place, or the record of a past exhibition. The computer would juxtapose pieces of information and help people make new connections about art. Annenberg liked the film and proposed giving the Met $20 million to build the place and another $20 million to run it for ten years. And then all hell broke loose.

What seemed too radical for New York in 1976 is, of course, commonplace now; with the Internet, millions of people have something approximating the Annenberg Center at home. A project that was denounced as a dangerous attempt to push the envelope of art education in the 1970s seems almost ho-hum at the end of the 1990s. The system the Eameses envisioned for the Met was really an early attempt at interactivity, and if it had been built, the Metropolitan would have been nearly a generation ahead of the rest of the world.

The Eameses were ahead of their time in quite a number of ways. Charles Eames, who was born in St. Louis in 1907 and died in 1978—his wife died ten years later to the day—was trained as an architect and designed chairs in molded plywood, fiberglass, and welded wire that are among the most technically advanced, not to mention famous, designs of the twentieth century. Along with his wife, a painter who had studied with Hans Hofmann, he was also a filmmaker, curator, scientist, inventor, graphic artist, toy designer, exhibition designer, and proto-techie. Charles and Ray Eames were the original nonlinear thinkers. They figured out that design was going to be different in the age of cyberspace long before William Gibson had given a name to such a thing.

The visionary Eameses all but invented the notion of using multiple projectors and multiple screens. When they were invited to produce a film explaining life in the United States for an exhibition sponsored by the United States Information Agency in Moscow in 1959—the exhibition at which Nixon had the famous kitchen debate with Nikita Khrushchev—they came up with a seven-screen display that bombarded Muscovites with more than two thousand images of freeway cloverleafs, buses, kite fliers, skiers, musicians, churches, skyscrapers, and Marilyn Monroe. Close-ups, wide shots, and distant views flashed from screen to screen for twelve intense minutes. "We wanted enough images going at the same time that it would completely discourage being absorbed in a single one," Eames said later. "If you got more than you could really take in, the effect of information was one that was greater than you had actually experienced."

Like the notion of a computerized catalog of art, the idea of carpet-bombing the viewer with hundreds of fleeting images is commonplace now. But it was startling in the 1950s, when almost every documentary film was a straightforward narrative with a beginning, a middle, and an end. Just as remarkable was the Eameses' response to Leland Hayward's request in 1960 for a short film on the music of the 1950s to run as part of a television special he was producing for CBS. They created nine minutes of images, seemingly disconnected, rapidly cut, and set against a musical montage—arguably the first music video.

Almost everything the Eameses did broke new ground. Their house overlooking the ocean in Pacific Palisades in California, which was constructed out of factory-made steel-and-glass parts, anticipated the high-tech fashion in architecture by a quarter of a century. In 1943, six years before the house was built, they had set up a general design studio in a sprawling former automobile-repair shop at 901 Washington Boulevard, in the Venice section of Los Angeles, that was the spiritual antecedent of the lofts that countless architectural firms and film companies began moving into thirty years later. The work that emerged from the loft also broke the mold: furniture, books, films, and toys that were at once matter-of-fact and elegant.

The Eameses were the king and queen of multimedia long before that word was coined. Their work had no particular style. Though the graphics tend to have a certain 1950s jauntiness to them, the things themselves make continual conceptual leaps far beyond their time. One of the Eameses' earliest films, *Blacktop* (1952), an art film that consists of nothing but footage of soapy water flowing over an asphalt playground, prefigures the films of Andy Warhol. *The Black Ships*, a documentary from 1970 that uses old Japanese prints to explain how nineteenth-century Japan viewed Commodore Perry, shows that the Eameses had figured out how to make a motion picture from exquisitely photographed stills a decade before Ken Burns began work on his documentaries about the Brooklyn Bridge and the Civil War.

An immense retrospective of the work of the Eameses opens on May 20 at the Library of Congress in Washington. It toured in Europe last year, in somewhat different form, and will move this fall to the Cooper-Hewitt Museum in New York and then to several other American museums. The exhibition should put an end to the automatic twinning of the words "Eames" and "chair." Only one of six sections of the exhibition is devoted to furniture; the rest is given over primarily to categories the curators have dubbed Space, Beauty, Culture, and Science. "We wanted to show that furniture was just one of their means of expression," C. Ford Peatross, the curator of the architecture and design collections at the Library of Congress, where most of the Eames archives are held, told me. "They were interested in problem solving, and furniture was just one way of solving problems. If they were alive today, they might not be doing furniture at all."

The greatest pieces of Eames furniture, the sinuous molded-plywood chairs of the 1940s and the sumptuous leather-and-rosewood lounge chair with ottoman of 1956, are remarkable objects, although Eames hated to think of them as works of art; he wanted them to be seen as proof that modern technology could create useful, beautiful, comfortable things that were affordable— mass-produced sensuous objects. And, as time went on, he grew less and less interested in the objects themselves, and more interested in finding ways to convey his belief that design was a means of teaching and problem solving, and that the good things in life should not be restricted to an elite. The Eames office continued to produce new furniture designs through the early 1970s, but as early as the 1950s, it was clear that what most excited Eames himself was devising new ways of educating people about history, culture, and technology.

The Office of Charles and Ray Eames, as the atelier in Venice was officially called, had consulting relationships with Westinghouse, Boeing, Polaroid, and the Herman Miller furniture company, which manufactured the Eames chairs. The Eameses designed showrooms and graphics for Herman Miller as well as furniture, and they were so trusted by D. J. De Pree, the head of the company, that he simply allowed them to design what they pleased and brought it out when they felt it was ready. There were no marketing studies and no direct assignments.

The United States government was also an Eames client, between 1959, when the Eameses made the film for the Moscow exhibition, and 1976, when they designed a vast, rambling exhibition, "The World of Franklin and Jefferson," for the Bicentennial. One of their design proposals for the government showed what a national aquarium in Washington would look like. The aquarium film, produced in 1967, is a guided tour through a building that did not yet exist.

It was a predecessor of the Metropolitan Museum film that would persuade Walter Annenberg to open his checkbook. The film was so vivid that I. Bernard Cohen, a historian of science who worked as a consultant to the Eameses, recalled years later that he and his wife, finding themselves in Washington with nothing to do, went looking for the aquarium. "We tried and tried and tried—we couldn't find the damn thing," Cohen said. "And then we both suddenly realized that there had never been an aquarium."

The Eameses' most collaborative and intimate relationship with a client was surely with the International Business Machines Corporation. The association began in the early 1950s as computers were just beginning to find their way into the public consciousness. The Eameses designed more than fifty exhibitions, films, and books for IBM. They crafted the company's thoughtful, public-spirited, and slightly whimsical image, no small achievement in the bland corporate culture of the postwar years.

I still remember one of the exhibitions that the Eameses created to explain computing to laymen: the IBM Pavilion at the 1964 New York World's Fair. They worked on the pavilion in association with Charles Eames's great friend Eero Saarinen—who died in 1961, just as the project was developing—and with Saarinen's successors, Kevin Roche and John Dinkeloo. It consisted of a huge, egg-shaped theater sitting atop a forest of columns designed to resemble trees. A bank of steep bleachers, called the "people wall," ascended on a hydraulic lift from ground level up into the theater. In the egg, displayed on twenty-two screens, was a thirty-minute multimedia film, *Think*, the point of which was to convince people that the mysterious things called computers were merely machines that could solve a lot of conventional problems very, very fast. In the film, a hostess is trying to plan a formal dinner party. She sits with a pad of paper, puzzling over how to arrange her guests around a table. The variables are that Bill will want to talk to Cindy, who can't be next to Harry, who doesn't like Alice, who is married to Sam. All computers really do, the film explains, is solve problems like this over and over again. And, just as a computer would have to be told that Harry couldn't be seated next to Alice, the quality of the results a computer yields is dependent on the quality of the information put into it.

The image of the woman and her dinner party remains in my mind vividly, thirty-five years after I first saw it. Indeed, it is so powerful that I barely remember the rest of *Think*, and was startled, when I saw an archival version of the film again the other day, to discover that the dinner-party sequence is only a portion of the film; it also includes a rather dreary sequence in which a group of urban planners sit around talking about how computers will help design cities—one of the only moments in the entire Eames oeuvre that seems dated.

Charles Eames came from the Midwest; his wife, from Sacramento. They were conventional, almost genteel people: calm, courtly in manner, and understated in appearance. He dressed in suits and bow ties, she in tailored pinafores. They had things custom-made to look ordinary. Charles Eames was folksy in a studied way. He sounded like Henry Fonda, and his lectures, like his conversation, were circuitous; he did not so much tell stories as present his mental processes for examination. You could almost say that while their work looked forward to the twenty-first century, their manner looked back to the nineteenth. They ran their lives with a kind of casual formality—picnics instead of sit-down dinners, but choreographed picnics. The loft in Venice was half factory, half atelier, with a cook.

Charles was less an aesthetician than a man who wanted to impose upon the world a kind of pleasant reasonableness. He had a way of seeing through mental clutter and getting to the essence of things, whether it was art, computers, mathematics, or history. He loved technology, he believed in systems, and he was something of a tinkerer. The office, to him, was a workshop, and he was the master, surrounded by loyal elves. Ray—whose stout form made her a kind of Mrs. Claus done up by the Bauhaus—actually had the better aesthetic sense of the two, and their relationship was complex and enriching to both, even though, like many women in creative partnerships, she often got short shrift in terms of public acknowledgment of her contribution. She had given up a promising career as a painter to join forces with Charles, and her sense of modernism as pure, abstract forms in space influenced his thinking. As the architectural critic Joseph Giovannini has pointed out, Charles loved to refer to his chairs as pure expressions of technology, the result of his having figured out how to mold plywood into curves, and never mentioned that "the implicit subject of the chairs is not only structure but richly dimensionalized space," which came from Ray. Her modernism was based on abstraction; his was based on ideas of industrial production. Their genius lay in the seamlessness of the combination.

The Eameses met in 1940 at the Cranbrook Academy of Art, in Michigan, a school known for its merging of art, architecture, urban planning, and crafts. Charles Eames was a relatively conservative architect in his early thirties, married, with a ten-year-old daughter. He had been invited to Cranbrook by the head of the school, the Finnish master Eliel Saarinen, who had seen photographs of a church designed by Eames which had a glimmer of sleekness to it. Eames was brought in as an architect, but, as Ralph Rapson, a Minneapolis architect who was also at Cranbrook, recalls, "Charlie spent no time in his architectural studio, absolutely none—he spent all of his time in the ceramics studio, in the photography studio, in the metal shop, in the weaving studio, obviously preparing himself for all the things he would do later on. He was learning the technology of all of these things." Eventually, Saarinen appointed Eames head of the industrial-design department, and he became close to Saarinen's son, Eero, an architect who would become not only his closest friend but a kind of aesthetic conscience. Eames and Saarinen collaborated on furniture designs, and Ray Kaiser, who was studying at Cranbrook after a period of living and painting in New York, helped them with their presentation drawings. Their entry won the Museum of Modern Art's "Organic Design in Home Furnishings" competition in 1940, and Eames's new career was launched.

Eames was apparently ready for all kinds of change: by 1941 he had divorced his first wife, married Ray, and embarked on an ardent conversion to modernism. His love of systems and technology had never fit comfortably with the relatively traditional architecture he had been working in, and that may be one reason he drifted away from conventional architectural practice so easily. Saarinen and Ray showed him that his instincts were those of a modernist.

Saarinen remained at Cranbrook to practice architecture with his father, and the Eameses moved west to try to manufacture the molded-plywood furniture that Eames and Saarinen had been designing. To pay the bills, Charles took a job in the art department at MGM, working under Cedric Gibbons, where he helped design the sets for *I Married an Angel* and *Mrs. Miniver*, among other films. The Eameses were at the center of the developing modernist culture in Los Angeles: they lived in Richard Neutra's sleek International Style Strathmore Apartments; Ray designed covers for *Arts & Architecture*, the California magazine that prided itself on being at the cutting edge. In 1942, the Eameses convinced the United States Navy that their plywood furniture forms could also be used to make an effective splint to hold an injured leg secure in the field, and they and several partners formed a company to fulfill an order for five thousand splints. The company eventually became the Molded Plywood Division of Evans Products, which in 1943 moved into the space at 901 Washington Boulevard. The Eames office remained there for forty-five years.

Visits to the studio were conducted according to a kind of ritual that brought out the understated propriety of the Eameses: guests were always given an extended tour, and usually an exotic multicultural meal and gifts. "There would always be something, some kind of little treat," Charles Moffett, a curator who worked at the Metropolitan Museum in the 1970s, recalls. "Once, Charles was working with Polaroid, and he made a film with some new type of camera to welcome me." This was gracious, but it was also a way of making clear who had the power, both creative and otherwise. Clients were supposed to feel privileged to work with the Eameses, not the other way around. It was the same for employees. The Eames office retained everything they did. "When you left, you didn't have much work to take with you—it was all theirs," Deborah Sussman, a graphic designer who accepted a summer job in 1953 and remained, on and off, for more than a decade, said to me. "They used it all or put it into their archives." Charlie Moffett nonetheless was so happy to work with Charles Eames on a film about the Degas collection at the Metropolitan that he considered giving up his career as an art historian to become an intern in the Eames office, and was dissuaded only when Eames told him they were both too old.

The Eameses shared a love of the ordinary and an ability to make it noble, even sacred. "They endowed material things with an extrasensory magic," Deborah Sussman said to me. Their house shows it. I first visited the Eames house, which is actually a pair of buildings—one a residence, the other a studio—in the mid-1970s, when Charles and Ray were still alive, and I went back to see it again last month. It is a stunning industrial form, made lyrical by its lightness and its precision. The spaces inside are at once grand and intimate. What I remembered most vividly was the way in which this modernist container was used to hold all kinds of objects: African art, dolls, toys, shells, vases, flowers, candlesticks, plants, fabrics, paperweights, and ashtrays, Victorian clutter arranged with modernist precision. Ray Eames put a slab of marble on the floor and set a candelabra and a vase of flowers on it, and the image of that brilliant explosion of the conventions of bourgeois domesticity has stayed with me for a quarter of a century. The floor! Ray overturned convention not by embracing minimalism, like so many modernists, but by making the entire house, in effect, a piece of three-dimensional sculpture, with objects hanging in space as well as sitting on shelves and in nooks. There was even, for a while, a pair of Hans Hofmann paintings hanging from the ceiling, facing down—placed, like most things in the house, to be seen by someone sitting. Almost everything is placed low, as if it had fluttered from the sky and come to rest in the perfect spot. It is a house designed for intimacy, not for crowds.

The house is now owned by Charles's daughter, Lucia Eames, and the studio is used as an office by Charles's grandson, Eames Demetrios, a filmmaker who manages the ongoing affairs of the Eames Office. (This spring, Demetrios expanded the operation to a storefront gallery in Santa Monica, not far from the old Washington Boulevard loft.) The family occasionally opens the house to visitors, although because of the fragility of the place, and the presence of all of Ray and Charles's possessions, guests are restricted to the grounds. Even a cursory peek through the glass, however, makes it clear that the Eames house is the critical monument of postwar California modernism. It is a house that belongs on the short list of great houses designed by architects for themselves, along with Monticello, Sir John Soane's Museum, Frank Lloyd Wright's two Taliesins, and Philip Johnson's Glass House.

Charles Eames was no theorist, but he was as devoid of fuzzy thinking as any designer in history, as is clear from a series of answers to basic questions about design he provided for an exhibition at the Louvre, which the Eameses in 1972 turned into a short film, *Design Q&A*.

Q: What is your definition of "design?"
A: A plan for arranging elements in such a way as to best accomplish a particular purpose.
Q: Does design imply the idea of products that are necessarily useful?
A: Yes—even though the use might be very subtle.
Q: Is it able to cooperate in the creation of works reserved solely for pleasure?
A: Who would say that pleasure is not useful?
Q: To whom does design address itself? To the greatest number? To the specialists or the enlightened amateur? To a privileged social class?
A: To the need.
Q: Does the creation of design admit constraint?
A: Design depends largely on constraints.
Q: What are the boundaries of design?
A: What are the boundaries of problems?

Even where he appeared to ramble a bit, he was focused, as in the series of Charles Eliot Norton lectures he gave at Harvard in 1970 and 1971. He showed films and spoke movingly of the beauty of common things, saying of a ream of paper, for example, that it was "absolutely beautiful stuff. Whatever you do with a ream of paper can never come up to what the paper offers in itself." What the Eameses loved most of all was, as Charles put it, "the uncommon beauty of common things."

One of the only projects on which the Eameses lost their footing was their big Bicentennial project, an exhibition, book, and film about two characters—Franklin and Jefferson—with whom Charles and Ray identified perhaps too closely. This time, their characteristic avalanche of information seemed busy and cluttered, not exhilarating, and the Eameses failed to realize that the story called for a clearer narrative line than they normally provided. When Ray showed up at the Paris opening of the exhibition wearing a Franklin coat, the gesture seemed pretentious, not clever. The poor reviews of the exhibition distressed them deeply—they had spent five years immersed in Franklin and Jefferson, and nobody seemed to get it.

Curiously, the Eameses are not revered by the current generation of cyber-geeks, who really ought to be idolizing them. Charles saw in the early 1950s that computers would change the world, and he was talking in the 1970s about communications systems that seem quite like the World Wide Web. Almost everything they designed prefigures the multimedia world of today. Yet the Eameses' very breadth of scope—they were graphic designers and filmmakers and educators and product designers and exhibition designers and architects and inventors—paradoxically makes them old-fashioned. Today you are supposed to blow everyone away by your brilliance in one thing, not everything.

The Eameses' personal style, their belief in ritual and propriety and dignity, makes them seem even farther away from the world of Silicon Valley billionaires. What possible connection could this genteel man in a bow tie and his pleasant wife have to the high-pressure madness that the technology business has become today? The answer is every connection, and none at all. Charles and Ray Eames were far ahead of our time, and way behind it.

The New Yorker, May 24, 1999

Courtesy Robert Polidori

Mies van der Rohe and Venturi, Scott Brown on Exhibit

HOUSE PROUD

In 1954, when Phyllis Lambert, an aspiring architect and the daughter of Samuel Bronfman, the head of Seagram, was asked by her father to decide who should design his new headquarters on Park Avenue, she considered every big name from Frank Lloyd Wright to Le Corbusier to Louis Kahn. She chose Mies van der Rohe because, she wrote, "the younger men, the second generation, are talking in terms of Mies or denying him." Forty-three years after the bronze-and-glass Seagram Building was finished and thirty-two years after Mies's death, they still can't stop talking about him. There is something about the purity of Mies's buildings, the Platonic perfection they aspire to, that generates awe, even in an age that has no

Ludwig Mies van der Rohe, Riehl House, Potsdam-Neubabelsberg (left);
Robert Venturi, Vanna Venturi House, Philadelphia (right)

interest in modernism's dreams. Mies's buildings look like the simplest things you could imagine, yet they are among the richest works of architecture ever created. Modern architecture was supposed to remake the world, and Mies was at the center of the revolution, but he was also a counterrevolutionary who designed beautiful things. His spare, minimalist objects are exquisite. He is the only modernist who created a language that ranks with the architectural languages of the past, and while this has sometimes been troubling for his reputation—it seems, falsely, easy to imitate a Mies building, in the same way it seems easy to knock off a Greek temple—his architectural forms become more astonishing as time goes on.

For a long while, Mies's legacy seemed defined less by his own buildings than by their awful progeny. The glass boxes on Third Avenue diminished the Seagram Building, or clouded its glory, anyway. Modern architecture made a mess of cities, and the architect who was the god of glass towers had to share some of the blame. But we have been through a full cycle now, not only of wretched modern skyscrapers in the 1960s and 1970s but also of second-rate postmodern skyscrapers in the 1980s and 1990s, those buildings that, in deliberate reaction to Mies's austerity, were sheathed in stone with lots of decoration. The aura of freshness that surrounds Mies these days comes, at least in part, from the authenticity of his buildings. They are not imitations, and they are not responses to something else, and they are not intended to make a rhetorical point.

It is finally possible to look at Mies with a clear head, and both Lambert, the founder of the Canadian Centre for Architecture in Montreal, and Terence Riley, the chief curator of architecture and design at the Museum of Modern Art, where the Mies archive is housed, have done exactly that in a pair of exhibitions which, taken together, constitute the most complete survey of the architect's work ever produced. The two museums split the turf. "Mies in Berlin," the exhibition at MoMA, tracks Mies from a house he designed as a twenty-one-year-old architect in Germany in 1907, through his years as the head of the Bauhaus, and ends in 1938, the year he fled Germany for the United States. (He was famously apolitical and was not so much escaping persecution as leaving a place that clearly was inclined to give more work to Albert Speer.) The Canadian Centre exhibition, "Mies in America," which has been mounted at the Whitney Museum in a simultaneous run with the Modern show (it will go to Montreal later), starts with his years as an eminent refugee in Chicago, where he designed the campus for the Illinois Institute of Technology, ran its architecture school, and before long became the philosopher-king of American modern architects.

Mies would seem to have been an odd man for that last role: his English was terrible, he wrote no books or significant treatises, he was more interested in building than in theorizing. Yet within a few years of his arrival in Chicago, he had become the most powerful aesthetic force in American architecture after Frank Lloyd Wright. Mies lacked Wright's passion for keeping himself in the public eye, but he appealed to the corporate executives who commissioned buildings. By the late 1940s, as Wright's career was waning, Mies was beginning to design high-rise apartment towers for real-estate developers. He had produced famous theoretical schemes for skyscrapers in Germany, but he had never managed to build much beyond some private houses and several portions of the huge Weissenhof housing project in Stuttgart. In America, he found businessmen who were willing to let him function in the real world. They must have mistaken him for a pragmatist. (Samuel Bronfman, for whom Mies designed what at the time was probably the most expensive office building ever built, had no such illusions, or lost them early in the game.) Mies was blunt, he smoked cigars, he didn't waste time rhapsodizing about the glories of architecture. His only real interest was in physical form, and he was fanatical in his search for ways to perfect it.

His obsessiveness led to a certain cultishness, and to the development of a group of Miesians who worked directly for him or, like the firm of Skidmore, Owings & Merrill, produced architecture in his mold. (The Skidmore firm was known as "Three Blind Mies.") As Mies became more important, a party line developed about his architecture: it was simple, it was pure, it was utterly rational. According to the canon, his career was a progression toward higher refinement and exactitude. A corollary to this was the belief that his architecture was better than what was around it and, for that reason, owed very little to what was around it. Mies's buildings stood aloof as Mies himself stood aloof. "Less is more," the master said, which explained everything.

The current exhibitions gracefully unravel the myths of Mies while doing no harm to his reputation. At the Modern, Riley and his cocurator, the architectural historian Barry Bergdoll, have turned up numerous early projects that show how Mies was connected to the cultural context of Berlin in the 1920s, and how his modernist vocabulary did not come to him in a moment of epiphany but grew gradually, poking its way at first into some early houses that could almost be mistaken for traditional German houses of the turn of the century. The most striking of these, the Riehl House, built for a philosophy professor and his wife near Potsdam in 1907, looks from the front like a two-story stucco cottage with a pitched roof and window shutters, but from the side it is almost abstract. A huge, plain gable overhangs a loggia, below which the land falls away, and the house appears to sit on a long, flat podium, with a sleekness that is prescient of the architect's later work. Although it was built when Mies was only twenty-one, in later life he was not interested in having been a prodigy. He discouraged Philip Johnson from including a photograph of the Riehl House in an exhibition of his work mounted at the Museum of Modern Art in 1947—the first significant introduction of Mies's architecture to American audiences. By that time, both Mies and Johnson thought that the traditional elements of the Riehl House and his other early houses subverted his image as the consummate rational modernist, and together they began to construct the view of Mies that is more or less what prevails today.

The truth is that Mies's architecture isn't much more rational than Stanford White's. Mies was a romantic, and what he was romantic about was the notion of beautiful and serene modern buildings. He would do almost anything to make them look like temples of pure reason. Most of Mies's buildings were a lot more complicated than they appeared, and he was as willing as any other architect to indulge in ornament when it suited his purposes. If you look carefully at the Seagram Building, you see that its exterior isn't flat, but is lined with little I-beams between the windows. They aren't part of the structure. They were put there to provide texture and to make the building softer on the eye—Mies's version of classical moldings. On the sides of the Seagram, where the structural engineers had demanded solid concrete walls to stabilize the narrow tower against heavy winds, Mies covered the surface with marble, then placed a grid of bronze I-beams on top of the marble so that it would look exactly like the framing around the windows elsewhere in the building. This is fakery, and it is lovely.

Mies's American buildings have been studied to death, and, while there is nothing like the little-known Riehl house to discover here, the Whitney show does—or it did for me—alter the perception of Mies as an architect who hated cities. He did several groupings of towers in his career—the 860-880 Lake Shore Drive Apartments in Chicago, the Federal Center in Chicago, Dominion Center in Toronto, Westmount Square in Montreal—that are generally thought of as collections of boxes plopped down with no regard for the pattern of city streets around them. But, in fact, in each case the towers are arranged to create an open space at ground level that is magnificently proportioned—at once intimate and grand. The open space and the masses of the tower slabs are expertly balanced, with void playing off solid. And every one of these compositions seems entirely at peace with the old streets that surround it. Mies opens the streetscape up, but he doesn't destroy it. Just as the plaza in front of the Seagram Building strengthens rather than weakens Park Avenue (unlike almost every other plaza, which feels like a useless gash in the street wall), the public space in Mies's other large projects relates to the old urban fabric with respect and gentleness. If "Mies in Berlin" connects the architect's work to a broader cultural context, then "Mies in America" connects it more clearly than ever before to physical context.

Of all the architects who have tried to take Mies on, the one who got the farthest, in a way, was Robert Venturi, whose remark "Less is a bore," in the opening pages of his 1966 book *Complexity and Contradiction in Architecture*, became almost as famous as Mies's original line. Venturi's position was that Miesian abstraction had nothing to do with real life, and not a lot to do with the history of architecture, either, since the great architecture of the past was never as simple as Mies wanted his buildings to appear to be. And, while Mies's pristine objects might be beautiful, Venturi argued, they had little to do with the realities of our difficult and ironic time.

For at least a decade following the publication of his book, Venturi and his wife and partner, Denise Scott Brown, were the most important architectural thinkers in the United States, the people who, like Mies in the 1950s, everyone else either followed or reacted against. When Scott Brown and Venturi, along with Steven Izenour, wrote *Learning from Las Vegas*, which argued that the commercial strip was to the United States what Baroque church facades were to Rome, they seemed to be deliberately provoking sanctimonious middle-brow good taste. But if Mies was the sort of architect who made real-estate developers think that they could elevate themselves by hiring him, Venturi and Scott Brown turned off the people who built major commercial and civic buildings. Their architecture is funky and elitist at the same time. They talk and write about popular taste, but for the most part they've built houses and cultural institutions for a sophisticated clientele.

Venturi and Scott Brown's home city of Philadelphia has never given them a major commission, unless you count the new building for the Philadelphia Orchestra, a project that they designed and lost to another architect, Rafael Viñoly, whose style was thought to have more appeal in the fund-raising department. Philadelphia is now making up for this with "Out of the Ordinary," an elaborate retrospective of the firm's work, curated by Kathryn B. Hiesinger at the Philadelphia Museum of Art. It is as important, in its way, as the Mies exhibitions or the huge retrospective of Frank Gehry's work now on view at the Guggenheim. (With Gehry, Venturi, and Mies running simultaneously, this is the greatest summer for architectural exhibitions I can remember.)

The main part of the exhibition is a mix of models, drawings, and photographs. Venturi has always drawn beautifully, and it is wonderful to see his old sketches. There are a few special objects, including a full-scale reproduction of a big three-dimensional coffee cup that Venturi hung above the door of a restaurant he designed in 1962 and, better still, a full-size reproduction of the facade of the house that he designed for his mother, Vanna, in the Chestnut Hill section of Philadelphia at around the same time. The facade, which you have to pass through to get to the part of the exhibition devoted to houses, is an exhilarating coup de théâtre. The Vanna Venturi house—pale green, with a split gable and simple moldings—may be the most famous American house by an American architect after Philip Johnson's Glass House. It is at once sweet and monumental, like a child's drawing of a house, but also a complex, subtle play on architectural history, with allusions to such masterworks as Blenheim Palace. It's a house with a subject: the image of a house. In the 1960s, when houses were either modernist boxes or replicas of traditional style, Venturi went off in another direction.

That direction eventually led to postmodernism, which Venturi and Scott Brown have come to disavow. I don't blame them, and not only because postmodern is now a term used mainly in the Sunday real-estate ads to describe McMansions. Venturi and Scott Brown are really modern architects, not postmodernists or historical revivalists. They didn't want to copy history, only to acknowledge it, and to weave allusions to other things into their work. They are modern Mannerists, really. Just as sixteenth-century Mannerists like Michelangelo distorted the elements of Renaissance architecture for greater effect, Venturi and Scott Brown play with modernism. They love thinness and lightness as much as Mies did, but for them thinness involves pictures of things. The quintessential Venturi object is his Chippendale dining chair, which looks like a cutout of a traditional carved chair with a pattern printed on it.

I don't think any other architects could have designed the Sainsbury Wing at the National Gallery in London, the firm's most sumptuous public building and perhaps the greatest essay in Mannerism of our time; or the checkerboard-fronted addition to Cass Gilbert's art museum at Oberlin College; or the Hôtel du Département de la Haute-Garônne, in Toulouse, France, a series of government buildings that constitute their largest built work to date. In each case, patterns in the form of traditional ornament are placed over sleek, modern surfaces, as if to proclaim both the importance of decoration and the futility of using it in the traditional, three-dimensional way.

Image is as important as reality to Venturi and Scott Brown, which isn't what you hear from traditionalists or postmodernists. It isn't even what you hear from Frank Gehry, who in some ways is a much more traditional architect than Robert Venturi. Gehry designs astonishing shapes, and they pack an emotional wallop. His work is easy to experience as something sensual, where Venturi is almost always cerebral. Gehry offers new shapes, and Venturi offers a wry take on old ones. No wonder Gehry is more popular.

Venturi could be called the most radical architect alive, however, just on the evidence of a project in the Philadelphia exhibition that was never built and has been almost forgotten—his prizewinning entry in a competition in 1967 for the National Collegiate Football Hall of Fame. He proposed what he called the "Bill-Ding-Board," a shedlike exhibition structure set behind an immense electronic signboard that was to rise to twice the building's height. The signboard would continuously project images of classic football plays, while the interior would contain a display of football relics and more projections of film on the barrel-vaulted ceiling. Venturi maintained that this was an electronic version of the painted ceilings of Baroque churches.

Today, we talk about how cyberspace is changing the nature of built space, but this project, designed thirty-four years ago, is the first instance I know of in which an architect said, in effect, that the information is the building. Frank Gehry would never dream of doing such a thing. It's more in the line of Liz Diller and Ric Scofidio, the team of architects who have built a career on the creation of projects that blur the distinction between media and architecture, and who use technology to create new kinds of spatial perceptions. Venturi was there first. The technology wasn't really even ready for his idea in 1967. He envisioned making his electronic football plays with two hundred thousand light bulbs. Today, his billboard would look like a vast television screen.

In some of Venturi and Scott Brown's work, like the small, shingled houses the firm has built in Nantucket and Westchester County, the desire to play around with the idea of image recedes somewhat, and convention is tweaked more quietly. Most of the time, though, their architecture is a dance through history that embraces everything from hamburger stands to cathedrals. The exhibition in Philadelphia ends with a section designed by Venturi and Scott Brown themselves—a sort of coda but with a tone very different from that of the main galleries. The rest of the exhibition is a bit dry and academic, and this last part is exuberant. It has one billboard-sized wall displaying a series of Venturi and Scott Brown aphorisms ("Ugly & ordinary is better than heroic & original"; "The validity of clutter"; etc.) and another containing Venturi's take on *The Architect's Dream*, Thomas Cole's famous painting of an architect contemplating a perfect classical city. In Venturi's version, there are McDonald's arches, Coca-Cola signs, and screens that parade video collages of buildings he and Scott Brown have done and things they love (Stickley furniture, Beethoven, Thai food, pumpkins, Italian palazzos, eggplants). The rest of the exhibition hasn't misrepresented Venturi and Scott Brown, however. They view the world with irony, but they take their own work straight, without much humor. They don't acknowledge that an ironic commentary about popular style isn't the same as popular style. Mannerism was never taken up by the masses, and it is never going to be, no matter how brilliantly Venturi and Scott Brown reinvent it for our time.

The New Yorker, July 2, 2001

Robert Moses

EMINENT DOMINION

For a generation, the standard view of Robert Moses has been that he transformed New York but didn't really make it better. This view was shaped by Robert Caro's epic biography *The Power Broker*—published in 1974 and in print ever since. Caro portrays Moses as a brilliant political operative who perpetuated his power by means of grand public works, filling the landscape with bridges and tunnels and parkways, heedless of people or neighborhoods that might get in the way of them. The notion of Moses as the evil genius of mid-twentieth-century urban design got a boost last spring in obituaries of and tributes to Jane Jacobs, a longtime antagonist, who was instrumental in defeating one of his most outrageously wrongheaded schemes, the Lower Manhattan Expressway, which would have destroyed much of Soho. Almost every article about Jacobs included a swipe at Moses, whose arrogance and lack of interest in the texture of the city seemed a harsh contrast to Jacobs's love of neighborhoods, streets, and, by implication, people.

Jacobs's book *The Death and Life of Great American Cities*, published in 1961, all but put an end to the idea that the way to improve old urban neighborhoods was to tear them down and replace them with towers and expressways. By the time Moses died, in 1981, his tendency to see public works as a form of machismo had fallen almost entirely out of fashion. Whereas he celebrated big things and his ability to build them, Jacobs changed the way people thought about cities by teaching them to focus on little things.

Moses—who began his marathon career under Governor Al Smith, in the 1920s, and was forced from power by Governor Nelson Rockefeller, in 1968—has been gone for more than a quarter of a century, and New York, which was decrepit and nearly bankrupt when Caro's book appeared, is a different place. Moses is clearly due for a reevaluation, and this week sees the opening of "Robert Moses and the Modern City," a huge exhibition that surveys his impact on New York. Organized by Hilary Ballon, an architectural historian at Columbia, the exhibition extends over three institutions. The broadest installation, at the Museum of the City of New York, is called "Remaking the Metropolis," and presents Moses's highway system and the big institutions, like Lincoln Center and the United Nations, that he helped build. "The Road to Recreation," at the Queens Museum of Art, documents Moses's new parks, playgrounds, and swimming pools; and "Slum Clearance and the Superblock Solution," at Columbia's Wallach Art Gallery, shows his inventive mastery of the federal government's Title I slum-clearance programs, and the results, both good and bad. Ballon and Kenneth Jackson, a prominent historian of New York based at Columbia, have put most of the visual material from the three exhibitions, along with several strong essays, into a book, *Robert Moses and the Modern City: The Transformation of New York*. The title is an obvious retort to Caro's subtitle, "Robert Moses and the Fall of New York," and the book presents itself as a cautious corrective to Caro's view.

Caro called Moses "America's greatest builder," and perhaps the most distinctive service of the exhibition is to bring home the sheer scale of his achievement to a new audience. There are models of many Moses projects and exceptionally elegant color photographs, by Andrew Moore, showing the current state of those projects. The photographs are so beautiful that they make you yearn for a time when enhancing the public realm was a serious calling. Moses built the Verrazano-Narrows Bridge, the Triborough Bridge, the Henry Hudson Parkway, the Henry Hudson Bridge, the Southern and Northern State Parkways, the Grand Central Parkway, the Cross Island Parkway, the Bronx-

Whitestone Bridge, the Throgs Neck Bridge, the Brooklyn-Battery Tunnel, the Long Island Expressway, the Meadowbrook Parkway, and the Saw Mill River Parkway. He built Jones Beach State Park (an early masterwork), Orchard Beach, the Niagara and St. Lawrence power projects, the New York Coliseum, and the 1964 World's Fair. By his own count, Moses added 658 playgrounds and seventeen public swimming pools to the New York City park system. In Central Park, he added the Conservatory Garden, the Great Lawn, and the Zoo. He played a major role in the creation of Shea Stadium, Stuyvesant Town, Lenox Terrace, Park West Village, Lincoln Towers, Kips Bay Plaza, Washington Square Village, and Co-op City. At one point, Moses held twelve New York City and New York State positions simultaneously. He served under seven governors and five mayors, and a popular joke had it that Moses wasn't working for them so much as they were serving under Moses.

Even more significant, perhaps, than Moses's productivity is the fact that he was one of the first people to look at New York City not as an isolated urban zone but as the central element in a sprawling region. In the early 1930s, he would charter small planes and fly back and forth across the metropolitan area to get a better sense of regional patterns. His vision of New York was of an integrated system with an urban center, a suburban ring, and a series of huge public recreational areas, all connected by parkways. Although the Regional Plan Association had proposed looking at the metropolitan area that way in 1929, Moses was the only public official who both grasped regionalism as a concept and had the ability to do something about it—which meant not only transcending local politics but also figuring out ways to pay for huge projects. He did this by establishing a series of public authorities, which allowed him to issue public bonds at favorable rates while leaving him with nearly as much autonomy as he would have had if he were running a private corporation. He moved among his various offices via a fleet of limousines—the highway-builder never learned to drive. His home base was in the headquarters of the Triborough Bridge and Tunnel Authority, a small building on Randall's Island, nestled under the Triborough Bridge, where he held court in lavish offices that were hidden from public view.

It is this image of Moses—unseen, omnipotent—that dominates Caro's biography. Thirty years after its publication, the book remains remarkable both for its exhaustive research and for its almost Shakespearean scale and complexity. At the same time, it can be melodramatic ("He had learned the lesson of power. And now he grabbed for power with both hands."), and it sometimes underemphasizes the extent to which, extraordinary as he was, Moses was still a product of his time. Caro points out, for example, how many subway improvements could have been bought with the money Moses spent on highways, but in Moses's day cities all over the country were building highways at the expense of mass transit, and New York was far from the worst. Some critics, like Jacobs and Lewis Mumford, were complaining that highways damaged urban neighborhoods, but most people didn't see this until long after the damage had been done. Moses's view of "urban renewal" was no different from that of officials elsewhere, and in some ways it was far more imaginative. Moses didn't bring down New York, and he didn't single-handedly sell its soul to the automobile. Indeed, New York probably comes closer to having a workable balance between cars and mass transit than any other city in the country.

One of Caro's most damaging accusations is that Moses was motivated by racism both in his designs for certain projects and in his decisions about what neighborhoods would be given priority for new parks and pools. In an interview with Paul Windels, a colleague of Moses, Caro turns up the bizarre detail that Moses believed that black people preferred warm water and decided to use this supposed fact to deter them from using a particular pool in East Harlem: "While heating plants at the other swimming pools kept the water at a comfortable seventy degrees, at the Thomas Jefferson Pool, the water was left unheated." The essays in the exhibition catalog go into the issue of racism in some detail but do little to rebut Caro's claims. They show a willingness to give Moses the benefit of the doubt, where doubt exists. The architectural historian Marta Gutman points out that the placement of swimming pools was in almost all cases determined by the location of existing city parks. She also confirms that the pool in East Harlem contained the same heating equipment as the others (although, of course, there is no proof that it was turned on). Kenneth Jackson makes a more general point: "The important questions, however, are not whether Moses was prejudiced—no doubt he was—but whether that prejudice was something upon which he acted frequently." Jackson argues that Moses's strong commitment to the creation of expansive public works more than compensated for his tendency to skimp on facilities for black neighborhoods. It's also worth pointing out that, no matter what planners think or do, architecture is ultimately defined by patterns of use that emerge over generations; today, Moses's pools, situated in multiethnic neighborhoods, serve entirely different communities from the ones he envisaged.

Whatever Moses's racial views, the swimming pools he built were monuments that conferred grandeur, even nobility, on their neighborhoods, and they suggest that Moses believed that the public realm deserved only the best design. In the summer of 1936, he opened one swimming pool per week. Each was architecturally notable; each was different; and the biggest ones could hold thousands of people at a time. A few, like the Crotona Pool, in East Tremont, and the McCarren Pool, in Greenpoint, were masterworks of modernist public architecture. Gutman writes that Moses managed "to integrate monumental modern buildings into the fabric of everyday urban life," and she persuasively asserts that the buildings were "unique in the United States during the New Deal."

Oddly, for all that Caro tried to destroy the myths about Moses, he never challenged the biggest one of all—that of his omnipotence. Moses is portrayed as rarely losing a political battle, but in fact he lost quite a few. One of the most important was the struggle, in the early 1950s, to extend Fifth Avenue south through Washington Square, splitting the park in two. It was as indefensible as the Lower Manhattan Expressway plan, a few years later, and Moses's inept handling of opposition to the Fifth Avenue plan from residents of Greenwich Village contributed directly to Jane Jacobs's radicalization and, ultimately, to the growing interest in preserving urban neighborhoods. In 1958, in a speech titled "Washington Square and the Revolt of the Urbs," the urban planner Charles Abrams said, "It is no surprise that, at long last, rebellion is brewing in America, that the American city is the battleground for the preservation of diversity, and that Greenwich Village should be its Bunker Hill . . . In the battle of Washington Square, even Moses is yielding." Lewis Mumford, writing in this magazine in 1959, described the fight to ban traffic from Washington Square as "a heartening sign of the way in which a stir of intelligence and feeling not only can rally far more support than one would expect . . . but can bring to a halt the seemingly irresistible force of a group of experts and 'authorities.'" Caro barely mentions the battle over Washington Square. By contrast, he devotes three chapters to the saga of the Cross-Bronx Expressway, in which Moses trampled over the neighborhood opposition.

Caro enhances the sense of Moses's power by minimizing the influence of less flamboyant players, such as Austin Tobin, the head of the Port Authority from 1942 to 1972. Tobin managed to wrestle control of the city airports from Moses, construct a container port, expand the Lincoln Tunnel and the George Washington Bridge, and build the World Trade Center.

When Caro's book was published, Jane Jacobs's views were on the ascendant, and it seemed reasonable to connect the city's troubles to Moses's imperious way of doing things. But Moses's surgery, while radical, may just possibly have saved New York. For every Moses project that ruined a neighborhood, as the Cross-Bronx Expressway did East Tremont, there are others, like the vast pool and play center in Astoria Park, Queens, or the Hamilton Fish Pool, on the Lower East Side, that became anchors of their neighborhoods and now are designated landmarks. Lincoln Center, whatever you may think of it, jump-started the revival of the Upper West Side; if Moses hadn't pushed it through, there is little chance that the high-rise condominiums, multiplex theaters, restaurants, and stores that now fill the neighborhood could have sprung up when they did. We are lucky, of course, that Moses's last big project, a bridge across the Long Island Sound connecting Rye and Oyster Bay, was defeated on environmental grounds, but it is difficult to imagine the New York region functioning without the Triborough Bridge or the Grand Central Parkway.

And Robert Moses got things done. In the age of citizen participation, this has become harder and harder. For more than five years, we have been fighting over what to do at Ground Zero, and the future of much of the sixteen-acre site is still unresolved. The idea of Moynihan Station—a conversion of the classical Farley Post Office, on Eighth Avenue, into an improved Penn Station—was first proposed a decade ago, and it still hasn't happened. By contrast, Moses's plan to cover miles of train tracks on the Upper West Side with an extension of Riverside Park took under three years from design to completion. In an era when almost any project can be held up for years by public hearings and reviews by community boards, community groups, civic groups, and planning commissions, not to mention the courts, it is hard not to feel a certain nostalgic tug for Moses's method of building by decree. It may not have been democratic, or even right. Still, somebody has to look at the big picture and make decisions for the greater good. Moses's problem was that he couldn't take his eye off the big picture. He was so in tune with New York's vastness that he had no patience for anything small within it. Caro brilliantly immortalized Moses's indifference to neighborhoods and people at a time when the city was weak, when the wounds from his high-handed approach were raw, and when Jane Jacobs's focus on the fine grain of neighborhoods held fresh promise. But there is a price to pay for thinking small, just as there is for thinking big. Thirty years later, we are still trying to find the balance.

The New Yorker, February 5, 2007

Burnham Plan for Chicago

TODDLIN' TOWN

In the mid-1890s, Daniel Burnham, then the most prominent architect in Chicago, met with a young architect named Frank Lloyd Wright. Burnham had been impressed by Wright's talent but felt that he could use some seasoning. He offered to pay Wright's tuition at the École des Beaux-Arts, in Paris, to support his family,

Daniel Burnham at home in Evanston, Illinois (above)

and to give him a job when he returned. Wright turned him down. It was one of the few times that Burnham, who was probably the most successful power broker the American architectural profession has ever produced, didn't get his way, and he told Wright that he was making a mistake: the Beaux-Arts style, of which Burnham was a leading exponent, was taking over the country, and Wright was deluded if he thought that his modern approach, with its open spaces and horizontal lines, would ever amount to much.

Burnham and Wright went their separate ways, but their paths kept crossing, because if you had anything to do with American architecture around the turn of the century, you inevitably ran into Burnham. He designed the Flatiron Building, in New York; Union Station, in Washington, D.C.; Orchestra Hall, in Chicago; Selfridges department store, in London; and more banks and office buildings than you could count. He got the train tracks that had despoiled the Mall in Washington for much of the nineteenth century removed and headed a Washington planning commission that, among other achievements, set the location for the Lincoln Memorial. Most important of all, a hundred years ago, in 1909, Burnham completed work on a document with the unassuming title "Plan of Chicago" that remains the most effective example of large-scale urban planning America has ever seen. Assisted by the young city planner Edward H. Bennett, he laid out the shorefront of Lake Michigan, quadrupling the amount of parkland and thus insuring that the lakefront would forever be public open space. He created the Magnificent Mile, the double-decker roadway of Wacker Drive, and the recreational Navy Pier, which extends into Lake Michigan. Envisioning Chicago as the anchor of an enormous region, he drafted a rough outline of highways to connect the city to the places around it. Quite simply, Burnham determined the shape of modern Chicago.

Chicago is marking the centennial of the Burnham plan with a yearlong festival of exhibitions and public events, including the construction, this June, of architectural pavilions in Millennium Park by Zaha Hadid and Ben van Berkel—odd choices, given that their avant-garde allegiance would have been anathema to Burnham. Still, the scale of the celebrations seems apt. Burnham is famous for the line "Make no little plans, they have no magic to stir men's blood." There is little evidence that he really said this, but everything he did suggests that he believed it. If Theodore Roosevelt had been an architect, he would have been Daniel Burnham.

Burnham was born in 1846, grew up in Chicago, and never went to architecture school. After trying his luck as a salesman, he fell into an apprenticeship in the office of William Le Baron Jenney, who built the first steel-framed skyscraper, and then set up a firm with John Wellborn Root. He and Root proved to be perfect partners: Root was a far more sophisticated architect, but Burnham excelled at bringing in business. The firm flourished in the construction boom following the Great Chicago Fire of 1871, and, in 1890, the partners were retained to advise on the plans for Chicago's first World's Fair. Burnham turned himself into an impresario, assembling a team of architectural rivals, including Richard Morris Hunt, Charles F. McKim, and

View looking north on the south branch of the Chicago River

Louis Sullivan, and assigning them each a building. (Root died of pneumonia early in the planning stage.) Chicago's 1893 World's Fair was a historic success. At a time when even the most prosperous American cities were dirty, squalid, and dangerous, the fair seemed to offer the promise of another kind of urban world entirely. Known as the White City, it launched the City Beautiful movement, giving the country a seemingly insatiable appetite for monumental courthouses, museums, libraries, and train stations that made every city look as if its roots went back to ancient Rome.

Burnham decided to make the fair a template for the future of Chicago and trumpeted the virtues of the City Beautiful to anyone who would listen. He had the instincts of a politician and skillfully worked himself into Chicago's power structure. In 1906 he secured the backing of an association of prominent businessmen, which paid for a staff; Burnham himself worked for nothing. He set up a penthouse office in the Railway Exchange Building, an enormous building that he had designed on Michigan Avenue, across from the Art Institute, and started by instructing his staff to gather data on major cities around the world. As the plan was coming together, he invited various influential people to the penthouse—the governor, the mayor, local politicians and businessmen, and fellow architects like Wright and Sullivan—to test his ideas. It didn't hurt that they could look out on the most spectacular view of the lakefront imaginable.

When the Plan of Chicago was made public, in 1909, it was published in a 150-page book. Along with Burnham's maps and plans, the book contained a series of stunning watercolors by Jules Guerin. Soft, hazy, and alluring, the pictures romanticized the immense metropolis, making it look like the seat of an empire. Burnham wanted to remake the city along the lines of Paris—the plan gained the nickname Paris on the Prairie—and, to a large extent, he succeeded, prescribing a series of projects that kept the city busy through the 1920s. Some things, such as a gargantuan civic center that would have made Les Invalides, in Paris, seem modest, were never built. But the campus of museums on the lakefront—including the Field Museum of Natural History, the Shedd Aquarium, and the Museum of Science and Industry—and the network of parks, boulevards, piers, and lagoons that have kept the area in public hands for a century is the plan's enduring legacy. It forms a startling contrast to the elevated highways and industrial buildings that have come to obstruct the waterfronts of most other American cities.

At the time of Burnham's death, in 1912, at the age of sixty-five, he was the most eminent city planner in the country, if not the world. But in later decades, the Olympian vision he put forth for Chicago came to seem formal and impersonal. According to Lewis Mumford, it showed "no concern for the neighborhood as an integral unit, no regard for family housing, no sufficient conception of the ordering of business and industry themselves as a necessary part of any larger achievement of urban order." Jane Jacobs called Burnham's ideas "irrelevant to the workings of cities" and suggested that his emphasis on monumental grandeur had actually made things worse in neighborhoods that, for her, were the soul of the city. To Jacobs, Burnham was Robert Moses with better taste.

It's true that Burnham's autocratic ways would be unthinkable today. But Mumford and Jacobs, writing when the automobile had begun to drain life from the urban street, failed to see that Burnham's monumental style strove for social betterment as well as aesthetic uplift. Before Burnham, Chicago was raucous and congested, growing helter-skelter with minimal concern for social welfare. Burnham understood the public's hunger for environments that would impart a hint of fantasy to the humdrum routines of daily existence. Certain that the time had come "to bring order out of the chaos incident to rapid growth," he said that "beauty has always paid better than any other commodity and always will." The architectural historian Kristen Schaffer, while preparing an introduction for a recent reprint of Burnham's plan, looked at an early draft and discovered that Burnham had some surprisingly radical social notions. He called for day-care centers, police stations in which all police activities would be open and visible to the public, and improved housing for the poor, "in common justice to men and women so degraded by long life in the slums that they have lost all power of caring for themselves." For Schaffer, Burnham's draft indicates a belief that cities were not only "for the capitalist, but for those who found themselves in police custody or those too poor to support their children." It's a pity that more of these amenities weren't built, but even the parts of the plan that were convey Burnham's public-spiritedness. Far from being forbidding, places like North Michigan Avenue and Navy Pier are usually teeming with people. Burnham's belief in the public realm was so powerful that it transcended all else, and it remains convincing.

Long after Burnham's death, Frank Lloyd Wright told a lecture audience, "Thanks to Dan Burnham, Chicago seems to be the only great city in our States to have discovered its own waterfront." Chicago, Wright said, was the most beautiful city in the country, and he gave the credit for this to Burnham, whose architecture he could never abide.

The New Yorker, March 9, 2009

NEW YORK

A HELLUVA TOWN

A couple of years back, in a memorable exchange in *Forbes*, the writer and social critic George Gilder referred to cities as "leftover baggage from the industrial era." Technology, Gilder felt, had liberated us from the tyranny of places full of crowds, noise, dirt, and crime. Why should people live among the general mess of a city like New York when they could buy, sell, and speculate from Greenwich instead, or Sun Valley? On a computer screen, Waco is the same as Wall Street. This thesis has been a given for some time among the technologically savvy. Cities emerged because people and buildings had to be jammed together in order to facilitate the manufacture of goods, making of deals, and delivering of advice. Now, at the end of the twentieth century, we are concerned less with objects than with information, and information—whether it be the blips on a bond trader's computer screen, the goods for sale on an Internet site, or the words being sent into the air by a broadcaster—has no tangible presence. It needs no place to shelter it. So why is it that New York, the biggest city of all, has boomed in the last decade? It can't be only because Rudy Giuliani got rid of the squeegee men.

That the information culture, which coyly pretends to need no city, has not killed New York but made it stronger will come as no surprise to readers of *Gotham: A History of New York City to 1898*, by Edwin G. Burrows and Mike Wallace. The story they tell, over the course of twelve hundred pages, shows that while the city's infrastructure may seem old and crumbling, New York is in many ways the first modern city, the first city to grow huge on the basis not of the things it made or even the objects it traded but on the information it exchanged. New York was never an industrial city in the sense that, say, Detroit or Pittsburgh was. It was the center of power because its financiers exerted nearly total control over America's money, and its publishers and journalists controlled the flow of information.

That New York figured out the twenty-first century's game back in the nineteenth doesn't explain why people continue to gravitate to its dense streets long after physical proximity theoretically has become irrelevant to doing business, and the reason, of course, is that physical proximity is not irrelevant to doing business: it matters. Dennis Weatherstone, the former chairman of J. P. Morgan, once remarked that financial centers wouldn't exist without lunch. And when you put enough people together, a lot more happens than business deals. Culture, for one thing, follows both money and density, and that is why the nation's center of capital soon became a place in which as much culture was created as was consumed. The sprawling, vaguely anarchic quality of New York made the city a kind of free port of disparate characters, a place with a rich sociocultural tapestry that stoked the fires of both entrepreneurship and culture. This may have led much of the country to view New York with a dislike bordering on contempt, but it gave the city its particular frisson.

The character of the city developed as publishing, shipping, trading, and the capital markets wove a common destiny early in the nineteenth century, creating a city of hustlers who specialized in knowing things before anybody else did. When the price of cotton on the Liverpool markets shot up unexpectedly in 1824, the news reached New York first because the Black Ball Line, a New York–based shipping company, had instituted regular shipping schedules. (Until 1818 ships wouldn't sail until their holds were full.) On learning of the uptick in the value of cotton, Burrows and Wallace tell us, the Black Ball's owner, Jeremiah Thompson, sent agents by fast pilot boat to New Orleans, where they bought cotton at the old, lower price and immediately resold it at a high profit. "Stories like this, repeated over and over as canals and steamboats quickened the flow of intelligence toward Manhattan, whetted the entrepreneurial imaginations of a new generation of publishers," Burrows and Wallace report. "By 1830 New York had forty-seven newspapers, eleven of them dailies, each determined to bring the news to its readers ahead of the others."

Newspapers were the medium of information in the nineteenth century, and having the information first was the point. "New York's hegemony as a clearinghouse for foreign and domestic news pulled in subscribers from every part of the country and compelled editors elsewhere to cannibalize Manhattan papers for stories," Burrows and Wallace write. "By 1828, 160,000 newspapers were shipped out monthly through the New York post office; by 1833, nearly a million."

All this was more or less concurrent with the completion of the Erie Canal, in 1825, which joined the Atlantic Ocean to the Great Lakes for the first time. When the canal opened, it was as if the nation had been tipped on its side, and Midwestern produce suddenly went tumbling toward New York Harbor, enriching the city's traders and virtually guaranteeing the short-term future of its economy. Burrows and Wallace understand that the completion of the canal did not create New York's strength, but confirmed it. It was a precursor of the vast man-made infrastructure that would eventually knit the disparate strands of the nation together. When DeWitt Clinton, the canal's most ardent advocate, spoke to a gathering of businessmen in 1815, he promised them that the canal would make New York "the greatest commercial emporium in the world." Never mind "greatest"; the word that really shows that Clinton knew what he was talking about is "emporium." Clinton, like Burrows and Wallace, knew that the city was a marketplace above all. New York embraced the idea of the service economy long before that dreary phrase entered the language.

New York firms failed more often than did "the dynastic enterprises of Boston," Burrows and Wallace tell us, but that is because entrepreneurs in New York continually went where businessmen in other cities feared to tread. Many of them came from other places, and they were supported by a business culture in which there were relatively few entrenched leaders and still fewer entrenched ideas. New Yorkers would sell anything to anyone, and they would keep on figuring out new ways to do it. With all due respect to Edith Wharton, Burrows and Wallace make it clear that new money and a certain raucousness did more to shape the character of New York, even old New York, than gentility.

The arrivistes here would always have the jump on the aristocrats, although freewheeling capitalists constantly came up against a powerful regulatory impulse. In 1800 the city payrolls included at least sixty-four public measurers, five weighmasters, twenty-two inspectors of hay, and thirteen inspectors of firewood. New York banned the sale of oysters in the summer and inspected the food sold in public markets. Bread prices were strictly controlled until 1800, when the Common Council experimented with allowing them to fluctuate according to the market, a decision that was so controversial that it did not become permanent until 1821. Sometimes regulation was the result of disaster, not of planning. The city's first tenement laws, enacted in 1879, were a weak response to a horrendous spectacle of overcrowded and filthy slums, and the regulatory impulse, however strong, managed to do little to improve health standards throughout the nineteenth century. Most of the city's regulations were reactive, and almost all of them were justified as a way to enhance commerce, not restrict it.

The most ambitious single event in the history of city planning in New York was the so-called Commissioners' Plan of 1811—the mapping of Manhattan's streets in a huge grid, stretching from river to river and from Fourteenth Street, then roughly the northern border of the densely settled portion of the city, to 155th Street. The state-appointed Streets Commission hired a young surveyor, John Randel Jr., to assist in laying out a plan for the city's inevitable northward expansion. Randal surveyed all eleven thousand four hundred acres of Manhattan and was then told to ram twelve avenues northward, parallel to Manhattan's central axis, and slice identical streets across them every two hundred feet. There were to be no circles, squares, or other punctuation marks of urban design in the manner of, say, the ones that Pierre Charles L'Enfant had sprinkled all over Washington. Such frivolities violated "the principles of economy," the commissioners said. "Like the proposed Erie Canal," Burrows and Wallace write, the grid "gloried in the supremacy of technique over topography. Manhattan's ancient hills, dales, swamps, springs, streams, ponds, forests and meadows—none would be permitted to interrupt its fearful symmetry."

Of course, plenty of things did break the grid—most notably Central Park, which was laid out in midcentury after a bruising political battle. But the Manhattan grid remains one of the most relentlessly single-minded acts of urban planning in the history of American cities, and also one of the most brilliant. In the spirit of New York, it is efficient, but even more in the spirit of New York, it is almost neutral in value. The grid may seem cruelly rigid at times, but it also makes possible the extraordinary sight of open views, from river to river. It is less a restrictive cage than it is the largest piece of graph paper in the world, offering a subtle hint of Cartesian order which plays off against New York's determined rambunctiousness.

Burrows and Wallace note that the grid in effect equalized all property. Streets were numbered rather than named, for instance. The grid, in its indifference to topography, foreshadowed the day when Manhattan's huge country estates would fall to real-estate development. All neighborhoods were equal, but that some would eventually turn out to be more equal than others was not the fault of the commissioners, who apologized for not laying out the grid beyond 155th Street, explaining that "it is improbable that (for centuries to come) the grounds north of Harlem Flat will be covered with houses."

Burrows and Wallace—who are professors of history at Brooklyn College and the John Jay College of Criminal Justice, respectively—have been working on *Gotham* for twenty years. In this first volume of their project, they lay out a saga that begins with the Lenape Indians in the sixteenth century and ends with the consolidation of Manhattan and Brooklyn and the creation of Greater New York in 1898. Wallace, whose main contributions are in the nineteenth-century sections, is now working alone on a second volume, which will carry New York through the twentieth century. The collaboration on the first volume was a smooth one, and it yielded an exceptionally readable chronicle that begins with some deft reflections on what might be called the city's primal story, the supposed purchase of Manhattan by the Dutch for twenty-four dollars, and on the origins of the city's longtime nickname, which was conferred on New York by Washington Irving. The original "Gotham" was a medieval village of legend whose inhabitants, depending upon which version of the story you believe, were either foolish, or foolish like a fox.

Gotham is a spectacle, a cavalcade, a parade in which people move on and off the stage with astonishing rapidity, and the scene shifts constantly from politics to finance and on to art and social reform and city planning and transportation. The book is at once a history of feminism, of social policy, of marketing, of public works, of health care, of architecture, of government, of religion, of philanthropy, and of culture—which is as it should be, since if it were anything less, the authors would not have understood their subject. It is also a history of people, and here it is hard not to feel a slight bit of disappointment. The pace of the narrative makes it difficult to deal with any character in depth, and some of the essential people in the development of New York get short shrift. I think particularly of Frederick Law Olmsted, the codesigner of Central Park, and the industrialist Peter Cooper, who is omnipresent in the narrative but is never quite graspable. Olmsted's story, of course, has been well enough told elsewhere, and it's fair to say that Burrows and Wallace have more than made up for these lapses by bringing to the fore certain figures who are not as well known as they deserve to be, and who, thanks to this book, may now take their proper place. It is no small part of the authors' achievement to have given people like John H. Griscom and Andrew Haswell Green, to name but two of the figures who play major roles here but are barely remembered today, their due.

Griscom was a Quaker physician who held the post of City Inspector in the 1840s and had the temerity to issue a report in which he said that much of the death and disease that befell poor New Yorkers could be avoided if better sanitary and living conditions were provided. Half a century before Jacob Riis became the city's most famous crusader for better living conditions for the poor, Griscom called the basements into which slumlords crammed the poorest tenants "living graves for human beings," and agitated for legislation that would guarantee minimum space and fresh air to every resident of a New York apartment, as well as for the replacement of politically appointed health wardens with nonpolitical medical experts. As a reward, Griscom was relieved of his position at the end of his term.

Andrew Haswell Green, a law partner of Samuel Tilden's, did somewhat better. He was a member of the Central Park Commission and perhaps the first New Yorker to argue that large-scale planning was useful as a means not merely of consolidating political power but of enhancing the quality of life in the city. Green, who was something of a proto–Robert Moses, managed to extend the Park Commission's mandate far beyond Central Park itself to include laying out streets, designing parkways, and overseeing planning for most of Upper Manhattan and the Bronx. But his greatest contribution was as the first advocate of an aggressive expansion of the city's borders. Green is, in effect, the spiritual father of the consolidation of Brooklyn, Queens, Staten Island, the Bronx, and Manhattan into Greater New York.

In a bibliographical note, Burrows and Wallace refer to themselves as "synthesizers," but they sell themselves short when they acknowledge their debts to previous scholars by saying that "it is they who have produced the strands of scholarship that we have woven into a narrative." Happily, *Gotham* is much too well written to be merely an amalgam (although when synthesis is this monumental, it is a massive scholarly achievement in itself), and, in fact, Burrows and Wallace have their own ideas about things. What I take to be the book's most important premise, that New York grew powerful by selling information and not just goods, is both original and true. And if the rest of Burrows and Wallace's thesis—the idea that the city belongs to no one group, that its lines of power are not easily demarcated, and that it has always been a place that no one fully controls—is not quite as original, it is every bit as essential to an understanding of why New York turned out the way it did.

The city has always been distinguished by a precarious—some might say an enchanted—balance between anarchy and order. In the mid-nineteenth century, as what remained of the old Dutch and British social, political, and economic order attempted to absorb the vast waves of immigrants who poured in, the clash of worlds was physically symbolized by the filth and degradation on the ordered, straight streets—decadence set off against Cartesian purity. The city's architecture, at once utterly banal and wildly exuberant, reflected the same pull of opposites. New York's builders were devoted in equal measure to squeezing in the greatest number of rentable square feet and sheathing their structures in the most ornate garb. The city's commercial and residential buildings were often meaner in their accommodations than those of other cities, but they were much more fun to look at.

In one sense, this architectural dichotomy represented an essential, if unconscious, aspect of New York's developing character. A city obsessed with image, it was always willing to sacrifice creature comforts if appearances could be served. At once pragmatic and flamboyant, New York saw itself, in a sense, as a continuous show. The fascination with appearances underscored the extent to which the city's architecture elevated the public over the private, implicitly giving more to the pedestrian who passed by than to the tenant. New York may not have had a Tuileries or a Champs-Élysées, but its facades—and, by the end of the nineteenth century, its skyscraper tops—collectively constituted a kind of grand public realm, focused on the life of the streets. And the creation of such monumental public constructions as Central Park and the Brooklyn Bridge, nineteenth-century New York's greatest achievements, gave this intense, determinedly capitalist place what in some ways was the finest public realm of any city in the country.

New York flexed its muscles, grew by leaps and bounds, was by turns awkward and graceful, and didn't bother to digest any stage before it moved on to the next. It was so intently focused on growth and the future that it paid little heed to its past and saved virtually none of its landmarks. It would take a long time—well past the midpoint of the twentieth century—before the city gained the maturity to look at its past as an enrichment, not an albatross.

In the mid-twentieth century, it was easy to be fooled about New York's true nature as the metropolis of information. Since the city was the headquarters for five of the nation's largest oil companies, three of its biggest airlines, and more Fortune 500 corporations than any other place, you could be forgiven for thinking of it as a vast industrial center. But even then it was never more than the front office for a business enterprise whose real work went on somewhere else. The oil companies were in New York because they felt it was more important to be near the source of capital than next to the oil wells; General Motors's financial officers needed to be closer to money than to cars. All of that began to change after World War II, when the siren call of the suburbs worked its magic on an inherently conservative and antiurban corporate class, and the huge industrial companies left, one by one, setting up shop in Stamford, White Plains, or Dallas. In the 1970s, the corporate exodus elicited a wave of angst about the depletion of the city's economic base. But these departures turned out to matter little, in the long run, to the health of the city, once finance, communications, law, and arts organizations expanded to take the place of the jobs lost. By the 1990s, the city had what could only be called an even purer service economy, driven almost entirely by jobs that had nothing whatsoever to do with manufacturing.

And so it is today. New York has become, in a sense, more true to itself. It is a city that was built on intangibles, and the people who deal in ideas and information and money are hunkered down here, making New York more and more dense. They know that proximity to others like them provides energy, that certain things happen faster and better in the metropolis than far away, and so they stay, and New York gets bigger, retaining its character as what Burrows and Wallace call "a city of capital, not a capital city."

The New Yorker, November 30, 1998

Christian de Portzamparc, LVMH Tower, New York

DIOR'S NEW HOUSE

"Small skyscraper" is one of the more pleasing oxymorons in the language. It glides smoothly over the tongue, and it calls to mind, nostalgically, something that is thought to have been lost in our age of gigantism. There were once lots of little buildings that strove to be high, and cities, including New York, were full of them. Most of the masterworks of Louis Sullivan—like the Bayard-Condict Building on Bleecker Street and the Guaranty Building in Buffalo—are not much more than a dozen stories high, but that was enough, in the 1890s, for them to establish the aesthetics of the modern skyscraper. Even as recently as the 1950s, buildings like Lever House and 500 Park Avenue, both designed by Skidmore, Owings & Merrill, were able to project an aura of height, dignity, and beauty without great size.

The notion that a tower that does not literally scrape the sky—or cast dark shadows on the street—can provide a rich architectural experience was doomed largely by economics. Land in the center of major cities is now too expensive to be used for anything less than the maximum square footage, and, besides, most tenants no longer want the small floors that little skyscrapers inevitably end up with. You probably couldn't fit Morgan Stanley's derivatives desk onto one of Lever House's minuscule levels, let alone an investment bank's whole trading floor.

We should be grateful, then, that Bernard Arnault runs a French luxury-goods conglomerate and not a financial-services concern. Arnault, the chairman of LVMH, has just given New York its first important small skyscraper in more than a generation. Designed by the French architect Christian de Portzamparc, who won the Pritzker Prize in 1994, the LVMH Tower is a twenty-four-story-high prism of glass on East Fifty-seventh Street. LVMH owns Louis Vuitton luggage, the Moët's & Chandon champagne and Hennessey cognac businesses, Guerlain perfume, and Christian Dior, among other brands, and the tower was built to serve as the company's American headquarters. Arnault must have intended to show the world that French design can be both innovative and chic. The order given to de Portzamparc, in effect, was that the tower's emblematic mission would take precedence over the practical concerns that dominate skyscraper design today.

This isn't to say that de Portzamparc was told to do whatever he pleased. LVMH certainly wanted to squeeze as much space as it could out of the building's small site, just off Madison Avenue. But de Portzamparc was building a symbol for the company, and Arnault gave him the same kind of creative leeway he would be expected to give his designers at Christian Dior. Sometimes that level of creative freedom doesn't work in architecture. This time, it has yielded a stunning, lyrical building, a sculpture in glass which manages to be at once exuberantly iconoclastic and perfectly appropriate for the proper, ordered streets of the Midtown Manhattan grid.

De Portzamparc's building is across the street from the huge, dark-granite facade of the skyscraper at 590 Madison Avenue and is tightly squeezed between a pair of genteel neighbors—a classic 1920s brick-and-limestone bank building at the northwest corner of Madison Avenue and a tower of gray granite which was built in 1995 as the American headquarters for LVMH's competitor, Chanel. The Chanel tower is a proper, tailored suit of a building which is deliberately evocative of older towers; its message to the streetscape is that to get along you have to go along. That was what most architects thought a decade ago, when people began to want buildings to make a harmonious whole on the street. Since modern buildings stuck out, the reasoning went, the best way to make a building fit in was not to make it modern but to make it look as much as possible like the ones that were already there. The success of de Portzamparc's building proves how tired that thinking is. There is nothing wrong with the Chanel tower, except that it is timid and conventional and altogether devoid of emotion. If the building were a person, we would call it repressed. The LVMH Tower proclaims its feelings, whether or not you want to hear about them.

The site was not an easy place in which to fulfill Arnault's desire for a powerful symbol of the company's style. The skyscraper across the street, which was built originally for IBM, looms ominously over the site, and the next-door neighbors encouraged the new building to join in their well-mannered but vapid dialogue. How to mediate between these conflicting demands? De Portzamparc correctly figured that the only thing to do was to treat the bank building and the Chanel tower like bookends that would enclose and frame a more assertive statement, and then to make that statement in glass to play off against the solid, dark wall of the tower across the street.

The LVMH building has a flat top and a fairly straightforward street floor, which contains a Christian Dior retail shop. The facade itself, however, is anything but flat. Between the straight lines at the bottom and the top, de Portzamparc has crafted an angular, faceted composition of great complexity. The building appears to fold in on itself, as if it were a huge piece of origami. The most powerful line in the composition is a diagonal, running from the upper-right corner down to the left side of the building; the section on the right side of the diagonal line projects outward, bending slightly in the middle. This is too good an abstract design to be discussed in terms of trite visual analogies, but the slanting, outwardly projecting section still makes me think a bit of a woman's leg crossed in front of her body, as if this part of the facade were a thirteen-story glass skirt.

The composition has other elements. The eleven-story base has its own set of nips and tucks, and the facade contains two different kinds of glass: the projecting section on the right is sheathed in milky-white glass, and the section on the left, in soft green. Half of each white-glass window has been sandblasted, and the other half is partly transparent. The transparent sections have tiny lines sandblasted cutting across them at varying intervals. Each window is thus a composition in itself, with an angular line dividing the translucent portion from the transparent portion. Together, the angular lines create a larger pattern on the facade. Meanwhile, the thin lines on the transparent glass make it look like a piece of shimmering fabric. De Portzamparc has created the equivalent of a curtain cut into the glass. At night, the windows, as well as the spandrels— pieces of plain, translucent glass below them—are lit, so that from the outside the entire white-glass section of the facade appears to glow, while the green-glass section appears to recede behind it.

It isn't easy to make a glass building appear sensual—glass is a cool material, and when it is used for an office tower the result is often bloodless. Glass can be light and elegant, but it doesn't usually have much presence. The glass in the LVMH building has a sculptural, emotional resonance that is very rarely achieved. The tower isn't beautiful and mute, like Lever House and 500 Park Avenue. It is more like an Expressionist building than a modern one. Even though the details aren't as inventive or as refined as those of many other modern buildings—the British architects Norman Foster and Richard Rogers, for example, produce modern structures with a much higher level of finesse—this building has a demonstrative and emotive quality that most other architecture in glass lacks.

Not the least of de Portzamparc's achievements is that he has managed to resolve the conflict between a love of shapes and a love of cities. Allegiance to the street is the first priority of all good urban architecture, and a lot of the time, this allegiance gets in the way of expressive shape-making. That's why so many architects, particularly in New York, give up and produce dutiful and uninspired buildings. De Portzamparc, by letting the surroundings function as a kind of frame for a tightly controlled, highly active composition, has managed to have his shapes and restrain them at the same time.

It's rare for a respected architect from abroad to have the chance to build in New York—it's rare for a respected architect from New York to have the chance to build in New York—and it's rarer still when his first effort turns out to be exactly right for the city at this moment. De Portzamparc's best-known work in France is the Cité de la Musique, a conservatory and cultural complex in the eastern portion of Paris that was finished in the early 1990s, and while it also demonstrates a desire to somehow merge strong, expressive shapes with urban restraint, it has nowhere near the lyricism of the LVMH Tower. De Portzamparc spent some time in New York as a student in the 1960s, and he says he remembers bringing back a pair of posters of the city skyline that were on his office walls for years afterward. He seems to have been something of a frustrated Manhattanite for much of his career. But his yearning to design a building here didn't manifest itself in a piece of architecture that tries too hard to look like the classic New York skyscrapers of the 1920s and 1930s. De Portzamparc seems to have wanted to move New York forward, not leash it to its past.

The interiors of the building, with one exception, are disappointing. They were designed by the Hillier Group, the architectural firm that served as de Portzamparc's American partner for the project and handled most of the day-to-day work of getting the tower built. But the responsibility for the interiors is de Portzamparc's. He produced dull, flat spaces for the office floors, which do not carry through any of the promise of the facade. Even the elevator lobby, which is lined with sensuous, glowing surfaces in a mixture of glass, pressed wood, and metal, is a letdown after the excitement of seeing the building from the sidewalk. The only really first-rate thing inside is the spectacular, thirty-foot-high, glass-enclosed space at the top of the building. Perhaps because they were frustrated by the lack of an appropriate term in the English language for a party place on top of a tower, LVMH officials have named it the Magic Room, but no matter; it is a magnificent space, a kind of glass box hovering twenty-four floors over Midtown Manhattan. The proportions are superb—it is twice as wide as it is high, but not so grand that it doesn't feel intimate. The main space, which fills the twenty-fourth floor, is overlooked by an arrival balcony on a mezzanine, so that guests can alight from the elevator, show their faces on the balcony, then descend via a curving staircase to the crowd below. This is what is known as making an entrance, and there are few architects—at least few modern architects—who would bother with it.

In the end, it's the height and the view that make the room, though. Because the LVMH tower is so short, being at the top doesn't yield a panoramic, picture-postcard view. It's more like being in a helicopter that has somehow ventured dangerously low to the ground. From this height, Central Park isn't a vast expanse, but a sliver poking out from between some other buildings. Fifty-seventh Street stretches out beneath you. When you look one way, you see the roof of a neighboring building; when you look another way, there is the side of a taller building. You feel you could reach out and touch everything around you. De Portzamparc has made of this room what he made of the tower itself: a place that is apart, shimmering and different, and at the same time intimately connected to the center of New York.

The New Yorker, January 31, 2000

New Architecture in Times Square

BUSY BUILDINGS

When you try to fix an image in your head
of any one of the skyscrapers that have
just been built or are going up around
Times Square, it doesn't hold. There isn't
a single clear shape that you can remember.
None of the new towers have the simple

Platt Byard Dovell, New 42nd Street Studios, New York (above) strength of the Empire State Building or the Chrysler Building or Lever House or the World Trade Center. Even the least appealing of the old skyscrapers, those that lack the iconic power of, say, the Flatiron Building or the Woolworth Building, have a certain clarity. The towers being built now aren't clear at all; they aren't intended to be. They are assemblages of parts, collages, that look different on each side, and their bottoms often bear no relation to their tops. The base of each new skyscraper is covered with electronic advertising signs (which the city's zoning laws have required since 1987 as a means of keeping the glitter of Times Square alive, long past the age when outdoor advertising was a necessary form of communication), and the buildings behind and above the clutter often seem every bit as hyperactive as the signs themselves.

Skyscrapers today are huge—bulky more than high—and yet they seem lighter than ever, in part because their shapes are so elusive. Is the new Reuters headquarters at 3 Times Square a curving object of reflective glass or a bunch of setbacks in granite? Are its windows holes in a wall of solid granite or sections of a glass wall? It all depends on what part of the building you are looking at. Viewed from Forty-second Street, the tower doesn't seem very big, since you see mainly a small light-gray section of granite, which pops out at you while a bigger mass of grayish glass behind it, the color of the sky, fades into the background. Across the street at 4 Times Square, the Condé Nast Building—home of a large law firm and sixteen magazines, including this one—looks like a round drum from one vantage point and like a tower of glass or a tower of stone from others. It is a virtual catalog of different kinds of sheathing covering different shapes. The architect of both 3 and 4 Times Square, Bruce Fowle, of the firm Fox & Fowle, says that he put five kinds of coverings on the Condé Nast Building and went up to six on the Reuters Building, all variations of granite and patterns of glass. Kohn Pedersen Fox, the architects of the tower that is rising on the south side of Forty-second Street—which will be called Times Square—decided that they wanted to express geometric patterns in glass, and the dominant feature of their building is a huge diagonal line slicing across the facade, separating a section covered in solid glass from one covered in reflective-glass stripes.

Why have architects of skyscrapers, who were for so long devoted to Platonic form—the perfect tower, standing alone—shifted their priorities? Plenty of tall buildings put up in the past were hemmed in by their neighbors, but they almost always showed a carefully ordered, formal face on whatever public sides they did have. The varying facades and fidgety, edgy forms of the new buildings are not simply a response to the visual cacophony of Times Square, since it isn't only at Times Square that you see this new kind of tower. In almost every major city in the world, restless, agitated, disconnected buildings are going up. The skyscraper has become a collection of parts.

It has been a long time since a group of new buildings in close proximity to one another in New York could be described as setting a tone for high-rise construction everywhere. But the new towers in Times Square show us, unambiguously, that the idea of the skyscraper as a pure object is dead. The new buildings have a fluid identity, and it is tempting to think of their dematerialization as neatly paralleling the shift toward cyberspace—from mechanization to electronics, from atoms to pixels. This notion is especially appealing as an explanation of why so many of the new skyscrapers have gone up in a place where media headquarters converge and the latest technologies enliven the signs. What better architectural expression of the new world could there be?

I wish we could attribute such ambitious intentions to Fox & Fowle or to Kohn Pedersen Fox or to Skidmore, Owings & Merrill, the architects of the intersection's fourth tower, which will rise on the south side of Forty-second Street, between Broadway and Seventh Avenue. (This building, to be called the Times Square Tower, is also a sleek kit of modernist parts, with an exceptionally zestful top and a section with visible diagonal trusses.) But it is more likely that the architects were preoccupied with new and vexing practical demands. Their clients are real-estate developers, and even in the age of cyberspace, developers want more actual space, and they want it in bigger chunks. Companies demand huge floors, not little rooms in the sky, which means that if you don't do something reasonably clever, your building will end up looking so bulky that it will make those 1960s boxes on Sixth Avenue seem cute and friendly.

The skyscrapers that everyone seems to love, like the Woolworth Building and the Chrysler Building, are slender towers. Even the GE Building, at Rockefeller Center, is a fairly narrow slab, magnificently sculpted; 40 Wall Street is thin, and 570 Lexington Avenue is a veritable spindle. Once, the challenge of skyscraper design was to express height gracefully. ("The skyscraper must be tall, every inch of it tall," Louis Sullivan admonished.) But designing a skyscraper today isn't all that different from designing a convention center. In both cases, the problem is in figuring out how to make the thing look less fat, less like a behemoth, and one way to do that is to break the enormous mass into parts.

It's no accident that the best new building in Times Square is the smallest one, a ten-story building on the north side of Forty-second Street between Seventh and Eighth Avenues. It opened in June and is intended to provide rehearsal space for performing-arts groups as well as offices and a ninety-nine-seat black-box theater. Designed by the firm of Platt Byard Dovell, it is a simple glass tower with stainless-steel brise-soleils, or sun grilles, covering the south-facing facade. The grilles create a splendid texture, and the building manages to appear pristine without being prissy, which is no small achievement amid the cheap, multiplex-theater glitz that has taken over most of the rest of the block. At night, thanks to a brilliant computerized scheme by the lighting designer Anne Militello, the facade of the building literally becomes a performance. It glows, it flashes, it changes from red to blue and then to yellow, orange, and green. Militello's design delivers no stock quotes or news; it exists to advertise nothing except the building itself, which it does in delicious silence. The lights do not cover up the architecture, like the commercial billboards up and down the rest of the street; they are completely in tune with the structure of which they are a part. They make it dance.

In 1981, when the state and the city's urban-renewal plan for Times Square was first announced, the centerpiece was to have been four towers by Philip Johnson and John Burgee that would have made a rather monstrous matched set. Each of them had a granite front that appeared to be pasted onto a huge mass that was topped by a glass mansard roof. There were big arches at the bases of the buildings, which were to have risen pretty much straight up, with almost no setbacks. They would have appeared even bulkier than the towers that are now being built—at once frilly and grotesquely large, sort of like elephants in tutus. The Johnson buildings were postmodernism's revenge, and it is not surprising that almost no one had a good word to say about them. A slow market for office space and political opposition to the redevelopment plan—and not just the awfulness of the design—did the buildings in, but the difference between the Johnson project and what has gone up in its place shows what enormous changes have occurred in the mainstream of commercial architecture in less than twenty years.

At one point in the early 1990s, Johnson and Burgee were sent back for another try, and they came up with a bizarre proposal for four towers that were identical in size to the first group, but this time each one was sheathed in a different architectural garment. One was vaguely in the style that was then coming to be called Deconstructivist, with all kinds of disparate parts; another was a variant on the mansard-roofed postmodernism of the first scheme; and still another had a kind of sleek, abstracted modernism to it. Nothing in the revised design seemed to have much to do with the site itself. There was something almost desperate about the proposal, but by throwing everything into the pot, the architects inadvertently hit on the beginnings of the kit-of-parts aesthetic that now holds sway.

If there's anything that raises the level of the new Times Square skyscrapers and makes their designs more than mere entertainment, it's the way that their architects have tried to relate the buildings to their surroundings. The Condé Nast Building, which occupies one of the busiest corners in the world, is a dynamic, zestful presence. On the other hand, sometimes architects try too hard to justify the complicated, inconsistent tone of their work as a reflection of the complicated, inconsistent tone of the cityscape. Bruce Fowle, for example, explained the design of the Condé Nast Building to me by saying that he put more granite on the east side, which faces the more formal and proper neighbor-hood closer to Bryant Park and Fifth Avenue, and more glass on the Times Square side because it is flashier. As for 3 Times Square, the Reuters Building, Fowle said that he wanted to give it a more corporate look from the north, and tie it into Times Square's glitter from the south, where he placed a curvilinear glass facade intersected by a stainless-steel wedge. "The struggle was how do you create corporate dignity and fit into the razzle-dazzle at the same time?" he said. But his solution—"We sliced it here, we sliced another plane there"—yielded a building that sometimes seems like a bunch of unintegrated pieces.

The slice-and-dice process is handsomely documented in an exhibition that opened in June at the Skyscraper Museum, on the ground floor of 110

Maiden Lane, in Lower Manhattan. The show traces the development of the Times Square towers that have already been built or are going up as well as two others, the Westin Hotel, by Arquitectonica (to be completed in the fall of 2002), and a tower to rise over the Port Authority Bus Terminal, by Skidmore, Owings & Merrill. There are more than a dozen models of each building, versions that were discarded because they did not please either the architects, the developers, or the officials of the 42nd Street Development Project. All the little models lined up on shelves demonstrate one of the raw truths of architecture: there are almost always multiple solutions to a project, and the finished building is usually a product of somewhat arbitrary options. The explanations given by even the most gifted architects for their choices are often not apparent to people looking at the completed buildings. William Pedersen explained the diagonal line on the front of 5 Times Square as an attempt to echo the diagonal line of Broadway. "The geometries of the building came from the geometry of Broadway and Seventh Avenue," he said to me. "The building is prismatic." But will pedestrians ever see the building's facade as a reflection of the street plan? And will they perceive the graceful curve of the Reuters Building as a gesture toward the intersection of Broadway and Forty-second Street, and the granite section on the north side as a statement of corporate dignity inserted into the glitz? The shapes may appear as a lot of architectural noise, trying to be heard above the visual din of all those signs.

Perhaps the purest new building in Times Square is the small tower of black glass designed in the early 1990s by Mayers & Schiff and Costas Kondylis for the Renaissance Hotel, just north of Forty-seventh Street. It was intended as little more than a backdrop for signs. The former Times Tower, at 1 Times Square, the tiny triangle in the middle of the intersection of Broadway and Seventh Avenue, at the south end of the square, has become literally a framework for signs, hardly a real building at all. Except for the ground-level store, there is virtually nothing functional inside. And maybe it's perfectly fine for these buildings to be perceived as benign blurs. Maybe that's the best way, right now, to deal with skyscrapers in contemporary cities, which are themselves blurs of rapidly changing images.

The posticonic skyscraper—the skyscraper that isn't so much a thing as a collection of things—isn't easy to love, but it does evoke a curiously traditional idea, one worth holding on to, which is that the concept of the city is more important than an individual building. Every one of the new buildings has been designed as a piece of a big, messy whole. The new towers both assert themselves within this environment and step back from it. Their shapes can't be separated from their surroundings. The signs, in the end, pull the new Times Square together, as the softer, whiter lights of another generation pulled the old Times Square together.

I'm not ready to relinquish the notion of the tall building as an icon. But putting up more such structures may make little sense in New York today. The Empire State Building remains a true spire nearly seventy years after it was finished, mostly because of the eccentricities of the neighborhood. Few other great towers have been so lucky. More often, their exquisitely crafted shapes have been rendered invisible by the rampant growth of the city around them. Towers want to be alone. The new, posticonic skyscraper loves crowds.

The New Yorker, September 4, 2000

Rem Koolhaas/Office for Metropolitan Architecture, Prada New York Epicenter (above); Joanne Newbold and Gensler, Toys 'R' Us, New York

HIGH-TECH EMPORIUMS

In 1948, Frank Lloyd Wright redesigned a home-furnishings shop on Maiden Lane in San Francisco for Lillian and Vere Morris. His plan called for a multistory interior space but no traditional display windows, which worried the Morrises, and Wright assured them that he was thinking of their commercial needs. "We are not going to dump your beautiful merchandise on the street," he wrote, "but create an arch-tunnel of glass, into which the passers-by may look and be enticed. As they penetrate further into the entrance, seeing the shop inside . . . they will suddenly push open the door, and you've got them. . . . Like a mousetrap!" Rem Koolhaas has given Prada more or less the same advice. Koolhaas doesn't think much of the old modernist idea of transparency, which says that you put goods in big, open windows and let them speak for themselves. He also believes that if Prada is to survive what seems to be overexpansion, it can't keep building those mint-green stores everywhere. Koolhaas, like Wright, has good marketing instincts, and after studying Prada's problems, he told the company that it should start selling architecture along with the handbags.

Koolhaas has suggested that to avoid "the Flagship syndrome: a megalomaniac accumulation of the obvious," Prada should create a series of "epicenters," or supersized stores, each a distinct work of design. This seems sensible enough. A company that has based the aura of its brand on cutting-edge design might be well advised to think in terms of a cutting-edge environment. Alas, however, the first of these new stores, the Prada shop at 575 Broadway, in Soho, is not a staggering reinvention of the retail environment, no matter what Koolhaas and his followers claim. The enormous new store, which cost somewhere in the neighborhood of $40 million, combines some hard-edged late modernism with some fancy technology (glass-enclosed dressing rooms that turn translucent at the touch of a button), and comes in a package that, like a lot of Koolhaas's work, mixes roughness with sleekness in a way that never manages to avoid seeming self-conscious. The architectural centerpiece is a set of zebrawood steps, like bleachers—what Koolhaas calls "the wave"—which descend from the street-level entry to the main selling floor, one level below. This creates both selling space and performing space, since the steps can be used as seating. But most of the time they are covered with shoes. What the wave does best is disguise the fact that most of this spectacular store is actually in the basement.

The wave reminded me of the huge Ferris wheel in the new Toys 'R' Us store in Times Square, which opened a few weeks before Prada Soho. Both Prada and Toys 'R' Us suffer from a sense that their brands are being diluted, and the New York stores were conceived as an antidote to this. The Toys 'R' Us store, like Prada Soho, has an underground selling area—although most of the store is above ground—and the designers wanted to camouflage what could be perceived as dark and unpleasant grottoes. The sixty-foot-high Ferris wheel makes customers think that they are in one big space, and it makes Koolhaas's wave at Prada seem tame. The Toys 'R' Us store was designed not by a famous architect but by a group that included Joanne Newbold, a store planner, and Gensler, a large commercial architecture firm. It is fair to say that the world of design did not greet the opening of the store with the same degree of reverence as it did Prada Soho, but the effect created at Toys 'R' Us is similar and a lot less pretentious. Of course, Toys 'R' Us is quite a bit bigger than Prada. The architects had the equivalent of a four-story atrium to work with, and more than a hundred thousand square feet of selling space.

I like the Times Square Toys 'R' Us a lot, in large part because it demonstrates Koolhaas's theories more clearly than Koolhaas's store does. It's exuberant and doesn't try to be important. It is probably the best indoor public space around Times Square. The Ferris wheel is a perfect blend of entertainment and hard sell. It has fourteen passenger cars, each of them an "individually themed cab," which is to say that one car is based on Mr. & Mrs. Potato Head and another on a Tonka truck. Mr. Monopoly has a car, as does Barbie. Much of the store is divided into environments with special themes, including a *Jurassic Park* exhibit where dinosaur toys are sold and a Lego shop containing huge Lego versions of the Empire State Building and the Chrysler Building so accurate that they should be given to the Skyscraper Museum. What I like best, however, is the store's glass facade, which is sometimes transparent and sometimes covered with a series of images on automated panels that roll down together, like shades. The facade is a continuously changing billboard. If you want to see how technology can render traditional space obsolete, Toys 'R' Us demonstrates it much more effectively than Prada.

It's easier to be loose when you're selling twenty-dollar Barbie dolls rather than $600 shirts, of course, but the new Soho Prada—which Koolhaas and his Rotterdam-based firm, the Office for Metropolitan Architecture, designed in association with ARO in New York—is particularly stiff. It makes you feel like you're being watched. Koolhaas has built his aesthetic on unexpected juxtapositions, mixing common elements of popular culture with refined, high-end objects, and the Soho store seems to adhere to a code that most of us aren't privy to. One part of the downstairs selling floor is covered in unpainted green plasterboard, decorated with white spackling over the joints and nails. It's a nice green, even though the unfinished look turns out to be fake. Koolhaas preferred the color of a British gypsum board that wasn't thick enough to meet New York City fire laws, so the wall is actually a veneer over another wall. An imported veneer, no less.

So much for roughness as the new face of luxury. There is real roughness, and there is, well, Prada roughness, which is as contrived as any opulent architectural detail. I'm sure that the architects who have been trooping through the space have been bedazzled by Koolhaas's elevator, a magnificent cylinder of glass perched on a hydraulic piston. It was fabricated in Italy, and it is so exquisitely detailed that you can't see any moving metal parts in the elevator cab, only sliding surfaces of glass. The elevator cost nearly a million dollars and took ten months to design, but I had trouble cracking the code here, too. I couldn't figure out why it called for rough walls and stunningly elegant elevators. Why not shimmering, elegant walls and a rough, industrial elevator?

On the street level, much of the Prada merchandise is displayed in uncomfortable-looking metal cages that hang from the ceiling and can be moved around, allowing the store to be, in effect, redesigned in an instant. Never mind that this, like a lot of things about the store, is an exceedingly expensive answer to a relatively simple problem. Plenty of stores have had movable, flexible display systems for years, although it was not considered a priority to hang them from the ceiling. You could probably build a dozen Gap stores for the price of some of Koolhaas's technology here.

Designing a store that attempts to combine shopping with entertainment and technology is nothing new, and, other than the juxtaposition of the raw and the refined, there isn't much at all in the way of architectural ideas at Prada Soho. Nevertheless, judging from the awe with which some of Koolhaas's pronouncements are received, you would think that he had the freshest take on the popular landscape since Robert Venturi and Denise Scott Brown. The latest Koolhaas screed, the *Harvard Design School Guide to Shopping,* written in collaboration with some of his students, asserts that "shopping is arguably the last remaining form of public activity. Through a battery of increasingly predatory forms, shopping has infiltrated, colonized, and even replaced, almost every aspect of urban life." This is the sort of thing that has given Koolhaas a reputation as a social critic.

It's too bad that he isn't more comfortable simply being an architect, because he is a very good one. The Prada store in Soho is full of wonderful elements, beyond its extravagant elevator; there's exquisite pink resin shelving in one section, and a marble floor that recalls Prada's main store in Milan in another. Koolhaas is consistently inventive in his use of materials, and at his best he is a brilliant maker of form. But, at Soho Prada, anyway, the whole is less than the sum of the parts. Koolhaas's current celebrity is based not on the beauty of his compositions but on the power of his rhetoric. He loves to rant about how outdated the traditional city is, and about the meaninglessness of public space in the age of technology. He seems to denounce consumerism, but then he winks and says let's make of it what we can, and you're never quite sure whether he intends to celebrate banality or complain about it, or if he's just figuring out how to profit from it.

There are no such conflicts at Toys 'R' Us. John Eyler, the chairman of the company, says that he wants the Times Square store to be a "destination icon," and he seems to have understood instinctively that the way to reinvigorate a retail brand is to make a new store that isn't just bigger than all the others but has an altogether different image—in this case, a kind of conflation of a theme park and the urban energy of Forty-second Street. When Eyler talks about how the store will demonstrate his "strategic vision for renewing the company's growth heritage over the next few years," he's saying the same thing as Koolhaas when he says that "the epicenter store becomes a device that renews the brand by counteracting and destabilizing any received notion of what Prada is, does, or will become."

Still, there is some question about how much any of this matters. People now expect to be entertained when they shop—they want something to justify going out and not ordering off the Internet—but I suspect that architecture gets them through the door more effectively than it can get them to part with their cash. You need products inside that people want to buy. When I went back to

Soho after leaving the cacophony of Times Square the other day, the store that was supposed to show us the future seemed quiet, serene, and almost genteel. Koolhaas seems to have envisioned the Prada store overflowing with crowds, but the reality is that almost everything he designed looks better when the place is nearly empty and you can see it not as public space but, like so much architecture today, as a private indulgence.

The New Yorker, March 25, 2002

MIAMI VICE

Guests at the new Westin Hotel, which stretches between Forty-second Street and Forty-third Street on Eighth Avenue, will have a pretty good view of one of the most revered modern skyscrapers in New York, the bluish-green McGraw-Hill Building, half a block to the west. A short walk in the other direction will bring them to what is probably the most beloved skyscraper anywhere, the Chrysler Building. When the McGraw-Hill Building was finished, in 1932, it was dismissed by the architecture critic of *The New Yorker*, George S. Chappell, as "a stunt and not a particularly successful one." Chappell, who wrote as T-Square, said that the Chrysler Building had "no significance as serious design." Lewis Mumford called it "a series of restless mistakes . . . this inane romanticism, this meaningless voluptuousness."

The Westin will probably be received in pretty much the same way, but I doubt that history will reverse the verdict. The building is not ahead of its time, like the McGraw-Hill Building, which is an early International Style tower. And it is certainly not the contemporary equivalent of a graceful exercise in Jazz Age syncopation, which is how people came to view the Chrysler Building. The forty-five-story Westin is the most garish tall building that has gone up in New York in as long as I can remember. It is fascinating, if only because it makes Times Square vulgar in a whole new way, extending up into the sky.

It is not easy, these days, to go beyond the bounds of taste. If the architects, the Miami-based firm Arquitectonica, had been trying to allude to bad taste, one could perhaps respect what they came up with. But they simply wanted, like most architects today, to entertain us. This is less a building than a concept, and you can imagine its being pitched to the developer, Tishman Realty & Construction, the way producers pitch a television show to network executives: audiences now don't want plain towers that go straight up, and they're not going to be satisfied with just a fancy top, so we've come up with a way to make the whole building into a vibrant, dynamic object. The developer bought this and ended up with a skyscraper split down the middle by a big, swooping white line on its north and south sides. To the east of the swooping line, the building is sheathed in a vaguely copper-colored, pinkish glass, set in horizontal panels. The west side is covered in blue glass, set vertically. The notion, according to Bernardo Fort-Brescia, who, along with his wife and partner, Laurinda Spear, heads Arquitectonica, is that the east side of the tower is "earthbound, anchored to the ground"—hence the horizontal lines and the warm color—while the blue-toned, vertical-lined side, which is taller, is "skybound."

Well, okay. This is no more superficial than the reasoning that goes into plenty of other buildings today. And I have to admit that the Westin looked rather sexy in the renderings that were shown around in 1995, when Arquitectonica and the developer won a competition, sponsored by the government's 42nd Street Development Project, to build a major hotel in the "new" Times Square. But, just as Hollywood concepts have a way of evolving, the Westin that has gone up bears only a slight resemblance to the drawings. It is both shrill and banal, less a piece of architecture than a developer's box in drag. The Westin forces you, as no piece of architecture in this city has in a very long time, to come to terms with exactly what makes a building so strident that it enthralls in the way a gruesome accident does.

The main problem isn't the shape, which, while self-conscious, isn't awful. In fact, from a couple of blocks south, on Eighth Avenue, where you can see the tower in full profile, the mass of the building is striking. No tower meets the sky quite like this one. The blue section swoops over the pink one as if it were slicing into open space. At night, the white line will be lit up on the Forty-second Street side of the building, and spotlights on the roof will pick up the motif and shoot a ray of light into the sky. But it makes no sense to design a single building to look as if it were two different, clashing buildings. The two parts aren't different structurally and they aren't doing different things inside. There is no logical reason to split a skyscraper vertically with a curving line, or to make one section play at hugging the ground and another section play at reaching to the sky. It's all pretense—not the kind of pretense that brings us fake Georgian or fake Renaissance but the pretense that the hoopla is somehow connected to a meaningful architectural idea. Everything Arquitectonica has done here is as superficially decorative as if the building had been sheathed in classical columns and pilasters. Fort-Brescia told me that the line just came to them. "Laurinda and I literally took a drawing and slashed a line across it," he said. "There is a rational side to our profession, but there is a lot that is intuitive."

I could live with the zooping and swooping if it weren't for the way the shape of the building is covered. The glass must be the ugliest curtain wall in New York. Make that the two ugliest curtain walls in New York, since the pink section and the blue section are ugly in different ways. They are both unpleasant to look at—tawdry colors, gaudy finishes. As if that weren't enough, the architects have decorated each section with stripes in darker tones that they call "brushstrokes," but which do not succeed in making the building look even remotely like a painting. It's as if Fort-Brescia and Spear had no faith in the shape they made and could not stop themselves from tarting it up.

The tower marks the northwestern boundary of the Times Square redevelopment project, which includes four office towers around Times Square itself, as well as new movie houses, stores, and a few restored landmark theaters along Forty-second Street. The main entrance to the hotel is through a blessedly ordinary modern base of clear glass on Forty-third Street. Things are quite different on the south side of the Westin, however, the side that faces Forty-second Street, where the redevelopment project's planners insisted that the hotel have a big, boxy base to tie it into the so-called "entertainment zone"—the open-air suburban mall, in other words—that Forty-second Street was in the process of becoming. The base, which the architects refer to as the building's bustle, is a seventeen-story-high box that contains a thirteen-screen multiplex, stores, restaurants, and eight floors of hotel rooms. The bottom floors are covered in advertising signs, and you have never been more grateful for the excesses of capitalism. (As in most of the new Times Square, the best architecture isn't bricks and mortar but moving lights and electronic images.) On the upper floors of the bustle, the architects could not hide behind flashy signs, and their solution for a facade yielded one of the strangest attempts at decorating a box that you are ever likely to see: plain, double-hung windows set into yellow, orange, and copper-colored metal panels in large, geometric shapes at slightly tilted angles. The facade is eerily like a child's drawing, complete with crooked lines, little boxy windows, and strange colors. What it does not look like is a wing of a $370 million commercial project in the center of New York City.

I'm not saying that a building in Times Square ought to look like a building at Rockefeller Center. Fort-Brescia told me that he wanted to respond to the atmosphere of Times Square. "We wouldn't do this on Wall Street," he said. "But Times Square is the entertainment district of New York. The building is performing. It has to be somewhat histrionic." Fort-Brescia is enthusiastic and engaging, and it's obvious why he is able to sell his designs to business people who want a little more pizzazz. Arquitectonica has an unusual history. It was established in the 1970s—Fort-Brescia and Spear are both fifty-one—and it grew very large very early, thanks mainly to the fame of a single building, the Atlantis, a waterfront condominium on Biscayne Bay in Miami. The Atlantis is a twenty-story slab with a square, four-story hole cut out of the middle. The cutout, in which a single palm tree grows, became the most famous void in contemporary architecture. It showed up in the opening sequence of "Miami Vice," and it expressed perfectly the way Miami wanted to see itself: daring, brash, and glittery. Now the building has been there so long it is practically as much a part of Miami's history as the Fontainebleau, and it looks almost quaint. But when the Atlantis was built, Fort-Brescia and Spear were barely past thirty, and the combination of pragmatism and exuberance that marked their work was unusual. They suddenly found themselves among the small group of architects whom developers seek out because their names add to a building's value.

The cachet of the celebrity architect is familiar today, when condominiums by Richard Meier in the West Village sell for more than many Park Avenue apartments, but it wasn't the norm in the late 1970s and early 1980s. Arquitectonica helped to create the architectural culture of this moment, such as it is, which is no small accomplishment for a young firm. And Fort-Brescia and Spear have had a singular effect on Miami, where they more or less created an architectural vernacular that mixes Latin energy and sensuousness with classic modernism. But I wonder if they haven't been hurt by too much success too soon. Michael Graves designs housewares for Target, there are Charles Gwathmey dinner plates, and condos created by Robert A. M. Stern, but those architects earned their stripes in the realm of more ambitious architecture before they went so heavily commercial. Big-time commercial work almost invariably involves big-time compromises, and Arquitectonica has often appeared a bit too eager to play the game. For all the promise of its early work, the firm didn't build up a big enough roster of serious architecture to leaven its participation in the culture of architectural celebrity, and now the thinness shows.

It's not easy to do architecture as entertainment. You see a building again and again and the jokes get old. That is not to say that architecture has to be stolid and dull to have staying power, but it does mean that it's harder to get away with being slick and superficial, even in a place like Times Square. The special qualities of Times Square as an urban space don't come from its architecture. The older buildings in the neighborhood, like the Paramount Building on Broadway or the Candler Building on Forty-second Street or the long-gone Astor Hotel, weren't all that different from buildings in other parts of town. The lights and the signs, the applied glitz, made the difference. Now, thanks to a new generation of technology, the lights and the signs are more spectacular than ever, and I wonder if we wouldn't be better off if architects recognized this and let the new buildings recede even more than the old ones did. Why try to upstage the electronic spectacle that defines Times Square?

Arquitectonica had a much firmer sense of how far to go inside the hotel. The lobby reminds me a bit of the big entry hall at the United Nations General Assembly Building, which is one of the most underappreciated 1950s rooms in New York. Many of the details, like the elevator cabs with curving, backlit metal panels, are splendid. Because the bustle is so deep—it fills the entire front half of the site—there is a lot of leftover space in the middle, and the architects have filled it with an atrium, which is enclosed on one side by the lower floors of the tower. Thus some of the elements of the facade, including the bottom end of the swooping white line that runs all the way up the south side of the building, are elements of the atrium, too. As much as I dislike that white line on the exterior, I like seeing it close up. In the atrium, it operates in a very different way than it does on the facade. It reveals how the building is made, and is completely engaging.

The hotel rooms themselves are appointed in a kind of mass-market Ian Schraeger manner, and they're not a bad example of that design sense: slate bathrooms with stainless-steel sinks; sleek furniture. I had assumed that, in addition to providing an environment of reasonable sophistication and comfort, the rooms would have the virtue of being the one place from which you could not see the exterior of the building, but when I looked out the window of one of the westward-facing rooms, I was confronted with a projecting side of that damn bustle. There is no escape from the outside of the Westin, even inside it.

The New Yorker, October 7, 2002

Diller and Scofidio, Reconceiving Lincoln Center, New York

WEST SIDE FIXER-UPPER

In the mid-1950s, when Robert Moses came up with the idea of Lincoln Center—a performing-arts complex that would make the depressed West Side of Manhattan respectable and provide the impetus for large-scale urban renewal—most of the city's performance venues were old, and people thought they should be replaced, not restored. The Metropolitan Opera House, on West Thirty-ninth Street, had sight-line problems, a cramped backstage, little room for storage, and inadequate rehearsal space. The company had been trying to relocate for nearly fifty years. The New York Philharmonic was particularly desperate, since its lease at Carnegie Hall was about to expire, and, in any case, the hall was going to be torn down to make way for an office building. The Philharmonic was the first tenant to move into Lincoln Center, in September, 1962. The New York State Theater opened less than two years later, then the Vivian Beaumont, and the Met in the fall of 1966.

There were complaints about the facilities at Lincoln Center from the beginning, and persistent squabbling among the various institutional constituents, so it didn't come as much of a surprise to hear, a year or so ago, that the New York City Opera was talking about putting up a new hall miles away, at Ground Zero. Having struggled for years to produce operas in a building that was designed to muffle the sound of toe shoes on the stage, why shouldn't City Opera have a place of its own? But when the Philharmonic announced recently that it was leaving, too—moving back to Carnegie Hall, which, of course, hadn't been torn down after all—it was pretty clear that Lincoln Center was in serious trouble.

It's not likely that either the Philharmonic or City Opera would have bolted if its hall had been more suitable. Avery Fisher Hall—which is what Philharmonic Hall has been called since 1973—is widely thought to be an acoustical disaster and has been resistant to tinkering, despite a complete reconstruction in 1976. But the raison d'être for Lincoln Center was dubious from the beginning. It originated with Robert Moses, not Leonard Bernstein, and Moses didn't care much for opera or theater or symphony orchestras. He just figured that they could serve as a magnet for development. Using culture in this way was a new idea in the 1950s, although almost everything else about Lincoln Center was stuck in the past. As a piece of design, it was as retrograde as the halls that it replaced—and much less successful.

Moses first proposed that the new arts complex be built at Columbus Circle. He would have set the Philharmonic and the Met behind the building that eventually became the New York Coliseum. When that plan didn't work out, he moved up the street to Lincoln Square and expanded the notion to include the New York City Ballet, the Juilliard School, and a new repertory theater. John D. Rockefeller III signed on as the first president of Lincoln Center for the Performing Arts, and Wallace K. Harrison, who had been more or less the Rockefeller house architect since the early days of Rockefeller Center, was asked to start making plans for the new Met, which would be the focal point of the complex, and to coordinate the choice of architects for the other buildings. Harrison asked a few of the architects he admired, including his partner Max Abramovitz, Alvar Aalto, Marcel Breuer, I. M. Pei, Pietro Belluschi, Edward Durell Stone, and Philip Johnson, to come to his office for a two-week-long charrette, or architectural work session. Pei and Stone did not respond, but the others came, and the charrette produced numerous schemes, including a proposal by Breuer to place all the buildings on stilts and one by Aalto that had a central plaza entirely enclosed by buildings, somewhat like the Piazza San Marco in Venice. Harrison and Abramovitz at one point concocted a plan that would have put the entrance to Lincoln Center at the corner of Sixty-fifth Street and Broadway, where Avery Fisher Hall now stands. There wasn't much of a consensus about what should be done, except in the case of Belluschi's idea of facing all the buildings in Roman travertine, which the architects reportedly agreed on instantly. Several months later, they decided on a roughly classical layout, with three buildings arranged around a formal, symmetrical plaza facing east.

In 1958, with a site plan in place, the board of Lincoln Center made the final selection of architects, rejecting Aalto because he was not based in the United States, and Breuer because he was believed to be too rigid. The roster was, nonetheless, a sampling of 1950s stars. Harrison gave Abramovitz the commission to design Philharmonic Hall, Johnson was assigned the dance theater that became the New York State Theater, Eero Saarinen the repertory theater, Belluschi the Juilliard School, and Gordon Bunshaft of Skidmore, Owings & Merrill the library and museum of the performing arts. Because Harrison tended to be a passive leader, the much more assertive Philip Johnson had a great deal to say about both the design of the central plaza and the architectural style of the three main buildings. Johnson was moving away from modernism and starting to embrace a kind of decorative classicism at the time, and the dominant architectural style of the main buildings reflected this, while the less conspicuous buildings off to the side were permitted to be more modern. (Johnson wanted to impose an even stronger classical sensibility on the place by running a delicate, columned arcade all the way across the east side of the plaza, meaning that you would have entered Lincoln Center through his gateway.)

The process of designing the individual buildings was something of a horror, since each architect had to produce a plan that would be acceptable not only to the people who ran the performing-arts organization that would occupy the building but also the organization's board of trustees, the board of Lincoln Center itself, and the city. It was architecture by bureaucracy, or, rather, by four layers of bureaucracy. Harrison's first designs for the new Metropolitan Opera House were spectacular, even daring. One resembled the General Assembly Building of the United Nations, for which Harrison had been the lead architect. Another seemed based on Jørn Utzon's Sydney Opera House design. But the Met had no more interest in being a patron of contemporary architecture than it had in being a producer of contemporary opera, and Harrison was sent back to the drawing board time and time again. In each instance, he returned with a design that was more conservative, more constrained, and more compromised than the last. The final version, his forty-third—produced after Rockefeller ordered that budgets be cut by 25 percent—was the smallest, meanest, and dullest of them all, and it got built. It bore almost no resemblance to Harrison's original concept. Abramovitz's concert hall and Johnson's dance theater endured similar if less severe compromises. The designs ended up awkward, overdecorated hybrids.

Like the World Trade Center, Lincoln Center epitomizes a certain kind of postwar urban design: formal, boxy, set on a podium, and altogether indifferent to the streets of New York. Architectural theorists of the time believed that the best way to save the city was to suburbanize it. The podium exists mainly to provide parking garages and automobile drop-off space underneath the buildings. It is the exact opposite of the situation at Carnegie Hall, which is enveloped in the swirling energy of the city streets.

People often say wistfully that we couldn't possibly afford to take on big projects like Central Park or the George Washington Bridge now, and that we probably wouldn't agree about how to build them if we did have the money. Yet they rarely talk of Lincoln Center that way. Lincoln Center would never be built today because the premises on which it was conceived are no longer convincing. The idea of a cultural campus set apart from the city never made much sense, even though Lincoln Center did, to be fair, promote the urban-renewal effect that Robert Moses intended. The neighborhood would probably have been gentrified without Lincoln Center, of course, but hardly in the same way, or on the same timetable.

As the surrounding area filled with condominiums and restaurants, however, Lincoln Center has sometimes seemed less the vibrant source of the neighborhood's energy than the empty hole in the middle of the doughnut. Often there is more buzz on the sidewalk in front of the multiplex theater a couple of blocks north, or amid the parade of mall-like retail stores that now line Broadway, than there is at Lincoln Center. Even though the center's various plazas are the major public squares of the neighborhood, they are for the most part cold and uninviting, and do not function as destinations in themselves, the way public space in a city ought to. Except for those occasional evenings when the weather is mild and the great central fountain is spouting, there is little about the plazas to attract anyone who is not heading to a performance. And if you approach Lincoln Center from what is supposed to be its front, facing the intersection of Columbus Avenue and Broadway, you have to navigate thirteen lanes of traffic. It isn't much easier to enter on the north side, from Sixty-fifth Street, where the plaza arches over a wide street and you feel as if you were going through a tunnel. From the west, the complex presents a solid wall, turning its back on the Amsterdam Houses, a public housing project. Although Robert Moses had little to do with the design, Lincoln Center reflected his social philosophy, which was on the side of public subsidies for middle-class amenities and against the visible presence of the poor. As for the wonderful benefits that would come from putting the city's major performing-arts institutions together on a kind of modernist acropolis—the other notion used to sell the project—it seems no more sensible than putting AOL and Time Warner together to create a hypothetical synergy.

The effort to remake Lincoln Center architecturally began in 1999, before the City Opera started talking about leaving, when the architects Beyer Blinder

Belle were asked to study the complex and figure out how to improve it. They evaluated the condition of the Lincoln Center buildings, all of which are aging and in need of serious renovation. Marshall Rose, a civic-minded real-estate developer on Lincoln Center's board, was put in charge of an effort to fix up the complex. He established a new organization called the Lincoln Center Constituent Development Project and hired Rebecca Robertson, who had run the Forty-second Street redevelopment project in Times Square, to head it. Rose then brought in the architectural firm of Cooper, Robertson & Partners (no relation to Rebecca Robertson) and asked them to join Beyer Blinder Belle in producing a master plan. In search of a big idea, Rose put Cooper, Robertson together with Frank Gehry, who suggested that a huge glass dome be erected over the main plaza. Gehry's dome was to be the centerpiece of a $1.2 billion program that would include another major renovation of Avery Fisher Hall, some updating at the Met, the New York State Theater, the Vivian Beaumont Theater, and the Juilliard School, and improvements to the public spaces.

Beverly Sills, who was then the chairman of Lincoln Center, had doubts about the Gehry plan. "A glass dome? We're going to have to heat it and air-condition it and clean the pigeon poop!" she said to the *New York Times*. "Which constituent would like to pay for that?" Joseph Volpe, the general manager of the Met, hated the idea of the dome, and he announced at the beginning of 2001 that the redevelopment plan was being handled so badly that the Met wanted nothing to do with it. Gehry was gone by the end of the year. The dome was a notable failure for him, if you can call something that never got past the preliminary design stage and was never even made public a failure. It wasn't so much an architectural failure—it might have been quite beautiful—as a conceptual and political failure. He seemed to be trying to keep a lot of dead architecture safe by putting it indoors.

Marshall Rose had resigned in October 2001, when Sills failed to back Gehry. Almost a year later, he was replaced as chairman of the redevelopment project by Peter Lehrer, the founder of a large construction management firm who had been involved in projects like the Statue of Liberty restoration and Canary Wharf in London. Lehrer resigned in mid-June this year, less than two weeks after the Philharmonic announced that it was going back to Carnegie Hall. Lehrer had clashed with Rebecca Robertson, and he told the *Times* that "a lot of money has been spent on planning with not enough to show for it."

Lincoln Center needs, desperately, a shot of adrenaline. In December last year, after the Gehry plan had been cast aside, the husband-and-wife architectural team of Elizabeth Diller and Ricardo Scofidio was interviewed by a committee made up of the center's trustees and administrators, which had started to look for another architect to redesign the complex's public spaces. Diller and Scofidio are best known for works that appear to straddle architecture and conceptual art, and they seemed less like serious candidates than like token representatives of the avant-garde, the sort of architects who get put on search lists so that the boards of large cultural institutions don't appear to be out of touch. Norman Foster and Richard Meier were also being interviewed, and feelers had been put out to Santiago Calatrava. It seemed likely that one of the megastars would be hired.

Diller and Scofidio designed three postcards to present to the committee. They called the first one "the image of Lincoln Center that you want to send to your friends." It was a picture of the fountain in the main plaza with the Metropolitan Opera House in the background—the view of Lincoln Center that everyone knows. The two other postcards were considerably less appealing. One showed the sterile landscape around the reflecting pool in front of the Vivian Beaumont Theater, and the oppressive platform-bridge over West Sixty-fifth Street, which connects the central plaza to Juilliard. The other postcard depicted the empty concrete bandshell in Damrosch Park, at the desolate southwest corner of the complex.

The postcards were meant to demonstrate that Diller and Scofidio could talk in terms that nonarchitects—like the financiers and arts patrons on the committee—would understand, and that they hadn't come to sneer, which is what some of the other architects being interviewed did. "One architect went so far as to say that more than Avery Fisher Hall should be ripped down," Bruce Crawford, who succeeded Sills as chairman of Lincoln Center, told me. "But Diller and Scofidio demonstrated there was something exciting you could do with this place without being in awe of it." Diller and Scofidio also exhibited a kind of modesty that, in the current economic climate, Lincoln Center was eager to embrace. (No one is talking about billion-dollar budgets anymore.) And by choosing to make two of their mock postcards views of ugly, uninviting parts of Lincoln Center, they showed that they had no illusions about how much work there was to be done.

Diller and Scofidio got the Lincoln Center job just a couple of weeks after a retrospective exhibition celebrating their career as radicals and architectural gadflies opened at the Whitney Museum. The exhibition didn't focus much on their architectural work, because there hasn't been much of it to show. They became famous for projects like the Blur Building, a pavilion at an international exposition in Switzerland in 2002 that consisted of a platform engulfed in mist. It was meant to dematerialize the experience of being in a building, to make it feel like standing in a cloud. More recently, they were commissioned to create art for Terminal 4 at Kennedy Airport, and they lined the long corridors leading from the planes to customs with a series of plasma-screen panels illustrating personal dramas involving travel—a couple breaking up in Paris, people losing treasured possessions. The narratives comment slyly on the difficulties of travel and the vapid nature of most travel advertising, but the installation is also a genuine attempt to relieve the boredom of walking through the corridors. Diller and Scofidio believed that a kind of high-tech interpretation of the old Burma Shave signs could transform the experience far more effectively than a conventional, decorative architectural element.

The Whitney exhibition included several hundred toy robots on a moving conveyor belt, which was intended to evoke the experience of passing through airport security. The robots' glass case looked as if it could have been designed by Mies van der Rohe. Diller and Scofidio love technology and architectural space, and they are fascinated by the ways in which they intersect. Some of their ideas will be put to the test in a new museum building they have designed for the Institute for Contemporary Art in Boston, but their greatest test, surely, will be at Lincoln Center. Two of this country's most determinedly avant-garde architects have been given the task of renovating what is probably the most conservative, not to say politically byzantine, cultural institution in New York.

"We opened our presentation by saying we really love Lincoln Center," Scofidio says. "They were shocked. They hadn't expected to hear that from an architect"—particularly from a firm with the reputation of being on the cutting edge. But Diller and Scofidio were expressing a growing affection among younger architects for the architecture of the 1960s. They seem to feel that if everyone else thinks the stuff is so bad, then maybe it's worth looking at more carefully.

Diller and Scofidio put together a video of computer-generated images that proposed such things as an enormous rectangular fabric roof, like a vast umbrella, that could be mounted on the corner of Avery Fisher Hall. It would rotate over the main plaza of Lincoln Center or over the north plaza in front of the Vivian Beaumont Theater, or back over Avery Fisher Hall, where it would turn into a tent covering a rooftop dining area. This wouldn't alter the main plaza permanently, as Gehry's dome would have, but it would protect it both from rain and from the intense sun that renders it nearly unusable on hot summer days. And it would provide a visual change. The plaza is now defined so completely by building facades and pavement that it looks oddly the same at all times of the year.

Diller and Scofidio's video also proposed carving out a section of the main plaza and turning it into a gigantic elevator platform that could ascend from the concourse level, bringing crowds up from the subway and the garages. When moved up a few feet higher, it would become a performance stage on the plaza. They suggested replacing Damrosch Park with a landscaped hill, beneath which would be tucked a structure containing office and rehearsal space. Actually, the hill would be more like an undulating, grassy roof that would be at its highest at the south end of Lincoln Center, and would form a kind of amphitheater as it descended toward the south side of the Met. Their most original ideas were focused on the north plaza, which now contains the reflecting pool in front of the Vivian Beaumont and the bridge across Sixty-fifth Street. The video included designs for ramps that would rise from the level of Sixty-fifth Street up to the plaza through a grid of trees planted at street level, so that you would feel as if you were ascending through the trees as you walked toward the main theaters. The architects also proposed carving out some of the space under the reflecting pool for public use and having the pool appear to cantilever out over this space, like a water-covered roof.

Diller and Scofidio were told to start work immediately on the first phase of the project, a redesign of the northern edge of Lincoln Center, which is the part no one likes. (Gehry had been fiddling with the main plaza around the central fountain, which is more likable, however seldom it actually gets used.) They are having discussions now with the various Lincoln Center organizations and will present a formal proposal sometime in the fall. It's unlikely that many of the ideas that Diller and Scofidio presented last winter will be intact in their final design, but they wouldn't have been chosen if the only thing they were expected to do was spiff up the old travertine. Hiring them was a commitment to rethinking the architecture of Lincoln Center in a way that is more radical, paradoxically, than anything Frank Gehry was preparing to do.

The plan will focus on West Sixty-fifth Street, which was bloated to interstate-highway width when the center was constructed. The street will be narrowed, the bridge over it removed, and restaurants and high-tech signage installed along the block. Diller and Scofidio want to make it a conventional street, but with a twist. They are also studying ways to reconfigure the traffic under the podium, and to reduce the number of entrances for vehicles and provide better access for pedestrians. The plaza around the reflecting pool will be redesigned, with more seating space and possibly another café. (The architect David Rockwell is already designing a pair of screening rooms for the Film Society of Lincoln Center that will go under the pool.) The empty triangle of space in front of Alice Tully Hall would be filled in with a building that could include a bookstore. The idea is to introduce the urbanity that Lincoln Center's original designers rejected.

Lincoln Center isn't going anywhere, whatever we think of it, and Diller and Scofidio are figuring out ways to weave the atoll back into the fabric of the city. They don't want to obscure the fundamental qualities of the architecture, but they feel that they can play with the podium itself. "Rather than thinking of the plinth as an object, think of it as a surface whose edges can be bent up and down," Diller said to me. "The street warps its way up to the plaza. The plinth is relentless, but we want to create a topography that is less relentlessly horizontal."

The strength of Diller and Scofidio's conception here underscores something that was clear from their retrospective exhibition earlier this year at the Whitney: for all their talk about architecture as a form of social criticism or performance art, their real passions are traditional. They believe that architecture should encourage social interaction, and they believe in the purity and power of formal composition. They love exploiting the latest technology, but they use it to embellish and reinvent traditional urban space, not to escape it.

The challenge of redesigning Lincoln Center is to know the difference between the parts of it that always worked and may simply be out of fashion, and the parts of it that don't work at all and have to be fixed. With the World Trade Center gone, Lincoln Center is the one true temple of 1960s architecture on a grand scale that New York has left. It's too important a place to get rid of, and it's too awful a place to leave the way it is.

The New Yorker, July 7, 2003

Diller Scofidio + Renfro, Alice Tully Hall, New York

CENTER STAGE

Alice Tully Hall, and the Juilliard School complex of which it is a part, were the last elements of Lincoln Center to be built, and when they opened, in 1969, they seemed like an ambitious attempt to bring cutting-edge Brutalism to the place. That's probably why so many architecture critics liked them and so many other people didn't. Amid the tepid classicism of so much of Lincoln Center, Juilliard stood out as something totally 1960s, all cantilevers and boxy geometries. Granted, it was covered in travertine, to match its genteel neighbors, but that served only to make the building seem ill at ease, like a wrestler dressed in a Sunday suit.

The building was a misfit in other ways, too. Alice Tully Hall, Lincoln Center's main venue for chamber music and recitals, was supposed to be its most conspicuous public element, but the entrance was half hidden behind a stairway that led up to a bleak, windswept plaza. It was also separated from the street by a small, virtually useless triangular plaza, a result of the insistence by the architects, Pietro Belluschi and Eduardo Catalano, on a rectangular building, even though the site, facing the diagonal of Broadway, was a trapezoid. If you were going to Juilliard instead of to Alice Tully, the front door was even harder to find—off the plaza, one level above the street.

So there is a certain justice in the way that this structure, designed with apparent disdain for the traditionalism of its neighbors, has turned out to be the first part of Lincoln Center to be radically rebuilt. (I'm not counting Avery Fisher Hall, the Philharmonic's acoustically challenged concert auditorium, whose interior has been redone four times, but whose exterior remains intact.) In February, Alice Tully will reopen as, for all intents and purposes, an entirely new hall. Large sections of the surrounding Juilliard building have been renovated, and almost nothing about approaching, entering, and being inside the complex is the way it was. The architects, Diller Scofidio + Renfro, have stretched Juilliard's rigid box all the way to Broadway, giving the building a shape that, at last, reflects the outline of the site. They have covered the new Broadway side of the building in glass—including a spectacular dance studio on the second floor which seems to float over the entrance. And they created a new front door by cutting a huge diagonal swath out of the southeast corner of the building. From some angles, it looks as if a giant had wrenched the building out of its foundation by lifting up the corner. When you get close to the door, the corner seems to loom over you, like an enormous triangular canopy. Forty years after Alice Tully Hall opened, it finally has an entrance that you notice.

Architects sometimes talk of design elements as "moves," as if they were playing a game of chess, and when dealing with problematic older buildings, the chess analogy is apt. You are more likely to succeed if you craft a strategy consisting of a lot of carefully considered small moves, not one big one. That's one reason for the failure of Frank Gehry's plan, a few years back, to solve Lincoln Center's problems by putting a gargantuan glass dome over the main plaza. Move by move, you have to take your cues from the architecture that is already there, but you can't let the older building dictate everything, either. Liz Diller, Ric Scofidio, and Charles Renfro, along with their associate architects, the firm of FXFowle, have figured out the balance. They joust with Belluschi's architecture, but they never try to kill off the old structure. They manage to be bold and subtle at the same time, making a dull building exciting without warping its identity completely.

Belluschi wouldn't have liked the renovation, an affront to his doctrinaire modernism, but almost every change has made this building better—both more alive and more functional. From Sixty-fifth Street, it looks almost the same, and where the architects have extended the south side to the corner of Broadway, they even copy Belluschi's travertine facade—perhaps as a gesture of homage, but also more likely because nothing else would make sense there. Yet from Broadway you see only the new material, and the building becomes another thing entirely, a vibrant composition of glass and metal that looks, and feels, strikingly new. Previously, once you found the door, you entered a cramped vestibule and then walked down several steps to a low-ceilinged, carpeted lobby that felt like a basement. Now, when you pass through the corner entrance, you find yourself in a vast glass-enclosed space—it includes most of the area where the triangular plaza used to be—that is full of light and open to views of the surrounding city.

In terms of its configuration and the precision of its details, this is probably the most urbane lobby at Lincoln Center. It avoids the grandiosity of Philip Johnson's space at the State Theater and the sappy romanticism of Wallace K. Harrison's Metropolitan Opera lobby. One wall of the new lobby is covered in muirapiranga, a Brazilian wood, set in narrow tongue-and-groove panels. There is a huge freestanding café bar made of Portuguese limestone, with one end sculpted in the form of a flying wedge. It looks like a model of a building by Zaha Hadid, but more elegant. From the lobby, you enter the hall by going down a steep staircase, as before, and the hall, unlike the lobby, isn't bigger, but the interior has been totally redone. At Lincoln Center, gold and red velvet have usually carried the day, but the new hall is paneled in a veneer of moabi, an African wood, and its contours are softer and more rounded than before. The seats are covered in dark-gray suede. It's reserved, but it's not cold—indeed, the gray of the seats and the rust-orange of the wood make the hall feel warmer and more intimate. Like the lobby, the interior of the hall shows how much richness and complexity can be teased out of the modernist vocabulary in the right hands.

It's somewhat amazing that Lincoln Center hired Diller Scofidio + Renfro, instead of opting for any one of several starchitects who were short-listed. Until recently, the firm had focused as much on multimedia installations as on real buildings, and even though their home for the Institute of Contemporary Art, on the Boston waterfront, finished in 2006, revealed their ability to produce significant architecture, it made clear that they would never have designed anything remotely like the original Lincoln Center buildings. Nonetheless, they have turned out to be exactly what the place needed. So far, their Lincoln Center work—which will include several additional phases of reconstruction, beyond Alice Tully—shows a rare talent for being assertive without being egotistical. The other work will be finished in stages over the next year or two, and it will address some of the key urban-design failures in the original Lincoln Center plan.

Chief among these is the treatment of West Sixty-fifth Street, which separates Alice Tully and Juilliard from the main campus. When Lincoln Center was designed, it was thought that a wide bridge extending the plaza over the street would be the right way to pull the two sites together. In fact, this ruined the street, turning it into a grim tunnel, and it brought no real benefit above. The genius of the redesign is to see the street not as a problem in need of covering up but as an asset whose energy can be harnessed. The bridge is gone, and Sixty-fifth Street is becoming a new spine for Lincoln Center, with street-level box offices, expanded facilities for the Lincoln Center Film Society, and a restaurant contained in a swooping new structure with a public lawn on its roof. The greatest design failing of Lincoln Center was its separation from the rest of the city, and the redo of Sixty-fifth Street will go a long way toward healing that breach.

But the most elegant thing Diller Scofidio + Renfro are doing is at Lincoln Center's main entrance, facing Columbus Avenue. The complex has always been difficult to approach, since you need to cross not only six lanes of traffic on Columbus (fourteen lanes if you count Broadway) but also a small roadway for taxi drop-off—an instance of the tendency of 1960s planners to put vehicles ahead of foot traffic. The architects are sinking the roadway and elongating the stairway to the main plaza out over it, creating a grand approach. The stairway will have lots of high-tech gimmicks, like electronic messages in the risers which you will see as you approach—this is a Diller Scofidio + Renfro production, after all—but that's just surface decoration. The really wonderful thing isn't the modern tricks but the classical symmetry. Lincoln Center's plaza will never be more than a weak echo of Michelangelo's Campidoglio, in Rome (the most famous plaza with pavilions on three sides), but by placing this grand staircase on an axis with the fountain and the Metropolitan Opera, the architects have enhanced its strength as a work of classicism. It wasn't such a surprise that they could give modernism new life at Alice Tully Hall. But who would have thought that they could rescue Lincoln Center's classical side, too?

The New Yorker, February 2, 2009

Courtesy Robert Polidori

Skidmore, Owings & Merrill, Time Warner Center, New York

THE INCREDIBLE HULK

The new Time Warner Center, at the southwest corner of Central Park, isn't a bad piece of urban design. The base of the building reflects the curve of Columbus

Circle in a sumptuous, even graceful arc, and it gives the circle a monumentality that it never had before. If you don't look up, you could like this building. Columbus Circle is one of New York's few true roundabouts, and almost every building put on it has ignored the architectural potential that the shape holds. Edward Durell Stone's sweet but hapless marble museum at 2 Columbus Circle made a gentle nod to the curving street, but you hardly noticed it when the monolithic New York Coliseum loomed on the site that the Time Warner Center now occupies. The tall glass stick that is the Trump International Hotel doesn't help much, either.

It may be going overboard to say that the curved base of the Time Warner Center is reminiscent of John Nash's glorious facades on Regent Street in London. A better comparison, perhaps, would be to a fine New York building that is often overlooked—the old Standard Oil headquarters at 26 Broadway in Lower Manhattan, by Carrère & Hastings, which has a tower set atop a convex base. The facade of the base reflects the shape of Broadway as it passes Bowling Green. The tower is aligned with the straighter grid of streets to the north, and thus can be seen from a distance. For the Time Warner Center, David Childs of Skidmore, Owings & Merrill (who is more famous at the moment for being at loggerheads with Daniel Libeskind over the shape of the Freedom Tower at the World Trade Center site) designed two huge glass towers that are positioned to be seen not just from Central Park but from along the axis of Fifty-ninth Street and Central Park South. The building hunkers over Fifty-ninth Street and blocks it, but the towers have been placed on either side of the atrium, where the street would be, so that as you view the building from afar, the open space of the street appears to continue. Childs added a striking sculptural fillip at the southern end of the base, which has a transparent glass skin under which you can see the steel frame.

Alas, the building itself is so big that Childs's well-intentioned gestures mean very little. The best you can say is that they prevent it from being worse than it is, or as bad as earlier versions, which date from the 1980s. The architecture above the rounded base is dull and conventional. The towers are nicely shaped but banal, and the glass is far too dark. (Strangely, the towers look brighter from across the Hudson River in New Jersey, where the afternoon sun gives their back side a light, glistening tone that the morning sun never seems to confer on the front.) Childs did add some small glass fins that project from the tower facades and provide a bit of texture, but they are not enough to give any real panache or dignity to the place.

The Time Warner Center is a hodgepodge, a sort of Rubik's Cube, with a luxury hotel, offices, condominium apartments, a big retail atrium, restaurants, and space for cultural events all thrown together. It is a theme-park version of a sophisticated urban building, slickly packaged to make city life seem attractive to people who aren't accustomed to it—the sort of thing you would expect to find on North Michigan Avenue in Chicago but not in a city that is as fully defined by its street life as New York is. The condos have spectacular views, but some of the rooms are oddly shaped, which isn't surprising, given that the towers aren't rectangles but parallelograms, designed to align the building with the angle of Broadway.

The 250-room Mandarin Oriental hotel was the first tenant to move in, with guests being officially accepted on November 15. The retail space and the restaurants will open early next year, which is more or less when the two hundred condominium apartments will be finished. They are being marketed now, those in the south tower under the address of One Central Park (which sounds more chic than Columbus Circle), and those in the north tower as the Residences at the Mandarin Oriental. One unit has reportedly been sold to a London financier for $45 million.

The interiors of the hotel were designed by Brennan Beer Gorman, and six other architects—including the eminent Rafael Viñoly, who designed performance spaces for Jazz at Lincoln Center at the top of the atrium—were involved in various parts of the building. David Childs had to cope with all of them while he wrestled with the problems of making a decent piece of commercial architecture in the middle of New York City. Viñoly seems to have made the most of the building's strong points. The firm of Elkus/Manfredi, which was put in charge of the atrium's retail space, has turned what might have been a stunning, curving arcade into something unpleasantly close to a suburban mall, full of fussy decorative columns. The hotel interiors are conventional—lots of marble and swirling decorations that are intended to distract the eye from the spaces, which are often cramped and awkward.

The Time Warner Center has a long and tortured history. In the early 1980s, the Koch administration and the Metropolitan Transportation Authority started talking about selling off Robert Moses's wretched old Coliseum, which was owned by the MTA. The Coliseum stood on one of the most prominent, and valuable, sites in New York, and city officials must not have thought too much about the fact that the more money a developer paid for the site the bigger the skyscraper he would have to build there, simply to justify the cost. Bigger was thought to be better. And, anyway, city planners of the time were enamored of the idea that new skyscrapers jump-started renewal in otherwise down-at-the-heels neighborhoods.

Thus we got, or almost got, Columbus Center, a pair of hulking towers designed by Moshe Safdie in 1985 for the developer Mortimer Zuckerman, whose firm, Boston Properties, offered the city $455 million for the Coliseum site, which it planned to turn into the headquarters of Salomon Brothers, an investment-banking firm that exemplified the 1980s boom. Safdie's design was widely thought to be grotesque, and it caused an outcry the likes of which New York hadn't seen since Marcel Breuer was commissioned to design a tower to go on top of Grand Central Terminal. The Municipal Art Society argued that the Safdie building would block the light on Central Park, and hundreds of people, including Jacqueline Kennedy Onassis, got together to hold black umbrellas along the outlines of what was purported to be the shadow it would cast. Zuckerman fired Safdie and replaced him with David Childs, who redesigned the building as an imitation of Central Park West architecture of the

1930s. Childs apparently assumed that if the building seemed familiar enough, people wouldn't mind that it was also enormous, although the protests faded only slightly. The urban theater provided by the people with the umbrellas was memorable, but, in the long run, a suit brought by the Municipal Art Society against the city was probably more effective. The society claimed that by selling off the site to the highest bidder, and granting zoning concessions, the city was in effect selling zoning rights, which is illegal. The society won, and the project was scaled down. Then, in 1987, the stock market crashed, and Salomon Brothers withdrew. The real-estate market collapsed a couple of years later, which put plans on hold.

The Time Warner Center is Columbus Center by another name. Mort Zuckerman is gone, and David Childs is now working with Stephen Ross of the Related Companies and William Mack of Apollo Real Estate Advisers, who won a competition for the project that the Giuliani administration initiated in 1996, early in a new real-estate boom. Ross and Mack paid less for the site than Zuckerman had offered, and the building is a little smaller than the 1980s versions, but it's still too big by half. Although Childs moved from Retro Central Park West to Anywhere Corporate Glass Sleek, the basic elements of Columbus Center remain. It's a mixed-use building with two large towers and shopping at the bottom. The most important addition, a nod to the Giuliani administration's demand that the project have a public component, is the performance spaces for Jazz at Lincoln Center. Giuliani had wanted a hall in which opera could be performed, and one of the spaces is outfitted to accommodate elaborate sets, just in case. The jazz spaces will not open until late next year, but even now, in their half-constructed state, they look terrific.

A jazz hall with spectacular city views almost, but not quite, justifies the whole overblown venture. The center originated when the government decided to sell off a piece of public land to private developers. A really big building would pay for a lot of subway cars. But that isn't the way to construct a city. Government should act as a referee in the game of real-estate development, and not as a player. Traditionally, it sets the rules, which is what zoning laws are. Developers are supposed to push for the maximum—after all, making money is their job—and the city is supposed to say no when a project threatens the public interest. But when the city joined forces with the MTA to squeeze as much money as it could out of Columbus Circle, the balance between public interests and private interests was endangered. The equilibrium of the development process was thrown out of whack. The city wasn't regulating the feeding frenzy; it was leading it. The people who protested the sellout, who went head to head against the forces with the money, did something important. But the fact that the city pulled in the reins a bit and agreed to take a little less money and have a slightly smaller building didn't change the story much. Money usually wins in this town.

The New Yorker, November 17, 2003

Norman Foster, Hearst Headquarters, New York

TRIANGULATION

Norman Foster is the Mozart of modernism. He is nimble and prolific, and his buildings are marked by lightness and grace. He works very hard, but his designs don't show the effort. He brings an air of unnerving aplomb to everything he creates—from skyscrapers to airports, research laboratories to art galleries, chairs to doorknobs. His ability to produce surprising work that doesn't feel labored must drive his competitors crazy.

Foster, who is English and lives in London, is an artist with the savvy of a corporate consultant. He knows how to convince chief executives that the avant-garde is in their interest. In the 1980s, he persuaded HSBC, the international bank, to spend nearly a billion dollars to build a tower in Hong Kong; the novel structure, in which five enormous steel modules were stacked on top of one another, was the most innovative skyscraper since the Seagram Building. In 2000, he secured a commission from the Hearst Corporation, the publishing firm, to design its new headquarters, in Manhattan. The gorgeous, gemlike tower, which will officially open in a few months, is Foster's first big project in America.

In the 1920, William Randolph Hearst commissioned Joseph Urban to design his company's first headquarters: six stories of megalomaniacal pomp on Eighth Avenue between Fifty-sixth and Fifty-seventh Streets. Despite its low height, everything about the yellowish stone structure suggests grandiosity, especially the monumental fluted columns that stretch higher than the building itself, giving it the look of a base for a much taller structure. (Hearst and Urban had planned to add a tower, but they never did.) The Hearst Corporation long ago outgrew this zany palazzo, dispatching most of its employees to rented space nearby. When the company decided to gather its operations under one roof, its executives smartly concluded that Urban's building was too much fun to give up. Hearst hired Foster to build something on top of it, and in October 2001, he unveiled a scheme to add forty stories to the original headquarters. It was the first major construction project to be announced in New York after September 11.

As with all Foster designs, the Hearst tower is sleek, refined, and filled with new technology. It looks nothing like the Jazz Age confection on which it sits. The addition is sheathed in glass and stainless steel—a shiny missile shooting out of Urban's stone launching pad. The tower's most prominent feature is the brash geometric pattern of its glass and steel, which the architect calls a "diagrid": a diagonal grid of supporting trusses, covering the facade with a series of four-story-high triangles. These make up much of the building's supporting structure, and they do it with impressive economy: the pattern uses 20 percent less steel than a conventional skyscraper frame would require.

Foster's brilliance can be seen in the way that he exploits this engineering trick for aesthetic pleasure. The triangles are the playful opposites of the dark Xs that slash the facade of the John Hancock Center, in Chicago. They give the building a jubilantly jagged shape. Foster started with a box, then sliced off the corners and ran triangles up and down the sides, pulling them in and out— a gargantuan exercise in nip and tuck. The result resembles a many-faceted diamond. The corners of the shaft slant in and out as the tower rises, and the whole form shimmers.

Such a scheme could have become a pretentious exercise in structural exhibitionism, but in Foster's hands it presents the perfect foil for Urban's building. The design avoids the two most obvious approaches: imitating the style of the base or erecting a neutral glass box. Joseph Urban's goal in the original Hearst Building was to create a respectable form of flamboyance, and Foster has figured out how to do the same thing with his tower, but in unquestionably modern terms, and without compromising his commitment to structural innovation. Foster is at his best when solving puzzles like this one; unlike most elite architects, he isn't obsessed with creating his own pure forms. His gift for building a meaningful conversation between new and old architecture became apparent six years ago, with the unveiling of the renovated Reichstag, in Berlin: Foster placed a glass dome atop an ornate nineteenth-century masonry structure, reinterpreting the building's monumentality in modernist terms. And, in 2000, he enlivened the courtyard of the British Museum with a steel-and-glass canopy that casts a delicate geometric shadow on the floor.

In some ways, the Hearst tower calls to mind a famous unbuilt design from a heyday of modernism: a six-hundred-foot skyscraper in Philadelphia, proposed by Louis Kahn and Anne Tyng in 1957, which would have had a zigzag shape based on a framework of triangular supports. Kahn and Tyng weren't the only designers to have understood that the triangle is an inherently strong and efficient structural form; Buckminster Fuller and the engineer Robert Le Ricolais made the same claim. Foster's use of triangles is, in this sense, a borrowed notion. But most of the older schemes had the visual appeal of something made with an Erector set. Foster took the ideas, updated them, and produced not just a real building but an exceptionally elegant one.

Indeed, the Hearst tower is the most beautiful skyscraper to go up in New York since 1967, when Skidmore, Owings & Merrill completed the stunningly serene 140 Broadway, in Lower Manhattan. After all the inchoate, collagelike skyscrapers that have been built around Times Square in the past decade, it's refreshing to see a tall building that clearly emerges from rational thought. Yet the Hearst tower also has a jauntiness that most modern buildings lack. The venerable modernist tradition of allowing a building's structure to determine its form has often led to pious, heavy-handed architecture. If you believe that there is something noble about a building expressing its structure, you will like the Hearst tower. But if you believe that it is more important for buildings to energize the skyline, you will like the Hearst tower every bit as much.

The pleasure of the Hearst tower doesn't end with the exterior. It has one of the most dramatic entrances of any tower in New York. You go in through Urban's original arch—which, along with the rest of the base's exterior, has been meticulously restored—and up a set of escalators. What comes next is an explosive surprise such as has not been seen in the city since Frank Lloyd Wright led people through a low, tight lobby into the rotunda of the Guggenheim. The escalators deposit you in a vast atrium that contains the upper floors of the old Urban building, which Foster has carved out and roofed over with glass. The inside walls of the old building have been covered with stucco, and you look up at three stories of windows—something one rarely sees, except perhaps in a cathedral—which give the space the feel of an outdoor piazza.

Hearst employees will be able to eat in a café within the atrium, and so will be on a par with their rivals at the Condé Nast Building, in Times Square, which features a sensuous Frank Gehry–designed cafeteria. But the Hearst space isn't just chic; it's majestic. The atrium is enhanced by huge, diagonal structural supports for the tower, which slice down into it, and skylights offer thrilling views of the tower rising directly above.

Unfortunately, it isn't easy to see the Hearst Building in the cityscape. It is blocked on the west by a banal brick apartment building, on the north by another apartment tower and, beyond that, by the new Time Warner Center, at Columbus Circle, which looks all the more uninspired in comparison. This situation isn't much different from that of most iconic New York skyscrapers, which are visible only in pieces. (The Empire State Building is a happy exception.) But the partial sightings of the Hearst Building that are offered up and down Eighth Avenue or along Fifty-seventh Street are so enticing that they end up increasing its allure—like a flash of leg in a slit skirt. The best view comes from the Upper East Side, around the Metropolitan Museum, since nothing blocks the Hearst Building to the northeast. From the Met's roof, you can see the tower emerge in its full glory, rising over Central Park, at once fitting into New York's skyline and transforming it.

The New Yorker, December 19, 2005

HOME

In 1921, Colonel Jacob Ruppert, the co-owner of the New York Yankees, needed to get his team out from under the thumb of the New York Giants, his landlords at the Polo Grounds, in Harlem, and build his own stadium. Having looked at a plot occupied by an orphan asylum in Upper Manhattan, some land in Long Island City, and an area on the West Side, over the Pennsylvania Railroad tracks, he settled on the Bronx. Just across the Harlem River from the Polo Grounds, he erected the largest and grandest stadium in baseball. Yankee Stadium, which opened in 1923, was a haughty structure designed to give the game a feeling of permanence lacking in earlier, scrappier ballparks, like Fenway Park, in Boston; Wrigley Field, in Chicago; and Ebbets Field, in Brooklyn. Unlike the builders of older ball-parks, Ruppert didn't have to contort the stadium to fit the lines of city streets. The stadium could spread out and lift high; it was the first ballpark to have three full tiers of seats. Nestled beside elevated subway tracks and across from the playgrounds and basketball courts of Macombs Dam Park, Yankee Stadium rose above its surroundings.

There is nothing so revolutionary in Yankee Stadium's replacement, which opens just to the north, across 161st Street, on April 3, when the Yankees host the Chicago Cubs for an exhibition game. (The first regular-season game is on April 16, against the Cleveland Indians.) The new Yankee Stadium, designed by the architectural firm HOK Sport, is effectively an attempt to atone for the brutal 1973 renovation of Ruppert's building, which removed the historic ambience without adding much in the way of modern amenities. HOK has reincarnated the old stadium, but with clearer sight lines, luxury suites, plenty of places to eat, and, finally, sufficient bathroom facilities. It has tried hard, very hard, to make us think of its predecessor, with sumptuous architectural effects that have the self-important air of a new courthouse built to look as if it had been there since William Howard Taft was president. When you first go in, you find yourself in the so-called Great Hall, an enormous space covered with a translucent roof, and from there you move into the concourses and toward the seats. Lest you forget that you are there not only to watch a baseball game but also to soak up the stadium's noble lineage, there's a reproduction of the famous scalloped frieze that adorned the old stadium's upper deck. Outside, there is a facade of limestone, granite, and cast stone, with high, narrow arched openings and entry portals that seem designed for the ceremonial arrival of the pope, Queen Elizabeth, or at least George Steinbrenner.

Also about to open is the New York Mets' new home—the first time that two major-league stadiums have opened in the same city at the same time. Citi Field, which people are already calling TARP Field, or Bailout Park, opens on March 29, with a college game. (The Mets play an exhibition game there on April 3 and their first regular-season game on April 13.) Like the new Yankee Stadium, Citi Field is right next door to its predecessor and was designed by HOK Sport. The firm has pretty much cornered the market in sports facilities in recent years; in 1992, it designed the most influential ballpark of modern times, Baltimore's Oriole Park at Camden Yards. The Orioles insisted that the new park have the ambience of an old-fashioned one and feel connected to the city, and HOK, scrapping an earlier design, obliged. Camden Yards launched a generation of so-called retro-classic ballparks, a style to which both of New York's new stadiums conform, even though they look vastly different from each other.

The previous home of the Mets, Shea Stadium, opened in 1964, at a time when architects seemed to think that their mission was to purge baseball fields of asymmetry, idiosyncrasy, and anything that seemed remotely related to a park's surroundings, and to offer up instead gigantic doughnuts of concrete that looked like highway interchanges. (Other notable examples of the genre sprang up in Pittsburgh, Atlanta, Cincinnati, and St. Louis.) Citi Field is pleasanter in every way than the harsh stadium it replaces. The park has a casual feel, with warm red brick inside, lots of amenities, great sight lines, and a layout that's easy to navigate. There are forty-two thousand seats, fifteen thousand fewer than Shea had, all a calm dark green and arranged in somewhat irregular tiers, bringing you much closer to the field than before. The complex has an energetic composition of brick facades, and dark-gray steel elements, which are said to have been designed with the great steel arch of Hell Gate Bridge in mind, and give the place a feel that is as much industrial as retro.

As for the retro-classic side of Citi Field, the Mets, having no ancient ballpark of their own to evoke, have appropriated someone else's. The architects, whose Camden Yards design incorporated features of several historic ballparks, have here wrapped an imitation of the facade of the much mourned Ebbets Field around the southern corner of the new structure, and the old Brooklyn stadium likewise inspired the form of the entry rotunda. The Mets treat the National League's New York history as if it were abandoned property, which, in a way, it is. But does that mean it is there for the taking? True, the identity of the Mets—whose colors combine the blue of the Dodgers and the orange of the Giants—has thrived on a magpie element, but there's something a bit dishonest about naming the rotunda for Jackie Robinson, who never wore a Mets uniform. A pastiche of the Dodgers' former field in Brooklyn pasted onto the facade of a different team's twenty-first-century ballpark in Queens is less a historical tribute than it is an act of make-believe.

Historically, ballparks have been urban places, gardens in the middle of the city. The greatest of them—Wrigley, Ebbets, Fenway, Forbes Field, Shibe Park—emerged out of the form and shape of their cities. Fenway has the Green Monster, the thirty-seven-foot wall that compensates for the truncation of left field; at Griffith Stadium, in Washington, D.C., the center-field wall was notched inward because the owners of houses next to the stadium refused to sell. Ballparks weren't the same because the urban places they belonged to weren't the same. One football gridiron is identical to another, but a baseball field, once you get beyond the diamond, is not—which is part of the reason that even the ugliest ones are loved so fiercely by the fans and become such repositories of civic feeling. A baseball outfield, technically, has no outer limits, just as a baseball game has no set time to end. The outfield stops where the stadium's builders decide it will stop. Urban ballparks had facades in front, to fit in with neighboring buildings, but were usually left low and open in the outfield, which had the effect of weaving the park into the neighborhood, so that, from the right place, you might catch an enticing glimpse of the green paradise within.

At the old Yankee Stadium, that place was from the elevated tracks of the Lexington Avenue subway, and one nice feature of the new stadium is that that, too, has been re-created. There is a break between the right-field stands and the scoreboard, and you can see the trains sliding by. The new stadium feels more tightly woven into the fabric of the city than the old one did. (It will feel even more so once a Metro-North station opens there, later this year, and once the city finally makes good on its obligation to replace the Macombs Dam Park facilities lost in construction of the new stadium with parkland on and around the site of the previous one.) If you approach it by driving along Jerome Avenue, you see a couple of the Bronx's finest Art Deco apartment houses across the street from the west facade, and you get a hint of the subtle counterpoint that once existed between a baseball park and an urban setting. The stadium is bigger and more imposing than everything around it, of course, but it seems to grow out of its surroundings, and this somehow rescues the building from its own pomposity. In a way, the apartment houses on Jerome Avenue, the jumble of storefronts and bars under the elevated tracks on River Avenue, and the constant presence of street life shape the stadium as much as its designers have.

At Citi Field, conversely, the Ebbets Field facade, stuck in the middle of acres of parking (as Shea was), seems more like a theme park than it would if it were in the middle of the city. HOK has tried to make the stadium feel more urban by placing a long brick building, containing the Mets' offices, just beyond right field, along 126th Street, where it faces a favela of auto-body shops in Willets Point. But, since the site is defined mainly by expressways and parking lots, the architects are fighting a losing battle. It's a pity that the Mets didn't build on the far West Side of Manhattan, where Colonel Ruppert first thought of putting Yankee Stadium, ninety years ago, and where the Jets recently tried to build a football stadium. A football stadium doesn't need to be in the middle of a city, but a baseball park, smaller and used much more often, does.

A stadium is a stage set as sure as anything on Broadway, and it determines the tone of the dramas within. Citi Field suggests a team that wants to be liked, even to the point of claiming some history that isn't its own. Yankee Stadium, however, reflects an organization that is in the business of being admired, and is built to serve as a backdrop for the image of the Yankees, at once connected to the city and rising grandly above it.

The New Yorker, March 23, 2009

Gensler and Renzo Piano, *New York Times* Newsroom, New York; Studios Architecture and Pentagram, Bloomberg Newsroom, New York (above)

TOWERS OF BABBLE

In 1999, when Arthur Sulzberger Jr., the chairman of the New York Times Company, was laying plans for a new headquarters, it was becoming nearly impossible to produce a newspaper in the rambling headquarters on Forty-third Street. The building was originally designed around the gargantuan printing presses that filled the basements and the delivery trucks that lined up in front. Writers and editors worked upstairs, in a crowded newsroom with few of the amenities of a conventional office. At one time—when it was filled with metal desks and clacking typewriters, the smell of ink and cigarettes and the yelling of city editors—this might have bestowed the kind of old-time newspaper mystique associated with plays and movies like *The Front Page*. But in the mid-1970s, with the first of a series of awkward attempts to adapt to the demands of the computer era, the noisy, competitive atmosphere began to dissolve. The deadline bells and the shouts of "Copy!" faded, and soon the newsroom felt more like the back office of an insurance company than like the nerve center of a great newspaper.

The tradition of having reporters and editors in one big space, called a newsroom or city room, arose largely because it was the easiest way to put out a newspaper on deadline. The fastest communication was face to face, and in a newsroom everybody could watch the same clocks, use the same news tickers, and keep an eye on one another. Everything depended on the flow of paper; in the old Times building, the Linotype machines were right above the newsroom, so that copyboys would only have to run up a single flight of stairs to deliver copy to the typesetters. Stories moved through the building in physical form, from paper to type to print, like an assembly line. Now, of course, stories are electronic blips, and page images are transferred in an instant to printing plants around the country. Almost none of the conditions that led to the creation of newsrooms still prevail.

So Sulzberger decided to start from scratch—something the New York Times Company hadn't done since 1904, when Sulzberger's great-grandfather Adolph S. Ochs put up the Times Tower in Longacre Square, at Broadway and Seventh Avenue. The building became an icon—soon after it opened, Longacre Square was renamed Times Square—but it was also impractically narrow and, within a decade, Ochs had to put up another building half a block away, which, presumably to save face, was called the Annex. Eventually, the entire operation moved into the Annex, and there it remained until earlier this summer, when it moved into a new tower.

Sulzberger, in building his tower, has been more methodical and less imperial than his ancestor. Having picked a site on Eighth Avenue, across from the Port Authority Bus Terminal, the Times Company joined forces with a real-estate developer, Forest City Ratner, and held a design competition. In the fall of 2000, the *Times* selected Renzo Piano, one of the world's most eminent architects. Piano, in partnership with the New York firm of FXFowle, designed a fifty-two-story tower of metal and glass, with screens of small ceramic rods running up the facade to make the building shimmer. The ceramic screens rise higher than the roof by about ninety feet, forming a light, ephemeral crown. Piano said that he wanted the tower to look as if it disappeared into the air, and while it doesn't quite do that—in part because of its steely, battleship-gray color—it has a tensile elegance that sets it apart from every other skyscraper in Manhattan.

For the reporters and editors, the most notable feature of Piano's design was his decision to put most of them in a structure known as the Podium, a separate, four-story glass wing behind the tower, facing onto a courtyard of moss and birch trees. Those involved with the building have made much of how apt a glass-enclosed building is to the openness at the heart of the journalistic mission. That seems a bit of a stretch—rapacious corporations and secretive government agencies like glass buildings, too—but clearly Piano, by making the newsroom a distinct architectural element, has tried to give reporters and editors pride of place. Inside, however, the newsroom feels enormous and austere, with a kind of corporate coolness. The interior was designed by the architectural firm Gensler, and it fails to emulate either the unusual quality of the building's exterior or the amiable rambunctiousness of an old-style newsroom. With its sea of cubicles partitioned by wood-veneer cabinets, it is vastly more sophisticated than any workplace the *New York Times* has ever had, but sleekness has brought a certain chill (though the effect will be pleasanter when the birch trees go into the still unfinished courtyard). You also don't get much sense that anyone has really rethought the idea of the newsroom in the electronic age. Ultimately, it's hard not to sense that the *Times*, so determined to have a building that makes a mark on the skyline, had a failure of nerve when it came to the interior.

Many of the reporters I spoke to didn't think much of their new digs. Journalists, of course, love to grouse, but they also don't like to be regimented, and just about every single workspace here is identical. In a nice, democratic gesture, most of the building's perimeter has been left open, bringing in lots of natural light, and the private offices for editors all have glass walls facing into the newsroom. One member of the editorial board, who gave up a large, enclosed office in the old building for one of these small fishbowls, growled to me, "There's no place I can change into a tuxedo." Undermining the egalitarian topography, Bill Keller, the executive editor, has rigged up a screen of frosted glass inside his office so that he can't be seen from the newsroom when he sits at his desk.

To see a newsroom truly designed for the electronic age, you have to head across town, to the headquarters of Bloomberg LP, on Lexington Avenue, which was completed two years ago. If the *Times* newsroom is an unadventurous space hidden within an architecturally important building, Bloomberg is the opposite: a dazzling work environment tucked inside a refined but conventional skyscraper, designed by Cesar Pelli. Bloomberg, working with Studios Architecture and the design firm Pentagram, has produced a workspace that could not have existed ten years ago. No one, not even the chairman and the chief executive, has a private office. Instead, some four thousand employees sit in uniform rows at identical, white-topped desks bearing custom-built Bloomberg flat-panel computer terminals. Although the desk of the CEO, Lex Fenwick, is larger and is set slightly apart—"I am not wholly pure," he told me—he sits just a few feet from the young employees who handle customer inquiries and complaints. "I wanted to make the point that we are a customer-service business above all," he said. Large, flat-panel monitors hang from the ceilings, flashing constantly updated numbers: how many customer-service people are working at that moment, how many calls they have answered, how long it's taking to answer the average call that day.

The most distinctive part of the office is a large central atrium, known as the Link, which overlooks a cylindrical courtyard at the base of Pelli's tower. The cylinder narrows toward the top, and so the Link's walls slant outward, making the most of the architectural quirk. A gathering place, with free snacks available all day to employees, the space gives an impression of maximal fluidity; it feels less like an office lobby than like the Palm Court of the Plaza, reconfigured for the computer age, when no one has time to sit down. Long screens, elaborately designed by Pentagram, relay news, market data, and other information. Elevators send all visitors and most staff members there first, and from there you can get to other floors on escalators, including one between the fifth and sixth floors that glides in a graceful curve.

Bloomberg, having started as a provider of financial data to corporate clients, is now a major news organization, whose radio stations, television studios, and significant online presence are all closely integrated. The workers are in much closer quarters than those at the *Times*, and you might expect the atmosphere to be one of a sweatshop, but sweatshops don't usually have rotating displays of contemporary sculpture or the tanks of tropical fish that are a feature of Bloomberg's bid for corporate cool. All in all, the Bloomberg newsroom is one of the most exhilarating workspaces I've ever seen, with both the high energy of a trading floor (where the Bloomberg products are consumed) and the buzz of the newsrooms of old. And, as with those newsrooms, visibility is key to the effect. On every floor, there are glass-enclosed conference rooms, couches for impromptu meetings, and even a series of small, glass-walled rooms for private one-on-ones—but you are always visible. Or almost always. Tucked away on a lower floor are a pair of tiny windowless, fabric-lined rooms where employees can retreat, presumably when the pressure of visibility becomes too much for them. With soft, glowing lights set into the floor, the room is a reminder that all this exuberance has its price, even if the snacks are free.

The New Yorker, August 6, 2007

**Frank Gehry, InterActiveCorp Headquarters, New York (above);
Atlantic Yards, Brooklyn**

GEHRY-RIGGED

Frank Gehry may be the most famous architect at work today, but, like so many of his peers, he has found it nearly impossible to build in New York. Twenty years ago, he designed a tower for the site of Madison Square Garden which never got built, and in recent years a number of projects—a redesign of One Times Square, a downtown branch of the Guggenheim, a hotel for Ian Schrager—have all foundered.

Now, at the age of seventy-seven, Gehry has completed his first freestanding New York building, a headquarters for Barry Diller's InterActiveCorp, in Chelsea. It is only ten stories tall, but you can't drive down the West Side Highway without seeing it—a white glass palazzo that looks less like a building than like a computer-generated image of one. On a cloudy day, it appears to fade into the mist. Gehry has likened the billowing forms of the facade to sails, and from a distance it seems to be made of some kind of plastic or fiberglass. All-glass buildings often feel stiff, but in Gehry's hands even glass is relaxed.

No Gehry building is ordered in a traditional way, but this one comes closer than most. There is a broad, nearly symmetrical five-story base, with a facade that zigzags in and out, making five roughly equal sections. On top of this is a narrower five-story tower of Gehry's swooping, rhythmic shapes. The facade, unusually for Gehry, is made of a single material: instead of a jumble of clashing forms, the glass is all you see, covering everything like a blanket. By Gehry's standards, this is serene, but behind the placid exterior are some daring technical maneuvers, including a number of concrete structural columns set at angles. During construction, the Georgetown Company, Diller's partner in the development, got calls from people who wondered if it knew that the building was going up crooked.

There are more than fifteen hundred panels of glass in the InterActiveCorp building, and almost every one is unique; they curve to fit the shape of the facade, gently concave one moment, convex the next. The white color is provided by ceramic dots, known as frits, bonded to the glass. Fritting is a common way of reducing glare in glass buildings, but Gehry has exploited its potential for drama. Each panel is densely fritted at the top and bottom but nearly clear at eye level. Viewed from the outside, the building exhibits dark, hazy horizontal stripes, as if the glass had been spray-painted. At night, when the offices are lit, the pattern will reverse, and the clear glass sections will appear lighter. "The whole building will glow like a lantern," Gehry told me.

The description is characteristic of Gehry, who, for all his experimentation, is always more interested in emotional impact than in architectural dogma. This helps explain the scale of his current celebrity. Last year, he made a guest appearance on *The Simpsons*, and this year saw the release of a worshipful documentary, *Sketches of Frank Gehry*, by the director Sydney Pollack. In the *Simpsons* episode, Gehry designs a satirically Gehryesque concert hall that ends up being converted into a prison, and there are moments when it seems that Frank Gehry's fame could be its own kind of prison, that his style will become mere shtick. Certainly Gehry is not good at saying no. He has designed watches for Fossil—his signature prominently displayed on the watch faces—and earlier this year Tiffany launched a line of his jewelry. (It features many of the twisting shapes familiar from his architecture, but what is revolutionary in a building is merely pleasant in a necklace.) The angst-filled artist we see in Pollack's movie is unlikely to round out his days as a brand franchise, but he clearly needs commissions that spur new discoveries rather than clients who just want his name on their projects.

Barry Diller is an ideal client for Gehry. He and his development partner Marshall Rose encouraged experiment, but Diller also has a company to run. Gehry has crafted interiors that balance architectural expression and practical concerns. Most of its offices will bear some hint of Gehry's style—a tilted wall, or a view that, because of the zigzagging shape, looks back at the building's own facade—but there is no space so oddly shaped that you can't work in it. People talk about the theatrics of Gehry's architecture, but he has an intuitive sense of when to express himself audaciously and when to be quiet.

It's a shame that this quality hasn't been more in evidence in Gehry's other New York venture, the Atlantic Yards development, in Brooklyn. This cluster of skyscrapers extending twenty-two acres around a new basketball arena for the Nets is the biggest project he has ever undertaken, and it has been the subject of bitter controversy for months. (Last month, following recommendations from the City Planning Commission, the plans were scaled back by 8 percent, but the project remains enormous.) Opponents complain that the sixteen residential towers will create a wall between the neighborhoods of Fort Greene and Prospect Heights. So far, they have cast the developer, Bruce Ratner, as the villain, suggesting that he is cynically using Gehry's name to add prestige to an ill-conceived scheme. In an open letter to Gehry published in *Slate*, the novelist Jonathan Lethem wrote, "I've been struggling to understand how someone of your sensibilities can have drifted into such an unfortunate alliance, with such potentially disastrous results."

Yet Gehry's design is a large part of the problem. He told me that he accepted the job in part because he has never taken on this kind of urban challenge, but his talents hardly seem suited to it. Gehry's great success has come from architectural jewels that sparkle against the background of the rest of a city—the Bilbao Guggenheim; the Walt Disney Concert Hall, in Los Angeles. In Brooklyn, the task is to create a coherent cityscape that relates comfortably to its surroundings. Gehry tried to do this by grouping some understated towers around a few very elaborate ones. (The 620-foot-high main tower, foolishly named Miss Brooklyn, is full of self-conscious Gehryisms.) Rather than giving a sense of foreground and background, the juxtaposition of plain and fancy just looks like a few Gehrys bought for full price next to several bought at discount.

Gehry has told me that he sees the project as a kind of homage to the old Manhattan skyline, but the romance of that vista is a happy accident of diverse buildings in a tight web of streets. Atlantic Yards, by contrast, involves eliminating streets, and has the look more of a single structure spanning multiple blocks than of a townscape that has grown organically. Gehry perhaps conceived of the whole thing as one huge object that could play off against the city—a gigantic version of one of his jewels. The problem with trying to do Bilbao on this scale is that it ceases to be an eccentric counterpoint to the context. It is the context.

Buried within the construction is the building that was the catalyst for the entire project—an arena for the Nets, the basketball team purchased by

Ratner and which he intends to move from New Jersey to Brooklyn. The arena is the best part of Gehry's plan. Its glass-enclosed spaces bring vibrancy to the intersection of Atlantic and Flatbush Avenues, and it will contain lots of public areas, not just for spectators but for anyone passing through. Such exclamation points in a cityscape are something Gehry knows how to create better than anyone. That's what Diller asked him to do, and it worked. Ratner's exclamation point, however, unlike Diller's, can't pay for itself, and Ratner is using it as a loss leader to justify an enormous real-estate venture. Although the site cries out for development, neither Ratner nor Gehry has a convincing idea of how this should be done. Ratner seems to have been less interested in using Gehry's architectural talent to best advantage than in trying to leverage his celebrity to make an unpopular development more palatable. Gehry, for his part, clearly loved the idea of taking on the biggest project in New York. But even the most famous architect in the world has limits.

The New Yorker, October 16, 2006

NEW YORK BECOMES LIKE AMERICA

By the way cities generally measure success, New York is healthier than it has been in more than a generation: employment is up, crime is down, construction is booming, and tourism has increased so much that you can't get a hotel room. The glow of prosperity emanates from most of the city, and almost everyone takes it as a truism that New York's revival represents a triumph over the antiurban sentiment that prevailed in the 1970s, when people and jobs seemed to pour out of the city with such zeal that the only question was whether they were headed for the suburbs or the Sun Belt. But if New York's resurgence seems to underscore the continued strength of cities, it also paradoxically proves the opposite. For the New York that exudes affluence today is—in its buildings, in its public space, even in its social patterns—not nearly as urban a place as it once was. New York has saved itself in part by becoming the very thing it had always claimed to despise: suburban.

I say this not because of the much-maligned "Disneyfication" of Forty-second Street, which for all the banality of its multiplexes and retail stores at least has brilliantly preserved historic theaters and, more important, some street life. In fact, the street life around Times Square has more energy than it has had in a long time. The new Times Square may be a bit sanitized for my taste, but it's clearly not a place that's like every other place—and its primary focus is still the street.

Once public life in New York was lived largely on the street. The street was the center, the heart of the public realm, and what had always made the city profoundly different from the places it now seems to want to resemble. The greatness of the public realm meant that we didn't need big houses, because we had the street. We didn't need big yards, because we had Central Park. We didn't need cars, because we had the subway. We didn't need a local church steeple, because we had the Empire State Building—and on top of that we had Carnegie Hall and Lincoln Center and Grand Central Terminal and Rockefeller Center and the Brooklyn Bridge and the New York Public Library and Bryant Park. Together all of these places make up as potent a public realm as any city in the world, remnants of a day when the notion of community was expressed in great physical places that were open to everyone and were intended to be shared.

The elements that always distinguished life in the city—once defined by walking along streets, by a certain serendipity, by a variety of shops and visual experiences, and by people you believed could not be duplicated anywhere else—are increasingly scarce, whereas the kind of experiences that exist everywhere else are increasingly common. Plenty of Manhattanites now do their food shopping by driving up the West Side Highway to the Fairway at 132nd Street, where the cramped parking lot and ominous entrance under the viaduct remind you that you're still in New York, but the immense shopping carts and warehouselike interior recall a discount food depot on Long Island. They crowd the Fairway in vast numbers, filling their carts with supersize boxes of cereal and megapackages of paper towels, the sort never sold at traditional space-challenged Manhattan markets. Then they load the trunks of their cars to overflowing and drive home, making the delivery of food to the better apartment buildings—which was once done at the back door by Gristede's deliverymen and building porters—now just as likely to occur via Range Rover at the building's front door. It is now the doorman's problem.

City life has been further changed by places like Chelsea Piers, which contains a pair of ice rinks, a gymnastics center, a bowling alley, a roller rink, a golf driving range, and a gym in a particularly lavish and un-Manhattan-like amount of space replete with on-site parking for more than four hundred cars right off the West Side Highway. Chelsea Piers is the mother church of the New Suburbanization. It has probably done more than any other place to convince Manhattanites who once thought of their cars only as a means of escape from the city to begin using them as a system of routine transportation, the way people do everywhere in the country except New York. Once Manhattan kids whose athletic ambitions extended beyond gym class were picked up by vans run by after-school sports clubs of the sort J. D. Salinger wrote about in "The Laughing Man," and parents had nothing to do with it except to pay the bills. Now they drive their children to Chelsea Piers—or to the West Side Soccer League, Little League, or some other program that has migrated into New York from the rest of America.

Just a few years ago, there were no chain stores like Kmart, Eddie Bauer, and the Gap, and far fewer national fast-food outlets like McDonald's and Burger King. Things in New York were different than in other places, by definition. We got our fast food at Nedick's and Chock Full o' Nuts—names that meant nothing outside of Manhattan (and today don't mean much within Manhattan either, except to people with long memories). We bought our children's clothing at local shops like Morris Brothers and Glad Rags, and food came from neighborhood markets that delivered. There is nothing of that world left in, say, the stretch of Broadway between Sixth-fifth and Sixty-eighth Streets, just north of Lincoln Center, where the Nevada Meat Market held sway for ninety years. Now there is Eddie Bauer, Pottery Barn, Barnes & Noble, and Tower Records, which share pride of place with a vast Sony multiplex. All that's needed to make those blocks into a perfect suburban mall is a roof over Broadway.

The New Suburbanization would seem to be more a matter of class than geography. You need to be able to afford a car to play Mamaroneck-in-Manhattan, and shopping at Banana Republic isn't cheap, be it on the conceptual mall of Broadway or in the real ones in New Jersey. But no one needs a car to get to the Kmart on Astor Place or Thirty-fourth Street, or to Old Navy or Bed Bath & Beyond, which have turned the old Ladies' Mile district on Sixth Avenue into a retail powerhouse. Throughout its reign the Giuliani administration made it easier for vast national retail establishments—the so-called big box stores like Staples and Toys 'R' Us—to establish a greater presence in the city.

Well, what of it? Places like that are often cheaper and more convenient than local stores, sometimes offer more variety, and inevitably offer a kind of glittery, sleek sex appeal that a little shop on Second Avenue, or a bodega on Ninth Avenue, can't touch. There is a reason that small towns and their old-fashioned Main Streets fall prey to Wal-Marts—they did not just happen because unsophisticated mayors succumbed to the lure of tax dollars. If people didn't want to shop in such places, there would be no tax dollars to be gained. Who in his right mind would rather shop in a cramped, run-down supermarket on Columbus Avenue when you can have something approaching suburban splendor? There is an exhilaration to space, cleanliness, and vast quantities of goods that makes a Manhattanite who first encounters them feel like a person who has just arrived from a Third World country. Anyone who thinks this is a simple matter of city culture good, suburban culture bad has a lot to learn about what people want in their daily lives.

Curiously, at the same time the city is becoming more suburban, the suburbs are becoming more citylike. Back in the days when arugula was to be found only at Balducci's and lattes at little cafés in the Village, food in the suburbs meant white bread. Now, with gourmet food shops everywhere and Starbucks having made its way even to the local mall, no bridges or tunnels need be crossed to satisfy more sophisticated cravings. Indeed, these cravings are now mainstream. Everything is available everywhere. And it's not just food. The *New York Times* reported that a woman in Scarsdale built a successful transportation business shuttling children from school to lessons and sports activities; it seems suburban mothers are now too busy to handle this sort of chore themselves. The notion of hiring someone to shuttle your children about is precisely the kind of thing that would have driven suburban mothers to sneer at Manhattan pretension a few years ago. In the age of ambiguous city-suburb identity, it plays just fine.

That the more troubling aspects of city life—crime, drugs, and violence in the schools—are often present in the suburbs muddles the distinction even further. So does the fact that the city is cleaner and safer than it used to be. (Does anybody even remember the squeegee men, who once seemed the bane of city existence?) For all the benefits this blurring of city and suburban identity may confer upon city people, who are liberated from supermarkets that feel like subway stations, and on suburbanites, who don't have to travel to Dean & DeLuca to find real espresso beans, there is a price to the blending of city and suburb. The loss is the uniqueness of New York. There was always a sense that city life was a matter of trade-offs, that you suffered through certain difficulties, even indignities, because you were in a place whose singularity gave it a kind of nobility. Yes, New York was inconvenient—but it was powerful and magnificent and far too sure of itself ever to want to look like any other place. You came here for life to be different.

But that makes the whole issue seem sentimental, as if it were merely a matter of losing Nedick's for McDonald's, or worrying that the uniform taste of the Pottery Barn will drive out the eccentric shops of the East Village. Actually, those are really just lifestyle issues. What is troubling about the New Suburbanization goes deeper than that. (In fact, on the lifestyle quotient, the suburbanized city wins. It's pleasanter, it's easier, and there's no upside in trying to convince affluent Manhattanites to give up their Land Cruisers.) The real question is what kind of physical place a more suburbanized city becomes, and what kind of community that physical place creates.

Suburbs historically haven't placed a high value on the public realm, in large part because the very idea of suburbia has always been to elevate the notion of private space—the single-family detached house, the yard, the automobile. Most suburbs now have even less truly public space than they once did. It's the older, villagelike suburbs that have parks, not the newer ones. And not only are malls taking the place of streets in the commercial life of many small towns, the privatization of the public realm has advanced even more dramatically with the huge rise in the number of gated, guarded suburban communities—places where even the streets are technically private. These communities exist to exclude, whereas cities traditionally existed to include, or at least had the effect of inclusion.

We have stopped valuing the street, which is the essential building block of any real city. It's understandable. Real streets are hard to control; they are by definition where everyone crosses paths and where the fundamental urban idea—that the city exists to create a maximum number of opportunities for encounter—realizes itself most fully. Put it all inside a big box and you may be safe from one kind of disruption, but you are equally safe from the stimulation and serendipity that makes a city what it is. And you have a recipe for the kind of disengagement and alienation that characterizes so many communities victimized by suburban sprawl.

Now in both city and suburb, expressions of urbanity—defined as the making of public places where people come together for commercial and civic purposes—increasingly occur in enclosed private places: shopping malls; "festival marketplaces," which straddle the urban/suburban models; atrium hotel lobbies, which in some cities have become virtual town squares; multiplex cinemas, which often contain a dozen theaters and exist at significant civic scale; and office building galleries and arcades. But there is a huge difference between the Rockefeller Plaza skating rink, which feels like a public place, and the Trump Tower shopping atrium, which in spite of its pretension to urban sophistication is a sterilized retreat from city streets.

That's the essence of the new urban paradigm—a kind of airbrushed urbanity that blends a whiff of urban sophistication with the separated, privatized space of suburbia. It's the model that gave us so-called edge cities like Post Oak, in Houston; Buckhead, in Atlanta; and Tysons Corner, Virginia, outside of Washington, D.C.—and it is now seeping into the middle of Manhattan.

This new urban paradigm doesn't just join the city and the suburbs—it also takes something from the ubiquitous theme park. In his brilliant 1965 essay "You Have to Pay for the Public Life," the architect Charles Moore observed that Disneyland was the only place in which southern Californians could have anything even remotely resembling a conventional urban experience. By allowing urban experience to take place in a safe and entertaining environment, Disneyland made the very notion of urbanity attractive. Moore was prescient: now the theme park has virtually taken over the landscape, a mutation running amok over both city and suburbia. The private realm—protected from the randomness and difficulty and challenge of real urban life on the streets—has given people everywhere the opportunity to play at urban life without getting their hands messed up in it. The triumph of the theme park as the new urban form has made its way most of all into retail life, where malls have taken over from the streets, parks, and squares. But it has also become part of art museums, where marketing art as entertainment has become part and parcel of the way business is done—and cafés and stores and events are sometimes more significant to the experience than looking at the art. We see it in science museums, where IMAX screens make dazzling, entertaining images the central attraction. We see it in megastores, such as the Barnes & Noble superstores with cafés that have become gathering places—the public places of the new urbanism.

Is this public-private mix a healthy development? Well, better to have a bookstore taking over the functions of a public square than to have no public square at all. Better to have an art museum behaving as an entertainment center than no art museum at all. In the age of virtual reality, when cyberspace so often seems to threaten the continued existence of physical space, there is a temptation to be grateful that anything at all is happening in the realm of the real. Then what is the problem? Isn't it simply a matter of urban form evolving to respond to new needs and technologies? Of course that's part of it. But to leave it at that—to say that the new model of urban form, in which a suburbanized private space morphs into something quasi-urban, is acceptable— is to deny an essential truth about great and even not-so-great cities. They are deeply, profoundly, and utterly public. In a real city we accept messiness as part of the deal. Unevenness, disarray, complexity, a mixture of people and things, and a certain amount of chaos are all part of the price we pay for the extraordinary creative energy that emanates from cities; for the presence of public space that can be described as true common ground; for that elusive, difficult-to-define quality called authentic experience.

There is a profound desire almost everywhere now to combine the comforts of middle-class suburban life with at least some of the excitement and entertainment that cities have traditionally provided, which is why the suburbs are feeling more citylike at the same time that New York is feeling more suburban. The horrifying prospect is that the two will eventually meet— that the suburbanizing city and the urbanizing suburbs will someday become indistinguishable, one homogeneous mass of middle-class sensibility awash in creature comforts and lifestyles that, however different their physical trappings may be, are essentially the same. Once you're inside a Barnes & Noble in Great Neck, does it feel any different from the one on the Upper East Side? Does the fact that someone gets into an elevator on West End Avenue before he climbs into his Saab to drive to the hockey rink make the life he leads as different as it once was from that of the man who starts the same kind of trip by walking down his driveway? I am not entirely sure that it does. I like to tell myself that it will take much more than Starbucks to make Scarsdale feel like the Upper West Side, and that the parade of Volvos and Jeeps heading into Chelsea Piers can't by itself turn the city into Scarsdale. But some days it is very hard to be sure.

Metropolis, March 2001

A NEW BEGINNING

In the lives of cities, boldness and vision rarely follow catastrophe. Chicago rebuilt itself in sturdy but mundane fashion after its great fire, in 1871; it was thirty-eight years before Daniel Burnham created the sweeping master plan that gave the city much of its grandeur. After the San Francisco earthquake of 1906, the city set aside a plan to remake itself with grand boulevards and focused instead on reconstructing as much as it could on its four square miles of burned ruins. Berlin tolerated the wasteland of Potsdamer Platz in its center for more than half a century, from World War II to the 1990s; the void at its heart was then filled with sleek but banal commercial buildings.

Still, it seemed reasonable to hope that things would be different at Ground Zero. In the anguished months after September 11, when people eventually began thinking about what should happen to the sixteen acres that had been the site of the World Trade Center, they talked either of ambitious, utopian projects—international centers for peace, memorials in the form of great towers—or of leaving the entire site as an open public space dedicated to the people who died in the terrorist attack. There were calls to hand over a portion of the site to Frank Gehry's audacious design for a new Guggenheim Museum, which had been proposed for another location in Lower Manhattan. Architects from Michael Graves to Paolo Soleri offered creative schemes for Ground Zero, and although many of the plans made little sense, they heightened the expectation that something extraordinary was likely to happen there—indeed, that something extraordinary had to happen, that vision and imagination were the only proper response to the tragedy.

Ground Zero, sadly, has become not a place of vision but, rather, the site of a planning and political catastrophe. In public, the planning process has been surrounded by lofty, often sanctimonious rhetoric; in private, the numerous officials and designers have squabbled ceaselessly over power and money. In the next few weeks, the planners will present a revised design for the project's centerpiece—the Freedom Tower, a seventy-story office building topped by a crown of latticed steel cables so enormous that it would have made the structure the tallest skyscraper in the world. The new design will undoubtedly look better than the present version, a clumsy hybrid of the work of two rivals: David Childs, known for his corporate skyscrapers, and Daniel Libeskind, the official master planner for Ground Zero, who is a creator of extravagant sculptural forms. Officially, the current design was derailed by security concerns. But Larry Silverstein, the tower's developer, had been struggling for months with the planners over whether he would pay for the latticed top, or for any other element that would make the tower more than an ordinary office building.

The Freedom Tower, with or without its fancy spire, is an unnecessary building. The planned skyscraper, which will contain 2.6 million square feet of commercial office space, doesn't have a single tenant—an unsurprising fact, since the demand for commercial office space in Lower Manhattan is so small that it can barely be said to exist. The tower, it seems, is being built not to ennoble, enliven, or enrich the city but to satisfy the narrow, self-interested agendas of Silverstein, who leased the Twin Towers in 2001, and the Port Authority, which built the World Trade Center and still controls the land. Silverstein, for his part, is largely building with insurance money instead of borrowing, as developers usually do, and he figures that he will be well positioned in the unlikely event that the Lower Manhattan office market rebounds. Meanwhile, the Port Authority receives $10 million a month in rent that Silverstein still pays, under the terms of his lease.

Governor George Pataki, who has overseen the rebuilding effort, bears the greatest responsibility for the failure of imagination at Ground Zero. Though he has spoken frequently about wanting to have an open and public planning process, his most important decision about the site was made in private. Not long after September 11, he agreed to let Silverstein and the Port Authority continue to treat Ground Zero as a platform for 10.5 million square feet of commercial office space. In the emotional atmosphere that followed September 11, it would have been easy politically for Pataki to have said he wanted to use some of the billions of dollars in insurance proceeds to buy the land back from the Port Authority and end Silverstein's lease. But Pataki, perhaps thinking that it was in his political interest to get something built as soon as possible, was unwilling to oppose these entrenched forces.

Pataki tried to cloak expediency in the garb of majesty, but he hasn't been able to carry off either one. The planning process has been presented as an effort to transform the site into a symbol of grace and renewal; in reality, the planners have been fixated on figuring out a way to cram a huge amount of office space into a small site. In addition to the Freedom Tower, the master plan calls for four additional office towers—even though there are no prospective tenants for them, either. Less than half of the site has been set aside for a memorial and cultural buildings, not enough to make public space seem central to the project. With the focus on generating profit, it is increasingly hard to see what makes Ground Zero different from any other real-estate project in New York, except for its size and, of course, for the way in which its land became available.

Since there has never been a true public dialogue about what Ground Zero ought to be used for, it's impossible to say what New Yorkers would prefer to see built there, but it's clear that the answer isn't a crowded cluster of office towers. (Donald Trump last week advocated building replicas of the Twin Towers one story higher than the originals, but the idea of spending billions to repeat one of the major architectural mistakes of the twentieth century is even worse than the current plan.) Ground Zero doesn't need simply to be rebuilt; it needs to be reimagined as a new district of the city, one that is both inspiring and useful. And what Lower Manhattan needs now, more than anything, is housing.

In the traumatic period after the Twin Towers collapsed, most people found the notion of living at Ground Zero to be upsetting, even ghoulish. Many apartments at Battery Park City were abandoned after September 11, and the Lower Manhattan Development Corporation, the agency in charge of revitalizing downtown, had to offer subsidies to persuade new tenants to occupy them.

This aversion to living in Lower Manhattan was surprisingly short-lived. There are now more residents in the area than ever before. As it turns out, September 11 only briefly interrupted a long-term trend. Manhattan has suffered from an apartment shortage for more than a decade, and people who once wouldn't have considered living below Fourteenth Street have begun exploring options on the island's southern tip. When the World Trade Center was built, in the 1970s, almost nobody lived in Lower Manhattan, but when the Twin Towers fell, there were more than fifteen thousand people living in their shadow. In the past few years, dozens of old office buildings have been transformed into apartments, bringing thousands of additional residents to Lower Manhattan, and the pace of conversions has made many of the area's slender prewar towers much more valuable as apartments than as offices. Even a building overlooking Ground Zero—an ornate, mansard-roofed 1907 office tower by the architect Cass Gilbert, which was badly damaged on September 11—is being converted into a luxury-apartment complex. New condominiums have, in turn, inspired the creation of restaurants, stores, gyms, and day-care centers. Wall Street now has nearly as many residential buildings as office buildings, and Whole Foods recently signed a lease to build a supermarket on Greenwich Street. An area that once contained a scattering of isolated homesteaders is coming to seem as domestic as Carnegie Hill.

There is still time to create an intelligent plan for Ground Zero, although it is going to be harder politically, and more expensive, than it would have been if Pataki had wrested control of the site from Silverstein and the Port Authority. Fortunately, we have one advantage that we did not have then, which is that we are beyond the time when we looked at the skyline of Lower Manhattan and felt a sense of shock at the absence of the Twin Towers. We can now comfortably make long-term decisions about the site.

In an ideal plan, most of Ground Zero would be devoted to housing, hotels, and retail space. Lower Manhattan currently has a range of housing options: the converted lofts of Tribeca, the converted office buildings of Wall Street, and the retro-style apartment complexes of Battery Park City. The one thing missing is experimental architecture. Ground Zero would be the perfect place for an inventive alternative to the prim, packaged urbanism of Battery Park City. Here is a chance to rewrite the city—to produce "green" buildings that generate their own energy or have walls made from recycled materials. Architects have developed a new generation of prefabricated modern houses, and Ground Zero could be the place to expand these sleek glass-and-metal boxes to monumental urban scale. Another possibility is to create modular lofts that could be easily adapted to the needs of a succession of tenants, or to integrate large gardens into high-rise living. With several blocks to build on, Ground Zero provides an opportunity to think not in terms of single buildings that are stand-alone works of sculpture but of ensembles that fit together to make coherent streetscapes and complete neighborhoods—something modern architecture has rarely succeeded in doing, in New York or anywhere else.

Daring residential design is finally beginning to appear all over Manhattan. There is, for example, a spectacular glass condominium by Winka Dubbeldam a dozen blocks north of Ground Zero, on Greenwich Street; Richard Meier's exquisite glass apartment towers, in the West Village along the Hudson River, may be New York's most coveted new address. A housing market that was once defined largely by white brick is more amenable to new architecture than it has ever been. We are at a point in time when strong architecture carries minimal risk.

What does seem risky is building office space. Not only does Larry Silverstein have to find tenants for the Freedom Tower, if he builds it, but he also has to fill another building, across the street from Ground Zero, which he has already constructed: a $700 million glass tower built as a replacement for

7 World Trade Center. That building, designed by David Childs, will be ready for occupancy next year. Predictably, it has no tenants.

These days, many planners and public officials try to justify building office towers at Ground Zero with words like "balance." They argue that the demand for housing in Lower Manhattan has become so great that the area is at risk of losing its identity as a strong commercial center. This view seems excessively dire: Wall Street is hardly fading into oblivion. Moreover, it seems foolhardy to interfere with the larger shifts in the evolution of Lower Manhattan, especially when those trends are so healthy.

Lower Manhattan hasn't been a truly diverse neighborhood since the nineteenth century, when the city's center of gravity began creeping uptown and office towers started surrounding Trinity Church, crowding out residential life. Now that the cycle has reversed, the planning for Ground Zero seems frozen in the past. Surely, it would be better to knit its sixteen acres into the vibrant new fabric of downtown.

The only element of the current plan that is worth salvaging is the need for a potent memorial. A memorial has to be not only the physical center of those sixteen acres but also the soul of the project. Daniel Libeskind, in his master plan for Ground Zero, adopted in 2003, had the brilliant notion of leaving a large section of the excavated site below ground level and incorporating a concrete retaining wall that survived the fall of the Twin Towers. This sunken space would break up the normal urban experience, creating a disquieting disruption in city life. But when a competition was held to design an actual memorial, the winners, Michael Arad and Peter Walker, produced a scheme that raised most of the memorial area back to street level. Libeskind, whose ideas for the site have been slowly undermined by Silverstein and others, was right in this case. Although the Arad and Walker plan is refined and intelligent, the danger is that the memorial will feel like an elegant park lost amid office towers.

In its current form, the memorial also feels squeezed by one of the two cultural buildings planned for the site: a wood-and-glass structure designed by the Norwegian firm Snøhetta, which will contain both the Drawing Center, a small museum, and the International Freedom Center, a new institution with the ambitious, if hazy, mandate of "helping people understand, appreciate and advance freedom as a world historical movement." The design, which consists of a large, boxy structure made of wood set with thousands of small glass prisms, is among the most innovative pieces of architecture so far proposed for Ground Zero—a shimmering object, neither opaque nor transparent. Unfortunately, it hovers on the edge of the memorial site and, as a result, may dwarf it. And if the master plan is realized, both the Snøhetta building and a performing-arts center across the street, which is being designed by Frank Gehry, will cower directly beneath huge office buildings. The Gehry building, for its part, faces an uncertain future, owing to funding problems, and its design remains incomplete. A replanned Ground Zero would put the public realm first and the private realm second.

Moreover, most of the cultural institutions involved are marginal. Ground Zero doesn't need expensive cultural buildings for small outfits that can't afford them. One of the many mysteries of the planning process is why strong cultural groups that wanted to come to Ground Zero, such as the New York City Opera and the New York Hall of Science, were turned away in favor of less well-known organizations, such as the Joyce International Dance Center and the Signature Theatre Company. Why wasn't space at Ground Zero given to City Opera? The planners adopted the misguided notion that smaller, populist groups were needed, when pride of place should have been given to major institutions that could make Ground Zero a cultural magnet. Perhaps City Opera was turned down because an opera house would have cut into some of Silverstein's lobby space in the Freedom Tower. An essential aspect of a revised plan for Ground Zero would be a much larger allotment for cultural buildings—enough land for an opera house, for example.

Ground Zero must also make an impression on the skyline. The Freedom Tower, for all its faults, would have soared higher than any other structure in New York. Yet an office tower is not the only tall structure imaginable. A great tower can also be a broadcast tower or a cloud-piercing observation tower. It could be a memorial in itself, or a part of a memorial, and if we called it the Memorial Tower, it would be a feature of the skyline that recognized the lives that were lost within the skyline. The tower would be, in effect, a twenty-first-century Eiffel Tower for New York, which would use the technology of our time as aggressively and inventively as Eiffel exploited the technology of the nineteenth century. It would be a perfect commission for Santiago Calatrava, the Spanish architect-engineer whom the Port Authority commissioned to design the new transportation center for downtown—a lyrical structure that resembles a vast, swooping tent of ribbed metal and glass. It's the one building proposed for Ground Zero, so far, that almost everyone seems to love.

A great tower by Calatrava or another architect equally adept at turning engineering into poetic form would give New York the defiantly proud icon it has craved since the towers fell. And it wouldn't require anybody to live or work a hundred stories above the street. Most important, it would be a way of transcending the false divide between commemoration and renewal. A soaring tower can be made to coexist with apartments and museums. The planners at Ground Zero have treated the sacred and the everyday as two distinct spheres. The answer isn't to split the site into a memorial sector and a business sector but, rather, to find ways to honor the dead while rejuvenating the city, to acknowledge the past while looking toward the future. Ground Zero is the first great urban-design challenge of the twenty-first century, and the noblest way to honor what happened here is to rebuild the site with the complexity and vitality that characterizes the best of Manhattan.

The New Yorker, May 30, 2005

PRESENT AND PAST

Benjamin Wood, Xintiandi, Shanghai

SHANGHAI SURPRISE

Modern Shanghai combines the soul of Houston with the body of Las Vegas. In Pudong, the city's booming financial district, flashing trails of colored lights race up and down the shafts of office towers, as if they were casinos. One freshly minted skyscraper, Aurora Plaza, has a facade of gold reflective glass that at night becomes even more garish, turning into a multistory LED screen on which huge smiling faces cinematically dissolve into bright corporate logos. The skyline of China's largest city has become a strangely exuberant version of the *Blade Runner* aesthetic, with simple geometries and sharp lines cutting into the sky; it may not be beautiful, but, in its staggering scale and intensity, it certainly is awe-inspiring.

The most provocative new architectural project in Shanghai, however, has none of the youthful brashness of the Pudong towers. Called Xintiandi, which means "New Heaven and Earth," and completed in 2002, it is a refined cluster of traditionally styled Shanghai brick town houses near the old French Concession district. Arranged along a two-block pedestrian street, the complex is filled with restaurants, cafés, nightclubs, and luxury boutiques, including Comme des Garçons and Christian Dior. The seven-acre development, which is highly popular, is what Western builders call a "festival marketplace." Like Baltimore's Inner Harbor, New York's South Street Seaport, and Boston's Quincy Market, Xintiandi is a stage set of an idyllic past, created so that people in China can experience the same finely wrought balance of theme park and shopping mall that increasingly passes for upscale urban life in the United States. Just as many of Shanghai's skyscrapers reiterate gestures that long ago became clichés in the West—enormous atriums; tall, pointy spires—the idea of a Disneyfied old downtown is a recycled one. Yet in China, a country with almost no tradition of preserving everyday commercial architecture or of putting up new buildings that look like old ones, the notion feels radical. Before Xintiandi, crowning a glass office tower with a pagoda was seen as a sophisticated homage to the architectural past.

The principal architect of Xintiandi is, not surprisingly, an American: Benjamin Wood, who once worked for Benjamin Thompson, the designer of Quincy Market. (Wood recently relocated from Boston to Shanghai.) Wood's design is a clever mixture of renovated old buildings and new construction imitating the style of *shikumen*, the gray brick town houses that were built in many Shanghai neighborhoods beginning in the 1860s. Three-story structures built along narrow alleys, with elaborate, stone-carved entries leading into small interior courtyards, *shikumen*—the term means "stone gate"—generally housed upper-middle-class families. (Under Communist rule, *shikumen* were converted to tenements, and as many as seven families were shoehorned into them.) Like many buildings in cosmopolitan Shanghai, a *shikumen* combines Asian and Western influences; it is a Chinese home with a Parisian sensibility, a hybrid form both delicate and monumental.

Authentic *shikumen* never looked quite as polished as the ones in Xintiandi. Wood's design seamlessly blends new architectural elements with original stone gates and carved lintels. To create a more open composition, Wood removed many of the crumbling houses on the site; of the houses that were kept, many had an outer wall or two replaced, and almost all the interiors were gut-renovated. The result is a cleaner and more orderly neighborhood, studded with public spaces that resemble Western piazzas. The architect also inserted large picture windows and glass storefronts into many of the original doorways, and created artful replicas of the narrow alleyways that provided the main circulation within *shikumen* complexes. It's fun to wander through these synthetic labyrinths, shopping bags in hand.

The building of Xintiandi required some awkward trade-offs. A large mansion in the neighborhood housed thirty families before the site's developer,

Shui On, took over the area; now the building has no tenants. The occupants were moved elsewhere—an easier matter in China than in New York. (In the end, more than two thousand families were relocated.) The developers then gave the mansion an exquisite restoration, turning it into what they call the clubhouse, which includes a conference center and a set of exclusive private dining rooms. Xintiandi's success has also increased the value of land in the immediate area, making it more likely that the aging *shikumen* surrounding Wood's ersatz neighborhood will be demolished. In time, the inauthentic may drive out the authentic altogether.

Shanghai has only a few parks and public squares, and they tend to be clumsily conceived. In the center of the city, the crowded new Renmin Square, built on the site of a former racetrack, is dominated by the huge Shanghai Art Museum and the Grand Theatre, two banal modern buildings, and the green space is almost inconsequential. Streets in Chinese cities have traditionally been used for transport and commerce, not for social encounters. The emblematic user of the Chinese street is the woman who bargains at an open-air street market. Nothing seems less Chinese than the notion of the flaneur, of the street as a place in which to observe other people.

Xintiandi has given the residents of Shanghai a place to experience the public realm as something pleasant. Moreover, it has encouraged them to acknowledge the affection they have for the historic parts of the city, even as bulldozers ruthlessly knock down one decaying neighborhood after another. In one section of Xintiandi, the developers built a full-size, painstakingly detailed *shikumen* for public display; it is furnished with antiques and artifacts that might have been owned by a typical Chinese family, and has rooms for a dowager grandmother, a married couple, children, and a boarder. The exhibit romantically proposes that the boarder—whose room is a small, dark chamber off a landing—is a struggling young writer.

The inspiration for the Xintiandi project was a gray brick building, no larger than a house, sitting in the middle of the site; it is where the Chinese Communist Party originally met, in 1921. (Mao himself attended the first meeting.) Vincent Lo, the developer who runs Shui On, was told by government officials that the buildings adjacent to the old meeting place had to be maintained, and that none of the garish commercialism that marks most Chinese retail establishments would be permitted beside it. Lo sought the advice of Wood, who argued that there was a way to mix historic preservation and commercial real-estate development. If Mao's old meeting hall had to remain untouched, Wood said, why not make older Chinese architecture the theme of the whole development?

The banks and the government were initially wary of the project. "We wanted to create a mixed-use neighborhood, and we wanted to keep the streets walkable—it is not easy to do in China," Albert Chan, a manager at Shui On, told me. "When we started this project, we showed it to people, and they said, 'No Chinese will eat outside.' But if you give them the right kind of place, they will."

As in Xintiandi's American counterparts, the crowds are a mixture of foreigners—it is one of the city's most popular tourist destinations—and locals.

When the project opened, it was mostly expatriates visiting, Chan said. "Now more than half the people who visit are locals." In this case, the locals tend to be members of China's elite professional class; dinner for two at one of Xintiandi's restaurants can easily cost sixty dollars or more, and a typical laborer's daily wage is less than five dollars.

Xintiandi is so successful that Shui On has been asked to replicate its formula elsewhere in China, and other developers are trying to build copycat projects. Christopher Choa, an American architect who lives in Shanghai, told me, "It has become a verb. Developers say to architects, 'Can you Xintiandi this project for me?' The young Chinese people come because they think it's trendy, the foreigners come because they think it's historically significant, and the old people come because they feel nostalgia." Since Xintiandi opened, Shanghai has begun to preserve much more architecture than it ever did before. During the first forty years of Communist rule, the city's main promenade, the Bund—a remarkable series of ornate stone office and bank buildings, many of them masterworks of Art Deco from the 1920s—fell into serious disrepair. But the area is now being restored, and it has become an extremely desirable address: one building, Three on the Bund, was renovated by Michael Graves and contains an Armani boutique, an Evian spa, and a Jean-Georges Vongerichten restaurant.

The Bund is Shanghai's most Western cityscape and its most celebrated vista. It faces the Huangpu River, with the new skyline of Pudong, which didn't exist fifteen years ago, on the other side, just as the old skyline of downtown Manhattan faces the new skyline of Jersey City across the Hudson. But this juxtaposition has even greater drama. The architecture of the Bund has always been thought of as a symbol of Western influence on Shanghai, which may be one of the reasons that these grand buildings were disdained for so many years. But now that they have been rediscovered, they demonstrate how potent another Western idea has become here: old architecture is a very good way to make new money.

The New Yorker, January 1, 2006

Mount Vernon, Virginia

WHY WASHINGTON SLEPT HERE

The more familiar a building is to you through photographs, the smaller it seems when you finally visit it—unless it is the Taj Mahal or the Eiffel Tower. Most famous buildings, like movie stars, loom much larger in the imagination than they do in real life. Small does not mean trivial, however. An iconic building's smallness can make the experience of seeing it for the first time more intense, as if all the building's symbolic force were compressed into a tight, taut, powerful package. I felt this when I first saw Frank Lloyd Wright's Fallingwater and Le Corbusier's Villa Savoye, buildings that I had spent my student years craving to visit. And I felt this way again just a couple of weeks ago, when I finally got around to seeing Mount Vernon, a house that I had never taken seriously as architecture at all. This year is the bicentennial of George Washington's death, and a spate of scholarly studies and exhibitions have drawn attention to Mount Vernon, making the case that Washington was as passionate an architectural amateur as Thomas Jefferson, and as much the author of his own house as Jefferson was of Monticello.

Monticello is much more revered than Mount Vernon, which does not even show up in most architectural histories, although Washington's house is as well known a building as any in the United States. Unfortunately, its fame has contributed to its banality. Mount Vernon's red roof, narrow cupola, and expansive colonnade have become generic, and have influenced everything from Howard Johnson's restaurants to suburban tract houses. Mount Vernon, or the idea of Mount Vernon, exudes a kind of kitschy Americanness that stems in part from its association with its owner. George Washington is a wooden figure to most of us, a farmer who had greatness thrust upon him. He isn't as interesting intellectually as Jefferson. It is an axiom of American architectural history that Jefferson was the finest amateur architect we have ever produced and that his life marked the first and last time that architectural talent has intersected with great statesmanship in this country.

While it is true that Washington was not as sophisticated as Jefferson, or as erudite, Mount Vernon has a kind of brazen panache that the more cerebral Monticello does not. Washington designed with a curious combination of caution and bold strokes, and his work as an "architect" turned out to presage American taste far more than anything produced by Jefferson, who was idiosyncratic and occasionally effete. On reconsideration, Mount Vernon appears, quite startlingly, to be the most influential eighteenth-century house in America, and one of the greatest.

A large house of white painted wood crafted to look like rusticated stone, Mount Vernon is integrated into the landscape more seamlessly than any other house of its time, and it combines grandeur and intimacy in a way that no house had done before. Like Monticello, which was begun in 1769 and which Jefferson expanded and radically changed over the years, Mount Vernon began as a much smaller house. When Washington leased it from the widow of his half brother, in 1754, for an annual rent of fifteen thousand pounds of tobacco, it was a one-and-a-half-story, eight-room farmhouse. Washington turned it into a mansion during several building campaigns, each of which lasted many years, and when he was finished, Mount Vernon was a house of three stories, with twenty-one rooms plus outbuildings. Washington had a kind of gut feeling about what he was after. His ideas, he wrote to his friend Dr. William Thornton, the first architect of the Capitol, "proceed from a person who avows his ignorance of Architectural principles, and who has no other guide but his eye to direct his choice."

It was an unusual eye indeed, for it led Washington to create four asymmetrical facades at a time when symmetry was considered a sign of refinement, particularly in a house that aspired to serious pomp. Many of the windows are off center, especially on the west side, and the cupola and the pediment, which in any self-respecting classical house line up, in Washington's don't. Washington also ran a colonnade of double-height, squared-off columns across one entire side of his house, facing the Potomac River; this was at once a plainer and more monumental device than anything in a comparable house. Outdoors, his eye inspired him to cut a path nearly three-quarters of a mile long through the woods between the house and the front gate, not as a road but purely as a scenic vista. These were not the decisions of a man who was uncomfortable speaking through architecture.

The scenic vista is what first made me realize that Mount Vernon is not a cliché but a work of genius. I got a whiff of it in the splendid photographs and drawings in *George Washington's Mount Vernon*, an elaborate coffee-table study edited by Wendell Garrett; it was not until I visited the house, though, that I truly understood what Washington was up to. I was given a tour by Allan Greenberg, a Washington architect who has been trying for years to get the world to put Mount Vernon on a par with Monticello, and who is the author of a new architectural study of the house (*George Washington: Architect*). Greenberg is a contemporary classicist who, in addition to designing such projects as the diplomatic reception rooms for the State Department, created a near-replica of Mount Vernon in Greenwich, Connecticut, even bigger than Washington's, for the art collectors Peter and Sandy Brant. (Greenberg's form of homage was a little odd. He corrected Washington's asymmetries and put an indoor swimming pool in the outer wing that had been Washington's kitchen.)

Greenberg, along with Robert F. Dalzell Jr., and Lee Baldwin Dalzell, the authors of a historical study also called *George Washington's Mount Vernon*, has made a strong case for the quality of Mount Vernon and for Washington's responsibility for every detail of its design. So committed was Washington to rebuilding his house that during the most intense battles of the Revolution, he kept the work going, and wrote weekly from the front to his construction managers. "As mastery of his troops, of Congress, of the larger military situation continued to elude him," the Dalzells write, "he had created in his mind a world at home wholly amenable to his control, one where his every wish would be followed to the letter."

Washington's plantations originally encompassed more than eight thousand acres, or upward of twelve square miles, much of which was sold off in the nineteenth century. Roughly 550 acres remain. They are owned by the Mount Vernon Ladies' Association, which is the corporate name for the entity that purchased the house, in 1858, for $200,000 from John Augustine Washington Jr., the son of Washington's nephew's nephew. Mount Vernon was badly run down by the mid-nineteenth century; John Augustine was not nearly as skillful a farmer as his celebrated ancestor had been, and he was further burdened by tourists seeking to visit the house, which even in its decline was viewed as a shrine. He offered to sell the house and two hundred acres to the federal government; it turned him down, but he was rescued by a thirty-seven-year-old semi-invalid from South Carolina, Ann Pamela Cunningham. Miss Cunningham's mother had been traveling up the Potomac on a passenger steamer in 1853 and wrote to her daughter about the shock of seeing how dilapidated Mount Vernon was. Miss Cunningham was moved by the plight of the great house and made saving it her life's work. She formed the Ladies' Association, the first organization in this country that was devoted solely to historic preservation, and set in motion what was to become the first successful rescue of a major landmark in the nation's history.

Mount Vernon sits in a part of Virginia that has become increasingly suburbanized in recent years; there are tract-house imitations of Mount Vernon within sight of its original gates. Development has been limited along the roads approaching the house, however, and as you drive up to it you feel, for the last few minutes, if not quite at Yellowstone, at least more than fifteen miles from Washington, D.C. Allan Greenberg introduced me to the property by showing me how Washington meant a visitor to come across it for the first time. He parked the car near the Ladies' Association office, a red brick building tucked into a corner of the grounds that looks more or less as though it might house a prosperous suburban medical practice. We walked away from the building and along a newly paved asphalt drive leading into the woods and down a steep hill, after which the asphalt gives way to a dirt road. We climbed another hill and kept walking through the woods for another quarter mile or so. Mount Vernon itself was nowhere visible, but in the distance, up ahead, was an old white painted wooden gate, closed and obviously little used.

When we reached the gate, roughly half a mile from where we had left the car, we turned around. Suddenly, there was Mount Vernon, about three-quarters of a mile to the east, a glimmer of white and red across a wide swath of meadow, framed by trees. The meadow itself dipped down into a ravine and back up; Washington had designed the vista so that the visitor's eye would be pulled straight across the undulating landscape to the house itself. "You can see from here why the roof was painted red, and there were dormers and the cupola," Greenberg said. "It was all scaled to be seen from here. This is the thing to see—this is the way into George Washington's mind. It takes the landscape and alters it in the most subtle way."

Washington merged the axes of French classicism—think Versailles—with the picturesque, flowing forms of English landscape design. His house pulls you in and appears to control the landscape; as you move toward it through the land-scape, it disappears; and then it reappears, closer and more formal, sitting at the head of an open lawn. This is a magnificently choreographed approach, which visitors now never see unless they walk away from the standard tourist route.

Washington planned the gardens, situated the trees that were added when the virgin forest was torn down, and laid out all the estate's outbuildings, including the unusual open, curving arcades that connect some of them to the main house. His most striking architectural innovation was what he called "the piazza," the two-story colonnade on the east side of Mount Vernon, facing the river. It was grander than a normal portico, although it was not the entrance to the house. Washington put Mount Vernon's front door on the side of the house facing west, away from the river. Yet the piazza is hardly a riverfront porch, either. It is more like a monumental grandstand, a sprawling private box from which to view the river and the passing boat traffic. It is also the place where the occupants of Mount Vernon could mix together most easily—what the Dalzells call "a remarkably open space in a social as well as a physical sense." The piazza affirmed Washington's democratic vision.

It is this aspect of Mount Vernon that distinguishes it most explicitly from Monticello. Jefferson studied classical architecture rigorously, and he encouraged its revival in the belief that classicism was the ideal style to represent American democracy. But Monticello, with its soft, low dome and inward focus, does not represent democratic openness so much as Jeffersonian refinement. Jefferson's extraordinary intellect is at the center of Monticello, both conceptually and physically. There is nothing universal about the architecture. Its meaning comes from its connection to Jefferson's psyche; and its pleasures, from the extent to which you can penetrate that psyche. Washington created a building that asserts the democratic idea so powerfully that it can only be called radical. Washington was hardly indifferent to privacy—one of his innovations at Mount Vernon is a two-story private suite within the house, a vertically stacked combination of study and bedroom which allowed him to move around out of view of guests—but the private spaces were not the driving force in the design. Pride of place at Mount Vernon goes to shared spaces, to entertaining space, and to the sweeping riverfront piazza.

Mount Vernon is a sometimes lyrical, sometimes awkward combination of elements which exposes a yearning for things English and yet is confidently American. It is full of signs of its owner's determination to show off his status and his fortune to the world. Washington fought the British on the battlefield, but he collapsed entirely before them aesthetically, filling his house with furniture, china, and architectural details typical of upwardly mobile British taste of the late eighteenth century. The taste was conventional; the uses to which Washington put it were not. No one has known quite what to make of the building's lack of symmetry, but Allan Greenberg is sure that it was intentional. "This man planned everything—everything was an aesthetic question to him," he said to me as we walked across the lawn, looking at the strange, off-center features of the west facade. "I can't believe he didn't intend the asymmetry— he would only have had to move four windows." But if Washington wanted the house to be asymmetrical, why? What made this man of relatively routine, upper-class taste break the rules so willingly?

It may have been simply that Washington was being practical—in an American sort of way. He was ambitious but deeply pragmatic, and he gave no indication of being particularly concerned with perfect order. He could be seen as a sort of enlightened CEO, one of those types who combine commanding leadership with a tentative but eager aesthetic sense. He had high aims for his house, but he was not obsessed with minutiae, and it may be that to him symmetry fell into the category of a minor detail. Washington wanted Mount Vernon to be a model for others—to be for houses what he wanted his presidency to be for presidents. He was less learned than Jefferson but more open to experience: he looked around, he observed, he saw all kinds of things he liked and synthesized them. He did not think about architecture as obsessively as Jefferson did, but he reveled in it. You can see how he must have infuriated Jefferson—this man who didn't study the classics, who probably never thought about Palladio, producing an American icon, by instinct alone.

The New Yorker, February 15, 1999

ATHENS ON THE INTERSTATE

Rodney Mims Cook Jr. insisted that I meet him at the Piedmont Driving Club as soon as I arrived in Atlanta, even though it was closed. He went to some trouble to make certain that the club, his club, opened its doors on a Monday—the one day of the week on which Atlanta society traditionally finds someplace else to eat and drink—because the Piedmont Driving Club very clearly demonstrates, if one had somehow forgotten, that Atlanta is not entirely a city of glass office towers set astride shopping malls. It is an easy thing to forget in much of the city. Atlanta's most famous thoroughfare, Peachtree Street, is Wilshire Boulevard with a Southern accent: a line of office and apartment towers, strip malls, gas stations, and hotels. For most of its length, it is not much pleasanter to stroll on than an interstate highway. Atlanta grew large and powerful in the age of the automobile, and underneath its thin Georgia veneer it has a lot more in common with Houston than with Savannah.

The Piedmont Driving Club, which attained a certain notoriety recently as the setting for satiric scenes in Tom Wolfe's novel *A Man in Full*, was established in the nineteenth century as the Gentlemen's Driving Club and provided a place for Atlanta's gentry to cavort in carriages and broughams. The clubhouse was built in 1887, but it didn't really come into its own until the 1920s, when it was renovated and expanded by Philip Trammell Shutze, one of the great classicists of modern times. Today, the building is a curious mixture of elegant neoclassical details and graceless remnants of fairly recent renovations, like the acoustical-tile ceiling in a room lined with exquisite mahogany paneling. The place has the feel of a rich, slightly bland country club that somehow cut loose from its golf course and drifted back toward the center of town. I liked seeing it empty: the Driving Club without its Drivers, except for Rodney Cook, who is a typical Old Guard member. Many of the newer members are more like Charlie Croker, Wolfe's over-extended real-estate developer protagonist, who made his fortune building glass office towers and created a private world surrounded by symbols of old money.

When you meet Cook, you wonder why Tom Wolfe didn't build a character around him as a foil to Charlie Croker, except that maybe it would have been too easy. Croker eats people like Rodney Cook for lunch. Cook is an affable and quiet man of forty-one who wears tweed jackets and khaki pants and projects the earnest demeanor of a missionary, which is more or less what he believes himself to be. He is a prominent member of a small band of young American classical designers, people who are determined to mark the end of the twentieth century with pediments and Doric columns. Many of them are based in New York, where new Wall Street money seeking to look old provides ample call for their services. Doing this kind of work in Atlanta is more of a challenge.

Rodney Cook aspires to be the kind of figure Philip Trammell Shutze was. Shutze, who died in 1982, at the age of ninety-two, scattered mansions of remarkable elegance, inventiveness, and finesse across the wealthier sections of Atlanta. Cook himself grew up frolicking in one of the greatest Shutze houses, which was owned by an uncle. His father-in-law, James Robinson III, the former chairman of American Express, was raised in another Shutze mansion—the house that Tom Wolfe purloined as the home of the tycoon Inman Armholster in *A Man in Full*. Wolfe described it as an "Italian Baroque palazzo . . . sheer homage to conspicuous consumption." Cook idolized Shutze, whom he met when he was going to school, and that kept him, he thinks, on track. "My friends were going in classical and coming out modern, to my horror," he says. "I mentioned this to Mr. Shutze, and he said, 'I'm sorry, Mr. Cook. You're going to have a life of misery.' But I pushed on."

Cook doesn't live in a Shutze house now. Until recently, he and his wife, Emily, and their two daughters lived in an apricot-colored mini-Italianate stucco palazzo of his design. They sold it so that they could buy a sixty-acre estate in Buckhead, a Beverly Hills–like mix of glass towers, shopping malls,

and megamansions where the richest citizens of the city live, and where Cook
is developing an enclave of classically styled houses. His office on the grounds
of the estate is a renovated stable, which he expanded into a residence for
his family. Until the house, a turreted structure that looks something like a
Russian dacha, was ready, they lived with Emily Cook's grandmother, Josephine
Robinson, in a huge modern high-rise apartment that Rodney Cook outfitted
with enough classical trim to obliterate all traces of the original architecture.

Cook wants classical architecture to be something more than fancy dress
for the rich. He wants to remake the whole cityscape. He has had one public
commission: a small museum for the work of the nineteenth-century painter
Jasper Cropsey in Hastings-on-Hudson, New York. A vaguely Baroque jewel box
of a building, it was finished in 1994. In Atlanta, however, he is under siege—
or, at any rate, that is how he sees it. "There is a climate of hostility here to what
I'm trying to do," he says, and explains that it is a kind of "hostility to beauty."

When Philip Trammell Shutze was designing buildings, the traditional
nature of the architecture expressed the certainty of the social order. Irony
was uncalled for, and the striking forms of modernism were barely known. But
these are ironic, not to say ambiguous, times. Modernism cannot be denied, and
neoclassical and Renaissance and Georgian and Baroque buildings, however
well executed, risk looking like chic stage sets, pretty but shallow. Cook talks of
beauty and proportion and history in a city that defines its architecture in terms
of depreciation and marketing and easy access to the interstate.

Real-life Charlie Crokers, of which Atlanta has plenty, should have made
quick work of Rodney Cook long ago, but, oddly enough, they haven't. Cook
has had an interesting effect on the city's corpus, if not on its soul. A couple of
years ago, he managed, with the cooperation and the financial support of Prince
Charles, the patron saint of contemporary classicists, to erect a fifty-five-foot-
tall monument at Pershing Point, one of Atlanta's prime intersections, along
Peachtree Street. A round structure with five columns crowned with bronze
figures holding up a globe, it was intended to suggest a tie between the classical
tradition in architecture and the Olympics, which were held in Atlanta in 1996.
It is officially called the World Athletes Monument, although it is popularly
known as the Prince Charles monument, and—for reasons that would have been
impossible to anticipate—it has ended up as a memorial to the prince's late wife.
When Diana was killed, grieving Atlantans seized upon the site as the locus of
their emotions, depositing flowers and lingering through the night.

Cook's success in getting the prince's monument built followed a failed
attempt to impose his vision on Atlanta in a more grandiose manner. In 1992 he
proposed putting a huge Beaux-Arts-style plaza of his design in Piedmont Park,
which is somewhat run-down and just happens to be beneath the windows
of the Piedmont Driving Club. An anonymous donor—who was thought in some
Atlanta circles to be connected with Cook and his wife's family—offered to foot
the $10 million bill. This project was also intended to mark the Olympics, but it
was soon mired in local politics and was ultimately rejected as being too fancy,
too much Rodney Cook's own, too much a piece of noblesse oblige to be in tune

with the democratic, free-flowing spirit that the city hoped to convey through its public spaces during the Olympic Games.

Not that there is much public space of any kind in Atlanta. When the Prince Charles monument suddenly became central to Atlanta's civic life, it was not only because of Diana's husband's connection to it but also because there aren't a lot of places in the city that fulfill the traditional function of a communal gathering place. If Atlantans feel like congregating, where are they to go? Do they pour into the parking lot at the Lenox Square mall? Take over the field at the Georgia Tech football stadium? Maybe they could assemble in the atrium of the Hyatt Regency Hotel. As the architect Charles Moore once noted about Los Angeles, where would you go to start a revolution?

The extent to which the monument seems to have settled into the fabric of the city suggests that traditional urban forms can still have an impact, even in a city as wedded to the automobile and urban sprawl as Atlanta is. Rodney Cook certainly saw it that way. He looked around the triangular, grassy site and noticed that there was an empty lot beside it, and he began to wonder if he could make the monument the focal point of something bigger; with a little effort, he thought, he could turn the traffic island into a traditional piazza, right on Peachtree Street. And so Cook and his partner, an Atlanta architect named Peter Polites (Cook himself is not technically an architect and collaborates with Polites on most of his work), designed an office building to fill the empty lot, closing off the west side of the site and giving the place at least the beginnings of the qualities of a real urban square. If the proposed structure is built—and Cook and others are trying to find financing to develop it themselves—it would be Atlanta's first office building with a facade inspired by the Farnese Palace, Sangallo and Michelangelo's mid-sixteenth-century Roman masterpiece.

The building proposed for the prince's monument site seems like an earnest and endearing affectation until you consider the grim legacy of architecture in Atlanta. There is no modern building that even approaches the stature of New York's Seagram Building or Lever House. In a city where most medium-sized office buildings look like pint-size versions of bigger ones, the notion of a structure that is a nicely proportioned seven or eight stories is itself radical.

The ersatz Palazzo Farnese would give Cook, who has thus far designed houses, apartment interiors, and the little museum in upstate New York, his first major civic building. (Neither Cook nor Polites actually created the design for the World Athletes Monument, it should be said, though Cook was very much its impresario. The specific design was the result of a competition open to students affiliated with Prince Charles's institute for the study of classical architecture. The winner was a young Russian, Anton Glikine.) The scheme makes sense not because the building is a piece of classical architecture but because, if it is built, it will be a piece of classical city planning. If there is one area in which modernism has failed abysmally, it is in creating civilized urban spaces.

Can you graft old-fashioned urban space onto a postwar city? That Cook wants to try makes his proposal something more than merely charming. Most cities defined by the automobile have been resistant to such attempts; cars are just too overwhelming, and the cityscape of freeway interchanges, wide boulevards, parking garages, and shopping malls that they create has such power and presence, not to mention scale, that small, pedestrian-oriented places inserted into the middle of it usually end up looking trite and silly. That's certainly the case with, say, CityWalk, at Universal Studios, in Los Angeles, a street of stores and restaurants and theaters; it's hard to tell whether it is a street masquerading as a theme park or a theme park masquerading as a street. So, too, with Two Rodeo Drive, the upscale little shopping mall in Beverly Hills which has been designed as a faux European street.

Cuteness is not the antidote to the plague of the automobile-oriented city. Not that anyone will dismiss Cook's new square, if it ever gets built, as too cute. While the piazza would indeed have the prince's monument as its centerpiece, it would also have a couple of on-ramps to Interstate 85 swooping through the middle of it. Apparently, the ramps cannot be moved, even though the Georgia Department of Transportation is a big supporter of the project.

The square could end up being no more than a sweet-natured irrelevance in the sprawl of the city, which is how many Atlantans view the Prince Charles monument already. Yet, while not a great work by any means, it resonates with a pleasant if not a particularly profound unself-consciousness, and manages to rise above kitsch. The monument does something else, too, which may in the end turn out to be its real justification. It addresses as nothing else has a certain schizophrenic aspect of the architecture of Atlanta. For the last couple of generations, traditional architecture and modern architecture in the city have been set on opposite sides of a firm divide. Not for nothing did Tom Wolfe portray Charlie Croker as living in an old mansion in Buckhead while making his money as a builder of glass office towers along the interstate. Wolfe had it exactly right. In Atlanta, once you hit a certain demographic category, classical architecture is what you live in, and modern architecture is what you work in. The number of modern houses of significant quality in Atlanta is very small. Atlantans want to live in Philip Trammell Shutze houses, but they expect to go to work in John Portman towers. Rodney Cook and Peter Polites are attempting to break through this divide, to build a public realm of traditional, rather than modern, elements, thus repudiating the gentleman's agreement under which architecture has been practiced in this city for generations. They want to bring classicism out into the open, coaxing from it some response to the wretchedly automobilized cityscape.

It may be naive to believe that classicism will succeed in doing that in Atlanta any better than it has managed to elsewhere: the paneled libraries of the real-life Charlie Crokers, self-indulgent symbols of an arriviste class, do nothing to push the art of architecture forward. And behind them lurks, as always, the danger of the theme park, the risk that the unpleasantness of the modern city will be replaced by the coy disingenuousness of a make-believe old-fashioned one. But it's hard to deny that Rodney Cook's vision of the city represents, at the very least, a break from the architectural sanctimony on which so much of Atlanta has been built.

The New Yorker, February 1, 1999

Prince Charles

A ROYAL DEFEAT

Last week Queen Elizabeth presided at the dedication ceremony of the new British Library, a sprawling, $850 million pile of brick and concrete within sight of St. Pancras Station. In a speech she called the building "remarkable" and "a labor of love." The queen was emphatically not accompanied by the Prince of Wales, whose opinion of the building had already been expressed, in somewhat less diplomatic language than his mother's. The British Library, Prince Charles said in 1988, would

Poundbury, Dorset, United Kingdom (above)

be "a dim collection of brick sheds groping for some symbolic significance" and would resemble "an academy for secret police." That royal excoriation was so harsh that the library's architect, Colin St. John Wilson, later claimed that it had led to the demise of his practice.

Until very recently, the prince has rarely passed up an opportunity to comment on a new building. His attempt to direct the course of British architecture toward more traditional designs has been the major project of his adult life, and no member of the royal family has been as outspoken on any subject as Charles has been in his jihad against modern architecture. Lately, however, the prince has been more or less silent on the subject. He has offered a few remarks in defense of Poundbury, a quaint neotraditional village that he commissioned in Dorset, but the sweeping pleas to reject modernism and bring back classical architecture have stopped. Charles's stoic silence about the new library, a banal and wildly unpopular building that even many modernists dislike, does not mean that he has changed his views. But he has evidently come to believe that his architectural crusade has interfered with his project of turning himself into the kind of heir to the throne that the British public seems to crave. And, indeed, Charles is no longer seen as an indifferent father and an amiable dingbat who talks to carrots. Rather, he is now spoken of in the respectful tones befitting a future king.

The refurbishing of Charles's public persona is only part of the story. The reality is that the prince's vision of Britain—equal parts Christopher Wren and Ralph Lauren—has been defeated, overwhelmed by a wave of sleekness that has given London more glass and stainless steel than New York and fresher architecture than Paris. Modernists dominate the British architecture world today as never before. Richard Rogers, the sixty-four-year-old architect who, in the late 1980s, led the opposition to the prince, is now Lord Rogers, and he and his fellow modernist Norman Foster, now Sir Norman, are the most powerful architects in the land.

The prince declared war on modern architecture in 1984, in a speech in which he called a proposed addition to the National Gallery "a monstrous carbuncle on the face of a much loved and elegant friend." With those words, he instantly became the world's most famous architecture critic, and a new age of British classicism seemed imminent, with him as its patron. With advisers like the classicist Leon Krier and the *Financial Times* critic Colin Amery at his side, Charles founded a school to teach classical architecture, started a magazine, wrote a book, produced a television special, commissioned Krier to design Poundbury, and watched with pleasure as plans for modern commercial buildings in London were tossed out in favor of more traditional designs. The future of architecture in Britain seemed to belong to architects like Quinlan Terry, a stuffy classicist best known for an office building, along the Thames in Richmond, designed to look like a series of classical false fronts—a building the prince called "an expression of harmony and proportion."

Modernists like Rogers and Foster decided to find work abroad. James Stirling, whose proposal in 1986 for an office building near the Bank of England had been described by the prince as looking "like a 1930s wireless," did a lot of his work in Germany and the United States, and declared that if he won the commission to design the Getty Center, in Los Angeles—he was one of three finalists—he would immigrate to the United States.

But today Charles's magazine, *Perspectives,* is defunct. His school, the Prince of Wales's Institute of Architecture, has had four directors in six years and has been denied accreditation by the Royal Institute of British Architects. The school's board now consists of lawyers and is run by Hilary Browne-Wilkinson, the solicitor who handled the divorce of Charles's longtime lover, Camilla Parker Bowles. Poundbury, partly built, is a theme park of 142 houses—pretty but of little significance beyond its connection to its royal squire. As far as Britain's architectural culture is concerned, the prince is now under a kind of intellectual house arrest.

Meanwhile, the exiles have returned in triumph. Foster and Rogers now head an entire school of British modernists, which includes Nicholas Grimshaw, who designed the glass-roofed terminal for the Eurostar, the Chunnel train, at Waterloo Station; members of the firm Arup Associates; Michael Hopkins; Lifschutz Davidson; and David Chipperfield. Together they constitute the most cohesive and vibrant group of modernist architects in any country in the world.

The work they are producing is very different from the Le Corbusier–inspired New Brutalism of the previous generation of British modernists, a style typified by Denys Lasdun's National Theatre, on the Thames. The new work is brighter, lighter, more exuberant, enthralled by technology, and as sensual as it is spare. For the first time in decades, there is a clear British architectural style, and most of it is very good. But it is nothing like what the Prince of Wales, who tried harder to put architecture on the public agenda than any leader since Thomas Jefferson, intended it to be.

Prince Charles has no formal training in architecture, but his sincerity has never been in doubt. Big, harsh modern buildings offended his sensibilities, and he knew that the difference between living in a council high-rise and living in Kensington Palace was not only a matter of how much space you had. The problem, friends say, is that Charles is not particularly interested in the twentieth century. He is reportedly happiest at Highgrove, his eighteenth-century country house, and is made uncomfortable by cities, going to considerable lengths to avoid spending the night in London. Charles's architectural education, one of his friends has remarked, consisted of "looking out the window of a Rolls-Royce listening to his mother and grandmother saying, 'Isn't all that ugly?' "

In launching his architectural crusade, the prince made an error in judgment. From the outset, he cast the issue of Britain's architectural future in moralistic terms, as an argument "between the inhuman and the human," he wrote in his book *A Vision of Britain*. The more he sermonized, the more he sounded like a well-bred reactionary. Charles got people talking about architecture, but his solutions were vague and sentimental, and he had no coherent plan for making things better. And he failed to understand a basic historical fact about British architecture: it has always valued eccentricity. Most of the greatest British architects—Nicholas Hawksmoor, John Soane, William Butterfield, Edwin Lutyens—have broken rules, not followed them, and have developed highly personal ways of building. But here was the prince saying that rules mattered more than ever, and were morally superior, too.

Stephen Bayley, a founding director of Sir Terence Conran's Design Museum, in London, recalls meeting with the prince to invite him to give the dedication speech for the museum's opening, in 1989. "We went to St. James's Palace and showed him the model, and all he said was, 'Mr. Bayley, but why does it have a flat roof?'"

Charles surrounded himself with people who shared his vision of Britain. Even so, several years into his campaign against modernism, schisms started to develop within his inner circle. Some of his advisers continued to argue that his crusade would bring him closer to the people, but others thought it was simply making him look stodgy. By the time the Labour Government took over last year, the antistodge camp was in the ascendancy. If Charles was ever going to convince the people that he had some of the contemporary touch that had made them love Diana, going on and on about how much he hated everything modern just wouldn't do.

"There have always been two conflicting issues—the agenda of the Prince of Wales and the agenda of the palace," an architectural historian who used to teach at the prince's institute told me. The palace, he said, wants "to smooth the route to the throne and remove the prince from any controversial activity. He ruffled so many feathers." (Another friend of the prince said to me, "Put not your trust in princes—they cannot run things, because they are run themselves.")

Now Charles is being advised by a group of people with no connection to architecture, image shapers who are said to be close to Camilla Parker Bowles. Since there seemed little chance of persuading Charles to moderate his views on architecture, these new courtiers have tried to shift him off the subject altogether. "He can no longer be the agent provocateur—he cannot be engaged in an intellectual battle with everyone else," Paul Finch, the editor of *Architects' Journal*, said to me. "They will not allow it."

When Charles first took on the architectural establishment, it was difficult not to applaud him. Back then, most modern architecture in Britain was awful. New Brutalism had been embraced with more enthusiasm in Britain than anywhere else, and London, for a while, seemed to be the world capital of concrete slabs. In Charles's second major speech on the subject, he declared that modern architects had done more damage to London than the Luftwaffe, and the British people cheered.

The prince's populist affection for old-fashioned buildings turned out to be right at home in the Britain of Margaret Thatcher. Even though the business and real-estate communities were at odds with the prince when it came to such big 1980s projects as the office complex at Canary Wharf, whose American-style skyscraper Thatcher loved and the prince despised, those communities could easily agree with him about architectural tastes in private homes. What better way to celebrate the newly created wealth of the boom years than with a shiny new neoclassical villa? Charles's architecture crusade, excised of its moral fervor, became closely associated with Thatcherism, almost in spite of itself. Classical architecture felt rich, and in the eighties rich was good.

Sometimes more than just a conceptual connection bound Charles's crusade to Thatcherism. There was, for example, the reconstruction of Paternoster Square, a site adjacent to St. Paul's Cathedral occupied by a dreary set of office buildings from the 1960s. In the 1980s, a developer planned a new Paternoster Square and invited six prominent modernist architects, including Richard Rogers, to submit schemes. Rogers's plan was reportedly the favorite, but the developer, worried that it wouldn't pass muster with Charles, chose a scheme by Arup Associates instead. Arup fared no better than Rogers; Charles's lack of enthusiasm led to the abandonment of the whole competition, and the decision was made to start all over again with an elaborate cluster of classical palazzi, intended to make Paternoster Square into a showpiece of London's new classical revival. That version, which was put together by a consortium of American, British, and Japanese developers and included buildings by John Simpson and the American classicists Allan Greenberg and Thomas Beeby, didn't get built, either. The project stumbled when it became obvious that the buildings, designed to please Charles, would be too expensive and were too awkwardly laid out to make sense as office space. It was an attempt "to produce seven masterpieces at the same moment—an impossible scenario," as one of the developers put it.

So the old Paternoster Square still stands, more desolate than ever, its empty concrete buildings facing a littered, windswept plaza. A few months ago, developers unveiled a new, more modest, more practical plan for the area. Even if the new project is built, it will do little to change the general view of Paternoster Square as a powerful emblem of how Prince Charles's architectural ideas have become increasingly irrelevant in the Britain of Tony Blair.

The architect Richard Rogers has been the prince's fiercest and most eloquent opponent. He was born in Italy into a family of English intellectuals, studied architecture at Yale, and first gained wide attention as the coarchitect, with Renzo Piano, of the Centre Pompidou, in Paris. The Pompidou, which opened in 1977, immediately reenergized the Paris art and architecture scene, and it gave Rogers instant status as a kind of radical within the establishment. In 1989, while most of the architectural profession in London was retreating in fear and confusion before Charles's onslaught, Rogers published a strongly worded counterattack.

"If princes want to argue, they should stop being princes," Rogers said in an interview in *Marxism Today*, and went on to call Charles's attempts to direct the architecture of public buildings "very vicious and questionable democratically. This is the reason that in the past some countries beheaded their kings." Rogers, whose socialist leanings and fondness for being in the public eye made him a natural spokesman of the architectural opposition, tried to meet with the prince. But, he said, three different meetings were canceled by Buckingham Palace.

Today, Rogers is the most politically influential architect in England. He has designed the Millennium Dome, in Greenwich, and has completed the sleek new London headquarters for Lloyd's and Channel 4. He and his wife, Ruthie, who operates the fashionable River Café restaurant, are among Tony and Cherie Blair's closest friends. He has been appointed to run a national government task force on reclaiming derelict urban land, and he has become an ardent environmentalist, arguing that advanced technology will allow architects to create modern buildings that will use less energy. Rogers has carved out a position for himself at the intersection of political and architectural power, giving him the very role Charles had presumed for himself as the nation's aesthetic conscience.

When Rogers speaks, he even sounds like a politician. "Britain and Tony Blair are saying we have to be seen as a creative society," Rogers told me. "There is a tremendous attempt to show that Britain is good at more than preserving the past."

The Prince of Wales's Institute of Architecture is housed in a pair of faded John Nash villas in Gloucester Gate, opposite the northern reaches of Regent's Park. Both the buildings and the location sound grander than they are; despite imposing Doric columns and six-over-six windows, the houses have seen better days, and the neighborhood is funky Camden Town, a long way from Belgravia. I had expected something with the polish of a wealthy foundation, but when I visited, on a recent spring afternoon, I found a set of shabby rooms embalmed in eerie silence. (Adrian Gale, the institute's current head, compares the premise to "a third-rate provincial hotel.") A bust of Charles stands in the lobby, not far from a small desk at which the institute's few publications are for sale.

Charles originally conceived of the institute as both a school and a research center, but it has developed a reputation as "a finishing course for people who weren't quite sure what to do—rich kids coming for a year of drawing or painting," in the words of one former faculty member. The only academic program that ever really got going is "the foundation," a one-year introductory course in architecture. At its busiest, the school has never had more than about sixty students.

From the beginning, the institute has been riven by turf battles among rigid classicists—for whom the place was a vehicle for promoting their own narrow vision of what architecture should be—more social-minded architects, and various New Age types to whom some of Charles's other interests appealed. (One such group, called Temenas, was described by a friend of the prince as "an alternative spiritual group—they begin their meetings by lighting a candle and talking about sacred geometries.") Architects, scholars, and critics figured that there was no better way to promote their own agendas than to get close to the prince. As one architect said, "A hopeless bureaucracy of people uninterested in architecture was created."

Since Charles does not finance the institute but gives it only his sponsorship, its program has been shaped in part by those who pay the bills, estimated at £2 million a year. The benefactors seem to be people who wish to maintain ties to the Royal Family, such as the philanthropist Drue Heinz and several Middle Eastern potentates, who in 1993 persuaded the institute to house a department devoted to Islamic design.

"I knew it was time to go when Lord Morris"—the institute's chairman from 1992 to 1997—"asked me who Norman Foster was," one former faculty member told me. Foster, in fact, gave a lecture at the institute in 1995, and was promptly attacked in an interview by Richard John, a dogmatic traditionalist who was the institute's director at the time. The turnover in directors has had less to do with Charles's management style than with the whims of the prince's courtiers, who have veered back and forth between trying to improve his image and trying to please him. "I remember him once saying, 'I can't stand being involved with so many people who don't agree with me,'" one of his friends said to me.

The appointment, in January, of Adrian Gale, a modernist who once served an apprenticeship with Mies van der Rohe, to run the institute was viewed by diehard classicists as the final admission that the prince's vision had failed. *Architects' Journal* published a cartoon of the prince kneeling before the Seagram Building, with Gale's head perched on the top. But Gale's hiring is both less ideological and more political than it appears. Gale's wife knows Hilary Browne-Wilkinson, who recently took over the institute's board. When palace spin doctors reportedly demanded a new and manageable chief, Gale, the retired head of an architecture school in Devon, was a comfortable known quantity.

I asked Gale why he had agreed to become the institute's director, and he replied, "This is not something I sought or expected or even necessarily wanted. I came here with one single purpose, which is to get this place taken seriously." Gale, an affable, white-haired man who was wearing a beret and a dark suit, acknowledged the distance between himself and the classicists who used to surround Charles. "'New' is a word that you can use at the institute, but 'modern' is not," Gale said. When he first met with the prince, he recalled, Charles "spat out the word 'modernism,' it flew past me and hit the wall, splat. He is deeply suspicious of technology and science, and he remains suspicious of modernism."

Gale sees himself as caught between what he calls "the princelings" in the palace, who would like to see Charles close down the institute, and the traditionalists, who complain that Gale is making a mockery of the prince's original vision. He believes that the institute can be saved only if it can be redirected toward more socially responsible ends than teaching students how to draw Corinthian columns. "The prince knows that we're in the Last Chance Saloon," he said to me. The institute, he says, has been "a laughingstock. The teaching has been superficial—about how you dress the building, not about space, not about soul."

The prince, Gale believes, sees architecture the way he does, as something profound. "Both Mies van der Rohe and the prince recognize that buildings have souls, that they have a spirit about them," Gale said. But he spoke of the prince almost wistfully; to Gale, it seems, Charles is the student he knows he could convince, if only the prince would pay attention.

Some of Charles's acolytes take a different view of the institute. "The prince's brilliant ideas have not been defeated—only his institute," Rodney Cook, an American classicist who helped start a foundation in the United States to support the institute, told me. "The modernist establishment waged a campaign against him, and they defeated him. It's pretty hard to fight the establishment, but that's what he tried to do."

If Britain's modernists weren't exactly in the mainstream in 1984, they are unquestionably the establishment today. While the prince remained stuck on the same idea for a decade, these architects worked on important commissions all over the world. James Stirling's Neue Staatsgalerie, in Stuttgart, a mixture of rich stone and bright, even garish color, brilliantly turned classicism inside out and became the most important museum of the mid-1980s. Foster's monument to custom-made high tech, the Hong Kong & Shanghai Bank headquarters, provoked skepticism with its billion-dollar price tag, but it was widely admired aesthetically. Rogers was the only one of the three to do his most notable work at home. His headquarters for Lloyd's, in the City of London, is a skyscraper with such richness and visual complexity that its very existence seems to refute the prince's argument that modern architecture has to be brutal, cold, and mute.

By the time the prince's classical crusade had peaked, Stirling, Foster, and Rogers were at the top of their profession, and the world recognized it, even if the Prince of Wales did not. They were having considerable effect on their fellow architects, too, replacing the Brutalist style of the previous generation with something that was lighter and more nimble and more sensitive to the need for public space.

Rogers, in victory, no longer sounds like the architect who took on the prince, whom he now describes as "slightly cornered by his own structure." Neither does Foster or Nicholas Grimshaw. "We've been very well treated by Prince Charles," Foster said to me, sitting at a round table at the end of his cathedral-like drafting room, across the Thames from Chelsea. "His heart is in the right place. There is a difference between him and the advisers who have clustered around him. I am not going back into that debate." He paused for a moment. "But can you name one single building that came out of that debate? One emblematic building? One Guggenheim Bilbao, one important thing? There was nothing."

Grimshaw is similarly relaxed about his former royal opponent. "I think you could give the prince some credit for starting the debate, and a lot of what he said was quite heartfelt," said Grimshaw, whose tiny office is decorated with a framed photograph of his classic Citroën DS-19. "But I believe that we represent the mainstream. We have a tradition in Britain of exploring materials, of shipbuilding, of good, construction-oriented design."

If there is a problem with British architecture right now, it is not with its quality but with its uniformity: Foster's work may be the sleekest, Rogers's the most futuristic, Grimshaw's the most structure-driven, but they are more similar than they are different, and there are not many lively voices dissenting from their mode of reserved modernism. British architecture is better than it has been in half a century, but the modernist establishment has become, in its own way, something of an academy. Modernism, however much it may be evolving, is hardly the avant-garde. (Indeed, at the end of the twentieth century it is a somewhat conservative force, which is why architects and politicians in Britain have become so comfortable with one another.)

The modernist victory feels almost too neat, particularly since James Stirling, by far the most idiosyncratic voice in British architecture of his generation, died in 1992, too soon to see things turn around. Despite having created a masterpiece in Stuttgart, Stirling died thinking that he was not respected at home. But he, too, has won: his building at No. 1 Poultry, in the heart of the City—the one that Prince Charles denounced as a 1930s wireless— was finally completed this spring, and its stone turrets and chartreuse and pink trim add the one note of joyous bombast to the otherwise cool sleekness of new London architecture.

Paradoxically, the man whose very name connotes the establishment, the Prince of Wales, is now an outsider, his power drained by his indifference to the forces at work around him. Charles wanted to be able to influence the course of architecture and, at the same time, to retreat behind royal prerogative when asked to account for his actions. Still, he has always managed to maintain a certain noblesse oblige. When he finally met the architects whose National Gallery design had provoked his famous carbuncle remark, he spoke politely to them and reportedly found them quite gracious. The prince said, "I'm sorry it had to be you."

They replied, "We're sorry it had to be you."

The New Yorker, July 13, 1998

Friedrich St. Florian, National World War II Memorial, Washington, D.C.

DOWN AT THE MALL

Few war memorials evoke deep, gut-wrenching emotion. Maya Lin's astonishingly simple Vietnam Veterans Memorial in Washington does, as does the USS *Arizona* Memorial at Pearl Harbor and Edwin Lutyens's Memorial to the Missing of the Somme, in France. But the majority of American memorials—

for example, all those classical auditoriums, parks, band shells, boulevards, museums, and parkways dedicated to the dead of World War I—are rather soft. Many of them were built for other reasons and then called memorials. That's not such a bad thing. The implicit message is that the soldiers and sailors did not die in vain; they died to preserve the civic life that these structures represent.

The new National World War II Memorial on the Mall in Washington seems to want to be majestic, but it's really an opulent, overbuilt civic plaza. The most important thing about it isn't the design, which is a vaguely classical set of colonnades by the architect Friedrich St. Florian, but the real estate it occupies. The memorial is set between the Lincoln Memorial and the Washington Monument. It is the first piece of construction to be placed on the great central axis of the Mall since those monuments were planned, more than a century ago.

The decision to give pride of place to the World War II memorial was made in 1995 by J. Carter Brown, the former director of the National Gallery of Art and, for much of his career, the powerful chairman of the Fine Arts Commission. The Iwo Jima memorial, across the Potomac in Arlington, a bronze statue based on the famous photograph of marines raising the American flag, had served as a kind of de facto memorial to all the men who had fought in World War II, but an idea took shape that the members of "the greatest generation" needed an official, all-encompassing memorial. They had fought the last war that had nearly unanimous support among Americans, and they were dying off. Brown was determined to make a grand gesture, and he rejected sites along the edges of the Mall, even after the American Battle Monuments Commission and the National Capital Planning Commission had agreed to put a World War II memorial in Constitution Gardens, a landscaped area near the Vietnam memorial. Carter Brown wanted it built around the Rainbow Pool, at that time a rather tired-looking body of water at the east end of the long Reflecting Pool, which extends from the Lincoln Memorial toward the Capitol. He usually got his wish as far as artistic matters in Washington were concerned, and the middle of the Mall it was.

The architectural competition for the memorial was run by the General Services Administration, which treated the process more or less like the search for an architect for a regular government building and stipulated that experience would be a factor in the decision, all but assuring that an unknown designer with a fresh idea wouldn't have a chance. The rule was eventually relaxed, but the die was cast. Applicants were told that designs had to work with the Rainbow Pool, which would be spruced up as the new memorial's centerpiece, and this put a further brake on creativity. There were only some four hundred entries for the competition, compared with more than a thousand for the Vietnam memorial and more than five thousand for the Ground Zero memorial competition last year. St. Florian, a seventy-one-year-old architect and teacher who works in Providence, Rhode Island, won with a grandiose scheme that included fifty columns, each thirty-three feet tall; a set of embankments rising thirty-nine feet above the plaza surrounding the pool; and forty thousand square feet of underground space. The columns were arranged in two semicircles, one on the north side of the Rainbow Pool and the other on the south. St. Florian lowered the pool so that the memorial would not intrude too much on the views from the other memorials along the Mall, but that did little to reduce the overbearing quality of the design. Almost everybody hated it. A group called the National Coalition to Save Our Mall complained that it would overwhelm the vista between the Lincoln Memorial and the Washington Monument, and Bob Kerrey, then a senator from Nebraska, persuaded more than a dozen other senators, including Strom Thurmond, to sign a letter objecting to the scheme.

St. Florian was sent back to the drawing board and returned with a plan for something smaller. The embankments and the underground space disappeared, and the columns turned into metal shields with openings that made the design more transparent. It continued to evolve—in 1999 the shields became flattened pillars bearing sculpted bronze wreaths—but the tone of stolid, bland classicism remained. The version that got built has two semicircles of pillars, each representing a state or a territory, arrayed on either side of two forty-three-foot-tall arched entry pavilions symbolizing the European and Pacific theaters of the war. There is a formal entrance on the Seventeenth Street side, directly in line with the Lincoln Memorial, but most people will probably enter through one of the pavilions, walking under a ten-foot-wide bronze laurel wreath suspended from a bronze ribbon held in the beaks of bronze eagles set atop columns. From there, one descends a gentle, curving ramp to the level of the Rainbow Pool and the granite plaza. The pool is the focal point, not only because it is huge and occupies the center of the plaza but because its newly restored fountains give the memorial much of its visual energy—what there is of it. The fountains and the curving granite ramps and the sculpted granite benches beneath them overwhelm the most sober aspect of the memorial, Freedom Wall, on the west side of the plaza, which contains more than four thousand gold stars, each representing a hundred war dead. The words "here we mark the price of freedom" are engraved in a low stone panel in front of the wall, but the dead are not identified by name, and there are no images of war anywhere in the memorial, except in some small decorative bas-reliefs by the sculptor Raymond Kaskey.

The bronze eagles, which were designed by Kaskey, are beautifully wrought, and the stonework—the memorial is built of silvery granite from South Carolina and Georgia—is stunning in its execution. In an age when cheap, thin veneers pass for real stonework, it is pleasing to see stone that has been treated like stone, and carved by craftsmen who know what they are doing. But the design, in the end, is banal and timid, overly concerned with being well mannered. And what, finally, is the connection between the states and the war? Soldiers fighting abroad were not grouped by states and did not, I suspect, particularly identify with them. And there is no connection whatsoever between the states that are attached to the Atlantic pavilion and those attached to the Pacific pavilion; the whole arrangement is a conceit, dictated by the desire to turn the names of places into the elements of a symmetrical architectural composition.

During the design process, it was the memorial's stripped-down classicism that seemed most likely to be a problem. A lot of critics, including me, fretted about Albert Speer and Fascist architecture. That turns out not to be an issue at all. Mussolini or Speer would have overpowered you, and this memorial is welcoming. But a memorial ought to tug at the emotions in some profound way. What strikes you when you stand in the center of the World War II memorial is the sweep of the vista from the Lincoln Memorial to the Capitol, which is exactly what was moving about being in this space before. That a chunk of the space is now paved in elegantly carved granite and has some handsome bronze sculptures and spectacular fountains doesn't tell you much that you didn't already know.

There is a deep, unresolved contradiction at the heart of this project, and it emerges from the specifics of the site. On the one hand, the Mall is a great public space, as essential a part of the American landscape as the Grand Canyon. It has to be respected. On the other hand, a war memorial is serious business, and honoring four hundred thousand dead and the millions who served with them is not the sort of enterprise that naturally takes on a low profile. It is fundamentally at odds with the right way to use this piece of land.

The Lincoln Memorial works as well as it does partly because it is at the end of the Mall, terminating the vista, and not near the middle, but also because the designer, Henry Bacon, had absolute clarity of vision. He didn't want to make a user-friendly memorial. He wanted to make an inspiring one, and he did. Bacon wanted classical architecture to show Lincoln's greatness and, through that, the importance of the Union. In Bacon's temple, you have no choice but to think of what Lincoln meant. You don't have a choice in Maya Lin's memorial, either. The stark reality of more than fifty thousand names engraved on Lin's stone wall is staggering, and the subtlety of the relationship between the wall and the landscape—we descend, then rise again, as if to return to the land of the living—is deeply moving. The descent to the Rainbow Pool doesn't lend itself to that kind of experience. The memorial is a perfectly fine plaza, such as it is, and it has turned out to be far less damaging to the space than many people had feared. But it exudes a kind of well-meaning hollowness. The layout comes from the site, and from the desire to make a pleasant public plaza that will not overwhelm the great monuments on either side.

The people who make decisions about architecture in Washington— government bureaucrats, members of the Fine Arts Commission, and city-planning officials—have never been particularly open to new kinds of architectural expression. As the years pass, the freshness and brilliance of Maya Lin's Vietnam Veterans Memorial seems increasingly like a lucky accident. A fear of modernism has led to weak and pompous buildings, like the Kennedy Center and the Rayburn House Office Building, which weren't simply a consequence of trying to save money, the way bad buildings often are in New York and other cities. In Washington, the government usually pays top dollar.

Of course, the fondness for watered-down classicism also brought us the Federal Triangle, an urbane collection of government buildings, erected in the 1930s, which knitted together several blocks of downtown Washington and gave it dignity. Classicism, even timid classicism, is a good urban tool. It creates a sense of coherence and order. But a memorial isn't supposed to be part of a larger urban order. It is supposed to be a special place. The genius of the Mall is that it juxtaposes the monumental and the everyday. The World War II memorial throws things off balance. It tries to make the Mall more important and more inviting at the same time, and it ends up doing neither.

The New Yorker, May 31, 2004

Hans and Torrey Butzer, Oklahoma City National Memorial

REQUIEM

The debate about how to memorialize
the victims of the bombing of the Alfred
P. Murrah Federal Building in Oklahoma
City—the only event in recent American
history that comes remotely close to
the terrorist attack on the World Trade
Center in Lower Manhattan—went on
for more than two years. Oklahoma City

is a small town compared to New York, with a population of roughly five hundred thousand, and it is relatively homogeneous. There was no pressure to restore the site of the bombed building to commercial use, as there is at the World Trade Center, and yet the Oklahoma City National Memorial, as the park on the site is called, wasn't dedicated until the fifth anniversary of the bombing. The other half of the memorial, an interactive museum and information center, opened recently, nearly six years after the event it was created to commemorate. It is difficult to imagine things being easier, or moving faster, in New York.

The main feature of the Oklahoma City memorial is a set of a hundred and sixty-eight chairlike objects, made of bronze and glass, one for each person killed. The chairs are arranged in rows and spread out across the footprint of the Murrah Building. They face a large reflecting pool and an elm tree that escaped damage in a parking lot across the street. The tree became known as the "survivor tree," and it is now surrounded by a stone terrace. Two monumental bronze-paneled walls serve as gateways to the site. One of them is inscribed "9:01" and the other "9:03," marking the minute before the bomb went off on the morning of April 19, 1995, and the minute after. The space between the two gateways represents 9:02.

I went to Oklahoma City late this fall, when fires were still smoldering at Ground Zero. Larry Silverstein, who held the lease on the Trade Center towers, was loudly vowing to rebuild the same amount of office space, possibly in four shorter towers. Since then, Silverstein has quieted down a bit, and concedes that there might be room for various other things on the site. The head of the new state authority charged with rebuilding, John C. Whitehead, has said that he expects to build a memorial that is the equal of the Lincoln, Jefferson, and Vietnam Veterans Memorials in Washington, D.C., although he didn't indicate what he meant by that. He has also talked about including housing, office towers, and cultural facilities on the site, which is certain to arouse the ire of many families of the victims of the attack, who want it to be treated as hallowed ground.

Oklahoma City faced many of the same issues. In *The Unfinished Bombing: Oklahoma City in American Memory,* Edward T. Linenthal writes that "conducting business as usual would defile the site in the eyes of many." Linenthal, who teaches at the University of Wisconsin and has also written about the struggle over the creation of the Holocaust Museum in Washington, sets out a narrative that prefigures many of the events surrounding the World Trade Center catastrophe. Firemen became national icons, fences became spontaneous memorials, covered with pictures, notes, messages, and memorabilia. Some people felt that "a new building would signal defiance of terrorism," Linenthal writes, and others suggested leaving the ruins in place as "an evocative reminder of loss, and of the enduring dangers of violence." The Oklahoma City wreckage became a kind of pilgrimage site, attracting both mourners and voyeurs.

Leaving the ruins of the Murrah Building as a monument in themselves was never much of an option. The governor of Oklahoma, Frank Keating, said that what was left was "an eyesore . . . a symbol of destruction and terror that people here would much rather put behind them." In the end, several nearby buildings that had been seriously damaged were taken down, the street that the Murrah Building faced was closed, and three acres was turned into a memorial district. A building that had been damaged and whose tenant chose not to return was used to house the museum.

Within days after the bombing, public officials in Oklahoma City had been deluged with suggestions for the obvious arches, obelisks, and fountains, as well as a statue of "two giant hands (God's hands)" and angels, doves, eagles, and hearts. The mayor of Oklahoma City, Ronald Norick, appointed a local lawyer, Robert Johnson, to head a task force to figure out what an appropriate memorial would be. Johnson was sensitive to the fact that people wanted to be heard, and he understood that the memorial had numerous constituencies— relatives of the people who were killed, those who escaped but were traumatized by the event, rescuers, and the general public. They had different priorities, different ways of mourning, and different aesthetic sensibilities.

The most important decision Johnson's task force made was to articulate the intentions of the memorial before thinking about any kind of physical design. The group struggled for months to create what it called a mission statement. The preamble to the final document declared that "we come here to remember those who were killed, those who survived and those changed forever. May all who leave here know the impact of violence. May this memorial offer comfort, strength, peace, hope and serenity." The task force had fought over every word. "Killed" won out over the soft-sounding "lost" and the harsher "murdered" (which would have excluded a rescue worker whose death was not a direct result of the explosion). The language of the mission statement was too sophisticated for angels and praying hands. The memorial was not to include a representation of any known person, "living or dead," which was a way of indicating that statues of firemen carrying babies were not particularly welcome.

An open architectural competition was held. The model was the competition for the design of the Vietnam Veterans Memorial in Washington, which yielded the best American memorial of modern times, a design by an unknown twenty-one-year-old architecture student, Maya Lin. The Oklahoma City task force asked Paul Spreiregen, the architect who managed the Vietnam-memorial competition, to oversee the process. Spreiregen felt strongly that he and other professionals should be the ones to choose the best design, and he made it clear that survivors and members of victims' families were to have no more than an advisory role. The families refused to accept that. Although Spreiregen complained that permitting nonprofessionals to make the design decision was akin to going "to an accountant to have my appendix removed," the families had their way, and Spreiregen was off the job before he had ever really started.

By almost every professional standard, Spreiregen was right. Victims' families can't be expected to make a knowing judgment about what constitutes the best public memorial. Giving them control would seem to be a concession to a kind of victims' culture, elevating sentiment over any other value. In the end, however, Johnson's gamble that he could trust the families proved to be right, in large part because the mission statement set forth a program for the memorial that made the kitsch that Spreiregen feared almost impossible. The competition eventually received six hundred and twenty-four entries, which were narrowed down to five finalists.

Not many big-name architects felt like putting their fate in the hands of a mostly nonprofessional jury, but the level of the finalists was at least decent. The winner, as in the Vietnam-memorial competition, turned out to be relatively young and unknown: a married couple, Hans and Torrey Butzer, Americans who at the time worked in Berlin. The centerpiece of the Butzers' design, which they prepared with the help of a German colleague, Sven Berg, was the rows of empty chairs. In this sense, it was not altogether unlike Maya Lin's Vietnam memorial, where the V-shaped wall of black granite is an abstract object and the names carved on it create a realistic counterpoint.

The Butzers are sophisticated but not as subtle as Maya Lin. The chairs are semi-abstract, with open bronze backs and bases made out of glass cubes that are lit from within (which makes the place look like a glowing field of votive candles at night), but they still resemble tombstones. They are arranged in nine rows, each of which represents one floor of the Murrah Building. The chairs commemorating the children who were killed are miniature versions of the adult ones.

The Oklahoma City memorial is most effective, I find, when it is viewed as a series of abstract shapes—the monumental gateways, the glowing cubes at night—although for a lot of people it is the very chair-ness of the chairs that is powerful. Great memorials use abstraction to engender feelings of peace and awe. The obelisk of the Washington Monument suggests George Washington's primacy in the history of this country in a way that no statue of him on horseback possibly could. The strength of the Lincoln Memorial comes at least as much from the rhythmic power of Henry Bacon's austere box of columns as from Daniel Chester French's seated figure of Lincoln, which it both encloses and ennobles. When you visit the Vietnam Veterans Memorial, you descend gently into the ground, on an axis with both the Lincoln Memorial and the Washington Monument, and you are uplifted by their grandeur while being drawn into a private, contemplative realm. The Butzers haven't achieved this in Oklahoma City, but they have made a place that is earnest and dignified, with architectural details on a high level.

Ever since Maya Lin inscribed the names of the Vietnam War dead on those black granite walls, it has been considered inappropriate to memorialize the dead as a mass, as they are at Gettysburg, for instance. The Oklahoma City mission statement stipulated that the memorial contain a hundred and sixty-eight pieces of something—it was left up to the architect to decide what. In addition to the field of chairs, the memorial has a section that lists survivors of the bombing on a granite plaque, and it also has a kind of children's garden, and the survivor tree. There is a lot going on, but in downtown Oklahoma City it is a welcome change to have a lot going on. The memorial is the most active piece of open public space in town, and the most elegant.

The adjacent museum is a mixture of conscientious history, special effects, and sentimentality. There is background material on the Murrah Building and testimony from people affected by the bombing, and one area is devoted to memorabilia and photographs of the people who were killed. Another section is a re-creation of the hearing room of the Oklahoma Water Resources Board, which was across the street from the Murrah Building. You enter, and the door closes behind you as a tape plays the first two minutes of a meeting, and then you hear the blast and the room goes dark. The museum provides a much more American experience, really, than the outdoor memorial, since it is grounded in the belief that almost anything, including the most horrendous events imaginable, can be made entertaining.

The New Yorker, January 14, 2002

MUSEUMS

Frank Gehry, Guggenheim Museum Bilbao

THE POLITICS OF BUILDING

Great architecture has always emerged out of politics or been deeply connected to it. The Pyramids, the Parthenon, Chartres— these were all, in their way, political statements. So it is with the latest great building of the world—the Guggenheim Museum Bilbao, in northern Spain, designed by the American architect

Frank Gehry. It is not Gehry's personal politics that lie at the root of the building; they matter no more than Michelangelo's politics did when he was asked to paint the Sistine Chapel. The politics of the Guggenheim Bilbao are evident in a single word, museoa, that is plastered onto the building's facade in enormous letters. The word is notable because museoa is not how "museum" is spelled in Spanish. It's how it is spelled in the language of the Basques, the determinedly independent people who are in Spain but not entirely of it. They have erected this building in the center of Bilbao, their largest city, as a means of asserting their presence in the world.

Imagine if Sinn Fein had put up the Sydney Opera House in the middle of Belfast, or the separatists in Quebec had decided to ask Philip Johnson to build them a new skyscraper. There is nothing about the design of Gehry's building that seems connected directly to Basque culture; moreover, most of the art inside comes from somewhere else. What kind of way is this for a nationalist movement to declare itself?

The art and architecture press has rushed to praise Gehry's building, with many critics traveling to Bilbao even before the museum was far enough along to have any works of art installed. They have written of it with such awe that one would have thought they had discovered a whole new aesthetic that had sprung full-blown from an architectural Zeus. Much of this praise is not misplaced. The museum is the finest work to date of an architect who is increasingly recognized as one of the century's most important figures in his field—perhaps the strongest creative force since Louis Kahn. But the critics who have celebrated him have shown relatively little interest in the striking paradox posed by Bilbao; namely, that nationalism, so often a restrictive force, has in this instance brought forth a most enlightened, culturally advanced internationalism. How did it happen?

The logical answer—that political radicalism has simply transformed itself into cultural radicalism—turns out not to be right at all. The Basques possess a radical separatist arm—ETA—which has shown itself capable of extreme violence, but you do not have to spend a long time in Bilbao, a city that virtually exudes bourgeois complacency, to see that the deeper currents in Basque politics and culture are conservative. Bilbao is Spain's historic industrial and banking center, and the Basque region's per-capita income is about 11 percent higher than that in the rest of the country. Clean, almost prim, its people well dressed, Bilbao is the generic European provincial city. The main intersections have plazas and statues and fountains; there is an old quarter that is dense, and a river that is murky. Bilbao sits in a valley between two high green ridges, and they enhance the city's sense of isolation, indicating that this is a place with vistas only of itself.

To understand the Basques, it is necessary to appreciate the way the bourgeois citizens and the political radicals are inclined to accept one another. The proper folk of Bilbao deplore the political killing, and ETA leaders sneer that the region's problems won't be solved by building museums. But despite their extreme differences, they are united by a powerful sense of identity as Basques first and as Spaniards second, if at all. The Basques were opposed to Franco in the Spanish Civil War—Guernica is only twelve miles from Bilbao—

and during Franco's reign it was forbidden to speak or write the ancient Basque language. Even today, twenty-two years after Franco's death, attitudes in the Basque Country toward the central government commonly range from disdain to hatred. King Juan Carlos will dedicate the Guggenheim at its gala opening this month, but he is doing so, many people in Bilbao feel, to capitalize on the Basques' achievement. They hope he will be wise enough to acknowledge that the museum was conceived, built, and entirely paid for by the Basques.

Not surprisingly, the project had its origins in the conservative mainstream of Bilbao, where separatist impulses are tempered by boosterism. What could be better than to channel the nationalist impulses into an art museum that would dazzle the world and blunt the harsh edges of ETA? Then the city could achieve its fondest wish: to have an identity apart from that of Spain. After all, architecture was working much the same alchemy in Barcelona, where the city's spectacular commissions for the 1992 Olympics reinforced the Catalans' sense of themselves as a distinct culture and conferred international status on Barcelona. And so, in 1991, the city fathers of Bilbao turned to the Solomon R. Guggenheim Foundation, in New York, whose hegemonic ambitions under Thomas Krens, its director, had made it something of a multinational presence. Krens was willing to share the Guggenheim's name, its expertise, and its collection; the only stipulation, beyond a hefty fee, was that the Guggenheim would retain control of the project. The Basque regional government was so eager to build the museum that it agreed to these terms, setting aside a budget of $100 million for construction and millions more for related costs.

The result could have been a disaster: ambitious American museum exploits rich but innocent provincial European city. But the Basques are a kind of cross between canny developers and political rebels. The city had earlier commissioned Norman Foster, the British architect, to design what must be the sleekest subway stations in the world, and Santiago Calatrava, the Spanish architect, to design both a new airport terminal and a stunning pedestrian bridge in the city center. Krens's first act was to convince the Basques that their original plan—to put the museum in a former warehouse— was insufficiently impressive; his second was to nudge them toward the city's industrial waterfront. The Guggenheim and the Basque government invited three prominent architects to submit schemes: the Japanese Arata Isozaki (who had designed the Guggenheim's Soho branch for Krens); the firm of Coop Himmelblau, from Vienna; and Gehry. Each of them was given the brief of producing a great building for the end of the twentieth century. Gehry was the clear choice, with a design that, from the moment the first sketches were revealed, has seemed to be not only startlingly beautiful but entirely new without being self-conscious.

Gehry's museum is voluptuous. A series of curving metal panels opens out of a limestone base like the petals of a flower, embracing a gracefully curving atrium of glass and metal. To some, the museum looks like a Spanish galleon set beside the River Nervión. To others, it suggests a rose, or a vast Constructivist artichoke, or is seen as simply an abstract play on Bilbao's industrialized heritage. As with most of Gehry's work, the elements at first glance appear idiosyncratic and irrational—not so much a building as a work of sculpture assembled at random. This is an old criticism of Gehry, whose genius, in part, has been to create buildings that seem to be arbitrary and irrational but in fact are deeply responsive to their surroundings and to the needs of their users.

In approaching Bilbao, Gehry's first concern was the museum's heritage— that of the Guggenheim Museum in New York. Frank Lloyd Wright's building on Fifth Avenue is, of course, one of the great architectural achievements of the twentieth century, and the designer of any new museum bearing the name Guggenheim must contend with as powerful a father figure as there is. The New York Guggenheim is also the spiritual parent of every modern museum whose architect has put his own expressive desires ahead of the art. Wright's Guggenheim injects a shot of adrenaline into the experience of looking at art, but it also compromises that experience, and the inflexibility of its circular interior makes it, at best, a problematic model. Gehry's challenge was nearly overwhelming—to design something that would match Wright's building in aesthetic power while functioning much better as a container for art.

And he has pretty much succeeded. Gehry takes Wright's great spiraling rotunda and turns it into a room so soaring, so swooping, so contorted, and so full of natural light and a sense of the city that it makes Wright's creation seem, by comparison, as staid as a tea salon. Wright showed in 1959 that architectural space did not have to be enclosed in a box; Gehry shows in 1997 that architectural space does not have to be defined by a single system of geometry or, for that matter, by any conventional order. To bring us to the brink of chaos and then hold us back is, in the end, to assert the strongest order of all.

Gehry taunts chaos, but he loves convention. That is one of the paradoxes of his work, and it is perhaps the Bilbao museum's greatest strength. Do you really think this building is so strange? Then spend a few minutes staring at it. The secret of Gehry's Guggenheim is that it isn't nearly as weird as it appears to be. Gehry's forms are exciting, but they're not perverse; they have a certain naturalness to them. The Guggenheim Bilbao meets the ground solidly and gets more expressive as it moves upward, like a Baroque finial. However much this building startles, there are no gimmicks about it—none of the cheap tricks that one sees in skyscrapers that are seemingly balanced on a single point or cantilevered above an empty corner. In short, there is nothing here to challenge our basic instincts about space, proportion, and order. Gehry has produced structural magnificence, not structural exhibitionism.

This is a surprisingly comfortable building to be in. If its overall form is guided by reason, the spaces intended for the display of art are positively sedate. Well, some of them. Of the nineteen galleries, ten are classically proportioned—rectilinear and with straight up-and-down walls. When I went through the museum earlier this month, several of these rooms had already been hung with art; one of them contained a spectacular series of Rothkos and de Koonings as well as Pollocks from the Guggenheim collection, none of which had ever looked so good in Wright's building.

The nine other galleries are more Gehryesque, with walls that swoop and curve, but they are nearly as accommodating—particularly since they are intended for large-scale art. One of the rooms is devoted to Anselm Kiefer, and one will house, among other works, found-object pieces by Joseph Beuys; others will display parts of the huge collection of minimalist and conceptual art which the Guggenheim bought from Count Giuseppe Panza di Biumo in 1990 and has had insufficient space to show in New York. Gehry is famous for his close connections to contemporary artists, several of whom have produced work specially for this museum. One two-story gallery will be covered entirely in a mural by Sol LeWitt. Richard Serra's *Snake*, three parallel immense, leaning panels of rusted steel which weigh 174 tons and bend in the shape of an elongated letter *s,* is a brilliant comment on the shape of the gallery—the museum's largest, which workers have taken to calling "the boat" or "the fish." Gehry himself thought that the space, at 450 feet long and 80 feet wide, was too big, and he wanted to punctuate it with two walls running partway up to the ceiling. Krens, who loves the idea of having the world's biggest gallery, rejected the walls. As it now stands, the gallery seems hospitable enough to the 104-foot-long Serra (it would be more powerful if it were bigger still) and the huge *Knife Ship* by Claes Oldenburg. Although Donald Judd's *Copper Stack*—a work that would command a conventional gallery space—is all but lost here, Gehry has, for the most part, figured out how to create a potent architectural experience that, far from fighting with art, rises to the challenge of it.

There is a rightness to this building which is not just exciting as pure form but speaks to its surroundings as well. Whereas Wright dealt with the Manhattan cityscape by ignoring it, Gehry's building engages with every aspect of Bilbao. From the sweeping curves of a vast highway ramp and bridge that cross the river beside the museum, through the industrial forms of the old riverfront, to the vistas from neighboring streets, everything about Bilbao has played some role in the shaping of Gehry's forms. Even his choice of titanium, the marvelous shimmering metal used to coat the petal-like steel panels, is appropriate to this setting. Instead of glaring like stainless steel, it ripples like the water that has supported this port city for seven centuries.

The Guggenheim Bilbao ends the century by summarizing the era's achievements. It does not cower in denial of modernism, the twentieth century's great artistic revolution, but, rather, enhances it by joining modernism's power to the civilizing forces of urbanism. And it does not reject the glory of monumental form, which in an age besotted by the notion that real space may someday give way to virtual space makes Gehry almost conservative. This is traditional architecture, taken to the limits. Gehry's feat has been to stretch what the century has made and end it on a note of optimism. His great, living museum stands as a metaphor for Basque culture and the relationship it aspires to have with the world: a thing apart, yet entirely willing to make a connection on its own terms.

The New Yorker, October 13, 1997

Richard Meier, Getty Center, Los Angeles

THE PEOPLE'S GETTY

It is a paradox of Southern California that you have to remove yourself from the city to have an urban experience—or at least an upbeat one. You get in your car and drive a long distance on the freeway so that you can walk around Disneyland, and who wouldn't rather stroll along Disney's Main Street USA than in downtown Los Angeles? People throng to CityWalk, at Universal Studios, which is a kind of theme park masquerading as a city street; in Beverly Hills, people come to play city at 2 Rodeo Drive, a shopping mall that is a stage-set version of a European street, its cobblestones rising gently over convenient underground parking.

The planners of the Getty Center, the billion-dollar complex of six buildings high atop a hill in the Brentwood section of Los Angeles, did not intend their work to be the latest addition to this list of alluring fantasy environments, but that is what it has become. In 1984, when the Getty Trust commissioned the architect Richard Meier to design this immense project, the goal was to create a campus for the display, conservation, and study of high art, housed in buildings as serious in their architectural ambition as the Getty would be in its scholarly mission. The Getty was not intended as a populist enterprise. Indeed, during the fifteen years of planning and construction, it was widely criticized as being the opposite—an elitist palace that would look down upon culture-starved Los Angeles with disdain.

And then, in December, the Getty opened, and the place that was supposed to be where California got a dose of serious culture has turned out to be, instead, where serious culture gets a dose of California. The most astonishing thing about the Getty could not be seen during the months of private preopening VIP tours, and that is the way in which the public has embraced what was supposed to have repelled it. The surging crowds, more than double what the planners had projected, have redefined the Getty as one of those Southern California monuments in which a fantasy environment becomes the setting for a kind of enthusiastic, if ersatz, urban life.

The crowds frequently reach more than ten thousand a day. They wait patiently in line at the bottom of the hill for the white tramcars that will take them on a four-minute ride to the summit. (As at San Simeon and Disneyland, automobiles are kept far away, so as not to spoil the purity of the stage set.) The crowds emerge onto a plaza that is the weakest part of Meier's design, but they swarm eagerly across it, buying cappuccinos, sitting at little café tables, and staring at Meier's sprawling compositions of glass, enamel panels, and stone as if they were looking not at high American corporate modernism but at a piazza in Tuscany.

Meier's style is a kind of romantic modernism, serious in intent, almost always beautiful in design and execution, but quite often viewed as cold. Yet the Getty is so popular that Meier has become something of a celebrity in Los Angeles. I walked through the Getty with him the other day, and I soon lost count of the number of times he was approached by strangers. People wanted to have their pictures taken with him; they asked him to autograph brochures, maps, napkins. It was like walking around with a rock star. The unexpected popularity of the Getty has made some critics uneasy: if the people like it this much, the thinking goes, it can't be that good, can it? The Getty's success proves something that we have known for a long time but rarely admit: high modern architecture of the sort Meier produces is now fundamentally a conservative style. It connotes elegance and stability, not innovation, and while it is certainly not warm and inviting, neither is it threatening or hard to understand.

As a work of architecture, the Getty complex possesses all of Meier's strengths and a few significant weaknesses. Meier, unlike some of the neomodernist architects who are his peers, is comfortable working at a monumental, civic scale, and he produces some spectacular effects. The rotunda at the entrance to the museum may be the finest interpretation of a classical rotunda in modernist garb ever built anywhere, and the long open courtyard within the museum turns out to be livelier, more serene, and grander as urban space than the piazza surrounding the tram stop. The galleries are excellent, with superbly controlled natural light, and Meier has organized them into a rhythm that allows frequent breaks onto outdoor terraces, so that the experience of looking at art is gently mixed with views of the city and the opportunity to sip still more cappuccino. Although Meier objected when the architect-decorator Thierry Despont was hired to soften up many of the interiors, Despont's colored fabric in the painting galleries does the architecture little harm. His classical details in the decorative-arts section, however, are clunky and banal, turning Meier's strong spaces into fake period rooms.

Meier had a freer hand in some of the other buildings, particularly the Getty Research Institute, which consists of the library and the scholarly center, and which is one of his finest works ever—an exquisite circular building that melds geometric grace with precision of form. In other hands, modernism can feel industrial; Meier makes it breathtakingly lyrical. Still, one feels frustrated because the overall effect of the Getty is so corporate and its tone so even. With a place as big as this, you need some other kind of element—a campanile, perhaps?—to punctuate the relentless consistency. The whole of the Getty always seems like less than the sum of its parts.

Visitors to the Getty spend most of their time in the museum, but they are encouraged to wander around the entire complex. With so many places to wander, to eat, and to shop, the average visit lasts almost four hours.

The allure of the place has also had an extraordinary effect on the way transportation works in Los Angeles. The Getty's planners had assumed that the limited number of parking spaces (there are only twelve hundred, allotted by advance reservation) would effectively control the number of visitors, so it put no limit on the number of "walk-ins" it would admit, walk-ins being a rare species in Los Angeles. So much for knowing your audience. It has turned out that people have come by foot, by Rollerblade, by bus, and by bicycle; the taxi industry in Los Angeles has never had such a windfall; and ridership on the two public bus lines that pass the Getty's gates has ballooned. A whole industry has sprung up to get people to the Getty. Ten dollars will buy a parking space in, for example, the Holiday Inn's lot, and another five dollars per person will provide a seat on its private Getty shuttle van. (Prime hours at the Getty's own parking lot are booked through July.) Whatever the Getty's ultimate contribution to culture, it has already accomplished something that was always thought impossible: to get Angelenos to use alternative forms of transportation.

When Barry Munitz, the new president and CEO of the Getty Trust, took over from Harold Williams, who retired after the opening, he pledged to steer away from the elitist image that had been established by his predecessor. Back then, no one realized that Williams and Meier, without particularly intending to, had done Munitz's work for him. Seeking to make a modernist cloister, they made a modernist town square. Now Munitz's challenge is to make sure that the Getty is remembered as something more than the most successful art theme park of all time.

The New Yorker, March 2, 1998

Machado and Silvetti, Getty Villa, Malibu

WHEN IN ROME

In the 1970s, the Getty Museum built itself
a home in Malibu, California, in the form
of an imitation Roman villa from the first
century. There was something undeniably
kitschy about the notion of putting a
make-believe classical villa atop a hillside
overlooking the Pacific Ocean and calling
it a museum, but nobody seemed to mind.
This was Los Angeles, after all, and so what
if the overdecorated galleries, with their

damask wall coverings and trompe-l'oeil murals, gave the museum's interior the feeling of a mogul's mansion in Bel Air? Then the Getty grew up. In 1976, its eccentric founder, the oilman J. Paul Getty, died, leaving the bulk of his multibillion-dollar estate to the museum, which suddenly became the world's richest cultural institution. The museum morphed into the Getty Trust and spent a billion dollars constructing the Getty Center, a pristine modernist campus by Richard Meier, on top of a steep hill in Brentwood, thirteen miles east of Malibu.

The trust was obviously eager to leave behind its arriviste beginnings, and the villa could easily have become the most upscale condo conversion in Los Angeles history. Instead, the Getty came up with a more imaginative, and more costly, idea: it decided to give its strange building a chance to be taken seriously. The trust announced that it would turn the Malibu villa into a museum of antiquities, filling it with objects that were created in the period that the building—a replica of the Villa dei Papiri, in Herculaneum—was intended to evoke. It was a risky move, since it wasn't clear if this approach would make the building look more dignified or even sillier.

It took a dozen years and $275 million to renovate the villa and surround it with a series of modernist buildings, including an entry pavilion, an amphitheater, a parking garage, a café, an auditorium, an education center, and a shop. The project's architects are Rodolfo Machado and Jorge Silvetti, of Boston, rigorous modernists who have a love of classicism and believe that an architect best respects history not by imitating it but by teasing its spirit into new forms. Machado and Silvetti are about as far as you can get from Norman Neuerburg, who designed the original villa, and it seemed an odd match: there is nothing overtly charming about Machado and Silvetti's work, while Neuerburg's design was a vast, sprawling exercise in cuteness.

The campus that Machado and Silvetti have created is a bracing collage of old and new, and the villa has been nearly magically transformed. The task was surely made easier by the fact that the French furniture and Old Master paintings are gone from the villa, and its new contents have a genuine connection to ancient Rome. (In fact, some items in the collection may belong to Rome; the Getty has been accused of acquiring a significant number of looted artifacts.) But it takes more than hauling away some gilded frames to make a ponderous building into a gracious one. Instead of slavishly replicating Roman architecture (although various touches, such as new floors of bronze, mosaic, and marble, reveal a high level of scholarship), Machado and Silvetti have acknowledged the past without imitating it. They have boldly reorganized the villa, creating more logical routes through it and adding fifty-eight windows and three skylights, to bring natural light into the galleries. One of the best things in the villa now is a new main stair, of bronze, glass, and hand-carved Spanish stone; a meticulous modernist composition, it is broad, sumptuous, and serene, and a crisp counterpoint to the classical-looking environment around it. The effect is playful and knowing: in Italy, contemporary alterations to ancient Roman structures are often made in such a bluntly modern style, to make clear which elements are authentically old. Here, of course, the "original" details date from 1974.

By treating the barely old as a revered object, Machado and Silvetti somehow make visitors feel that this building is no longer an object of ridicule but, rather, worthy of respect. It is an understated, sly maneuver, and they do it without taking the easy path of irony. Machado and Silvetti have recast the villa not only through their upgrades but in the way they have surrounded it with a series of new structures, changing its context. The villa is no longer its own little theme park: it is now an architectural folly in the center of a carefully conceived, impeccably wrought modern campus. In the English landscape tradition, the folly was not a trivial object but a noble act of historical connoisseurship, playing off against a great manor house that was designed in a more contemporary style. Machado and Silvetti have saved the once outlandish villa by connecting it to this honorable architectural heritage.

The ring of modernist structures doesn't intrude on the villa, nor do the buildings form a neutral backdrop. They are the architectural equivalent of cupped hands, holding the original structure within a firm, protective grasp. In this scheme, the new buildings—mainly horizontal structures, some of which are set into the side of the canyon—are gateways that deliver you to the old. You start with Machado and Silvetti's monumental entry pavilion, and then zigzag up a series of staircases, through a carefully choreographed sequence of modernist areas, until you reach the amphitheater, where the space finally opens up. Only then does the renovated, painted concrete villa come into view— brilliant in ivory and white, with a glistening red tile roof.

The facades of Machado and Silvetti's new buildings contain a few portions of travertine, a warm and handsome stone that here serves as a deft allusion to the dominant material on Meier's Getty Center campus. But the new buildings are clad mostly with striated concrete, a more provocative material that is at once harsh and delicate. Here, it is sometimes layered with marble, bronze, wood, and other forms of concrete, to create what the architects call a "strata wall." The details are exceptionally refined—the retaining walls around the entry pavilion are capped by floating panels of translucent onyx, for example— and there are lots of climbing vines, lest anyone get the idea that these architects were trying to surround the villa with the rough and austere Brutalism that was fashionable in the 1970s. (Using the modernism of the villa's own period would have been a nasty, if clever, joke.)

Machado and Silvetti seem determined to show that modernism can have texture, richness, sensuality, and scale. Their architecture recalls that of the great Italian modernist Carlo Scarpa—like Scarpa, Machado and Silvetti can slip a sheet of glass or a crisp bronze rail into a stone facade, and make it seem not a coy juxtaposition of different periods but a real engagement of the modern with the classical, so that architectural styles separated by two thousand years appear to have something to say to each other.

One of the new sections, a tall structure containing the café and the museum store, has a large outdoor colonnade. Little slabs of onyx are set atop each column, forming modernist versions of capitals. The arrangement of the onyx layers varies with each column, and the effect is of piles of books stacked at random atop cylinders. A beautiful flourish, it's as subtle, and as gently witty, a comment on the dialectic between modernism and classicism as I've ever seen.

Elevating an object of architectural derision into something serious is no small achievement. This act seems particularly noteworthy in Southern California, where the line between good and bad taste has often been blurred beyond recognition, and the experience of being in public space often consists not of strolling along a city street but of parking your car and entering some kind of artificial environment. At the Getty villa, you still park your car and enter a fantasy world, but it's no longer a glib one: it's sincere, cerebral, and elegant. By adding modern buildings, Machado and Silvetti haven't made the Getty's Roman villa any less a part of Southern California, and they haven't made it any less entertaining. They have given it the one thing it always lacked: a proper sense of history.

The New Yorker, February 27, 2006

Renzo Piano, Reconceiving Centre Pompidou, Paris

BEAUBOURG GROWS UP

When it was new, the Centre Pompidou—or the Beaubourg, as it is usually called, after its site, the Plateau Beaubourg on the edge of the Marais district in Paris—seemed to be the most modern, not to say the most radical, museum building in the world. Its architects, the Italian Renzo Piano and his English partner, Richard Rogers, had wanted the building to look like a factory. Actually, it looks like a cartoon version of a factory, with enormous, bright-painted pipes and ducts running up and down the exterior. It was designed in a style that was, in the mid-1970s, just beginning to be called high tech, but Piano and Rogers managed to avoid the solemn Puritanism that would soon come to characterize architecture of that type. More than anything else, their building seemed like a slap in the face at gentility.

In 1971, when they won an international competition for the commission to design the museum, Piano was thirty-three and Rogers was thirty-seven. "We were terrible boys," Piano said to me recently. "The building was designed by young, insolent people." Influenced by the exuberance and irreverence that characterized the student uprisings in Paris in the late 1960s, they felt that the building should symbolize openness and change, and they put huge, unobstructed floors in the interior rather than a series of permanent galleries. Then they put all the structural workings of the building on the outside, as if to say that hiding the truth was to be avoided in architecture, as it should be in politics. They envisioned the Beaubourg as a people's museum that would represent the aspirations of the late twentieth century the way the British Museum had represented the aspirations of the nineteenth.

The Beaubourg was a popular success on a scale that far exceeded its architects' intentions. They had planned for about five thousand visitors a day, and more than four times that number came, on average, many of them tourists who took free rides up the glass-enclosed escalator that is attached to the facade and offers a spectacular view of the Paris skyline. The plaza in front of the building became a hangout for jugglers, street musicians, fire-eaters, and drug dealers. By the mid-1990s, there had been so much wear and tear on the building that it was looking shabby, and the exterior underwent an elaborate refurbishment. Then the whole building was shut down for more than two years, and the interior was renovated. It reopened in January, and, depending on how you view these things, it is now either a perfect museum for the twenty-first century or a travesty of what it was intended to be. Renzo Piano says that the redesign was simply a response to the need for a building that is "more rational, maybe as a mirror of a more rational culture." Richard Rogers, now Lord Rogers, is less sanguine. He told me he thought that the building had been "bureaucratized" and that the renovation "undermined the basic principles of the original design."

Piano and Rogers had entered the competition for the commission, which was sponsored by the French government, thinking that they didn't have much of a shot at winning. They doubted that the jury, which included the architects Philip Johnson and Oscar Niemeyer, would be sympathetic to their taste, and they assumed that if, by some miracle, they were selected, the government of France would be unwilling to go along with the decision. Piano and Rogers and their collaborators, the most important of whom was the British engineer Peter Rice, of Ove Arup & Partners, put together the kind of plan that is submitted by young architects who feel they have nothing to lose. No one was more startled than they were when the jury gave their design the only prize among 681 entries, and President Georges Pompidou, who had initiated the project, ordered it built.

It was as if the Metropolitan Museum of Art needed a new wing and asked a couple of young architects at Columbia who dabbled in radical ideas to design it.

Pompidou died during the construction of the center, and it became a memorial to him. It also became something of a watershed in museum building. The Beaubourg, more than any building since Frank Lloyd Wright's Guggenheim, made architecture the focal point of museum design and shifted the priorities of the contemporary museum from connoisseurship to public entertainment. But the Beaubourg pretty quickly looked neither radical nor sophisticated. Throughout the 1980s and 1990s, new museums were built in other cities that, if not equal to the Beaubourg in sheer, dazzling energy, possessed a degree of finesse that was lacking in Paris. When you compare the Beaubourg with buildings like Renzo Piano's Menil Collection in Houston, Richard Meier's Getty in Los Angeles, or Frank Gehry's Guggenheim in Bilbao, it seems like an overeager adolescent. By the late 1990s, the place had settled into a kind of arrested development, its brashness no longer exciting, its frame tired and faded. The fact that it needed a paint job didn't help. It is something of a paradox that in order to look good, the rough-and-tumble structure has to be kept in as pristine a condition as a building by Mies van der Rohe. But the real problem was that the very concept of its design, which depended on a certain degree of shock, had come to seem as comfortable as an old shoe. In twenty years, the Beaubourg had become a relic.

That it was the most endearing contemporary relic in Paris—the only large-scale structure built in the city in the last quarter-century that was not only admired but loved—wasn't enough to justify leaving it alone, in the view of the bureaucrats who manage it. For one thing, the principal mission of the building has always been to house the Musée National d'Art Moderne and a public research library, and although for a few years the building's success inspired a resurgence of Paris as a venue for contemporary art, the open floors of the Beaubourg were graceless and awkward and didn't provide a sympathetic environment for artworks. There wasn't enough wall space to exhibit much of the museum's collection, and the research library wasn't well laid out. The place was most successful as a magnet for tourists. "There were people who didn't even know there was a museum here," says Werner Spies, the director of the Musée National d'Art Moderne.

Spies and his colleagues, including Jean-Jacques Aillagon, the president of the center, tried to respect the original architecture of the building during the long reconstruction period. They started with the paint job, which made the place look as crisp and as fresh as it had in the 1970s. And they asked Piano and Rogers, who have practiced separately since 1977, though they remain close friends, to oversee an internal reorganization of the building which would expand the galleries by 50 percent, relocate and update the library, move the administrative offices outside the building, and change the public space in the main entry hall at the ground level. The famous outside escalator was redesigned so that it is accessible only to people who have bought tickets to the museum. The library now has its own entrance, off the main lobby. The open spaces for showing art were replaced with a series of small white galleries designed by the French architect Jean-François Bodin. The new galleries are closed, rigid, formal. They are also dull, which is the one thing the original Beaubourg never was. The entry hall now has signs with lists of corporate sponsors, led by Yves Saint Laurent, lest anyone doubt that the days when the French government paid all the bills are over.

Rogers so hated the way the building was being changed that he walked off the job midway during the design process, leaving it to his former partner. Rogers is not known for holding his tongue when he thinks that his social conscience is being compromised—he was the only prominent architect in Britain to speak out against Prince Charles when the prince was making a career of bashing modern architecture—and he felt that the renovation destroyed the very essence of the building he and Piano had designed. "The museum was never supposed to be a traditional museum—everything was supposed to be on the outside to give you those great football fields of space to allow total flexibility," he said to me. "In the original concept, there was no real differentiation between the library and the museum. It was a cultural center, and now it is a set of departments." Renzo Piano is more philosophical. "Architecture is a bouillabaisse," he says. "We wanted a flexible building, and we have to accept it. I am unhappy about making people pay to go up the escalator, but these are inevitable things."

Being "flexible" enough to accommodate the needs of the institution meant relinquishing the kind of "total flexibility" of layout that Rogers was talking about. Of course, that kind of flexibility is often antithetical to the display of art. If being able to shift partitions at will were all that mattered, then paintings would look better at the Javits Center than at the Met. But there is something of a conundrum in Piano's attempt to justify the changes at the Beaubourg as being in the spirit of the architects' original idea of openness to change, since these particular changes have created an interior space that is firmly fixed in a conventional mode. The renovated building is a triumph for those who believe that art should be shown in neutral settings, which is not what Piano and Rogers had in mind.

The Beaubourg isn't suitable for a permanent installation of art under any circumstances; it is too big, too sprawling, too full of its own energy. Unfortunately, the small-to-medium-sized works of modern art which are in the museum's collection look best in the kind of scaled-down galleries that obscure the building. Although there are a couple of exceptions in the renovated space—like the windows at the end of the hopelessly long central spine of rooms, where there are open views of the city—most of the new galleries seem to overpower Rogers and Piano's original architecture and, at the same time, to appear weak and trite inside it. The escalator ride up the exterior is as glorious as ever—nowhere else does a panoramic view of the roofscapes of Paris reveal itself at such elegant, measured speed—but when you get to the fourth and fifth floors, where the permanent collection is housed, you feel as though you had stumbled onto a Hollywood soundstage on which someone has constructed a set for a movie about the Museum of Modern Art.

The Beaubourg was intended to provide a circus tent for culture; it was not to be just a Kunsthalle. I think that Piano and Rogers were more prescient in their design than even they knew. The Beaubourg has always seemed suitable for a time when art would be less fixed than it was in the early 1970s—for a time when media and entertainment and technology and art blurred together. This is a building that predates the computer revolution, and yet it positively shouts New Media. It would have been wonderful to see what architects like Liz Diller and Ric Scofidio, the gifted New York–based designers who specialize in using new media as the inspiration for architectural form, could have done with the assignment of updating the Beaubourg.

It isn't Piano's fault that the building has been eased into the role of a temple of culture. After Rogers left, Piano seems to have stayed around largely to prevent the building from being compromised still further, and his sensibility, which I would describe as a benign and tolerant humanism married to exquisite aesthetic judgment, has surely given the renovation project what conscience it has. The building was extraordinarily difficult to change, in fact, because its fundamental nature is embodied in its brashness. Beaubourg may be the only celebrated monumental work of architecture in which youthful innocence could almost be said to have been the controlling architectural idea. "We didn't know when we won the competition what the culture was," Piano said to me. "At that age, we wanted to make a joke. At that age, you don't really know, so we said this is like a factory, come and enjoy . . . We had an innocence, an innocent energy."

Most monumental buildings, whatever their architectural style, are grounded in adult authority. The Invalides and the Louvre, for instance, project propriety, formality, and the sense that there is a set of rules that public buildings follow. The Beaubourg was designed to thumb its nose at authority. It is a very beautiful and exciting building, but it was conceived almost as a piece of adolescent rowdiness, and from the beginning this presented a problem. If the Beaubourg was so likable that everyone, even the government, could fall in love with it, then it wasn't much of a threat to authority after all.

Rogers was more attached to the vaguely socialist leanings of the original design—right this way to the escalator, free views on top of the cultural circus for all—which is why he has been more bothered than Piano about the building's reconstruction. He has had a harder time giving up on the youthful irreverence and subversive intentions of the original design. But how can adolescence be sustained for more than a generation? That is one of the paradoxes the Beaubourg presents, and maybe there is no real solution. To turn the Beaubourg into a grown-up museum, as has just been done, violates the basic nature of its design. On the other hand, that design, at least on the inside, never worked very well, and there was little practical justification for retaining it. To have done so would have been merely sentimental and would have required us to believe that the earnest innocence out of which this building was born meant something still.

The New Yorker, May 22, 2000

Norman Foster, British Museum Courtyard, London

THE SUPREME COURT

The British Museum has long embodied eighteenth- and nineteenth-century notions of what a museum should be— notions that were more enduring in Europe than in the United States. It was essentially a storehouse for great artifacts of Western culture: the Elgin Marbles, the Rosetta Stone, Egyptian sarcophagi, and busts of Roman emperors, all arrayed in long, dark, gloomy halls. Now, however, large museums have difficulty surviving unless they adapt to the American model of entertainment center and marketplace. Both the Louvre and the Tate Modern, for instance, have been designed to accommodate the kinds of crowds a sports arena gets. Not that the museum as agora is necessarily a bad thing. Since so many formerly communal experiences—shopping, working, strolling about—take place in cyberspace, there is something to be said for an institution that lures people out of the house.

In any case, there are budgets to be balanced and ever bigger audiences to cater to. So it is not surprising that the British Museum, whose sooty columns and musty classical grandeur set the tone of Bloomsbury for more than a century, has undergone a $150 million renovation and acquired a new set of shops and cafés and multipurpose auditoriums and a vast, glass-covered courtyard designed by Norman Foster. The project, which received nearly half of its funding from the national lottery, was overshadowed by all the hoopla about the Tate Modern across the river, but the Great Court of the British Museum may turn out to be the most important addition to London's cultural scene in many years. It's also an inspiring example of how a large museum can recast itself without totally selling out.

The new courtyard is stunningly beautiful. The graceful glass-and-steel roof manages both to respect the classical architecture of the original building and to provide a gentle counterpoint to it. Norman Foster seems to relish stylistic clashes. His glass dome atop the Reichstag, in Berlin, for example, has a kind of blustery bravado. But he refers to the new latticework roof at the British Museum as a "veil" over the building, and although the project is as elegant and as sleek as everything else Foster designs, it is also pleasingly deferential. He seems to have let a bit of tentativeness creep in, and this has strengthened rather than weakened the project.

The Great Court has an unusual architectural history. The museum was designed by Robert Smirke and was constructed in stages between 1823 and 1847. Smirke's design called for an open courtyard in the center, which the architect envisioned as an elaborately landscaped space where visitors could promenade. But money was tight, and the courtyard was never developed as Smirke intended. Instead, after lying empty for a few years, it was given over to the British Library. In 1857, a spectacular round reading room designed by Robert Smirke's brother, Sydney, was built in the middle of the space, and the room was soon surrounded by several other structures that held book stacks. Sydney Smirke's reading room, which is topped by a 106-foot-high cast-iron dome, is one of the great interior spaces in Europe, and until now it has been off-limits to the public. As far as most of the people visiting the British Museum knew, there was no courtyard at all. They experienced the museum as a sequence of dull interior rooms.

I have never understood how scholars could concentrate in the reading room—where Karl Marx did his research for *Das Kapital* and where Joseph

Conrad, Virginia Woolf, and T. S. Eliot worked. It is a distractingly sumptuous place, nearly as large as the domed interior of the Pantheon, in Rome, and more ornate. Sir Anthony Panizzi, an intense, demanding Italian scholar-administrator who was appointed Keeper of Printed Books in 1837, came up with the idea of a round room with a desk in the center and readers' tables radiating out like spokes. His plan was not universally admired. The Keeper of Manuscripts, Sir Frederic Madden, said that the room was "splendid," but "perfectly unsuited, I think, to its purpose, and an example of reckless extravagance occasioned through the undue influence of a Foreigner."

The reading room is a round drum roughly three stories high. The inside is lined with books and narrow balconies that give access to them. A series of twenty double-arched windows runs around this base, and above them the great cast-iron dome extends toward a glass lantern at the very top of the building. The dome, which is covered in copper on the outside and with a form of papier-mâché on the inside, is exuberantly delicate and a masterpiece of engineering. Its iron ribs constitute an exceptionally light framework for such a large structure. Smirke emphasized the delicacy of the dome by painting the interior a soft French blue and a cream color and by adding a lot of gilding.

By the middle of the twentieth century, it was pretty clear that the library no longer fit in the museum building, despite several attempts to shoehorn more stack space into odd corners. In the early 1970s, the two institutions were formally separated, and funds were found for a new structure to house the library on a site near St. Pancras Station, a mile away from the museum. The functions of the round reading room, along with the books and papers that were stored in the space Robert Smirke had intended to be a courtyard, would be transferred to the new building. Thus the museum had an unusual opportunity to expand without engaging in the messy issue of finding additional land to build on.

Initial discussions about new uses for the courtyard took place without much sense of urgency, since the design of the library was controversial, and the project had run into so many political and financial problems that no one had any idea when construction of a new building would actually begin. (It took sixteen years, from 1982 to 1998, to complete.) In 1993 an architectural competition was held for the museum redesign. Norman Foster won with a plan that called for demolishing the book stacks that filled the courtyard and preserving just the reading room itself, which would become a freestanding cylinder inside a glass-covered square. The reading room's exterior walls had never been visible, and Foster covered the newly revealed cylinder with Spanish limestone. Then he wrapped a pair of monumental staircases around it to bring visitors to a restaurant on a platform built out over the north side of the piazza space. He tucked small museum shops underneath the staircases and put two lecture halls underground, beneath the court. The shops and the restaurant are relatively unobtrusive. When you walk into the Great Court from the museum's main entrance, you see open space punctuated by a couple of pieces of monumental sculpture. Straight ahead, there is a small doorway that leads into the reading room. Eventually, there will be an abstract sculpture in front of it, which may be the one jarring note in the entire undertaking. But the key thing is that commerce is out of the line of sight. Unlike many other institutions, the British Museum doesn't blur the distinction between the things displayed and the things for sale.

The cylinder is rather too big for the area it inhabits, although there is plenty of breathing space on the south side. Visitors who enter there move from openness into compression, guided by the gentle curves of the cylinder, and then back again into roomier areas. The use of a freestanding drum to turn a rectangular space into something dynamic recalls the concrete cylinder containing a staircase in one of the atriums of the Yale Center for British Art designed by Louis Kahn. Foster is working on a much bigger scale here, but there is the same sense of a space made transcendent by the way in which roundness plays off against straight lines.

At first, the Great Court seems French in its spatial arrangement—formal, symmetrical, a straight-on axis from the entrance. But then you realize it is really more like an Italian urban space, somewhat eccentric in the way it pushes and pulls you in different directions. The porticoes Smirke designed to face the courtyard (which have been unseen for more than a century) are revealed not at a great distance but right up close, and often at unexpected angles, the way you might come upon a Baroque church on a narrow street in Rome. Actually, only three of the porticoes are Smirke's. The one on the south side, through which visitors pass from the museum's main entrance into the courtyard, was demolished years ago, and Foster has replicated it, more or less as originally designed, though with slightly deeper proportions and with additional openings in the facade behind it.

Smirke used Portland limestone, and the new portico was supposed to be constructed of the same material, but it turned out that the contractor substituted a cheaper French stone. This caused something of a scandal, and preservationists insisted that the new portico be dismantled so that the offending stone could be replaced with the one called for in the original design. ("We were mugged," Suzanna Taverne, the museum's managing director, said.) In the end, the portico stayed, and a few hundred thousand dollars was taken off the contractor's fee. Actually, the French stone looks perfectly decent, especially when one considers that any new stone is going to look different from stone that has been exposed for more than a hundred years. The most striking thing about the new portico is not what it is made of but that an ardent modernist like Foster chose to build such a piece of historical replication at all.

He did so, I think, because of the strange Chinese-puzzle nature of the architectural problem he was given. The reading room is something old set inside something new (the newly revealed courtyard) that, in turn, is set inside something old (the museum building). Foster wanted his glass roof to provide a counterpoint to something old on all four sides, not something old on three sides and something new on the fourth. Thus he was willing to copy a historical form, something that modernists almost never do. It seems that he has come around to thinking that there are instances in which appropriateness to place means more than appropriateness to time.

The round reading room is now a library as well as a kind of museum of its own past. Sydney Smirke's original color scheme, which had been obscured by various other decorations over the years—including, in 1907, a list of the great figures in British literature (nineteen men, no women)—has been restored. Opening up the room to public view after nearly 150 years would have been enough to justify the entire Great Court project. But Foster's new courtyard is as exhilarating as Smirke's masterpiece, which it both coddles and reveres. The Great Court is vastly more graceful than any of the contemporary wings at the Metropolitan Museum in New York, including the Temple of Dendur enclosure. (Of course, it also has an affinity with the Temple of Dendur, which seems to exist primarily as a high-end catering hall.) Norman Foster has rarely been so eager to embrace complexity and ambiguity. He has made the whole complicated architectural history of the building visible. In the new Great Court, Robert Smirke gets along with Sydney Smirke, and Norman Foster spreads a peaceful blanket of glass over them. Foster has reached out to embrace classicism, at least symbolically, and he has made modernism seem less hard-edged.

The New Yorker, January 8, 2001

Santiago Calatrava, Milwaukee Art Museum (above); Tadao Ando,
Pulitzer Foundation, St. Louis

ART HOUSES

The new Quadracci Pavilion at the
Milwaukee Art Museum does not so much
resolve the struggle between art and
architecture as dodge it. Santiago Calatrava,
the Spanish architect-engineer who
is known for some of the most beautiful

bridges of our time, has designed a spectacular building that has nothing to do with the display of art and everything to do with getting crowds to come to the museum. The main part of this $75 million building, technically an addition to the museum's older sections, which were designed by Eero Saarinen and David Kahler, is a huge, flamboyant structure of metal and glass that looks like an enormous bird, or a white version of Picasso's famous sculpture in downtown Chicago, blown up to monumental scale. It has masts, cables, a 250-foot-long suspended pedestrian bridge, and, as its coup de théâtre, a pair of movable wings made of metal louvers that form a gigantic brise-soleil, or architectural sunscreen. The only art in this portion of Calatrava's building is a Calder mobile near the front door. The big attraction is the brise-soleil, which opens to a wingspan of two hundred feet. The wings flap on schedule, like the eruptions of Old Faithful. Watching the brise-soleil open and close is a lot more fun than seeing one of those lumbering stadium roofs retract. The building is exquisitely light, and it seems almost to lift off the ground.

Most of the museum's art collection is housed in renovated galleries in the old buildings, a couple of hundred feet away. But one now enters the museum through the Quadracci Pavilion, which has a ninety-foot-high interior space, a kind of glass-and-steel tent, that the museum calls its reception hall. Tying this to the older galleries is a long, low section, also by Calatrava, that contains a large gallery for temporary exhibitions flanked by a pair of windowed promenades, one of which looks out over Lake Michigan. Calatrava's gallery is both handsome and flexible, but no one is ever going to mistake it for the main event. It can't compete with the reception hall and its brise-soleil, which— judging from the numbers of people who visited on the opening weekend, last month—has made Milwaukee feel rather good about itself.

Calatrava has neutralized the dilemma that has been at the center of museum design for more than a generation. Ever since Frank Lloyd Wright designed the Guggenheim in New York, architects have been accused, some-times rightly, of making museums in which architectural excitement is more important than showing art to its best advantage. Many of the new museums have been great buildings and wildly popular. They prove not only that you don't need to show art in a plain, neutral box but also that people are often more eager to see a thrilling container than what is contained in it. But no one, not even Frank Gehry in the Guggenheim in Bilbao, has been able to erase the tension between the desire of architects for self-expression and the desire of curators for simple spaces that don't compete with art.

Calatrava's solution is deft, to say the least. By putting the art—or that small amount of art that his building is expected to contain—in a low, matter-of-fact connecting structure that clearly defers both to the flashier part of his own new design and to the museum's original complex, Calatrava was able to provide plain-vanilla galleries and an icon at the same time. It's not all that different from what, say, I. M. Pei did more than twenty years ago in the East Building of the National Gallery of Art in Washington, where a splashy space wows crowds and, meanwhile, the art is tucked into ordinary galleries off to the side. Calatrava is just more honest about it.

It is logical, and also morally comfortable, to believe that, since art is the art museum's reason for being, the spaces that house it should be the most important ones in a building. Art uplifts, and, if the art museum is designed as a temple to art, it uplifts, too. But for at least two decades, the art museum has functioned less like a temple than like an agora. So what if Calatrava's building feels a little like the Guggenheim rotunda without the spiral, or the Great Hall of the Metropolitan Museum without the galleries? It is a kind of urban event, and one of the most pleasing exercises in structural exhibitionism in a long time. Since the main part of the building barely engages with art, it need not be compared with recent museums by architects such as Gehry, Renzo Piano, and Peter Zumthor. It's an extravaganza that says something about the exhilaration of well-crafted structures and about the ennobling potential of public places.

This is Calatrava's first building in the United States, and it bears some resemblance to American architecture that he admires, particularly Eero Saarinen's TWA Terminal at Kennedy Airport. The interior of the reception hall is an homage to that building, with the same swooping space, but it is lighter and more graceful. Calatrava is a lyricist. His architecture soars, and it celebrates light, transparency, and soft, sensuous curves. All of Calatrava's structures are tensile, and even the ones that don't literally move, as this one does, suggest movement in their forms.

Calatrava is so adroit a designer that he has even managed to make something lovely out of the museum's basement parking garage, which has a few swoops and curves of its own. The entrance to the garage is reminiscent of Frank Lloyd Wright's Johnson Wax headquarters, thirty miles south of Milwaukee, in Racine, and the huge, arching trusses recall Antonio Gaudí, with whom Calatrava has often been compared. The hundred-car underground garage even has natural light, brought in via skylights along the perimeter. It's a shame to waste it as a place for parking cars, since it is about as good a space for the display of contemporary art as you could ask for.

Attracting the multitudes has become an entrenched priority for art museums, and it is hard to know what to make of a new institution that goes into business by announcing its intention to keep visitor counts low. The Pulitzer Foundation for the Arts, in St. Louis, opened its new building last month, and, so that the galleries won't feel too crowded, it plans to allow the public in only two days a week, and only by appointment. There is no café, and there is no gift shop. The *New York Times* reported that some people thought the place might be a bit too elitist to deserve its tax exemption.

I don't think Tadao Ando, the Japanese architect who designed the Pulitzer Foundation, and Emily Rauh Pulitzer, the collector who built it, would have known how to make a museum any other way, and they have created one of the finest small museums of our time. Ando's two-story concrete building is the greatest work of architecture to go up in St. Louis since 1891, when Louis Sullivan's Wainwright Building—the first skyscraper that can be called a fully resolved, mature work of art—opened. The Pulitzer Foundation and the Wainwright are both small, dense, and emotionally powerful buildings. Ando has thought through the idea of the small museum with the same freshness and honesty that Sullivan brought more than a century ago to the idea of the high-rise office building.

Where Sullivan is ornate, Ando is austere. But Ando, who won the Pritzker Prize in 1995, is not like most minimalists, and his work is not simple. His buildings, which are almost all of concrete, are subtle compositions of masses and planes that play against light and, often, against natural elements such as water and plantings. An Ando building is an object in the light, an object in the sun, an object in the wind. It is continually acted upon by nature. This is not the machine in the garden, to use the classic metaphor of early modernism and its relationship to nature.

Perhaps alone among the world's important architects, Ando is essentially self-taught. He was apprenticed to a carpenter in Japan, and he spent some time as a professional boxer, which may account for the intense physicality of his buildings. When you are in one of them, you have a sense of your body in an open space, or in an enclosure, or you feel that you are floating, or lifted up by light. The Pulitzer Foundation is Ando's first public building in the United States—he designed a private house in Chicago a few years ago, and a gallery at the Art Institute of Chicago—and it has already led to other commissions, including the Museum of Modern Art in Fort Worth, which is now under construction, and the Calder Museum in Philadelphia.

Emily Pulitzer and her husband, Joseph Pulitzer Jr., the owner of the *St. Louis Post-Dispatch*, approached Ando in 1991 and asked him to renovate an old industrial building in the midtown neighborhood of St. Louis to house their collection of contemporary art. The project stalled when Joe Pulitzer became ill, but after his death, in 1993, his widow went back to Ando and asked him to design an entirely new building for an adjacent site. The building is roughly U-shaped, with a reflecting pool between two parallel wings. One of the wings is two stories high and contains the main gallery, which is 170 feet long; the other wing is one story high and has a glass-enclosed pavilion, a terrace, and a garden planted with pygmy bamboo on its roof. At the bottom of the U is an enclosed entry court, an interior vestibule, and a stair hall leading up to a mezzanine that opens to the roof garden.

The building is not large—the total gallery space is less than seven thousand square feet—but it is complex, and its overall shape cannot be grasped easily from the outside. From some viewpoints, it seems to allude to Mies van der Rohe's Barcelona Pavilion; from others, it could be an abstract version of Wright's Unity Temple or just a concrete fortress. You don't get the layout instantly once you go in, either, but this doesn't seem to matter, since with Ando there is a joy in discovering space as it unfolds. He has created an extraordinary series of rooms, and you want to move through them slowly, since they are powerful spaces in themselves and, at the same time, remarkable exercises in the subtle relationships between art and architecture. One gallery, a twenty-three-foot cube, contains a pair of Rothkos and a dark Richard Serra on linen that wraps around a corner; the room at once forces you to focus inward and lifts you up, like Borromini. The main gallery, which contains three Roy Lichtensteins, two Andy Warhols, and a Philip Guston, among other works, has a six-foot-high band of windows along one side, running down to the floor and looking out to the reflecting pool; midway in this complex space, a monumental staircase descends to a lower level, turning the end of the gallery into a double-height space top-lit by a skylight. Under the skylight on that far wall, and anchoring the entire area, is *Blue Black*, a twenty-eight-foot-high, two-panel work by Ellsworth Kelly that is one of two works of art that Emily Pulitzer commissioned for the building. The other is Richard Serra's torqued spiral, called *Joe* in honor of Joseph Pulitzer, which fills an outdoor courtyard. Both the Kelly and the Serra, like the building itself, inspire a literally physical mixture of joy and awe.

Ando's architecture is not easy or superficially entertaining. Yet it is deeply sensual. Architects have always struggled with ways to express the spiritual, and, of all architects alive today, I think Ando has come more consistently close to achieving a sense of spirituality in the spaces he makes and in the walls he wraps around them. The walls of the Pulitzer Foundation are made of a poured-in-place concrete that is satiny smooth. The building is comparable to the work of Louis Kahn, but it seems more rigorous and less fussy than Kahn's. The only small museum in America worthy of comparison to the Pulitzer Foundation is Kahn's Kimbell, in Fort Worth, yet the Kimbell seems almost busy beside the Pulitzer.

Ando owes plenty to Kahn, of course, as he does to Le Corbusier. But there is a lot about his work that is utterly Japanese, particularly the way in which it seems to connect to the notion that one can, within a limited amount of space and with limited gestures, evoke a broader world. Ando's rooms, his spaces, are metaphors, the way a Japanese alcove full of precisely composed objects is a set of symbols. His work sometimes seems to resemble a classic Zen garden rather than other architecture. It is precise and controlled, and it contains enormous compressed power. Ando boils things down to their core. His architecture is not plain, but richness distilled to its essence.

The New Yorker, November 5, 2001

Tadao Ando, Modern Art Museum of Fort Worth

A DELICATE BALANCE

The Kimbell Art Museum in Fort Worth is an architectural masterpiece. It was completed in 1972, just two years before its designer, Louis Kahn, died, and it has become probably the most revered museum design of the second half of the twentieth century. The Kimbell isn't very large, but a move to expand it a few years ago was beaten back by those who believe that Kahn's composition of travertine walls and concrete vaults washed by natural light is so close to perfect that it should be left alone.

In 1996, the trustees of the Modern Art Museum of Fort Worth acquired an eleven-acre site across the street from the Kimbell and commissioned the Japanese architect Tadao Ando to design a new building for them. This was a little like asking someone to put up a church next door to Chartres. The commission seemed even more daunting because Ando, who is sixty-one years old, had never taken on a major public building in the United States, although he had designed a small private museum for the Pulitzer Foundation in St. Louis, which was completed last year, and a house in Chicago. Ando's work is refined and restrained. It has an austere delicacy that seemed unsuited to a large-scale project.

In fact, Ando has much in common with Louis Kahn. Both are masters of concrete and know how to coax a sense of spirituality out of harsh materials. They have both made something of a fetish of natural light, and both have an almost visceral repugnance toward frivolity and commercialism. Ando's new building opened this month. It is taller and wider than the Kimbell, but its expansiveness is not the reason it has become the dominant presence in the Fort Worth Cultural District, which also includes the Amon Carter Museum, by Philip Johnson, and the Will Rogers Memorial Center, a sprawling, vaguely Art Deco auditorium. The Kimbell is the work of a brilliant, highly self-conscious master. It is small and dense, and you sense Kahn's anguish in the building. Ando's swaggering new Modern, on the other hand, has a kind of easy poise.

For much of his career, Ando, who was awarded the Pritzker Prize in 1995, has synthesized Western modern architecture with a Japanese sensibility, and he has taken the synthesis to a new level here. The traditional Japanese controlled landscape with a courtyard garden has been blown up to Texas scale. Ando's Modern is shaped roughly like a fat, bulky L, and it faces two streets, from both of which it looks like a sprawling box sheathed in aluminum panels with vertical fins, set underneath a flat, overhanging roof. A parking lot separates the building from the streets—perhaps a reticent number of parking spaces by Texas standards, but still too much for the building. A tall, curving sculpture by Richard Serra stands at the corner of the lot. You could easily mistake the place for some corporation's headquarters.

But then you enter the building and all is forgiven. Actually, you don't even have to go in. As you approach the main entrance, where the aluminum gives way to glass, you can see a huge, two-story lobby crossed by a concrete bridge, with an acre and a half of lagoon on the other side. The landscape around the lagoon is a rolling lawn punctuated by trees. Three rectangular glass pavilions appear to float on the lagoon, as does an oval-shaped glass café. Unlike Kahn, who made a quiet exterior to house a jewel-box interior, Ando has used a quiet exterior to mask what is really another set of exteriors, turned away from the street. It's an extraordinary space, at once tranquil and exhilarating.

Of course, Fort Worth is not Kyoto, and there are problems. For instance, a yellow-and-blue billboard promoting a local personal-injury lawyer glares over a wall separating Ando's meticulously crafted landscape from the street. ("Well, that's probably a pretty lucrative billboard," a museum spokesperson said to me when I asked about it.) Then again, the Japanese have always been skillful at tuning out the garishness of contemporary life. Ando's response to Fort Worth sprawl is neither to embrace it nor to try to destroy it but simply not to see it when it interrupts his line of vision. The Japanese have also traditionally made much of what they call "borrowed scenery," or attractive distant vistas, and the Modern has plenty of borrowed scenery as well. Some of it is along the lines of the billboard, but since the cultural district that contains the Kimbell and the Modern is on a slight rise about a mile from downtown Fort Worth, there are enticing views of the skyline.

Many of Ando's early sketches for the Modern, which are now on display in the lobby, show his building in relation to Kahn's, but Ando is too strong an architect to pay homage by copying, and there are only two places in the new building where you sense that he is evoking Kahn. One is a vaulted ceiling that loosely echoes the shape of the Kimbell ceilings, and the other is a rounded concrete wall (actually the end of an elliptical gallery) that looks very much like a concrete stairwell in one of Kahn's other celebrated buildings, the Yale Center for British Art.

Not the least of the virtues of Ando's building is how well organized it is. You walk into the large, formal lobby, and the entire layout is apparent: museum shop to the left; auditorium to the right; lagoon straight ahead, with the café visible at the right side of the water and the pavilions jutting out to the left. The pavilions, which contain elegantly proportioned glass-enclosed galleries, are covered with concrete roofs that extend over the water on three sides and are supported by unusual, Y-shaped concrete pillars. The pillars could be considered abstract trees or human figures with raised arms, but I doubt that is what the architect had in mind. I suspect that he was just making sure that the vista across the water was not static. He need not have worried. The water ripples in the wind, and the light changes it, so that one moment it is reflecting the architecture and the next distorting it. This is hardly the first building to be set against a reflecting pool—Ando uses the trick all the time, and so have plenty of Western architects—but it feels new here. Ando is brilliant at inventing ways to make you experience the connection between the building and the water not just from the outside but also from within. For example, at one end of the main galleries, there is what appears to be a corridor leading to a stair, but as you move along the solid wall, it becomes glass, and you discover that you are gently descending toward the water, almost being set into it.

Ando's galleries are not tucked into leftover space, as they are in so many museums of the previous generation. They are gracious, clear, generous, and varied. A few of them are two stories high, but they never feel overwhelming, and there are enough intimate areas for exhibiting smaller pieces. Most of the galleries on the second floor are lit by natural light. There is fifty-three thousand square feet of gallery space spread over the main body of the building and the pavilions, making this one of the largest museums of modern art in the country.

Michael Auping, the museum's chief curator, installed its admirable collection with great sensitivity to Ando's architecture. Putting Anselm Kiefer's vast lead-tin-and-steel sculpture *Book with Wings* all by itself in a small concrete-walled elliptical gallery and Andy Warhol's chilling green-and-black *Self Portrait* of 1986 at the top of the main staircase is the kind of thing that can be done only by a strong-willed curator who feels confident about working with a strong-willed architect. Ando has described the galleries as "concrete volumes encased in a glass-skin box," and Auping's brilliant eye for hanging art in them is particularly evident in the three pavilions over the lagoon. The concrete walls don't come right up to the glass. Room was left for a walkway between the concrete and the glass, and when you are strolling along, you can't decide whether you are in a cathedral ambulatory or on a pier. There is a single piece of art at the end of each pavilion: a thin sculpture by Cy Twombly in one, a set of steel panels by Carl Andre in another, and a Michelangelo Pistoletto sculpture of an Etruscan figure against a mirror in the third. One piece holds the center of its space, another anchors the floor, and the other engages the wall. All three occupy less of the gallery than you might expect them to, and each comes as a surprise.

Many museums these days look their best before any art is installed in them. This is the first great museum building in a generation that gets even better when art is added.

The New Yorker, December 30, 2002

Zaha Hadid, Contemporary Arts Center, Cincinnati (above); Frank Gehry, Fisher Center for the Performing Arts, Annandale-on-Hudson, New York

ARTISTIC LICENSE

Zaha Hadid is famous for producing extraordinary drawings of visionary projects, such as a nightclub in the hills of Hong Kong that looks like a series of broken shards. She is a cultish figure who has built very little of note, save for a fire station in Germany—which was converted into a museum shortly after its completion—and a building designed for a ski jump in Innsbruck, Austria. Hadid was born into a cosmopolitan Iraqi family in Baghdad in 1950. Her father, Muhammad Hadid, was a businessman and a leader of the National Democratic Party, which advocated social democracy and parliamentary reform during the postwar years of the Hashemite monarchy. He had studied at the London School of Economics, and Zaha went to the University of Beirut and did graduate work at the Architectural Association in London, where Rem Koolhaas was her mentor. After working with Koolhaas for several years, she established her own atelier in London.

A medium-sized city in the American heartland is the last place you would expect a Zaha Hadid project to come to fruition, but Cincinnati is about to open her first American building, the new Contemporary Arts Center. The center was founded in 1939 as the Modern Art Society and for years was run from the basement of the Cincinnati Art Museum. It moved downtown in the 1960s and has been making do with galleries over a Walgreen's drugstore. That's where its most famous show took place, in 1990—the "Perfect Moment" exhibition of the photographs of Robert Mapplethorpe, which resulted in the arrest of the center's director on obscenity charges, followed by a high-profile trial about artistic freedom, in which he was acquitted.

The Mapplethorpe flap made Cincinnati look like a redneck hotbed, but it has always had a fairly progressive arts community, and the Contemporary Arts Center, under the leadership of Charles Desmarais, who took over in 1995, grew so steadily that its mediocre galleries became an embarrassment. The board decided to build a real museum, and a committee led by Richard Rosenthal, the primary patron of the new building (it is officially the Lois and Richard Rosenthal Center), conducted an international search that was narrowed down to Bernard Tschumi, Daniel Libeskind, and Hadid. The committee chose Hadid, Desmarais says, "because she has a real understanding of the contemporary art world and what we are trying to accomplish." It probably doesn't hurt that her building puts the center on the international architecture-star map.

Hadid's first designs, which were shown in 1998, were conceptually heavy and were difficult to understand except as a series of fragmented, disconnected masses floating in space. It was easy, back then, to wonder if Cincinnati, in its eagerness to embrace the avant-garde, would be willing to challenge its architect to stay within the bounds of reality. I remember thinking that Hadid might have sold the museum a bill of experimental goods. But Desmarais, Rosenthal, and their colleagues turned out to be clients of quiet, firm sophistication, and Hadid performed with considerable flexibility and great sensitivity. The result is a spectacular building. Hadid uses architecture as a way of enlivening the street and creating an incentive for entering the building, and then she lets the architecture recede in stages, from the street through the lobby into the galleries. We have become accustomed to the notion that architecture can be an energizing factor in the experience of museum-going, but Hadid knew when to turn down the voltage. The galleries feel more like loft areas of varying sizes and ceiling heights than like aggressively sculpted spaces. They are not sublime, as are the rooms Tadao Ando designed for the new Modern Art Museum in Fort Worth, but, even though they don't offer enough space for enormous sculptural pieces or monumental canvases—this is not going to be where Richard Serra shows his major work or Anselm Kiefer mounts a show—it is easy to imagine them displaying a wide range of contemporary art.

The limited size of the galleries isn't so much Hadid's doing as the result of the decision to situate the new building in the heart of downtown Cincinnati, a block from Fountain Square, the city's main public space. (Cincinnati has a real downtown, where people walk on the streets.) But a tight site on a major urban corner turns out to have inspired Hadid, not confined her. From the outside, the building looks like a mixture of concrete and black aluminum boxes that float over a glass-enclosed base. (Imagine the facade of the Whitney Museum broken into pieces and reshuffled.) This is a virtuoso composition, in which the masses hover in graceful counterpoint to one another. And, like very few other modern buildings, the Contemporary Arts Center addresses the corner—more confidently and ingeniously than any building since Paul Rudolph's Art and Architecture Building at Yale, which was finished forty years ago. Hadid wants her building to embrace the city, not to defy it, and to that end she designed the sidewalk as a concrete plane that continues into the building as the lobby floor, then curves upward and becomes the back wall. She calls this the "urban carpet," and, while it is not the most successful element of the building, it underscores her determination to present the arts center as inseparable from the streetscape.

Hadid has managed to give the building a hint of formal, institutional grandeur without making it feel formal or institutional. It is reminiscent of the work of Rudolph; of Marcel Breuer, who designed the Whitney; and of Edward Larrabee Barnes's Walker Art Center in Minneapolis. Hadid's real love is composition, and it is impossible to look at her building and not think also of Malevich, and of El Lissitzky and the other Russian Constructivists who sought a new, grandly asymmetrical modernist order. They are her true forebears, yet Hadid does not, like some architects today, approach early-modern architecture with sentimental nostalgia. She is interested in making something of her own, using a language that connects her to the early modernists who inspired her.

The arts center in Cincinnati suggests that Hadid is a better maker of facades than of space. I don't think there is a single room inside that provides quite the pleasure that the public faces of this building bring to downtown Cincinnati. What comes closest is the remarkable center stairway, which zigzags up through the building against the backdrop of the concrete "urban carpet." The stairway is made up of long runs of steel beams, painted black, and it looks almost like a series of huge gangplanks that switch back and forth. This is one building in which no one should take the elevator unless he has to.

The Contemporary Arts Center ought to stifle doubts about Zaha Hadid's work being either buildable or workable. This has been built, and it works. My greatest worry, in fact, is that Hadid will now be perceived as something of a sheep in wolf's clothing—as a gentler, easier architect than she was supposed to be. You do not have to redefine the idea of what a building is, or of what space is, to understand this building, but your ideas will be stretched. Hadid is expanding the notions of interpenetrating space and geometric composition that have preoccupied modernist architects for more than a hundred years.

With buildings by Peter Eisenman in Columbus and Cincinnati, and by Frank Gehry in Toledo, Cincinnati, and Cleveland, the state of Ohio is beginning to seem as hospitable to cutting-edge architecture as the Netherlands. But avant-garde architects are getting commissions from small cities and institutions all over the country, not only because such places are eager to use architecture as a way of establishing their cultural credentials. Smaller cities are less likely to be encumbered by the political and economic pressures that affect projects in big cities, and, these days, they are more likely to take risks. Hadid is designing a new museum in Bartlesville, Oklahoma, as an addition to Frank Lloyd Wright's Price Tower, which has been turned into a hotel and arts complex. And at Bard College, 120 miles up the Hudson from New York City, Gehry's first major public building on the East Coast, the Richard B. Fisher Center for the Performing Arts, has just opened. At a time when New York is mired in bureaucratic uncertainty over what to do with the banal buildings of Lincoln Center (and when Gehry has not been able to get anything of his built anywhere in the city, despite several proposals), Bard, under the leadership of Leon Botstein, has ended up with what may be the best small concert hall in the United States.

The building, which is set on a bucolic site of rolling, grassy hills close to the Hudson River, contains a nine-hundred-seat hall suitable for an orchestra, chamber music, or full-scale opera productions; a two-hundred-seat "black box" theater; and four rehearsal halls. It is clad in the curving metal panels characteristic of Gehry's recent architecture, but it is actually a simple set of boxes. There is no pretense that the powerful shapes are anything other than decoration. From the start, the design was determined by acoustical needs, which required a fairly conventionally shaped auditorium, and by the tightness of the budget. But, just as Zaha Hadid responded creatively to the restrictions of building on a city corner, Gehry has been stirred to brilliance by things that might have frustrated him. The undulating surfaces of stainless steel (not the more expensive titanium of the Guggenheim Museum in Bilbao) swaddle the boxes, protecting them and at the same time raising them to monumental grandeur. The swooping forms stretch out far beyond the auditorium on three sides and create a profile for the building that gently echoes the Catskill Mountains in the distance, across the Hudson. From within, they define powerful lobby spaces and raw, almost industrial rooms that repeat the complex shape of the roofline. Within the auditorium, which has concrete walls and wood details, the task of providing a sensual experience is left largely to the music. (The sound, crafted by the acoustician Yasuhisa Toyota, has an exceptionally crisp brilliance.) In a sense, the relationship between the exterior, the lobbies, and the auditorium in Gehry's building parallels that of the exterior and interior of Hadid's arts center in Cincinnati. The architecture pulls you in and then steps back, as it were. The architect defers to other artists.

It is interesting to see how Gehry's voluptuous metal forms, which always seem so right in the middle of a city, are even more dramatic in a grassy meadow. The roof hovers over the main mass of the building with nearly perfect symmetry, as if the hall were a great country house or a classical villa. In the rear, it all falls away, and the building turns into a set of plain white stucco boxes. This is one of the best things about the building, and not because it represents architectural honesty or some such nonsense. Gehry's work, despite the consistency with which it expresses the priorities of architecture—space-making, responsiveness to a functional program, connections to a particular site—is often misunderstood as primarily sculptural. But when you have what is obviously a fancy front and an ordinary back, not to mention a box in the middle, it is hard to interpret a building as anything but a building.

The Fisher Center reminds me of another great academic building for the public consumption of culture, Louis Kahn's Yale Art Gallery, which opened in 1953. The Kahn building is also somewhat hard-edged, and uses a lot of concrete, but it is nimble in a way that bespeaks both love of art and a determination to see it clearly, free of heavy-handed trappings. The Yale Art Gallery was the first great postwar modern museum, and Gehry's Fisher Center is the first great concert hall of our time. Neither one of them is the largest or the most spectacular building of its kind, but each is the freshest and the most reverent.

The New Yorker, June 2, 2003

OUTSIDE THE BOX

The first building that the Museum of Modern Art put up for itself, in 1939, wasn't sumptuous, like the Met, or extravagantly sculptural, like the Guggenheim, two decades later. It was a crisp, blunt box. Philip L. Goodwin and Edward Durell Stone's International Style architecture was defiantly austere—a retort to the idea that museums should resemble grandiose palaces. The white marble building burst out of a row of genteel brownstones on West Fifty-third Street, forcing its way into the Manhattan cityscape. It was a matter of pride that the new building looked nothing like its neighbors.

The museum's idiosyncratic appearance was always a bit of a pose, however.

Though the building's original design emphasized its difference from the old architecture around it, the ultimate goal of the Modern's curators was to make all the old stuff go away. In 1951 a new wing by Philip Johnson was built along the museum's western edge, and in 1964 another, larger Johnson addition appeared on its eastern flank. The Modern grew again in 1984, with a new section by Cesar Pelli, who also designed a companion fifty-two-story apartment tower. And with the opening, this month, of the largest expansion yet, a $425 million addition and renovation by the Japanese architect Yoshio Taniguchi, the Modern has pretty much taken over the block. The museum stretches along Fifty-third Street from just west of Fifth Avenue to just short of Sixth, and it reaches north to cover most of Fifty-fourth Street, too. You couldn't ask for a clearer symbol of how modernism has moved from the cultural fringe to the mainstream. Not only has it been years since the art at the Modern has challenged anyone—its Matisses and Pollocks are beloved by all—but Taniguchi's strict geometries of stone and glass feel as conventional as a Doric colonnade.

When the Goodwin and Stone building opened, Lewis Mumford wrote that "it possesses, to a degree not dreamed of even by the designers of Rockefeller Center, the luxury of space." But it wasn't particularly big; it was barely larger than the neighboring brownstones. Arthur Drexler, who headed the architecture and design department for decades, liked to observe that until the 1984 expansion, you could fit the entire Museum of Modern Art into the Great Hall of the Met. The Modern didn't have any enormous galleries, and most of its exhibition spaces were domestic in scale. In fact, the affection that many people felt for the museum was formed by the experience of seeing paintings in fairly small, low-ceilinged white rooms.

The 1984 expansion was an attempt to make the museum bigger without changing its basic qualities, and it didn't work very well. The galleries got somewhat larger and there were many more of them, this time connected by a prominent set of escalators—yet the place felt unnaturally attenuated, like a stretch limousine. The general feeling about the expansion was summed up by Kirk Varnedoe, the chief curator of painting and sculpture, who said, "We squeezed the last juice you could get out of that model and maybe killed it in the process." In 1996, when Varnedoe made that remark, it was clear that if the Modern were to grow again, it would have to break from small white rooms and neutral International Style architecture. Ronald Lauder, the museum's chairman, reinforced this idea, saying that, as far as the trustees were concerned, the architecture should be "as exciting as possible."

That isn't what happened. The Modern talked to dozens of architects, including Rem Koolhaas, Bernard Tschumi, Jacques Herzog and Pierre de Meuron, and Steven Holl, as well as Taniguchi, and it commissioned casual studies from ten architects and then more detailed plans from three. In 1997 the museum snubbed the radicals and hired Taniguchi, who represents not the cutting edge of architecture but, rather, a carefully wrought, highly refined modernism—a cool and reserved aesthetic that has more in common with the Modern's original credo than with the expressive direction of recent architecture and museum design.

The decision, I suspect, was based in part on disappointment with the avant-garde architects' proposals but mostly on the realization that the Modern is fundamentally a conservative institution. The choice of Taniguchi wasn't so much a failure of nerve as a moment of institutional self-knowledge. This museum wouldn't have wanted Bilbao if Frank Gehry had done it for nothing. The Modern has supported, collected, and celebrated architectural design more than any other museum in America, but it has never allowed its identity to be defined by any architecture of its own. It is one thing to display Frank Lloyd Wright models inside your galleries; it is quite another to have Rem Koolhaas design your building. The Modern chose Taniguchi, a sixty-seven-year-old architect who was educated at Harvard but has done almost all of his professional work in Japan, because it thought that he could best preserve the museum's DNA.

That doesn't explain why Taniguchi's new Modern is as good as it is. Taniguchi clearly understood a paradox that underscores this project—that his success at keeping the museum the same would come, in part, from his ability to recognize how much had to change. His Modern was going to be nearly twice the size of the previous one, and he knew better than to simply distend the old spaces. With its sleek glass walls and sharp, rectilinear lines, Taniguchi's huge building superficially resembles the Modern of old, but in many ways it represents a greater change than the oddly shaped buildings proposed by some architects the museum considered, like Herzog and de Meuron, who suggested adding a prismatic glass tower, but would have left the museum's most celebrated paintings in the old Goodwin and Stone galleries.

Although Taniguchi has created some superb display spaces, his design is most splendid, and subtle, in its urbanism. Until now, the Modern has had an unresolved, almost hesitant relationship with Midtown Manhattan. When the benign tension between the 1939 building and the old houses disappeared, nothing replaced it. The museum didn't feel connected to the city, except in the sculpture garden. When the Modern bought and demolished the Dorset Hotel, on Fifty-fourth Street, along with numerous small brownstones, its site grew not only bigger but also more complex, and Taniguchi saw this as a chance to weave the building into the fabric of the city. He gave it a new entrance, on Fifty-fourth Street, and he provided a public passageway through the block to Fifty-third Street, a huge lobby that anyone can use as a shortcut through a busy section of Midtown. The museum now faces both streets, and it has finally become part of the connective tissue of Manhattan. The old Modern occupied the street in sullen isolation; this one dances with its neighbors. Taniguchi even sliced away a bit of his building in the southeast corner of the garden, where it might have blocked a portion of St. Thomas Church, which adjoins the museum to the east. On the inside, he has set skylights on the top floor, right against the base of Pelli's tower, creating dazzling views right up its side toward the sky.

Taniguchi's facade of absolute black granite, aluminum panels, and white and gray glass is elegantly restrained. It proves that you can ensconce a building within a kind of classic modern tradition and still imbue it with freshness. And the design works on a large scale—so well that Pelli's apartment tower, which always seemed too big, now feels like a natural part of a composition. It is balanced by a new, smaller tower at the west end of the site, which houses the museum's offices, and by two monumental, portico-like gateways at the east and west ends of the sculpture garden. Those porticoes, which resemble gigantic bookends, frame the garden from inside the building, and from the outside they ennoble the transition between the garden and the museum. The sculpture garden has been restored to its original Philip Johnson design (Pelli encroached on it with a greenhouselike structure containing escalators), but the new surroundings that Taniguchi has made for it give the garden a greater intensity.

The interior is a little less reserved than the outside, but not much. The new lobby offers glimpses up to a six-story skylit atrium that cuts through the new gallery floors, Taniguchi's acknowledgment that a building this big needs vertical as well as horizontal space. The atrium contains precisely positioned openings, projections, balconies, and overlooks; it is a pristine exercise in proportion, scale, and light, not the kind of razzle-dazzle hotel architecture that the word "atrium" calls to mind.

Once inside the museum, visitors follow a sequence that is quite different from that of the old Modern: contemporary art is shown mainly in a set of large double-height galleries on the second floor, and you move backward in time as you rise through the building and the ceilings get lower. The famous paintings that once hung on the second floor are now on the fifth, in rooms that are only slightly larger than the old ones. At the top of the gallery wing, on the sixth floor, are grand, loftlike galleries for temporary exhibitions.

The main difference is that there is no longer a single sequence of movement, as there famously was at the Modern: one route through obsessively linear galleries that presented the history of art as a straight shot from Cézanne to Picasso to Matisse. The Modern's singular view of art history came, over time, to take on the stature of myth, and these days politically correct critics call it into question, but the fact is that the gallery scheme was as much a result of physical limitations as of curators' sensibilities. In the narrow confines of the old Modern, there wasn't really room to arrange things any other way. Now, though, the building is vast, and its galleries aren't episodes in a narrative but hyperlinks, offering connections in multiple directions. Terence Riley, the head of the museum's department of architecture and design, refers to the layout as resembling the child's game Chutes and Ladders—you can move straight through, or you can slip down a stairway or up an escalator and find yourself in an entirely different moment in the history of art. This approach is more liberating than confusing, because the basic order of the building is always apparent; this museum is not a structure that, like the Met, rambles so much that you get lost in it.

Some of the most pleasant aspects of the design are in the details: a magnificent cantilevered staircase of wood and metal between the fourth and fifth floors is an expert homage to Mies van der Rohe. Taniguchi makes a complex array of balconies, bridges, porticoes, stairs, openings, vistas, and passageways seem serene rather than hyperactive. The building won't feel busy enough for people weaned on the nonstop stimulation of a lot of today's architecture, and it won't feel modest enough for people who insist that God meant the Museum of Modern Art to be small. But I suspect that it will please almost everybody else.

The architect has also restored the facade of the original Goodwin and Stone building, whose Thermolux translucent panels were covered up long ago to provide more hanging space. The restoration is exquisite, and it is both uplifting and saddening. The old building looks better than it has in half a century, both inside and out. But it has been spiffed up like a grande dame who has been dressed to be put on display at her grandchild's party. When you look at the old building from Fifty-third Street, it seems almost embalmed—a beautiful relic trapped inside a sprawling temple.

The New Yorker, November 15, 2004

**Renzo Piano, Morgan Library & Museum, New York (above);
Whitney Museum Expansion, New York**

MOLTO PIANO

Renzo Piano comes from a family of
builders in Genoa, and his firm is called
Renzo Piano Building Workshop, as if
he weren't a superstar architect but just

your friendly neighborhood problem solver. Unlike most other architectural stars, Piano has no signature style. Instead, his work is characterized by a genius for balance and context, an ability to establish inventive correspondences between his buildings and those that surround them. Until now, New York hasn't had a building by Piano, but his expansion of the Morgan Library, which has just reopened as the Morgan Library & Museum, is the beachhead for what may become a significant presence in the city. A skyscraper that will serve as the new headquarters for the *New York Times* is nearing completion, and Piano's addition to the Whitney Museum of American Art is expected to begin construction within the next two years.

Piano's achievement at the Morgan is to have created a satisfying composition out of three not particularly compatible landmark structures. The old Morgan buildings are awkwardly placed around the intersection of Thirty-sixth Street and Madison Avenue. The best of them, a dazzling Renaissance palazzo that Charles F. McKim designed as J. P. Morgan's personal library in 1906, is tucked away on Thirty-sixth Street. A dull classical annex next to it, erected by Benjamin W. Morris when the library was opened to the public, in the 1920s, has the choice location, on the corner, and north of this is a staid nineteenth-century brownstone. The challenge was to link these disparate buildings while also increasing the institution's space by half. Piano's solution is simultaneously subtle and radical. To avoid overwhelming the existing structures, he hid most of the new space underground, sinking storage vaults and a concert hall four stories into the bedrock. At ground level, an elegant glass-and-steel structure weaves between the older buildings and meets the street in two rectilinear facades, one on Madison Avenue and the other on Thirty-sixth Street.

Piano has reorganized everything so that the Madison Avenue facade is the new entrance, but it is from Thirty-sixth Street that you see most clearly how he has both preserved the Morgan and transformed it. The two limestone buildings, McKim's palazzo and Morris's annex, formerly tethered by a dreary connecting walkway, had an uncomfortable relationship with each other. Piano replaced the walkway with a compact steel cube painted a color that echoes the limestone. (Inside it is a gallery of medieval religious objects.) The cube is divided into eight ridged panels, to give it scale and texture, and it provides a firm counterweight to the mass of buildings on either side. It suggests that Piano is less concerned with form-making than he is with balancing masses, materials, and scales. I'd always found Morris's annex bland, but now it seems crisply defined, while McKim's opulent palazzo has acquired a new solidity, at no cost to its elegance.

Piano does something similar on Madison Avenue, but it is less effective. The limestone buildings on Thirty-sixth Street always had an innate competitive tension, but the austere side wall of the Morris annex and the grand old brownstone are two structures with little to say to each other, and they are separated by a wider gap. Piano fills the gap with an elongated version of his steel cube—which houses a new reading room—but the proportions aren't as enticing as they are on Thirty-sixth Street. Below the reading room, the new entrance consists of glass doors stretching across the facade, an improvement over the cramped front door in the old annex, but still a little conventional.

Inside, however, the ingenuity of Piano's conception becomes gloriously apparent. He has essentially created a piazza: a fifty-two-foot-high, glass-covered atrium in the middle of the complex, with access to all parts of the institution, new and old. Too often, when exterior walls of old buildings get turned into interior elements of stylish new spaces, they take on the precious air of stage sets. But Piano's loose embrace of the other buildings is free of self-consciousness, and the result makes you think of one of those oddly shaped squares in Italian villages that feel so comfortable. He has done nothing to disguise the irregularity of the space, enhancing its casual ambience with a café off to one side and a couple of ficus trees sprouting through openings in the floor.

This is one of the greatest modern rooms in New York, not by virtue of grandeur or scale but because of the subtle links it establishes between the Morgan's older buildings and the rest of the city. Piano's piazza is defined by its complex sight lines around the rest of the collection and to the street outside. A glass wall at the east end of the piazza abuts the backs of brick apartment buildings, a jumble of ordinariness that here feels familiar and warm. You are connected to New York in this space, yet magically removed from it, as if in a garden. If you position yourself at the right point, near the center of the room, and look through the glass ceiling, you glimpse the top of the Empire State Building poking above a Madison Avenue office building.

When the Morgan hired Piano, in 2000, it had just rejected the work of the three distinguished architects it had invited to submit plans, each of whom proposed large new structures that risked overwhelming the older buildings. (A disclosure: I was an adviser to the Morgan during this competition.) Two of the schemes proposed towers where Piano has placed his court, and, as it happens, a tower is exactly what Piano has come up with for his redesign of the Whitney Museum, some forty blocks north on Madison. Here, too, he succeeded other distinguished architects—Piano's ability to take on troubled projects is a testament to his versatile aesthetic—but the Whitney poses a very different set of challenges. Marcel Breuer's inverted ziggurat is so assertive that nothing marries easily to it. Against its brooding dark granite, a treatment as gentle as Piano's Morgan project would be all but invisible; conversely, previous proposals, by Michael Graves and, later, by Rem Koolhaas, would have loomed over the building and undermined its monolithic power. Piano's solution again shows a mastery of balance, but in an entirely different way from the Morgan. He has proposed a squarish tower, sensibly set as far back from the existing structure as the rather tight lot allows. The design doesn't compete with Breuer's building, but there's nothing timid about it. The plans—a nine-story tower sheathed in stainless-steel panels—promise a softly shimmering presence that will be the precise opposite of Breuer's blunt block. The keynote is quiet assertiveness.

The drawbacks of Piano's approach are becoming discernible, however, as his new headquarters for the *New York Times*, a fifty-two-story skyscraper, rises rapidly on Eighth Avenue. For skyscrapers, quiet assertiveness isn't enough; once they get above street level, their job is not to balance other buildings but simply to be. The Times building, which Piano has designed in collaboration with the New York firm of FXFowle, is a glass tower set behind a curtain of thin rods which form a sunscreen all the way up the facade. At 748 feet, that is a lot of rods. Up close, the tower has the pristine, tensile quality of Piano's smaller work, but seen from a few blocks away, the rods blur into something that looks like corrugated metal, and the building takes on a strange, thin blandness. It's one thing to design a tower that will play beautifully off the granite of the Whitney, but the Times building has to play off against a whole skyline. If the graceful interweaving of modernism and classicism at the Morgan demonstrates the power that brilliantly conceived, intense pieces of small-scale architecture can possess, the Times building, so far at least, shows the opposite. It comes off as dainty, even flimsy, as if inside this huge tower a little building were struggling to get out.

The New Yorker, May 29, 2006

Bitter Bredt Fotografie/Courtesy Studio Daniel Libeskind

Daniel Libeskind, Denver Art Museum

MILE HIGH

Daniel Libeskind's architectural career has had an unusual trajectory. He went from being a theoretician whose highly academic designs were so obscure that most people couldn't understand them to being a celebrity architect whose work is dismissed by many of his peers as too crowd-pleasing. The transformation began with the Jewish Museum in Berlin, which he designed less as a home for artifacts than as a de facto Holocaust memorial, using architecture to produce a sense of discomfort. The building, which opened in 2001, drew well over half a million visitors a year, and Libeskind discovered the allure of popular acclaim. When he won the competition to design a master plan for the reconstruction of the site of the World Trade Center, in 2003, he cloaked his familiar angular shapes in patriotic rhetoric. But, as reconstruction has moved forward, his plan has been compromised almost out of existence, and his continued attempts to claim ownership of the project have sometimes made him a figure of fun in the press. All the buildings at Ground Zero have been assigned to other architects, and very few of Libeskind's ideas will be visible.

In Denver, however, Libeskind's ideas are becoming very visible indeed. His new building for the Denver Art Museum, which opens this fall, is his first American work to be completed. It's already so popular in Denver that Libeskind was invited to construct a pair of condominium buildings and a hotel next door, and to design a neighborhood plan for a "cultural district" surrounding the museum. Marketed as the creations of "world renowned architect Daniel Libeskind"—whose face is all over the brochures—the apartments are among the highest-priced condos in town. Such success is a reminder of the fact that second-tier American cities have often proved more willing to take architectural risks than supposedly sophisticated cities like New York. In giving Libeskind the freedom denied him in New York, Denver is taking a risk: Does Libeskind have the ability to design a building that will exert the magnetic pull of an icon and still work well as a museum? And can he set out a plan for an entire neighborhood, as he tried to do in New York? Libeskind's new Denver Art Museum is an eruption of hard-edged rhomboids that suggests gargantuan quartz crystals. This is a bold building, and it is neither an inaccessible theoretical work nor a brazen piece of entertainment, but somewhere in between.

The building, officially called the Frederic C. Hamilton Building, is technically an addition to an eccentric structure by Gio Ponti, an Italian architect best known for designing the Pirelli Tower, in Milan. Ponti's museum is a forbidding, fortresslike block, clad in a million triangular tiles of reflective gray glass, with what looks like castellation along the top. The only Ponti design that ever got built in America, it's an earlier example of Denver's adventurousness, but when it opened, in 1971, not everyone was pleased: it was described as "an Italian castle wrapped in aluminum foil." Ponti's building is an all but impossible structure to add to, so Libeskind didn't really try. He just did his own thing next door, juxtaposing his crystalline forms with Ponti's sternly rectilinear style. The two buildings are connected by a glass-covered bridge across the street that separates them. The bridge itself is somewhat perfunctory, but above it Libeskind daringly extends one triangle of the building over the road like the prow of a ship. An origami fold, blown up to monumental scale, the prow is a powerful gesture: its point seems aimed directly at Ponti's building, a colossal siege engine set to storm the castle.

The Libeskind addition is sheathed in more than nine thousand titanium panels, which are not completely flat, so that as the light bounces off them, they seem to ripple gently, as if the building were covered with a thin film of liquid. Since none of the exterior walls are perpendicular to the ground and each surface slopes at a different angle, at any moment the sun strikes each of them differently, making some sections seem richly textured while others appear to have no texture at all.

As a purely sculptural feat, this building is a thrilling affirmation of the idea that museums can be artworks as well as merely containers. It is also willful and arbitrary, and wildly self-indulgent. Some people will praise Libeskind for creating the most exciting place in downtown Denver since the exuberant Gilded Age atrium in the lobby of the Brown Palace Hotel, and others will denounce him for creating a building that appears to put an architect's love of certain shapes above any commitment to the functions that a museum is supposed to serve. They will both be right.

How do you display art in such a building? Not easily, and not entirely successfully, but a lot better than you might expect. Like Frank Lloyd Wright at the Guggenheim, Libeskind has designed a building that never recedes into the background but that is surprisingly sympathetic to certain kinds of art. His angular spaces—in which walls slope inward or outward, many ceilings are raked, and every corner becomes a slanting line—are full of energy, which may be why they work best with big contemporary works. In the largest of the temporary exhibition galleries, the architect's determination to ignore conventional notions of rooms and galleries seems to make common cause with bold, large-scale works by artists like Damien Hirst, Matthew Richie, and Takashi Murakami. Elsewhere, Libeskind's design makes for bizarre challenges: a wall that slopes away, like the side of a pyramid, has been used to display textiles—the effect is winning, if faintly reminiscent of a fashion boutique—and, in another gallery, a huge striped painting by Gene Davis is hung from a wall that slopes the other way. The canvas dangles in space as the wall recedes behind it.

But most of Libeskind's walls are empty, since there really isn't much to be done with them. The task of making surfaces that you can actually hang paintings on has gone, instead, to Daniel Kohl, the museum's installation designer. Kohl has created interior partitions that zig and zag in a way that recalls Libeskind's angles but never directly mimics them; they are often painted in muted colors—plum, yellow, mossy green—to differentiate them from the white of Libeskind's, so that there is no uncertainty about who did what. To the extent that Libeskind's building is workable as a museum, it is Kohl who has made it so.

Much of the building's interior matches the visual drama of the exterior. Libeskind's spectacular atrium contains a characteristically odd version of the traditional grand staircase. His stairs ascend in a jagged, irregular corkscrew, like something out of *The Cabinet of Dr. Caligari*. This produces a sense of vertiginous complexity, which is accentuated by the fact that the wall against which the staircase is set slopes away from you. The climactic point of Libeskind's composition comes on the sculpture terraces that are tucked under the prow, where the square forms of a large Donald Judd piece play off perfectly against Libeskind's angles, and the architect's sloping walls create an outdoor room that seems to engage all of downtown Denver. At moments like this, Libeskind's assertiveness comes off not as bombastic but as masterly, and the museum convinces you that complaints about form not following function are beside the point.

But for every one of Libeskind's spaces that feels exultant, there is another that is deeply disquieting. Many of the first galleries you see are so awkwardly shaped that they leave you feeling only uneasiness. Does it really make sense to have a gallery with a floor plan that is bent like the letter "L," slanting walls, and a ceiling that is eight feet high at one end and slopes sharply up to thirty-four feet at the other? It's not just that it's hard to show art in here; it isn't pleasant to be in a room like this when it's empty. As for the museum's celebrated collection of art from the American West, unlike the brash contemporary works that thrive in Libeskind's unconventional rooms, these pieces look forlorn and out of place.

In the neighboring condominiums, now nearing completion, Libeskind has reined himself in. The buildings are long and low, and are clearly intended to defer to the museum: the cloisters to Libeskind's cathedral. Almost all the internal walls here run perpendicular to the ground, and the exterior has fairly standard glass-curtain walls, interrupted every so often by trapezoidal projections that look as if a piece of the museum had spun off and lodged there. Libeskind has figured out how to get beyond the standard box without making spaces that feel intractable; the rooms aren't square, but let's just say that you can put furniture into them a lot more easily than you can install paintings in the museum across the way. George Thorn, a developer who worked with the museum and others to erect the condominiums, says that the units that sold most easily were not the ones that offer a distant view of the Rockies, as is usually the case with Denver real estate, but the ones that face the museum. It's easy to see why. Many of these places have big windows that look right into the side of Libeskind's crystalline shards, a mere fifty feet away. Perhaps this view is what Libeskind had in mind all along. From there, the museum no longer feels like a piece of architecture. It is more like an enormous titanium sculpture that was created to decorate your living room.

The New Yorker, August 28, 2006

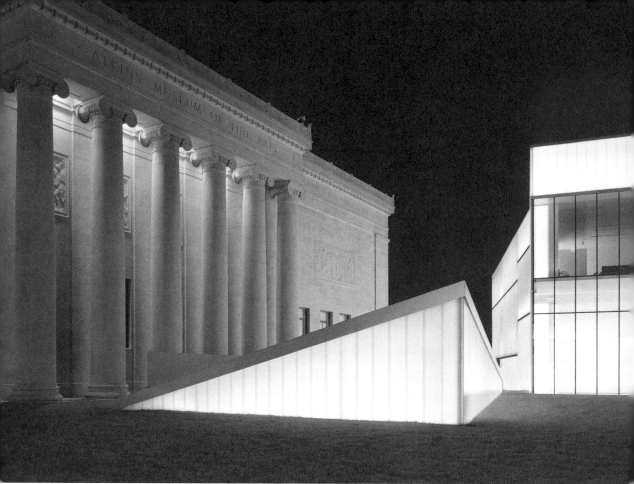

Steven Holl, Nelson-Atkins Museum of Art, Kansas City

LENSES ON THE LAWN

No art museum in the United States has a better site than the Nelson-Atkins, in Kansas City. Its austere, columned classical building, which was finished in 1933, sits on a hill overlooking a vast lawn that slopes down in terraces and gives it the air more of a royal palace than of a civic building in the Midwest. When the museum embarked on a major expansion, in 1999, it was taken as a given that this magnificent frontage was sacrosanct. There was plenty of room to build at the back, and that is exactly what five of the six architects who competed for the commission proposed. The sixth architect was Steven Holl. Born in 1947 and active since the mid-1970s, Holl is viewed as assertive by people who are trying to be complimentary, and as a bull in a china shop by people who aren't. Not surprisingly, he had no interest in hiding his building around the back. He came up with the idea of irregularly shaped boxes of translucent glass, which he called lenses, cascading down one side of the hill and linked underground by a series of galleries. They would change the view of the old museum forever.

Holl, whose major buildings include the Kiasma Museum of Contemporary Art, in Helsinki and a dormitory at MIT, has tended to present himself as an architect driven by impulses other than an interest in solving practical problems. His writings contain many exhortations like "Only by forcefully and passionately asserting our existence can we access what Mallarmé termed the 'force of the negative.'" Holl's buildings have always been intellectually provocative, but they have not always been accommodating to the needs of clients (with whom his relationships have sometimes been stormy) or even to accepted notions of beauty. Some, such as a recent brass-sided house in upstate New York with twenty-four windows that are meant to correspond to the twenty-four chapters of Homer's *Odyssey*, seem fanciful conceits bearing only a dim connection to normal life. But the Nelson-Atkins board chose Holl anyway, and his design was carried out with fewer alterations than is usual for a project of this scale. "Steven was the only one who had a real idea," Marc Wilson, the director of the museum, told me recently. "We knew in an instant that this was what we wanted."

As it turns out, the building, which will open in June, is not just Holl's finest by far but also one of the best museums of the last generation. Its boldness is no surprise, but, in addition, it is laudably functional, with a clear layout, handsome and logically designed galleries, and a suffusion of natural light. Furthermore, Holl's five glass structures, punctuating the hill, don't mock the old building as you might expect; they dance before it and engage it.

The original Nelson-Atkins Museum has always seemed relentless in its symmetry, its classicism tinged with a certain 1930s squareness. Colonnades on either side brought you into an enormous, columned central hall, a ceremonial space that seemed suited more to signing treaties than to viewing art. Holl's lenses, placed to the right, disturb this symmetry and form a row roughly perpendicular to the older building and following the gradient of the hill. At the top of the hill, the first and largest of the lenses forms an L with the rear facade of the original museum, and the new and old structures form a rectangular forecourt from which either can be entered. In the middle of the forecourt is a square reflecting pool with a placid sculpture by Walter de Maria.

With multiple levels woven around a constantly changing topography, the Bloch Building, as the new structure is called, is highly complex. It never feels overwrought, however, because Holl, working with his senior partner, Chris

McVoy, has constructed simple, clear paths through it. In contrast to the old building's ornate vestibule, suggestive of decorous repose, a three-story atrium in Holl's design—irregular in shape and crisscrossed by ramps and stairs and balconies—makes you want to keep moving. Long and narrow, it is finished with polished white plaster and flooded with natural light. You can enter this lobby either from street level, in which case a long ramp eases you down toward the galleries, or directly from an underground parking garage, in which case you enter at gallery level and meet the ramp coming down from above. Extending the glass-wall design of the building's exterior below ground, Holl has insured that the entrance from the garage is as appealing as the one from the street. The Bloch Building is one of the few museums anywhere designed in the recognition that, whether we like it or not, most people will arrive by car.

The atrium leads to the sequence of new galleries. You can proceed directly from one gallery to the next, walking a few steps downhill each time, or take a long, ramped promenade that passes to the side, like an indoor street. In most of the galleries, high clerestory windows allow natural light to filter through the cloudy, translucent glass and bounce down off a vaulted portion of the ceiling. Holl has written that architecture should heighten, even challenge, our sensations of light, sound, shadow, time, color, and movement, and throughout the Bloch Building, he treats light as if it were a building material in itself. Illumination from the clerestory windows, as well as from sections of translucent glass wall, diffuses gently through the galleries (sometimes cunningly enhanced by artificial lighting discreetly placed in alcoves), producing an interior of cool, even light. On an early drawing for the project, Holl suggested that the lenses would be like ice.

From the outside, too, the lenses make one aware of light's inherent drama. Although they lose some of their magical quality in bright sunlight, when the translucent glass has less depth and mystery and can seem like hard plastic, their effect in the light of an overcast day is ethereal. And at night, lit from within, they are transformed into a family of weightless objects, a composition of immense light sculptures, and every surface glows with the softness of moonlight.

Highly elaborate art museums by famous architects have become common in recent years, as cities strive for the so-called Bilbao effect. (Tourism to Bilbao has quintupled since Frank Gehry's Guggenheim building opened there.) Often, it has seemed as if the relationship between architecture and art were becoming a zero-sum game: the more exciting and unusual the architecture, the more it detracted from the experience of viewing pictures. Even I. M. Pei's famous 1978 East Building of the National Gallery, in Washington, D.C., arguably a forerunner of the current trend, succeeds mainly as a spectacular atrium; it does not provide convincing spaces for art, and its taut marble facade is even less relaxed than that of the sumptuous classical gallery beside it. At the Nelson-Atkins, a project in many ways comparable to the National Gallery, Holl has produced as striking and inventive a piece of architectural form as anything by Gehry, Herzog and de Meuron, or Jean Nouvel, and yet it is a serene and exhilarating place in which to view art. The building's unusual design pulls you toward it like a magnet and then recedes, in stages, once you are inside. By the time you reach the galleries, the architecture has deferred to the art.

Almost everything the Nelson-Atkins has put into the building—for example, its excellent collection of Abstract Expressionist and contemporary art—looks better than it did before. (Meanwhile, on the roof of the Bloch Building, landscaped to fuse with the rest of the lawn, the spaces between the lenses have yielded sculpture courts.) Walking around the galleries, you never feel that you are below ground, and sometimes you are not, thanks to the ingeniously uneven line of the terrain: in the small, chapel-like gallery devoted to the work of Sol LeWitt, or the expansive gallery containing the sculptures of Isamu Noguchi, you can look out across the lawn toward the old building.

Framed by such views, the grandiose temple of the Nelson-Atkins looks better than ever. Holl's design initially seems to pay scant attention to the old building, and to be the opposite of everything that the classical vocabulary represents. But Holl has avoided the trap of honoring an older structure by closely echoing its architectural cues, a choice that would surely have resulted in a mass of masonry overwhelming a beautiful setting. Instead, the lightness and softness of his buildings, and their asymmetry, bestow on the classical museum a kind of perpetual gravitas, as well as ceding it pride of place. Going his own way, Holl has produced a far finer homage to the old Nelson-Atkins than he would have if he had copied its Ionic columns.

The New Yorker, April 30, 2007

Kazuyo Sejima and Ryue Nishizawa/SANAA, New Museum, New York

BOWERY DREAMS

In the past few decades, American museums have discovered an easy way to get themselves noticed: put up a building by an international architect who hasn't built much in this country before. Too often, though, these exciting debuts go nowhere. Mario Botta's San Francisco Museum of Modern Art, Josef Paul Kleihues's Chicago Museum of Contemporary Art, and James Stirling's Sackler Museum, in Cambridge, all failed to earn their creators any more American museum commissions.

In 2002, when the New Museum of Contemporary Art in New York began to plan for a new building on the Bowery, east of its previous location, in Soho, it decided to limit the search to younger architects who had not built anything in New York. "We thought we should be consistent with our mission of supporting new art," Lisa Phillips, the director, told me. The search led the museum to SANAA, a twelve-year-old firm in Tokyo, whose principals, Kazuyo Sejima and Ryue Nishizawa, are known for buildings of almost diaphanous lightness. When the museum hired them, Sejima and Nishizawa had just one American commission, the Glass Pavilion, at the Toledo Museum of Art, an eye-catching structure of curving glass walls, which opened last year. Their best-known work includes a low-slung circular art gallery with no clear front or back, in Kanazawa, Japan, and a design school in Essen, Germany, that is a concrete cube a hundred feet high, punctuated, seemingly at random, with windows of assorted sizes.

SANAA's refined style might seem odd on the Bowery, one of the grittiest streets in New York. The site, a former parking lot at the intersection with Prince Street, was framed by blocks of restaurant-supply stores, whose owners seemed to be the only property holders on the Lower East Side who showed no interest in selling out to condominium developers. But after two decades in Soho, the New Museum had seen both the upside and the downside of gentrification. Marcia Tucker established the museum in 1977—the day after she was fired from the Whitney for curating shows that it found too controversial— in order to focus on cutting-edge art. Yet as the museum grew larger, it drifted from its radical beginnings, just as the Museum of Modern Art had done two generations before. The decision to move to the Bowery was perhaps a clever way of assuring its supporters that its agenda remains radical.

But things have changed since the New Museum purchased the lot, in 2002. There is now a Whole Foods nearby, several luxury condominiums within view of the museum's front door, and expensive shops, including a Ralph Lauren, amid the former tenements around the corner. The area hovers between a grungy past and an overpriced future. The New Museum may have left Soho, but it is powerless to prevent Soho from following it to the Bowery.

Sejima and Nishizawa have designed a building that is just right for this moment of the Bowery's existence. It is a pile of six boxes, stacked unevenly, like a child's blocks. Sometimes the blocks mount up in a pattern of setbacks like that of a traditional New York building; sometimes they jut out over open space in a way that suggests the architects had something more radical in mind. The building is original but doesn't strain to reinvent the idea of a museum. Sejima and Nishizawa have a way of combining intensity with understatement.

What makes the museum unlike any other building in New York is its surface—corrugated-aluminum panels painted silvery gray, with an aluminum mesh suspended an inch and a half in front of them. The mesh is a standard industrial material, but it gives the building the lightness of glass and the porosity of fabric. The visual signals this building sends—it is at once crisp and pliable, solid and permeable—seem deliberately ambiguous. When you look from a block or so away, the facade seems semitransparent—less like a wall than a scrim.

The depth and shadow and texture of the facade can be almost magical in the changing light. When you get near, however, the mystery is lost. You see that Sejima and Nishizawa have performed their magic with routine elements, and when you stand right in front of the building, its metal mesh looks harsh, even abrasive. Once the museum opens, next month, the effect may be more welcoming: the ground floor is sheathed entirely in glass, and a gallery and bookstore will be visible from the street. At the moment, the museum is enticing from afar but off-putting up close.

Things get good again when you go through the door. SANAA's ability to design places that look simple but actually have a lot going on has resulted in galleries that combine the clear, flexible quality of loft spaces with some shrewd architectural intervention. The second, third, and fourth floors have large, white-walled exhibition spaces, with ceiling heights of as much as twenty-four feet. The galleries, illuminated in part by natural light (through skylights), have some of the virtues of neutrality but are more inviting than plain white boxes. The main gallery spaces are almost, but not precisely, rectangular. One wall is angled just a bit, reflecting the diagonal of the Bowery, but the shift is so subtle that you don't notice it until you look up and see that the front wall is not quite parallel to the steel beams that run across the ceiling. This gives the room a slight frisson, without making it any less flexible or hospitable to art. The floors are all finished in a richly toned polished concrete that has been poured without the usual expansion joints, allowing it to develop small cracks as it sets. It looks both ancient and modern, and has a stunning resonance against the stark walls. ("It almost looks like an Anselm Kiefer," Lisa Phillips said as we walked through, and she was exaggerating only slightly.)

There are more flourishes once you get away from the main exhibition area: aluminum-lined elevators painted a kind of electric chartreuse; shelves that snake through the lobby in a sensuous curve, the one counterpoint to the building's straight lines. The most exciting space in the building is only four feet wide and some fifty feet high, and is tucked behind the elevators: it contains a stairway connecting the third- and fourth-floor galleries. I have never been anywhere at once so eerily narrow and so gloriously monumental. The stair hall, if you can call it that, has a large window with a view to the north, and a landing that opens onto a tiny exhibit area, barely more than a balcony.

In keeping their architectural tricks away from most of the art, Sejima and Nishizawa establish a certain kinship with the original building of the Museum of Modern Art, by Philip Goodwin and Edward Durell Stone. When that building burst onto West Fifty-third Street, in 1939, you could create excitement simply by sticking a modern building into a row of brownstones. The New Museum, similarly, derives its drama from the way it breaks with its surroundings. The original Modern lost much of its architectural power from the 1950s onward, as the brownstones gave way to a series of additions extending the museum up and down the block, and modernism became the new architecture lingua franca. Right now, the New Museum looks, as the Modern once did, like a thunderbolt from another world, but, as the spread of condos and boutique hotels across the Lower East Side continues, it is at risk of becoming a victim of its own success.

The New Yorker, November 19, 2007

Brad Cloepfil, Museum of Arts and Design, New York

HELLO COLUMBUS

Huntington Hartford's old Gallery of Modern Art—the white marble bonbon that stood at 2 Columbus Circle from 1964 until a couple of years ago—was a hard building to love but became an even harder one to hate. Excoriated by critics when it went up, then championed by preservationists when it was threatened with destruction, the building provides an object lesson in the inexorable march of architectural fashion and may point to an even more basic truth about people and buildings: we get used to things we don't like and then come to like things we've gotten used to. The eventual decision to refurbish the building entirely has also provided a young Oregon architect named Brad Cloepfil with a dauntingly controversial commission.

The Gallery of Modern Art, one of several quixotic cultural projects launched by Hartford, an heir to the A&P fortune, who died earlier this year at the age of ninety-seven, was originally intended to house his collection of figurative works and to stand as a riposte to what Hartford saw as the reign of abstraction at the Museum of Modern Art. The architect was Edward Durell Stone. Stone had been a leading American exponent of the International Style, but, in the 1950s, his new wife, a fashion writer he met on an airplane, encouraged him toward elegance and decoration, and he began to fill his buildings with glitter and marble and screens and gold columns.

As a museum, the Columbus Circle building was a disaster. The galleries, tricked out with expensive wood paneling and brass fixtures, were cramped, and the institution closed after five financially ruinous years. And yet somehow the structure's dainty columns, tiny portholes, huge arches, and vast windowless expanses of flat, unadorned white marble embedded themselves more deeply into the consciousness of New Yorkers than many better buildings. So what if it looked like a Bauhaus version of the Alhambra—or, as Ada Louise Huxtable, then the architecture critic at the *New York Times*, put it, "a die-cut Venetian palazzo on lollypops"? Amid the austere glass boxes of the 1950s and 1960s, it seemed to strike a blow for quirky individualism. Huxtable's harsh judgment gave rise to a nickname—the Lollipop Building—that was as much affectionate as mocking.

The building eventually wound up in the hands of the city, which, in 1998, decided to sell it to the highest bidder. The city repeatedly refused to have its own Landmarks Preservation Commission consider giving 2 Columbus Circle landmark status, a move that provoked outrage but kept the building salable and more or less sealed its fate. Whether or not the building deserved landmark status depends on what you think a landmark should be: it wasn't great architecture, but it had unique qualities and some historical importance. In 2002 the city agreed to sell it to the Museum of Arts and Design, formerly the American Crafts Museum. The museum was eager for an architect who had never built in New York before and hired Cloepfil, whose firm, Allied Works Architecture, in Portland, was just completing its first major project, the sharp and serene Contemporary Art Museum in St. Louis. Cloepfil started work on his design while the legal struggle to preserve the building was in progress, but in 2005 the preservationists lost in court, and construction began. The building will open next month.

Cloepfil ended up all but demolishing the original building and creating a new one of exactly the same shape and size, and almost the same color.

He kept the gentle curve reflecting the shape of Columbus Circle but changed just about everything else. To let light into the interior, he made long linear incisions, two feet wide, in the facade. These glass channels—Cloepfil has called them "ribbons of light"—make a number of right-angle turns across the facade. In place of Stone's marble are twenty-two thousand terra-cotta tiles specially made with a slightly iridescent glaze. Depending on the light, they look white or off-white or sparkle with tiny hints of color. Cloepfil told me that the use of ceramic and glass tied the new building to its role as a museum of craft, while its echo of the original marble's color would suggest continuity with the earlier building. Fair enough. But that dual goal encapsulates the building's main problem. Cloepfil is trying as hard as he can to be different while trying also to be the same. Rarely has an architect been pulled so completely in opposite directions.

In some respects, he probably didn't have much choice. He couldn't make the building taller, because of zoning laws, and he couldn't make it bigger, because it already filled every inch of its site. And, since museums require mostly solid, windowless walls, he was stuck with those, too. Cloepfil is a sophisticated architect who, at his best, can endow simple geometries with a powerful dignity. His style couldn't be more different from that of Edward Durell Stone's late period, which dances on the edge of kitsch, and he has tried to transform Stone's fussy marble froufrou into something serious and tasteful. Sometimes, as in the long, turning lines of glass, he manages to assert himself firmly enough to keep the old building at bay. At other times, like at the base of the building, where he has kept all but one of Stone's lollipop-shaped columns and put them behind glass, he seems to have given up altogether and settled for a curatorial role. Ultimately, Cloepfil has been trapped between paying homage to a legendary building and making something of his own. As a result, if you knew the old building, it is nearly impossible to get it out of your mind when you look at the new one. And, if you've never seen Columbus Circle before, you probably won't be satisfied, either: the building's proportions and composition seem just as odd and awkward as they ever did.

But if you go inside, entering through the glass-enclosed lobby, from which an elegantly detailed staircase of wood and steel leads up to four floors of galleries, it turns out that Cloepfil has done the impossible—making the building's interior at long last functional, logical, and pleasant to be in. He figured out early on that Stone had made a huge mistake putting the building's core—its elevators, stairs, and rest rooms—in the center, because that left just a tiny doughnut of usable space around the perimeter. Cloepfil moved two staircases behind the elevators, opening up space on every floor and making decent-sized exhibition galleries possible.

This move also enabled the building to address Columbus Circle more effectively than before. Galleries now have windows looking out over Central Park and, on the ninth floor, there will be a restaurant featuring an entire wall of glass, something the museum insisted on despite Cloepfil's objections that it would damage the composition of his facade. This might seem a little precious—why shouldn't the restaurant have a nice big window?—but Cloepfil was right. The window, running between two vertical glass ribbons, creates a huge "H" on the facade, a pity, because the ribbons are the heart of his design and its most brilliant feature. Once you are inside, you discover that they run not only up and down the facade but also horizontally, into the museum itself: from each vertical window notched into a gallery's wall, a glass ribbon stretches across the floor and you seem to be walking on thin air. Looking down can be vertiginous at first, but the glass channels allow light to permeate up and down the building, and tie the entire building, inside and out, together in a way that underscores what is new about it. It's not just that they look different from anything in Stone's original museum; requiring a completely different structure and engineering, they remind you that this is in almost every way a new building, albeit trapped in the body of an old one, screaming to get out.

The New Yorker, August 5, 2008

WAYS OF LIVING

New Residential Architecture in New York

A TOUCH OF CRASS

Residential glamour in New York has always been represented by apartment buildings, not private houses. Even in Chicago, the only other American city in which a substantial chunk of the upper middle class shares a roof, apartments are not deeply ingrained in the culture the way they are in New York, where you

Frank Williams, 515 Park Avenue, New York (above)

hear people refer to the most desirable addresses by a shorthand; "834" and "740" and "101," for example, mean 834 Fifth Avenue, 740 Park Avenue, and 101 Central Park West. These buildings and a couple of dozen others from the period between the world wars have an aura that comes partly from the sheer grandeur of the apartments they contain, partly from the wealth and celebrity of their occupants, partly from the outrageous prices the apartments command. But much of the luster is due to the early-twentieth-century architecture itself, especially the discreet ornamentation—usually neo-Renaissance, sometimes Art Moderne, sometimes a hint of Georgian or even Gothic.

The 1920s and 1930s have been viewed for a long while as a kind of golden age of apartment-house design. The 1920s had the Beresford and 960 Fifth Avenue, the 1930s had River House and the Majestic. We got white brick. There were sporadic attempts to construct modern buildings of distinction in the 1960s, 1970s, and 1980s—the United Nations Plaza apartments, Trump Tower, Museum Tower, 500 Park Avenue—but for the most part new luxury housing in New York was tacky. In the lexicon of real-estate brokers, "prewar" became a code word for "trust me, it isn't a tawdry piece of junk."

I've always wondered why real-estate developers and architects didn't try harder to copy the buildings everyone professed to admire. Did they really think that people wanted to live in little boxes of plasterboard set into bigger boxes of white brick, or was that simply what the builders found most efficient to produce? Whatever the case, they seem finally to have abandoned modernism. The latest crop of high-rise condominiums (most new buildings are condominiums, not co-ops) are determinedly retro. Developers—who are promoters and salesmen as much as dealmakers—are hawking prewar elegance as if they had just invented it. Almost every one of the new buildings has an elaborate sales center—a lounge where prospective buyers can view videos that contain computer-generated images of model apartments. An ambitious brochure for Ninety East End Avenue opens with fold-out pictures of the East River and the trees of Carl Schurz Park and the words "Where the River Never Hurries By . . . and the Sun Prefers to Linger . . . Comes the Perfect Place to Call Home." At the Chatham, which is going up on Sixty-fifth Street at Third Avenue, the selling point is the architect, Robert A. M. Stern, whose picture appears in all the promotional literature. He is identified as the man "some call the world's greatest residential architect." The brochure also includes a drawing of the lobby, which is to be "reminiscent of the Pantheon."

The passion for the past reaches its apotheosis, surely, in the grandest of the new buildings that have been finished, 515 Park Avenue, at the corner of Sixtieth Street, a tower of French limestone, mud-colored brick, and cast stone that is being promoted as "The Evolution of the Classic Park Avenue Residence." It's hard to know quite what the developers, the Zeckendorfs, believe represents an evolution here, unless it's the notion that expanding the traditional fourteen-story Park Avenue building of the 1920s into a forty-three-story tower constitutes a form of progress. In fact, 515 Park Avenue is particularly ungainly. The building has a base that is similar in bulk to its venerable ancestors, but two narrow towers extrude from it, like sections of a telescope, and they seem to be stretched and pulled to the point where all sense of proportion is lost.

The fact that 515 Park Avenue is taller than most of the neighboring office buildings wouldn't matter if the design made sense in itself. But the architect, Frank Williams, seems not to understand that a classic Manhattan apartment house from the 1920s and a tall, slender tower are completely different beasts. The early-twentieth-century buildings were not just well detailed but well proportioned; they weren't weirdly gangly. Many of them were no higher than the base of Williams's new building. A handful, mostly hotels, were taller, including the Ritz Tower, just three blocks south of 515 Park Avenue. Designed by Emery Roth, one of the masters of the classic New York apartment building, and finished in 1926, the Ritz is thirty-seven stories tall. But it has several setbacks, which give it a kind of lilting rhythm, and the imitation-Renaissance details on its facade are soft and understated.

I visited the clunky new building at 515 Park Avenue the other day with Williams, a friendly, gray-haired man whose enthusiasm for his creation is apparent. "Twelve-foot ceilings! We have twelve-foot ceilings! Nobody's built that in this day and age!" he exclaimed. He is right on that score—twelve-foot ceilings (some, but not all, of the floors of 515 Park Avenue have them) are unusual today. And some of the apartments do indeed approximate the gracious layouts of classic Emery Roth apartments, with large foyers, well-proportioned living rooms, and separate bedroom wings. (Williams's versions have better bathrooms and much better kitchens.) If you lived in this building, you might be able to convince yourself that you owned a rough approximation of a prewar apartment, but if you simply walked past it, you would not get that impression. Williams's favorite word is "patina," and he described how carefully he had replicated that of the old buildings on Park Avenue. But patina is not a quality that can be replicated. And, for all his scrutiny of the architecture of Park Avenue, Williams seems not to have picked up the most important characteristic of the city's older apartment buildings—their quiet dignity. The corners at 515 Park Avenue are lined with cast stone, a concrete derivative intended to simulate limestone, and there is too much of it. The corners come off as heavy and awkward. (Williams told me that the cast stone was cut into pieces small enough so they could be laid by the bricklayers' union, cutting the cost of labor.) The base floors are lined with Magny stone, a French lime-stone that the cast stone is supposed to resemble. The cast stone starts above the thirteenth floor, where we can't see it as clearly, and we are supposed to assume that the real stone has been used all the way up. But it's obvious that the material is different, and not as good. Add the murky-colored brick, which doesn't mix well with the color of the cast stone, and some awkward fake pilasters, and you have a facade that is a pretentious muddle.

Hugh Hardy, of Hardy Holzman Pfeiffer, did somewhat better at 145 East Seventy-sixth Street. Hardy, who designed the building along with the firm of Schuman Lichtenstein Claman Efron, had a reasonably modest assignment—

a fifteen-story luxury building that would contain large apartments and sit comfortably amid the older buildings of the neighborhood. No need to go high, and no need to create one of those useless plazas that zoning laws once encouraged in front of apartment buildings, and which led to a generation of slender towers. Here the shape could be traditional, which made covering the thing in traditional garb seem less contrived. Hardy has an exceptionally knowing eye, and he has inventively blended elements taken from the vocabulary of classic New York apartment architecture into his building. Never mind that the developer, the Macklowe Organization, insists on calling the truncated terraces "Juliette balconies." The building, which has numerous setbacks, is restrained, and the rusticated limestone detailing demonstrates a clear sense of proportion and scale. This isn't a masterpiece. It's just decent background architecture, which is exactly what we seem to have so much trouble producing these days. And, while rooms are not huge, the apartments are laid out with at least some sense of expansiveness.

It's quite possible that 90 East End Avenue, a thirty-eight-unit building designed by the architect Costas Kondylis, will have the same virtues of understatement on its exterior, though it looks as if the apartment layouts will be tighter. Less promising at this point is the Empire, a thirty-two-story tower of limestone and red brick designed by the Washington, D.C., firm of Hartman-Cox, along with the Schuman firm. The building's gabled, vaguely Queen Anne–style roof seems clearly inspired by the turret of a great lost Chicago landmark, Burnham & Root's Masonic Temple, of 1892. Or is it inspired by Philip Johnson and John Burgee's 1987 skyscraper in Chicago that was itself inspired by the Masonic Temple? In the world of retro architecture, it's not easy to tell the difference between imitating the imitator and imitating the original. Perhaps the real question is what the point is of putting luxury apartments on Third Avenue in New York into a container that looks like a nineteenth-century Chicago skyscraper.

Alas, the apartments in the Empire are uninspiring. They have the same short, narrow corridors that can be so oppressive in buildings of the white-brick genre. One layout at the Empire even contains a "maid's room" that is not off by itself but next to other bedrooms. I presume that the designers produced a bedroom that was so small they didn't think anyone would accept it, so they called it a maid's room. Whatever else you can say about Emery Roth, he never made that kind of mistake. The one virtue of the Empire's gabled top is that it will be a striking presence on the skyline, as will Stern's Chatham, with its elegantly detailed brick-and-limestone tower. I wonder, though, how much any of that matters, at least in the case of towers like these, since neither a fancy top nor a limestone-clad bottom can hide the fact that what we have is more very tall buildings being squeezed into already overcrowded parts of Manhattan.

What made the apartment buildings of the first three decades of this century important as works of architecture, and what makes them still so valuable as real estate, is the quality of their physical construction and of their apartments, and the sense they project of being part of a whole. Park

Avenue, Fifth Avenue, and Central Park West, not to mention West End Avenue and Riverside Drive, are all coherent works of urban design in which each architect's statement plays a secondary role. The street itself is the most important element, and each building serves the people who walk past it as much as it serves the people who live inside it. The architecture of a building like 515 Park Avenue pretends to be doing this, but it's a hollow claim.

It's sad that New York has not developed a strong tradition of modern residential design. If it had, we might be talking about buildings that excite the eye in new ways rather than about buildings for which the highest praise is to say that they evoke the golden age with modesty rather than with arrogance. Indeed, the mediocrity of most postwar luxury housing in New York is the main reason for the current retro trend. It certainly isn't the result of larger architectural forces, which dallied with retro in the 1980s in a slew of office towers and institutional buildings but few apartment buildings. The early postmodern period yielded the neotraditional 1001 Fifth Avenue facade by Johnson & Burgee and an apartment house at Seventieth Street and Third Avenue by Kohn Pedersen Fox, but nobody paid much attention to them back then, in part because not much other luxury housing was being built. Then came the 1990s boom, a wild leap in housing prices, and a market that was desperate for luxury. With investment bankers outbidding each other right and left for the real prewar apartments, it's no surprise that real-estate developers decided that the answer was to start producing more of them, like the savvy furniture makers who turn out "genuine reproduction antiques." The newly rich who didn't want to settle for a 1960s brick box and couldn't manage Emery Roth could have Robert Stern. After all, if there isn't enough of the old to go around, why not make more of it?

The New Yorker, August 16, 1999

Robert A. M. Stern, 15 Central Park West, New York

PAST PERFECT

In an essay titled "The Plight of the Prosperous," published in 1950 in this magazine, Lewis Mumford dismissed the living accommodations of upscale

New Yorkers as little better than slums. "I sometimes wonder what self-hypnosis has led the well-to-do citizens of New York, for the last seventy-five years, to accept the quarters that are offered them with the idea that they are doing well by themselves," he wrote. The typical Upper East Side apartment, he said, was dark, airless, and badly laid out. Mumford was mostly right, but, by the time he was writing, design and construction standards were heading downhill so fast that the prewar buildings he was sneering at had come to evoke the grand living of a bygone era.

Today, if you want such luxuries as high ceilings and a dining room, an old building is pretty much the only place to find them. Forget Richard Meier and Jean Nouvel and their sleek glass condominiums: for connoisseurs of Manhattan apartments, the real celebrity architects have always been Rosario Candela, J. E. R. Carpenter, and Emery Roth, who designed the best buildings put up between the wars. That period—when Roth built the San Remo, on Central Park West, while Candela produced the somber citadels of 740 Park Avenue and 834, 960, and 1040 Fifth Avenue—ended up being the glory years. Such buildings still represent the apogee of New York residential design. Brokers often mention Candela in their ads, because people will pay a premium to live in one of his buildings.

Candela has been dead for more than fifty years, but he should get at least partial credit for 15 Central Park West, a new apartment building, designed by Robert A. M. Stern, that occupies the full block between Central Park West and Broadway and Sixty-first and Sixty-second Streets. I have never seen anything quite like it: historical pastiche is common enough in country houses or museums, but it's rare on the scale of a skyscraper. Stern's entire building is covered in limestone (it took roughly eighty-five thousand pieces), outdoing even Candela, whose fanciest buildings still had brick at the back. The 201 apartments have casement windows, ten-, eleven-, or fourteen-foot ceilings, dining rooms, plenty of moldings, and plenty of light, Stern having devised a floor plan that gives nearly every room an open view. I am not sure what Mumford would have found to complain about, other than the fact that the building looks as if it had been put up seventy-five years ago.

But that very conservatism may be why 15 Central Park West has become the most financially successful apartment building in the history of New York. All the apartments were sold before the building was finished, at prices that started at more than $2,000 a square foot and were subsequently raised nineteen times. Demand was so extreme that brokers started to worry that the building was taking all the business away from other high-end buildings nearby. Someone I know who bought an apartment early on for about $12 million was offered the chance to resell it for potentially more than $16 million before ever moving in. (He didn't bite.) The average three-bedroom, four-bath apartment went for more than $10 million, and the total selling price of the building was close to $2 billion. Among the buyers have been celebrities like Denzel Washington, Sting, Norman Lear, and Bob Costas, but, in truth, the more spectacular units went for prices that would make even a movie star blanch.

The most expensive of all—a $45 million penthouse bought by the hedge-fund manager Daniel Loeb—was for a while the most expensive apartment ever sold in the city. A plurality of the buyers come from the world of finance, including Sanford Weill, the former head of Citibank, and Lloyd Blankfein, the CEO of Goldman Sachs.

So what does $20 million buy you these days? When the building opens, this fall, it will have a private dining room for its residents, a walnut-paneled library, a screening room, and a chauffeurs' waiting room. There is also a wine-storage area, with thirty private wine cellars, sold separately, and, on a low floor, twenty-nine maids' suites, also sold separately. The layouts resemble those of classic apartments from the 1920s, but instead of tiny kitchens and butlers' pantries and maids' rooms there are eat-in kitchens and picture windows, not to mention bathrooms big enough to bathe your polo pony in and closets the size of some studio apartments. The idea is to create, ready-made, the kind of place you would get by renovating an old apartment. Some occupants will take this a stage further, treating their apartment, or apartments, as raw space, stripping out the walls and starting over, perhaps to produce temples of luxury beyond even Stern's imagining.

A building like this leaves you two choices: you can resist it or you can yield to it. On one level, there's something unsettling about the whole thing—is costume-drama luxury the best that our new century has to offer? And what are we to make of the feeding frenzy surrounding it, in an already hypertrophied real-estate market? (Perhaps it's worth remembering that 740 Park Avenue, the 15 Central Park West of its time, went into construction a few months before the 1929 crash.) But the building itself is deeply seductive. For years, developers have been claiming that this one or that one of their latest creations signaled the restoration of prewar elegance, but it usually turns out to mean that they sprang for a powder room. This time, the assertion is not so hollow. Rooms are laid out in sumptuous procession around formal central galleries, and New York probably hasn't seen such exquisitely crafted marble trim in a residential lobby since the days of Cole Porter.

Stern, who is the dean of the Yale School of Architecture, has spent much of his life as a writer and a teacher, and the architecture of New York is his main subject. He began his career as a postmodernist, with a propensity for ironic quotations, but as the years have gone by (and he has become more successful) he has tossed away the pastiche in favor of replicating models of the past more directly. Stern is big on fitting into context: his business school at the University of Virginia is pure Thomas Jefferson, his Norman Rockwell Museum in Stockbridge looks like a classic New England meeting house; he's done sprawling Shingle Style houses in East Hampton and Spanish Colonial ones in California. Stern knows how to do a building like 15 Central Park West better than almost anyone, which is why the details—such as the book-matching of marble slabs in the bathrooms—ring true and don't look like cheap imitation.

The building consists of two parts: the House, a twenty-story structure on Central Park West that mimics the pattern of terraced setbacks characteristic of its prewar neighbors; and the Tower, a thirty-five-story slab that rises behind it, on Broadway, topped by an ornate, asymmetrical loggia (hiding a cooling tower) based on Candela's rooftop design at 1040 Fifth Avenue. The House and the Tower are separated by a spacious courtyard containing a round glass pavilion with a copper-and-glass cupola. Dividing the full-block site like this was an ingenious piece of urban design: the traditional-looking front wing blends into Central Park West as if it had always been there, and the tower behind it looks at home among the taller towers of Broadway. A formal entrance on Central Park West leads to a lobby that evokes the world of one of New York's lost prewar hotels—the Marguery, perhaps, or the Park Lane.

In some ways, the building seems less a piece of architecture than a creation along the lines of Woody Allen's *Manhattan*, an homage to the city by someone who not only loves the New York of the 1920s and 1930s but actually believes that he can will it back into existence. But, like Woody Allen, Stern is also smart enough not to be shackled by his infatuations. This building invokes the past to solve a set of contemporary problems: can you reproduce the grandeur of the past without any of the inconveniences that annoyed Mumford? And how can you make money on a piece of land for which the developers, the brothers Arthur and William Lie Zeckendorf, paid the seemingly outrageous price of more than $400 million? You don't recoup that kind of investment by putting up studio apartments, or monoliths of the type that have been going up all over town. Ubiquitous as glass condo buildings have lately become—glass is the new white brick—New York's wealthy, unlike their Mies van der Rohe–dwelling counterparts in Chicago, have always equated stone with substance. Even the Time Warner Center, after all, looks like the sort of development you might find in Hong Kong or Shanghai or Dubai. Whatever else you can say about 15 Central Park West, it could only be in New York.

The New Yorker, August 7, 2007

GLASS IS THE NEW WHITE BRICK

Cities are shaped by their vernacular as much as their monuments, and New York has always been a city of masonry. Whether the brownstone and terra-cotta and red brick of the nineteenth century or the limestone and white brick of the twentieth, the ordinary workaday buildings of New York have been solid objects first, exemplars of architectural style second. They are masses, and the streets along which they line up are voids. Philip Birnbaum's garish white-brick residential towers from the 1960s are hardly the equal of Rosario Candela's sumptuous and understated limestone apartment buildings from the 1920s, but at least the cheap arriviste and the self-assured aristocrat always had one thing in common: their masonry facades had the quality of dense objects.

Now the vernacular is shifting again. This is no surprise—after all, the white-brick apartment towers of the postwar decades have grown as old as the great buildings of the 1920s were when they were built. Some are even older: Manhattan House on East Sixty-sixth Street, the first of that breed and still the finest, opened its doors fifty-six years ago. So it is more than time for something else. But this change is more striking than the shift from brownstone to limestone, or from one kind of brick to another. We are now seeing for the first time the end of the notion of the building as solid object. There is a new residential vernacular in New York: glass.

It's a bizarre moment in the city's architectural history. Glass is nothing new. The United Nations Secretariat Building is so old that it is all but falling apart, Lever House has already had its entire curtain wall replaced, and the Seagram Building is as revered as the Dakota. But the city has never before embraced glass towers as a way of making ordinary residential buildings. Of course, we have had a few high-end exceptions: Harrison & Abramovitz's United Nations Plaza towers in the late 1960s came first, then the Olympic Tower and Trump Tower and Museum Tower and the handful of elegant slender buildings erected by the developer Sheldon Solow on the Upper East Side. By and large, however, New Yorkers were much more likely to work in glass towers than to live in them.

No more. In fact, I suspect there are now plenty of people for whom the opposite is true: they live in new glass buildings in Soho or Tribeca and work in old converted industrial buildings. Glass has become the new brick. You see it everywhere, and not just in small highly touted and precious examples of starchitect marketing: Richard Meier's pristine boxes on Perry Street, Winka Dubbeldam's rippling facade on Greenwich Street, Gwathmey Siegel's undulations at Astor Place, and the promise of Jean Nouvel on Mercer Street. This is the high-end stuff, and a lot of it is quite good—especially Meier's buildings and Nouvel's renderings—but these projects represent a cultural phenomenon as much as an architectural one, driven more by the selling power of a handful of architects' names than the allure of glass.

But that isn't the case with the glass residential slab on West Thirty-fourth Street—so huge you think it is an office tower. This isn't innovative design but the architectural equivalent of trickle-down aesthetics. So too with the Orion, a huge new tower on West Forty-second Street. These are standard-issue boxes with standard-issue apartments inside them, and there seem to be more of them all the time. The Durst Organization has put up the full-block Helena on Eleventh Avenue and Fifty-seventh Street, sheathed entirely in glass; there are also glass buildings on Ninety-ninth Street and Riverside Drive. Glass is not just the new brick—it is the new white brick, the default symbol of Manhattan banality.

The new condos by Meier and Nouvel and Gwathmey Siegel have the same relationship to these buildings that Manhattan House—the masterwork by Mayer & Whittlesey and Skidmore, Owings & Merrill—had to the white-brick buildings that followed it, or that the Seagram Building and Lever House have to the ordinary office towers of Third Avenue. New York has a long tradition of starting a genre with a first-rate work, and then instead of building upon its example, watering it down in ever plainer, less imaginative versions for a broader market. And so the list keeps lengthening, to include not only the glass mega-residential buildings on the West Side but projects like Place 57, on Third Avenue between Fifty-sixth and Fifty-seventh streets, advertising a "sophisticated Baccarat crystal lobby and garden," which is a clever way to use associations other than architecture to establish a connection between glass and luxury; and the Hudson, in Midtown, which urges young professionals to "parlay your bonus into a sound investment just two blocks from the Time Warner Center." The Hudson sells itself as the starter version of the high-end glass condo, promising "state-of-the-art" apartments with "floor-to-ceiling windows," not for zillions but for hundreds of thousands of dollars. And while we're talking about marketing, we shouldn't forget the Urban Glass House, the downtown building that Philip Johnson's firm produced at the end of his life, with apartments by Annabelle Selldorf—notable mainly for the brazen attempt to promote it as the city version of Johnson's masterwork in New Canaan.

Since even a mundane curtain wall looks fresher and more elegant than a white-brick facade, most of these new glass buildings are better looking than the brick boxes of the last generation. So in what passes for market-rate housing, New York now produces a higher grade of mediocrity than it used to (progress of a sort, I suppose). But the improvement tends to be limited to the facades. Most of these buildings are designed by pedestrian firms that follow the aesthetic directions set by others (some are even produced by SLCE Architects, which is the contemporary name for Schuman, Lichtenstein, Claman & Efron, one of the firms most responsible for the old brick boxes). The new interiors are straightforward. While the lobbies lack the imitation Louis Quatorze furniture of the white-brick buildings, they aren't exactly crisp Miesian spaces either. There's no imagination to the floor plans, and in some cases there aren't even the floor-to-ceiling windows that the glass facades would suggest. In the Helena, for example, many of the facade panels are spandrel glass, covering solid portions of exterior wall.

When glass residential buildings were rare, they had a graceful effect on the cityscape: light objects playing off against masonry. But just as the Seagram Building lost some of its luster when its masonry neighbors on Park Avenue were replaced by inferior glass buildings, we are beginning to run the risk of seeing glass become not the appealing counterpoint to the stone city but the new standard. And it doesn't work well at that. The allure of glass—its brittleness and precision, the way it seems to bedazzle and at the same time keep you at a distance—can sometimes make beautiful buildings, but it's less likely to make appealing streetscapes. This is not the place to get into modernism's urbanistic failings, which involve far more than material choices, but walking alongside a glass building doesn't provide the subtle embrace that richly textured stone or even brick does. It is a paradox: stone, heavy and opaque, pulls you closer; glass, light and transparent, keeps you at a distance. I have tried to avoid using words like warm and cold, but it is hard not to conclude that glass is cold and masonry, warm. A cold object can be stunningly beautiful, but one cannot make a whole street out of them, and streets are the mortar of civilizing cities. Masonry buildings make streets; glass buildings make objects.

There is, of course, a counterrevolution, and it began even before modernism had completed its trickling down to the vernacular. Thanks in part to pressure from adjustments in the city's zoning intended to discourage setback towers, and in part to the prestige of architects like Robert A. M. Stern—who brings as much marketing clout to neo-1920s buildings as Richard Meier does to modernist ones—there are a fair number of structures designed to look as much as possible like the great buildings by Candela, Emery Roth, and others from eighty years ago. Some of these, such as 515 Park Avenue by Frank Williams, are as mediocre as the ordinary glass ones; others, such as Stern's Chatham or his immense planned double building at 15 Central Park West, are more subtle. All of them respect the street. But what does it say when our choice for new housing seems to be between huge towers that look vaguely like office buildings and huge towers that knock off the details of the 1920s at gargantuan scale? Our residential architects seem to alternate between defying their predecessors and bowing meekly before them.

Metropolis, April 2006

Rocio Romero, LV Prefabricated House

SOME ASSEMBLY REQUIRED

It may be that the future of American housing is visible on a seventy-acre farm in Perryville, Missouri, a town of some eight thousand people in the rolling hills of the southeastern part of the state. The farm is owned by Rocio Romero, a thirty-four-year-old architect. In 2000, her parents asked her to design a simple, inexpensive vacation home in Chile, where they grew up. Romero came up with a sleek, metal-clad box that she named the LV, for the place where it was built—Laguna Verde, a beach town an hour and a half west of Santiago. It wasn't quite as cheap as her parents had hoped it would be—the cost was $35,000—but during the construction process, Romero realized that she had some ideas about how to attack a problem that has frustrated architects for most of the past century: the fact that modern houses aren't produced in a more mechanized manner. Apart from the mobile-home industry, no one turning out houses on an assembly line has made an impact in the housing business. Most mobile homes are aluminum-sided banalities that are supposed to look like traditional suburban houses but fool nobody, and whose sole virtue is that they are cheap. Modern architecture, of course, tends to be expensive. It often looks machine-made and features the latest technology, yet modern houses are almost always built largely by hand, even when they are intended to embody the aesthetic of the computer age.

Romero's original LV fit the usual pattern of a laboriously designed house that looked, deceptively, like a mass-produced industrial object. In 2001 she resolved to make a house that could be manufactured in one place and erected in another. The LV, she decided, could be replicated ad infinitum and sold as a prefabricated kit. She and her husband, Cale Bradford, a health-care executive, were living in St. Louis, where Romero had set up an office—Bradford comes from Missouri—and they bought a farm seventy-five miles south of the city. On a clearing overlooking a broad meadow, Romero erected an improved version of the LV house, which she could use as a sales model as well as a weekend getaway.

The LV is 1,150 square feet, with two bedrooms, two bathrooms, a large living-dining area, and a small kitchen. (A stretched-out version, which Romero calls the LVL—Laguna Verde Large—has room for a third bedroom or an expanded master suite.) Romero's farm now features a second prototype, the Fish Camp, a one-room metal cottage on stilts, which she placed overlooking a winding creek; sliding glass doors flood the interior with light, making it an ideal artist's studio. Later this month, she plans to erect a sample of her third design, the Base Camp, a medium-sized guest house, as soon as it rolls off the assembly line at a factory in Fort Wayne, Indiana.

Romero's farm recently became her full-time residence. She has turned a pair of old hog barns into a workshop, where two employees assemble the wall panels that make up the LV kits; the process takes about a week. So far, Romero has sold twenty-five kits, starting at $32,000 each. If you buy one of Romero's LV kits, you do not get an entire house. You get the exterior walls and the floors, the roof framing, special assembly tools, and lots of instructions. It is up to builders to construct a foundation according to Romero's plans, and to add such items as windows, doors, electricity, plumbing, and a roof, for which the architect provides exacting specifications. Buyers pay for shipping their future house on a flatbed truck, which runs roughly $2.25 per mile from Perryville. (One of the reasons Romero leaves out a lot of the house, she says, is that her system allows contractors to finish the work in accordance with local building codes. It also allows her to fit the parts she manufactures onto a single truck.) The final cost of one of Romero's houses depends on the cost of transportation, labor, and materials—it is cheaper to build an LV in Toledo than in East Hampton—but it tends to be roughly three to four times the price of the kit, or around a $110 per square foot. Today, most architect-designed houses cost more than $300 a square foot, and in many parts of the country, they can easily be twice that. Even with all that is left out, Romero's house is a bargain, especially when you compare it with putting up a modern house by the likes of Richard Meier or Charles Gwathmey.

When you drive along the country road that leads to Romero's farm, you go through a landscape of fields, passing a colonial house or two and a couple of mobile homes that have been fixed up to resemble suburban tract houses. It's not Tobacco Road, but it's not Greenwich, either. Romero's farm looks, at first, as if it had seen better days. The hog barns are close to the road and appear forlorn and abandoned. I drove around the barns, and the landscape opened up. In front of me was a silver box, roughly fifty feet long and twenty-five feet wide, that appeared to float a few inches above the ground. Part of the facade was covered in corrugated Galvalume, a zinc-alloy-coated steel, and the rest of it was a mixture of flat metal panels and glass. It shimmered in the sun, a benign alien in the landscape.

The LV is an exceptionally beautiful house. Other designers, such as Charlie Lazor and the firm Resolution: 4 Architecture, are building innovative prefabricated structures, but Romero's designs stand out for their clarity, simplicity, and grace. There is nothing funky about the LV. Romero has hidden the gutters inside the structure and made the exterior walls higher than the slightly downward-slanting roof, so that when you look at her house, all you see is a clean, pure box. The proportions are pleasing, and the details elegant; the foundation supports have been recessed slightly, giving the house that appearance of hovering.

The interior of Romero's LV is clean, white, and pointedly austere. Light pours in: the sides have floor-to-ceiling glass windows in a handsome grid pattern, and the back wall consists of a series of sliding-glass panels. The living room contains four black leather chairs, a glass coffee table, and a flat-screen television mounted on one wall. There are only three decorative objects: an old jukebox and a pair of Kennedy and Nixon posters from the 1960 presidential election. They all belong to Bradford, who has a collection of objects from the 1950s and 1960s that he displays in strict accord with the minimalist restraint of his wife.

There is something almost retro about Romero's modernism—she's on the cutting edge of process, but her aesthetic is comfortably familiar. She wants to build houses for the sort of people who, if they were rich and living in Chicago, would probably be on a waiting list for apartments in Mies van der Rohe's famous towers on Lake Shore Drive. "One of my clients calls this her poor man's Mies," Romero said to me soon after I arrived at the house. "I always wonder if I should take that as a compliment. To be compared to Mies is one thing, but to be called the poor man?" She paused. "But I want this to be affordable," she said. "I want to bring modern design to people. Otherwise, what's the point of prefab?"

Romero's parents emigrated from Chile in 1973, two years after she was born, and she grew up in San Diego. She went to Berkeley and then to Sci-Arc, an independent architectural school in Los Angeles known for its commitment to environmentalism, avant-garde design, and alternative methods. She has not shaken off her Southern California roots, even though she hasn't lived there for three years and says that she feels completely settled in rural Missouri. When I met her at her farm, last month, she was wearing black slacks, a white T-shirt, and Chanel sunglasses. She has bluntly cropped black hair and an easygoing manner that is both cheerful and vague, but she focuses quickly when the talk turns to I-joists or bolting systems. She couldn't quite remember whether she and Bradford had bought their farm two years ago or three, but she knew every aspect of her manufacturing system, and when we walked into one of the hog barns, she pointed to an eight-foot-long sandwich of foam, corrugated metal, and particleboard coated with a veneer of resin—one of the panels for the next LV kit to be shipped—and explained in detail how she had engineered the panel to withstand the winds of a Category 5 hurricane.

"A lot of the people who come to me say they like modern architecture but never felt comfortable with architects," she said later, over lunch at a local diner. "They have heard nightmare stories, and they don't want to be someone's guinea pig. Or they've seen things in the magazines, and they don't want to take on the challenge of doing it themselves." Romero decided that if she was going to succeed in the business of manufacturing modern houses, she had to do something more than produce a good-looking design; she had to make it easy to build. She devised the assembly process so that contractors, who are often wary of factory-made houses, would think of themselves as her partner, not her adversary. With this in mind, she created a system of color-coded stakes and cables of specific lengths to help contractors position the wall panels. "Not everyone is an architect," she said. "To empower people, you have to come up with this stuff—it's not goofy. My mom, she isn't very visual, so I had to keep coming up with stuff for her. You have to assume that people will make mistakes; a design needs wiggle room."

Putting together a house like the LV involves all the frustrations of assembling a china cabinet from Ikea, but on a much larger scale. Instead of small pieces of wood, there are hundred-pound panels. "It can take three people to push the floor panels tightly together," Romero said. The kit contains straps that facilitate this process. It also includes a video of her own house being assembled, because, she believes, people don't read manuals.

Romero originally thought that the primary market for the LV would be California, but most of her customers have turned out to be in the East or in the Midwest. The first kit Romero sold was to a couple in Virginia, Barry Bless and Jennifer Watson, who put it on a six-acre site in the Blue Ridge Mountains. Bless, a musician, and Watson, an architectural photographer, finished their house this past March. They did much of the construction work themselves, and it took about a year; the final cost was $95,000. The couple christened their LV the Luminhaus. As soon as it was done, they put up a web site filled with Watson's photographs of the house amid fall foliage and winter snow, offering the house for rent at $800 a week. In six weeks, it was booked for the rest of the year.

The couple first saw Romero's model in a slick coffee-table book titled *Prefab*. The book contains images of more glamorous, and more impractical, designs by elite architects such as Shigeru Ban and Greg Lynn. Bless and Watson, who have both worked as carpenters themselves, have mixed feelings about the chic aspect of modernist prefabricated houses. Romero's design, they found, was handsome but unpretentious. "A neighbor said to me that the house looked like a trailer—a very nice trailer," Bless said with satisfaction. He relishes the curiosity that his new home has aroused. "This house is aware that it doesn't belong, and I really like that," he said. "We didn't pretend to blend in."

Romero's customers seem to become not just clients but acolytes. Bless, for one, said that he would like to acquire more land and put up a colony of prefab houses for rent near his house in Virginia. Romero seems eager to see the creation of her own Levittowns. I asked her how big she wanted her business to become, and how many prefabricated houses she would like to produce. "Oh, millions and millions," she said immediately. "The more product you can push through, the better you can be."

The New Yorker, October 17, 2005

The Houses at Sagaponac, New York

HOMES OF THE STARS

In the late 1950s, J. Irwin Miller, the chairman of the Cummins Engine Company, decided to liven up Columbus, Indiana, where his company was based, by commissioning work from famous architects—I. M. Pei, Kevin Roche, and Robert Venturi, among others. Pei designed a library; Roche, a post office;

Hariri & Hariri, Sagaponac House (above)

and Venturi, a firehouse. Skidmore, Owings & Merrill designed the city hall. Charles Gwathmey built subsidized housing. Richard Meier and Hardy Holzman Pfeiffer built elementary schools. This made for a place that certainly isn't like any other small town in Indiana, but almost none of the buildings rank among their architect's best work, and Columbus, for all the good intentions, is pretty much the architectural equivalent of one of those art collections that consist of a Henry Moore, a Picasso, a Calder, and a Dalí—an assemblage of names rather than a coherent set of works.

Thirty years after the Columbus project was begun, the dean of the college of art and architecture at the University of Cincinnati also had an idea about using glamorous buildings to attract attention, and the school hired Peter Eisenman, Frank Gehry, Michael Graves, and Henry Cobb. Eisenman designed the architecture school; Graves, an engineering building; Gehry, a molecular-research lab; and Cobb, the music school. This project had a master plan, but the whole turned out to be much less than the sum of its parts, and the parts themselves were not first-rate.

In the mid-1990s, Coco Brown, a developer who lives in New York and Bridgehampton, Long Island, acquired about a hundred acres of scrub in the hamlet of Sagaponack, hard by the East Hampton Airport. This is not the part of Sagaponack where Ira Rennert has built the Versailles-like complex that is the largest house in the Hamptons, although it is only a five-minute drive away. Brown's land is not beachfront property. He picked it up cheaply when another developer went bankrupt after putting a handful of houses on it. Brown figured that he needed to do something to distinguish the land, and, like Irwin Miller and the University of Cincinnati, he decided to start collecting architects. He hired Richard Meier as an adviser, and they selected venerable figures such as Graves, Cobb, Richard Rogers, and Philip Johnson, along with younger celebrity architects—Zaha Hadid, Steven Holl, Shigeru Ban, and Eric Owen Moss—to design houses. They also chose several architects who are less well known to the general public but have substantial reputations in the academic world—people like Stan Allen, Lindy Roy, Winy Maas, Jesse Reiser, Nanako Umemoto, and the sisters Gisue and Mojgan Hariri. This project may be the closest such architects will ever come to designing a freestanding house.

The project seemed like a publicity stunt at first. Designs for the houses were published in a coffee-table book, and there were reports of conflicts between Brown and the architects. Brown, who is seventy years old and tends to dress in the white linen garb of a plantation owner, is accustomed to telling creative people what to do, and he sent Philip Johnson, among others, back to the drawing board. He rejected Thomas Phifer's first design and told Steven Holl that he didn't like a lot of what he had done. "I talked back to Steven Holl and he got a lot less difficult," Brown said to me. "The architects are all stars—it's like a Robert Altman movie." Nevertheless, he signed off on several of the designs and started construction on five houses, including Henry Cobb's, which he even managed to sell. Late this spring, the first house was completed: a sprawling riff on Mies van der Rohe's Barcelona Pavilion by the Hariri sisters,

Iranian-born architects who have practiced in New York since 1986. Three others—the house by Cobb and houses by Annabelle Selldorf and Shigeru Ban—are due to be finished later this year.

The Hariri house looks a lot better than it did on paper. It has a kind of sumptuous, self-assured grandeur that plays on the floating planes and transparent volumes of Mies without ever directly imitating him. It is both elegant and sensual, and the architects seem to have a reasonable understanding of the patterns of normal life. There is a huge master suite, an enormous open kitchen, and a guest wing that is separated from the rest of the house by a modern version of an open loggia—all arranged in an L-shaped structure organized around a pool set into terraces of off-white Turkish travertine. Whatever else you can say about the Hariri sisters, they know how to produce minimalism with a certain majesty.

Not all the houses in the Houses at Sagaponac project (Brown dropped the final "k" of the village's name for his development) are as accommodating to conventional life. Some of the designs seem more like student theses than plans for real buildings. Winy Maas, of the Dutch firm MVRDV, for example, came up with a three-thousand-square-foot house that looks like an amoeba, with the living space raised to the height of the treetops and set in three small huts sandwiched between enormous elevated decks. Lindy Roy's house is to be made of a series of eight interlocking S-shaped steel frames, with a cascading sheet of water that connects to the pool and also serves as an interior wall. Zaha Hadid's house is a sharply angled structure that looks like a small airport terminal. It's hard to imagine that these houses will get built, at least in their original form. One obvious problem with the project is that the star architects have had no relationship with the people who will end up owning—and living in—the houses.

What you are getting, if you choose to buy into Brown's project, is not a house designed specifically for you but a slice of contemporary architectural culture. As if to emphasize this, even the relatively reasonable houses tend to be described with rhetorical excess. The Hariri sisters have said that their house was inspired by a Giacometti sculpture and that "the spatial configuration of the house invites a variety of personalities and occupants, from hermetic individuals to sociable couples or groups, to be 'original' and invent their own way of habitation in this structure." Every house is a stage, but only the most narcissistic architects believe that the shapes they design make them directors.

Since the Hariri house was finished, this spring, Brown has been trying to sell it for $2.95 million. Custom architecture does not come cheap. Even so, less than $3 million in the Hamptons is considered a moderate price. Shingled McMansions on a couple of acres of former farmland near the ocean can go for more than twice that, depending on how the stock market is doing, since buyers are often young hedge-fund managers and investment bankers who are spending their bonuses. "I don't want twenty-five Wall Street guys here," Brown told me as we walked through the Hariri house earlier this summer. There is little danger of that. Not only is the location less than fashionable; there may not be twenty-five people on Wall Street who would want to live in the houses

Brown is building, even for the weekend. The taste of people with large bank accounts tends not to be on the cutting edge.

For two decades now, the prevailing fashion in the Hamptons, Nantucket, Martha's Vineyard, and everywhere else on the East Coast where people with money build beach houses has been to replicate the rambling, gracious architecture of gables and porches that dates from the late nineteenth and early twentieth centuries. When they first appeared, these traditionally styled houses were a welcome relief from the arrogant, simplistic modern houses that had made the seaside fields look like an exhibition of gigantic, second-rate minimalist sculpture. But the neo–Shingle Style houses have themselves become a plague. There are more and more of them, and they are bigger and bigger.

The first modern houses in the Hamptons were gentle, understated wood-and-glass buildings put up in the 1950s and 1960s by architects like Peter Blake, George Nelson, Robert Rosenberg, and Barbara and Julian Neski. Many of them have disappeared. If they had the misfortune of occupying a coveted piece of land, they were replaced by one of the huge new Shingle Style mansions. Now there is hardly any land left in the Hamptons, and almost no sense of the elegantly simple modernist tradition with which the postwar phase of development there began. Coco Brown wouldn't mind if all the McMansions disappeared, and his development strikes a welcome and strong blow for the besieged forces of modernism. But he doesn't want to go back to the sweet modernist boxes of another time, either. He wants modernism to keep innovating, as it should. You might say that the best thing about his project is also the worst thing, which is that the architects are all determined to do something different.

This year marks the seventy-fifth anniversary of Radburn, New Jersey, the extraordinary utopian suburb designed by Clarence Stein and Henry Wright at the edge of Fair Lawn, in Bergen County. Radburn, which its founders billed as a new "town for the motor age," contains relatively ordinary suburban houses, each one more or less the same as the others. But the town was laid out so that the houses turn their backs to the street, making it a service area. They face a wide, rambling greenbelt—a park, in effect. Radburn, almost alone among suburbs, manages to do what cities do, which is to emphasize public space over private space. There is a coherence to it, at no cost to the tranquil pleasures that people seek when they leave the city. Stein and Wright reinvented the idea of suburban development, and in three-quarters of a century, their work hasn't been bettered.

Although Coco Brown intends to add some trails and set aside common park space (as yet undesigned) in Sagaponack, his project is, at heart, a plain-vanilla subdivision. There is nothing about it that advances new ideas for community development, or any ideas about community at all. It is a series of private-house lots of one to two acres, strung together along streets—the most reactionary type of planning there is, wasteful of land and discouraging to a sense of the public realm. If the other houses in the project turn out to be as good as the first one—and those under construction look promising—there will be plenty of notable architecture. But in some ways the spectacular architecture undercuts a sense of community. Even the best houses are likely to clash with each other, and all of them cry out to be hidden by landscaping.

Underneath their flashy surfaces, these houses aren't nearly as different from the banal McMansions as they aspire to be; they're attention-getting structures disconnected from their surroundings. Houses at Sagaponac is being billed as a radical experiment in suburban development, but it is really an old suburb in high-design drag. Radburn was a lot more daring.

The New Yorker, September 13, 2004

GREEN MONSTER

The first thing you think when you see the new luxury apartment building at Astor Place—a slick, undulating tower clad in sparkly green glass—is that it doesn't belong in the neighborhood. The tone of Astor Place is set by places like Cooper Union, the Public Theater, and the gargantuan former Wanamaker store on Broadway: heavy, brawny blocks of masonry that sit foursquare on the ground. Louis Sullivan once described one of Henry Hobson Richardson's great stone buildings as a man with "virile force—broad, vigorous, and with a whelm of energy." The new building, designed by Charles Gwathmey, is an elf prancing among men.

Of course, cities are often enriched by architecture that seems, at first, to be alien:

the pristine glass towers of Mies van der Rohe and the sylphlike bridges of Santiago Calatrava have brought grace to countless harsh, older cityscapes. But this new building, which is on one of the most prominent sites in Lower Manhattan, does not have a transforming effect. If, as Vincent Scully proposed, architecture is a conversation between generations, this young intruder hasn't much to say to its neighbors. Its shape is fussy, and the glass facade is garishly reflective: Mies van der Rohe as filtered through Donald Trump. Instead of adding a lyrical counterpoint to Astor Place, the tower disrupts the neighborhood's rhythm.

In an inelegant way, Gwathmey's building has exposed a truth about this part of Lower Manhattan: inside those rough-and-tumble old masonry buildings is a lot of wealth. By designing a tower with such a self-conscious shimmer, the architect has destroyed the illusion that this neighborhood, which underwent gentrification long ago, is now anything other than a place for the rich. The thirty-nine apartments inside the Gwathmey building start at $2 million.

It is a paradox of the New York real-estate market that nothing breeds gentility like harsh surroundings. Once, it all happened indoors—grimy factory floors in Soho became expensive lofts. Sleekness was a private pleasure, not a public display. But the pair of exceptionally elegant glass towers designed by Richard Meier that went up on the western reaches of Greenwich Village a few years ago changed the rules. High-gloss modernism, preferably attached to the signature of a famous architect and dropped into an old industrial streetscape, became the hottest thing in Manhattan apartment architecture since Emery Roth invented the foyer.

Gwathmey was asked to design the tower soon after Meier's buildings were completed. The land on which Gwathmey's new building sits is owned by Cooper Union, whose main building is right across the street. It used to be a dreary parking lot. Cooper Union tried for years to build something noteworthy on the site, coming up with several ambitious schemes—several years ago, Rem Koolhaas, collaborating with Jacques Herzog and Pierre de Meuron, designed a striking, angular boutique hotel—but none came to fruition. Eventually, Stephen Ross, the head of Related Companies, who built the Time Warner Center at Columbus Circle, took over and commissioned Gwathmey to create a small, sophisticated apartment tower that would attract the same kind of people who had bought apartments in Meier's buildings—people who were tired of living on Park Avenue, or who might otherwise have settled in Tribeca lofts but would be tempted by sexier views and architectural glamour.

What architect wouldn't want to design a building here? Gwathmey's site, at the corner of Astor Place and Lafayette Street, is nearly as free and open as that of the Flatiron Building. Framed by streets on three sides, it faces a large, open intersection containing one of the city's best-known pieces of public sculpture: Tony Rosenthal's black cube, *Alamo*. The site dominates this part of downtown the way the Plaza anchors the southeast corner of Central Park.

Gwathmey responded to this opportunity with a piecemeal design: a four-layer cake. A chunky trapezoidal base is topped by a twenty-one-story section of curved glass; above this rests a boxy minitower, which is crowned by another curved section. For a while, the base of the building was surrounded by scaffolding on which was painted the words "sculpture for living— undulating, provocative, reflective, iconic, curvaceous," which is surely a more sophisticated approach to marketing than "4 rms river vu," even if it left you wondering whether it referred to a condominium or a stripper.

As the marketing campaign suggests, Gwathmey was less interested in fitting in than in stopping people in their tracks. He wanted to make freestanding sculpture. That, in itself, was a good idea, especially at a time when so many New York apartment buildings are knockoffs of prewar brick boxes, based on the idea that blending in is the greatest virtue. At least Gwathmey is above that. At one point, he told me that the building was inspired by Mies van der Rohe's famous unbuilt designs for a curving glass skyscraper. Yet the architect didn't follow Mies enough. He put Mies in the middle, but not at the bottom, where the squat limestone base tries too hard to fit into the surrounding streets, or at the top, with its crown of miniboxes.

Furthermore, the highly reflective glass the architect chose is inexplicable. It is the sort of pastel hue you would expect to see in a suburban office park. There's no need for that today, when glass manufacturers are able to produce clear, almost colorless glass that is as energy-efficient as older, reflective varieties. The green glass contrasts baldly with the white limestone masonry, further fragmenting the facade and making the whole structure look like a catalog of architectural parts.

A peculiar aspect of glass buildings is that they almost always look better when they are surrounded by something else. The Seagram Building seemed a lot more elegant when it had masonry buildings all around it on Park Avenue; so did Lever House. They felt like diamonds in the rough. That's actually a good metaphor for a certain kind of urban building. Frank Gehry's Guggenheim Museum, in Bilbao, and his Walt Disney Concert Hall, in Los Angeles, respond brilliantly to their neighbors by subtly playing off the shapes surrounding them. And diamond in the rough certainly describes Meier's towers, which have an almost ephemeral lightness, and rise gently amid the uneven jumble of the West Village.

Gwathmey has long been noted for his carefully detailed modernist houses and interiors. He and his partner, Robert Siegel, are the architects whom people like Steven Spielberg and Jerry Seinfeld hire for a kind of design that is expertly crafted, staggeringly expensive, and not particularly avant-garde. The apartment units at Astor Place were designed by Gwathmey Siegel in association with the architect Ismael Leyva. The spiffy baths and kitchens, designed by the master himself, are prêt-à-porter Gwathmey, remarkably close to those he creates for custom clients. Every apartment has at least three exposures, and most units have a spectacular section of curving glass wall. These are assertive, sensual spaces that evoke the classic modernist houses of

Le Corbusier, who in the late 1920s began experimenting with romantic curves as a counterpoint to straight lines. (Think of his famous leather chaise.) Being inside one of Gwathmey's living rooms feels, delightfully, like being inside an enormous, transparent grand piano.

The beauty of the interiors, however, only underscores the failings of the exterior. Gwathmey hasn't done many high-rises; he is more comfortable on a small scale. He thrives on intricacy, and that skill doesn't always translate to New York City streets. Gwathmey's building doesn't rise quietly—it thrashes about. It's as if he believed that its complex shape and its eye-popping glass would somehow provide a strong counterpunch to the powerful surrounding architecture. The diamonds in the rough that succeed are all, in one way or another, serene. There is an almost Zen-like quality to Meier's towers. Gwathmey's building is hyperactive. It alludes to Mies and it tries to be a sculptural marker and it tries to fit into the complex streetscape, all at the same time. This building could have been one of the best new buildings in New York—if only the architect had kept it simple.

The New Yorker, May 2, 2005

The Cell Phone Life

DISCONNECTED URBANISM

There is a connection between the idea of place and the reality of cellular telephones. It is not encouraging. Places are unique— or at least we like to believe they are—and we strive to experience them as a kind of engagement with particulars. Cell phones are precisely the opposite. When a piece of geography is doing what it is supposed to do, it encourages you to feel a connection to it that, as in marriage, forsakes all others. When you are in Paris you expect to wallow in its Parisness, to feel that everyone walking up the Boulevard Montparnasse is as totally and completely there as the lampposts, the kiosks, the facade of the Brasserie Lipp—and that they could be no place else.

So we want it to be in every city, in every kind of place. When you are in a forest, you want to experience its woodsiness; when you are on the beach, you want to feel connected to sand and surf.

This is getting harder to do, not because these special places don't exist or because urban places have come to look increasingly alike. They have, but this is not another rant about the monoculture and sameness of cities and the suburban landscape. Even when you are in a place that retains its intensity, its specialness, and its ability to confer a defining context on your life, it doesn't have the all-consuming effect these places used to. You no longer feel that being in one place cuts you off from other places. Technology has been doing this for a long time, of course—remember when people communicated with Europe by letter, and it took a couple of weeks to get a reply? Now we're upset if we have to send a fax, because it takes so much longer than e-mail.

But the cell phone has changed our sense of place more than faxes and computers and e-mail because of its ability to intrude into every moment in every possible place. When you walk along the street and talk on a cell phone, you are not on the street sharing the communal experience of urban life. You are in some other place—someplace at the other end of your phone conversation. You are there, but you are not there. It reminds me of the title of Lillian Ross's memoir of her life with William Shawn, *Here But Not Here*. Now that is increasingly true of almost every person on almost every street in almost every city. You are either on the phone or carrying one, and the moment it rings, you will be transported out of real space into a virtual realm.

This matters because the street is the ultimate public space, and walking along it is the defining urban experience. It is all of us—different people who lead different lives—coming together in the urban mixing chamber. But what if half of them are elsewhere, there in body but not in any other way? You are not on Madison Avenue if you are holding a little object to your ear that pulls you toward a person in Omaha.

The great offense of the cell phone in public is not the intrusion of its ring, although that can be infuriating when it interrupts a tranquil moment. It is the fact that even when the phone does not ring at all, and is being used quietly and discreetly, it renders a public place less public. It turns the boulevardier into a sequestered individual, the flaneur into a figure of privacy. And suddenly the meaning of the street as a public place has been hugely diminished.

I don't know which is worse—the loss of the sense that walking along a great urban street is a glorious shared experience or the blurring of distinctions between different kinds of places. But these cultural losses are related, and the cell phone has played a major role in both. The other day I returned a phone call from a friend who lives in Hartford. He had left a voice-mail message saying he was visiting his son in New Orleans, and when I called him back on his cell phone—area code 860, Hartford—he picked up the call in Tallahassee. Once the area code actually meant something in terms of geography: it outlined a clearly defined piece of the earth; it became a form of identity. Your telephone number was a badge of place. Now the area code is really not much more than three digits; and if it has any connection to a place, it's just the telephone's home base. An area code today is more like a car's license plate. The downward spiral that began with the end of the old telephone exchanges that truly did connect to a place—RHinelander 4 and BUtterfield 8 for the Upper East Side, or CHelsea 3 downtown, or UNiversity 4 in Morningside Heights—surely culminates in the placeless area codes such as 917 and 347 that could be anywhere in New York— or anywhere at all.

It's increasingly common for cell-phone conversations to begin with the question, "Where are you?" and for the answer to be anything from "out by the pool" to "Madagascar." I don't miss the age when phone charges were based on distance, but that did have the beneficial effect of reinforcing a sense that places were distinguishable from one another. Now calling across the street and calling from New York to California or even Europe are precisely the same thing. They cost the same because to the phone they are the same. Every place is exactly the same as every other place. They are all just nodes on a network— and so, increasingly, are we.

Metropolis, November 2003

THE SAMENESS OF THINGS

At the San Francisco headquarters of Williams-Sonoma, Gary Friedman operates what amounts to a mass-market taste laboratory. Several dozen designers and buyers work here, surrounded by vases and chairs and picture frames and glasses and clocks, charged with turning the things they see in the world into objects they can sell through the company's various holdings, which include Hold Everything and Pottery Barn. It is the opposite of alchemy: money is made not by rendering each object more valuable but by rendering it less valuable and less rare, so that it can be owned by anybody.

"We travel the world, looking for inspiration," Friedman says. "Then we edit it down to what we think is most

appropriate for our customer. But it's what we like—we are all the customer."
Friedman, who is the chief merchandising officer, takes his buyers and
his product development people to places that he thinks will inspire them.
He flew them all to South Beach in Miami to see Philippe Starck's Delano
hotel, for example, which led to the increased presence of whiteness in the
Pottery Barn's spring product line: from cutting edge to mass market in
a couple of years.

"We sit down around a table and talk about what we see, what's happening
in design, what any of us has seen that's excited us," he says. "Then we try
to boil that down to a target. Someone will say a modern thing is happening.
Someone else will interrupt to say, 'But everyone still cares about being soft
and comfortable.' And we will distill all of that into a general product direction."
Eventually this "general product direction" becomes a set of products,
organized in compatible combinations that are photographed for the catalog
and displayed in the stores in more or less the same arrangements, crafted to
enhance their allure.

If all of this sounds slightly, well, corporate, it is supposed to. Gary
Friedman and the Pottery Barn—along with his major competitors like the
Chicago-based Crate and Barrel and clothing merchants like the Gap and J.
Crew—have raised standardization to a high art. Together, these companies
have brought to the mass marketplace a level of design quality that once existed
only at a high price.

Nothing, of course, comes free: the cost of this achievement is that while
everything may be better, it is also increasingly the same. The khakis and
sweatshirts the Gap sells in Dallas shopping malls are the same as the ones
it purveys along Columbus Avenue in Manhattan—in nearly identical stores.
Perhaps even more to the point, they are not so different, aesthetically speaking,
from what's available at Benetton or J. Crew.

Call it the ubiquitous middle-class American taste culture. It manifests
itself in everything from the white-slipcovered sofas of Crate and Barrel to
the solid-colored polo shirts of A/X Armani Exchange; its symbolic church is
the Gap, whose president, Mickey Drexler, may have had a greater impact on
the quality and look of design in the last twenty years than anyone else in the
United States. Drexler is the man who transformed the Gap from a chain of
stores selling jeans to teenagers into what is probably the most effective mass-
market design engine in the world. Its volume is not the largest in American
clothing retailing—the Limited and the TJX Companies, parent of T.J. Maxx
and Marshalls, take in more than the Gap's $5.3 billion in annual sales. But the
Gap, with 1,682 stores in the United States, has been the driving force behind
the shift in American taste toward the simple.

"I have never understood why certain things in America can't be available
to everyone," says Drexler, fifty-two, a short, wiry man who combines the
enthusiasm of an undergraduate with the passion of a missionary. Sitting in his
San Francisco office, dressed in his usual Gap blue jeans, a white Gap T-shirt,
and a striped Hermes dress shirt, he looks out at the Bay Bridge and explains

that he envisions the Gap not just as a purveyor of clothing but also as a brand name that can be used to sell design to the masses.

Indeed, the Gap, along with its upmarket cousin Banana Republic and its new low-priced brand Old Navy, throws itself into standardization with almost military enthusiasm. The Gap stores—sleek combinations of pale wood, white walls, and brushed aluminum—are, like the clothes, modern and yet relatively classic, unambiguous and easy to look at. Warmth and accessibility come before innovation and challenge, managing the neat trick of appearing to celebrate casualness and spontaneity even as they honor continuity.

A directive from headquarters to Banana Republic store managers, for example, presents in photographs an environment for "Men's Relaxed Style II" and reads in part: "The shirt cabinet has been formatted so that every other shelf houses a bright color program, with the blue shirt styles housed on the shelves in between. Placing the colored shirts in the same order on each shelf reinforces the color expression and creates a very straightforward presentation."

Mass marketing has been transformed from a business that depends on sheer volume into one driven, like high-end clothing sales, by image: buy the T-shirt, get the lifestyle. What was once communicated by, say, highly styled photographs of beautiful young people in rural settings in the J. Crew catalog is now also communicated by the ambiance in the store. Ralph Lauren pioneered this approach in 1986 when he transformed the Rhinelander Mansion into a temple of retailing designed to evoke an aristocratic upbringing. The one-woman conglomerate of Martha Stewart plays a part in selling an identity along with the goods, as do designers like Calvin Klein and Tommy Hilfiger. But what stores like Urban Outfitters, Crate and Barrel, Pottery Barn, and the Gap have done is to create a taste machine, a veritable assembly line of aesthetics that knocks off both high-end, innovative design and eccentric, subculture notions, spitting out objects that appeal to people with sophisticated taste but that are also priced within the reach of a huge segment of the population.

Twenty years ago, there was little consistency and almost no design quality to moderately priced clothing; you pushed your way through the messy racks at Kmart or Wal-Mart or made do with the stock of a local merchant, and the best that could be said was that it was cheap. If there was any style at all, it was the kind that had trickled down slowly, getting more garish with each step. In household goods, it was the same story: dowdy imitations of traditional objects, and the more fake-wood-grain laminate, the better. Modern design was seen as something rarefied; stores like Design Research in Cambridge, Massachusetts, and New York, or Bonnier or Georg Jensen in New York sold modern furniture to a small, upscale audience, while progressive design was sold almost exclusively through special showrooms open only to decorators. The whole system seemed organized to prove the point that high design was the province of an elite.

In one sense, the new taste factories represent the triumph of the long-frustrated dream of the Bauhaus, which was that modern design would be available to everyone and would erase, as it were, class distinctions. That dream didn't have a chance in the 1920s and 1930s, when the Bauhaus first began to bring modern design to the German public, but ended up producing expensive objects of limited appeal. And it didn't happen in the 1940s and 1950s, either, as mass-marketing expanded its reach, but not enough to bring good design to a broad public.

But the 1960s brought stores like Azuma in New York, whose brightly colored plastic and rattan modules seemed to merge a modernist utilitarianism and counterculture breeziness, perfect for college dorm rooms and starter apartments. The bigger and longer-lasting Pier 1 began importing examples of modern design, bringing bentwood rockers and Indian print pillows to market cheaply, just as places like the Door Store and Workbench began selling imitation Marcel Breuer dining chairs or bentwood Prague chairs to baby boomers eager to show that they were no longer undergraduates.

It took the convergence of several trends—homogenization, mass communication, and the arrival of a new, more visually sophisticated young professional class—to make design marketable in the way that it has become today. Now, class distinctions are pretty much beside the point: the moment I realized that the Gap was truly a broad social and cultural phenomenon was when I heard Brooke Astor tell someone that it was her favorite place in New York to shop.

The consumers who are now in their twenties, thirties, and forties share an aesthetic that brings them toward things like black T-shirts and khakis and (except as a kitsch exercise) away from television sets with fake-wood Formica casing, "Mediterranean" kitchen cabinets, or avocado-colored refrigerators. They take their visual cues from advertising, magazine layouts, CD covers, movies—all orchestrated by itinerant stylists who serve as the messengers of what is cool, hip, and appropriately ironic. The well-oiled design machine then cranks out facsimiles of crumbly Ionic columns (to use as TV or plant stands), rotary-style phones with touch-tone pads (for a faux-1940s film-noir effect), and other design accents suggesting a critical "eye." The machine has no allegiance to any particular style, and its vigor and longevity lie specifically in its preemptive adaptability: no trend is too extreme or idiosyncratic for it to co-opt.

Sir Terence Conran saw much of this coming in 1977, when he opened his first Conran's as the baby boomers were hitting their thirties. Though his American stores were not nearly as sophisticated as his Habitat stores in England, the idea still worked, at least for a while, and surely set the stage in the late 1980s and early 1990s for Crate and Barrel, Ikea (whose vast blue-and-yellow stores combined European design with the American superstore concept), and the various outposts operated by Williams-Sonoma. Every one of these has become a brand name, selling a kind of cozy minimalism that is far from the cutting edge but consistently high in quality.

But there's a downside, connected to the global homogenization of products and culture and shared with McDonald's, *USA Today*, and Starbucks: the stuff may be good but it ain't special. As the floor of design quality is raised, the ceiling comes down a bit, too. Everything seems more and more the same, wherever you are. Eccentric and idiosyncratic things fill the shelves of these mass stores, but they have been devalued by their very accessibility. The truly special and inventive is harder and harder to find, unless you are very, very rich or have lots of time to look. Since the new common denominator is high, maybe it doesn't matter much. Still, we pay the price in a gradual but very real loss of individual variation: our houses and our wardrobes, like our entertainment, become part of mass culture, wherein we all increasingly consume and display the same thing.

Choice—the most bewildering thing to the consumer—is rendered magically simple. Everything looks (and is) acceptable, and almost everything goes with everything else. The white shirt goes with the sweater, which works with the khakis, which look fine with the denim shirt, all of which sits nicely on the slipcovered sofa next to the forged-iron coffee table, which looks good beside the metal picture frame and the brushed-metal lamp.

All merchants edit; the merchants of the new mass-taste culture edit especially heavily. They are like small boutiques where the owner's taste is the chief attraction—only here the taste is generic, and the boutique is a multimillion-dollar business operated worldwide. There was a time when good taste was something earned, something that signified a worldliness born of education and travel. These stores offer a shortcut.

"One of our home accessories buyers found a pocket watch in a London flea market, and she had this marvelous idea to turn it into a bedside clock," says Friedman. "So we designed a stand and found a manufacturer willing to make the clock in a big size and bring the whole thing to market for twenty-nine dollars. Now we've sold thousands of them. Who else could do that?"

Friedman picks up a beaded-shade lamp. "I've always loved these, and I wanted to buy something like this for my house, but it turned out to cost $800. So I went to our lamp buyer, and I said, I have a challenge for you, you are going to be the first person in the world to bring a lamp like this to people at a price they can afford. The buyer found a factory in India that made beaded emblems for British school blazers. One of our designers had the brilliant idea to do a modern base that works just right." The lamp, with a handsome cast-metal base, now sells for $129.

"It took a while, though," Benno Duenkelsbuehler, one of Friedman's lieutenants, says. "This is the first beaded shade they produced"—he holds up what looks like a green Slinky—"and when it came I was totally depressed."

The failed lamp has no place in the Pottery Barn, of course, but neither does the eccentricity it represents. That's the sad thing: that as uniformity becomes more and more what stores are selling—uniformity of presentation as well as uniformity of merchandise—a kind of high-level blandness begins to take over. The beaded lamp is a lovely little thing, and more power to Pottery Barn for letting us all have it. But it is now a mass-market object, no longer capable of providing a spark of original magic in a room.

Is there such a thing as too much good taste? It's easy to think this is exactly what has happened in the retail world. You begin to yearn for some off note, something wrong, something even a bit vulgar, just to show individual sensibility.

Paradoxically, these stores often market themselves as vehicles for creative expression: shop at the Gap and be yourself, buy your furniture at Pottery Barn so that you can discover the real you. But is the real you quite so much like the real me? Somehow I doubt it. Truly creative design has almost always come from breaking molds or finding new patterns, from someone doing something different from what has been done before. My house isn't supposed to look like your house. After we both finish shopping at the Pottery Barn, however, it probably will.

The New York Times Magazine, April 6, 1997

INDEX

Note: Page numbers in **bold** refer to illustrations.

Aalto, Alvar 133–34
Abramovitz, Max 133–34, 135
Abrams, Charles 95
airports 38–41
Alfred P. Murrah Federal Building 207–11
Alice Tully Hall **140**, 140–43
Allen, Stan 297
Allianz Arena **28**, 29–30, 43
Allied Works Architecture 273
American Crafts Museum 273. *See also* Museum of Arts
    and Design
Amery, Colin 194
Amon Carter Museum 243
Ando, Tadao 237, 239–41, 242, 243–45, 248
Andre, Carl 245
Andreu, Paul 39, 66
Annenberg, Walter 75, 76, 79
apartment houses 287–90. *See also under specific building
    names*
Arad, Michael 174
Architects' Journal 196, 199
Arnault, Bernard 112
ARO 124
Arquitectonica 9, 10, 120, 127–31
Art Institute of Chicago 35, 97, 99, 240
Arup Associates 195, 197
Astor, Brooke 311
Astor Place Tower 9, 166, 288, **301**, 301–4
Atlantic Yards, Brooklyn **160**, 162–63
Auping, Michael 245
Avery Fisher Hall 133, 134, 136, 137, 138, 141

Bacon, Edmund 64
Bacon, Henry 205, 210
Ballon, Hilary 92
Banana Republic 166, 310
Ban, Shigeru 295, 297, 298
Barcelona Pavilion 240, 297
Bard College 17, 249
Barnes, Edward Larrabee 248
Barnes & Noble 166, 169
baseball parks 152–55
Basques 9, 215, 216
Bauhaus 80–81, 85–86, 273–74, 310–11
Bayley, Stephen 196
Beaubourg. *See* Centre Pompidou, Paris
Beeby, Thomas 22, 197
Beijing
    airports in 38–41
    brief history, current state of 67
    CCTV Headquarters **64**, 65–66
    hutongs 46, 64, 66, 67
    new architecture in 8, 64–68
    Olympic architecture in 29, 32, 42–47
    Tiananmen Square 43, 67
Beijing Capital International Airport **38**, 39–41
Belluschi, Pietro 133–34, 140, 141–42
Benetton 57, 309
Bennett, Edward H. 98
Bergdoll, Barry 86
Berg, Sven 210
Berlin Philharmonic Hall 18

Beuys, Joseph 218
Beyer Blinder Belle 135, 136
Bird's Nest. *See* National Stadium, Beijing
Birnbaum, Philip 287
Blair, Tony 197, 198
Blake, Peter 299
Bloomberg Newsroom **156**, 158, 159
Bodin, Jean-François 230
Boston Properties 146
Botstein, Leon 249
Botta, Mario 269
Bowery 6, 268, 269, 270, 271
Bowles, Camilla Parker 195, 196
Brennan Beer Gorman 146
Breuer, Marcel 133–34, 146, 248, 258, 311
British Library 193–94, 233
British Museum 150, 228, 232–36
British Museum Courtyard **232**
Bronfman, Samuel 84, 86
Brooklyn Bridge 78, 109, 165
Brown, Coco 297, 298, 299
Brown, J. Carter 203
Browne-Wilkinson, Hilary 195, 199
Bryant Park 119, 165
Bunshaft, Gordon 72, 134. *See also* Skidmore, Owings
    & Merrill
Burgee, John 119, 281, 282
Burnham, Daniel **97**, 97–101, 170
Burnham & Root 281
Burrows, Edwin G. 105–10
Butterfield, William 196
Butzer, Hans and Torrey 207, 210

Calatrava, Santiago 33–37, 45, 137, 175, 216,
    237–39, 302
Calder Museum, Philadelphia 240
Camden Yards 153, 154
Canadian Centre for Architecture 85, 87
Canary Wharf 27, 136, 196
Candela, Rosario 284, 286, 287, 290
Carley, Christopher T. 34, 35, 37
Carnegie Hall 133, 135, 136, 165
Caro, Robert 91–96
Carpenter, J. E. R. 284
Carrère & Hastings 22, 145
Castro 51, 54, 57. *See also* Havana
Catalano, Eduardo 141
CCTV Headquarters **64**, 65–66
cell phones 305, 306. *See also* technology, effect on
    daily life
Central Park 76, 93, 107, 108, 109, 115, 135, 144, 145, 146,
    151, 165, 274, 302
15 Central Park West **283**, 283–86, 290
Centre Pompidou, Paris 6, 197, **227**, 227–31
Chanel 112, 113, 294
Chappell, George S. 127
Charles de Gaulle airport 39
Charles, Prince of Wales 11, 190, 191, 192, 193–201, 230
Chartres 214, 243
Chatham 279, 281, 290
Chelsea Piers 165–66, 169
Chicago
    1893 World's Fair 99
    and Mies van der Rohe 85, 87, 286, 293
    Ando, Tadao, architecture in 240, 243
    Burgee, John, skyscraper 281
    Burnham Plan for Chicago 97–101, 170
    Calatrava, Santiago, tower (Fordham Spire) 34–37, 238
    John Hancock Tower 149

Chicago (continued)
   library 22
   Masonic Temple 281
   Museum of Contemporary Art 269
   Wrigley Field 153
Chicago River **99**
Childs, David 145, 146, 147, 171, 174. *See also* Skidmore, Owings & Merrill
Chipperfield, David 195
Choa, Christopher 181
Chrysler Building 117, 118, 124, 127, 128
Citi Field 152–55
City Beautiful movement 99
CityWalk, Universal Studios 192, 219
Clinton, DeWitt 106
Cloepfil, Brad 272, 273
Cobb, Henry 297
Cohen, I. Bernard 79
2 Columbus Circle 145, 272–75
Columbus Circle 133, 145, 146, 147, 151, 272, 273, 274, 302
Condé Nast Building, New York 117, 119, 151
Conran, Terence 196, 311
Contemporary Art Museum, St. Louis 273
Contemporary Arts Center, Cincinnati **246**, 247–48
convention centers, design of 24–27
Cook, Rodney Mims, Jr. 188–92, 200
Cooper, Peter 108
Cooper, Robertson & Partners 136
Coop Himmelblau 216
Coyula, Mario 50, 58, 59
Crate and Barrel 309, 310, 311
Crawford, Bruce 137
Cropsey, Jasper 190
Cross-Bronx Expressway 95
Cuba, preservation in 50–59
Cunningham, Ann Pamela 185

Dalzell, Lee Baldwin 184, 186
Dalzell, Robert F., Jr. 184, 186
Damrosch Park 137, 138
Davidson, Lifschutz 195
Davis, Gene 262
Delano hotel 309
de Maria, Walter 265
Demetrios, Eames 82
de Meuron, Pierre 28, 43, 252, 302. *See also* Herzog and de Meuron
Dennis Pieprz 47
Denver Art Museum **260**, 261–63
de Portzamparc, Christian 111, 112–15
Desmarais, Charles 247
Despont, Thierry 221
de Young Museum 28, 30–31
Diana, Princess of Wales 190, 196
Digital Beijing 42, 44
Diller and Scofidio 89, 132, 136–39, 141, 231
Diller, Barry 161, 162, 163
Diller, Liz 89, 136, 141, 231. *See also* Diller and Scofidio; Diller Scofidio + Renfro
Diller Scofidio + Renfro 140–43
Dinkeloo, John 79
Dior, Christian 112, 113, 179. *See also* LVMH Tower
Disney Hall. *See* Walt Disney Concert Hall
Disneyland 62, 168, 219, 220
Drexler, Arthur 252
Duany, Andrés 52
Duany, Douglas 52, 53
Dubbeldam, Winka 173, 288
Duenkelsbuehler, Benno 312

Eames, Charles and Ray **75**, 75–83
90 East End Avenue 281
145 East Seventy-sixth Street 280–81
Ebbets Field 153, 154, 155
Eiffel Tower 61, 63, 175, 182
Eisenman, Peter 249, 297
Elizabeth, Queen of England 193
Elkus/Manfredi 146
Empire State Building 29, 117, 120, 124, 151, 165, 258
Erie Canal 106, 107
ETFE 29, 44
Excalibur, Las Vegas **60**

Fentress, Curt W. 63
Fiera Milano **24**, 25–27
834 Fifth Avenue 279, 284
1040 Fifth Avenue 284, 286
Fine Arts Commission 203, 205
Fisher Center for the Performing Arts, New York 17, 246, 249–50
Fisher, Norman and Doris 73, 74
Flatiron Building 98, 117, 302
Forbidden City 43, 46, 64, 65
Fordham Spire 34–37
Forest City Ratner 157
Fort-Brescia, Bernardo 128, 129, 130. *See also* Arquitectonica
Fort Worth 243, 244
42nd Street Development Project 120, 128, 136
Foster, Norman 8, 38, 39–41, 114, 136, 148, 149–51, 194, 195, 199, 200, 216, 232, 233–36
Fowle, Bruce 117, 119. *See also* Fox & Fowle; FXFowle
Fox & Fowle 117–18
Frederic C. Hamilton Building 261. *See also* Denver Art Museum
Freedom Tower 35, 145, 171–73, 175
Friedman, Gary 308–9, 312
Fuksas, Massimiliano 24, 25–27
Fuller, Buckminster 150
FXFowle 141, 157, 259

Gale, Adrian 198, 199
Gallery of Modern Art 272–73
Gap 125, 166, 309, 310, 311, 313
Garrett, Wendell 184
Gehry, Frank
   and Ground Zero 171, 174
   and Kahn, Louis 71, 73
   and Lincoln Center redevelopment 136, 138–39, 141
   architectural style of 34, 35, 89
   as jewelry designer 161
   Atlantic Yards, Brooklyn **160**, 162–63
   Condé Nast cafeteria 151
   Fisher Center for the Performing Arts, New York 17, 246, 249–50
   Guggenheim Museum Bilbao 9, 17, 162, **214**, 214–18, 229, 238, 239, 253, 266, 303
   InterActiveCorp Headquarters **160**, 161, 162
   retrospective of 88
   University of Cincinnati research lab 297
   Walt Disney Concert Hall **16**, 16–19, 162, 303
   work in Ohio 249
Gensler 122, 123, 156, 158
Getty Center, Los Angeles 195, **219**, 219–22, 224, 225
Getty, J. Paul 224
Getty Museum 223–24
Getty Research Institute 221
Getty Trust 220, 221, 224
Getty Villa, Malibu **223**, 223–26

Gilbert, Cass 89, 173
Gilder, George 104
Giovannini, Joseph 80
Giuliani, Rudy 105, 147, 166
Glikine, Anton 191
Goodwin and Stone 252, 253, 255
Goodwin, Philip L. 251, 270. *See also* Goodwin and Stone
Gotham: A History of New York City to 1898 105–10
Grand Central Terminal 146, 165
Graves, Michael 130, 171, 181, 258, 297
Greenberg, Allan 184, 185, 186, 197
Grimshaw, Nicolas 195, 200
Griscom, John H. 108
Ground Zero 12, 19, 35, 95, 133, 170, 171–75, 203, 208, 261
Guerin, Jules 99
Guggenheim Museum Bilbao **214**, 215–18, 229, 238, 249, 253, 266
Guggenheim Museum New York 88, 217, 238, 239, 251, 262
Gutman, Marta 94
Gwathmey, Charles 9, 10, 130, 288, 293, 297, 301–4
Gwathmey Siegel 9, 288, 301–4

Habitat 311
Hadid, Zaha 27, 29, 46, 98, 142, 246, 247, 248, 249, 297, 298
Hardy Holzman Pfeiffer 280, 297
Hariri, Gisue and Mojgan 297. *See also* Hariri & Hariri
Hariri & Hariri 296, 297, 298
Harrison, Wallace K. 133–34, 142
Hartford, Huntington 272, 273
Hartman-Cox 281
Haswell Green, Andrew 108
Havana **50**, **55**, 50–59
Hawksmoor, Nicholas 196
Hayward, Leland 77
Hearst Headquarters **148**, 149–51
Hearst, William Randolph 149
Heathrow Airport 38, 40
Heinz, Drue 199
Herzog and de Meuron 8, 28–32, 42–47, 252, 253, 266
Herzog, Jacques 28, 43, 252, 302. *See also* Herzog and de Meuron
Hiesinger, Kathryn B. 88
Highgrove 195
Hillier Group 114–15
Hideki Hirahara 66
HOK Sport 152, 153–55
Holl, Steven 66, 252, 264–67, 297
Holocaust Museum 208
Hong Kong & Shanghai Bank 200
Hopkins, Michael 195
Houses at Sagaponac, New York **296**, 296–300
Houston 26, 67, 168, 178, 189, 229
Hunt, Richard Morris 98
hutongs 46, 64, 66, 67
Huxtable, Ada Louise 273

IBM 79, 113
Institute of Contemporary Art, Boston 138, 142
InterActiveCorp **160**, 161
Isozaki, Arata 17, 216
Iwo Jima memorial 203
Izenour, Steven 60, 61, 62, 87

Jackson, Kenneth 92, 94
Jacobs, Jane 67, 92, 93, 95, 96, 100
Javits Center, New York 25, 230
Jazz at Lincoln Center 146, 147
Jefferson, Thomas 13, 94, 183, 195, 285. *See also* Monticello

Jewish Museum, Berlin 261
John Hancock Center, Chicago 36, 149
John, Richard 199
Johnson & Burgee 282
Johnson, Philip 56, 71, 72, 82, 86, 88, 119, 133–35, 142, 228, 243, 252, 254, 281, 282, 289, 297
Joyce International Dance Center 175
Judd, Donald 218, 263
Juilliard 133, 134, 136, 137, 140, 141, 142
Jun, Wang 67

Kahler, David 238
Kahn, Louis 36, 56, 69, 69–74, 84, 150, 215, 235, 241, 242, 243, 244, 250
Kahn, Nathaniel 70, 71, 72, 73
Kahn, Sue Ann 70, 71, 73, 74
Keating, Frank 208
Kelly, Ellsworth 241
Kiasma Museum of Contemporary Art 265
Kiefer, Anselm 218, 245, 248, 270
Kimbell Art Museum, Fort Worth 69, 74, 241, 242, 243, 244
Kleihues, Josef Paul 269
Kohl, Daniel 262
Kohn Pedersen Fox 117, 118, 282
Kondylis, Costas 120, 281
Koolhaas, Rem 9, 20–23, 29, 32, 64–66, 122, 123–26, 247, 252, 253, 258, 302
Kramer, Hilton 76
Krens, Thomas 216, 218
Krier, Leon 194

Ladies' Mile district 166
Laguna Verde. *See* LV Prefabricated House
Lambert, Phyllis 84, 85
Landmarks Preservation Commission 273
Lasdun, Denys 195
Las Vegas **60**, 60–63, 87, 178
Lauder, Ronald 252
Lauren, Ralph 194, 269, 310
Lazor, Charlie 293
Leal, Eusebio 51, 57, 58
Learning from Las Vegas 61, 87
Le Corbusier 17, 36, 57, 71, 84, 138, 183, 195, 199, 229, 240, 241, 255, 286, 293, 297, 302, 303, 304
Lehrer, Peter 136
Le Ricolais, Robert 150
Lethem, Jonathan 162
Lever House 112, 114, 117, 191, 288, 303
LeWitt, Sol 218, 267
Libeskind, Daniel 27, 35, 145, 171–74, 247, 260–63
Lincoln Center 19, 92, 95, **132**, 132–39, 140–43, 146, 147, 165, 166, 249
Lincoln Memorial 98, 203, 204, 205, 210
Linenthal, Edward T. 208
Lin, Maya 202, 205, 209, 210
LMN Architects 22
Loeb, Daniel 285
Lois and Richard Rosenthal Center 247. *See also* Contemporary Arts Center, Cincinnati
Los Angeles 17–18, 77, 81, 191, 219–20, 221, 223–24, 303
Los Angeles Philharmonic 17
Louvre 42, 82, 231, 233
Lo, Vincent 180
Lower Manhattan Development Corporation 172
Lutyens, Edwin 196, 202
Luxor, Las Vegas **60**
LVMH Tower **111**, 112–15
LV Prefabricated House **291**, 291–95

Maas, Winy 297, 298
Machado and Silvetti 223, 224–26
Machado, Rodolfo 224. *See also* Machado and Silvetti
Macklowe Organization 281
Mack, William 147
Madrid Barajas International Airport 38, 39–41
Mall, Washington, D.C. 6, 52, 98, 202, 203, 204, 205, 206
Mallarmé 265
Malmö. *See* Turning Torso Tower
Mandalay Bay, Las Vegas **60**
Manhattan House 288
Man in Full, A 189
Mao 43, 65, 68, 180
Mapplethorpe, Robert 247
Mars, Neville 67
Marxism Today 197
Massimiliano Fuksas 24, 25–27
mass-market design 308–13
Mayer & Whittlesey 288
Mayers & Schiff 120
McDonald's 90, 166, 167, 311
McGraw-Hill Building 127, 128
McKim, Charles F. 98, 257. *See also* McKim, Mead
    & White
McKim, Mead & White 22, 145
McMansions 88, 298, 299, 300
McVoy, Chris 265
Meier, Richard 37, 130, 136, 173, 219–22, 224, 225, 229,
    284, 288, 290, 293, 297, 302, 303, 304
Memorial to the Missing of the Somme 202
memorials and monuments 43, 53, 82, 94, 98, 175,
    190–92, 200, 202–6, 207–10, 220, 243, 287
Metropolis 4, 12, 92
Metropolitan Museum of Art, New York 35, 75, 76, 79, 81,
    133, 134, 136, 138, 151, 229, 230, 236, 239, 251, 252, 254
Metropolitan Opera House 133, 134, 136, 137, 138, 142
Metropolitan Transportation Authority 146, 147
Mets 153, 154, 155
Mies van der Rohe, Ludwig
    architectural style of 71, 84–85, 86–87, 138, 229, 298,
        302, 303
    Chicago 255, 293
    growing popularity of 85–86
    Riehl House **84**, 86, 87
    Seagram Building 36, 84, 85, 87, 149, 191, 199, 288, 289,
        303
Milan Trade Fair. *See* Fiera Milano
Militello, Anne 118
Miller, J. Irwin 296, 297
Milwaukee Art Museum 34, **237**, 238–39
Modern Art Museum of Fort Worth **242**, 243–45, 248
Modern Art Society 247
Monticello 13, 82, 183, 184, 186
monuments. *See* memorials and monuments
Moore, Andrew 92
Moore, Charles 168, 191
Morgan Library & Museum **256**, 257–59
Morris, Benjamin W. 257
Moses, Robert 51, **91**, 91–96, 100, 108, 132, 133, 135, 146
Moss, Eric Owen 297
Mount Vernon **182**, 183–87
Mount Vernon Ladies' Association 184, 185
Mumford, Lewis 11, 93, 95, 100, 127, 252, 283–84, 286
Municipal Art Society 146, 147
Munitz, Barry 221, 222
Musée National d'Art Moderne 229
Museum of Arts and Design **272**, 273–75
Museum of Modern Art, New York 30, 80, 85, 86, 87, 230,
    251–55, 269, 270, 271, 273

Museum of the City of New York 92
Museum Tower 279, 288
museums. *See under specific museum names*
MVRDV 298

Nagata Acoustics of Tokyo 18
Nash, John 145, 198
National Aquatics Center, Beijing 42, 43–47
National Center for the Performing Arts, Beijing 66–67
National Gallery, London 89, 194, 201
National Gallery of Art, Washington, D.C. 203, 238, 266
National Stadium, Beijing **42**, 43–44, 46, 47
National World War II Memorial **202**, 203–6
Nelson-Atkins Museum of Art, Kansas City **264**, 264–67
Nets arena 162–63
Neuerburg, Norman 224
Neue Staatsgalerie, Stuttgart 200, 201
Neutra, Richard 81
Nevada Meat Market 166
Newbold, Joanne 122, 123
New 42nd Street Studios **116**, 118
New Museum of Contemporary Art **268**, 269–71
newsrooms, brief history of 157
New Suburbanization 165–69
New York (city)
    brief history of 104–10
    brief history of residential architecture in 279
    new residential architecture in 278–82, 287–90
    Robert Moses's effect on 92–93
    urbanism in 164–69
New York City Opera 133, 135, 175
New York Coliseum 93, 133, 145, 146
New Yorker, The 4, 8, 9, 10, 11, 12, 47, 110, 115, 127, 147,
    206, 304
New York-New York, Las Vegas **60**
New York Philharmonic 133, 141
New York Public Library 21, 22, 145, 165
New York State Theater 133, 134, 136
New York Times 4, 11, 12, 70, 76, 136, 156, 167, 239, 273
    Newsroom 156, 157–58, 257, 259
1964 New York World's Fair 79
Niemeyer, Oscar 228
Nishizawa, Ryue 268, 269, 270
Noguchi, Isamu 267
Norman Rockwell Museum 285
Nouvel, Jean 266, 284, 288

Ochs, Adolph S. 157
Office for Metropolitan Architecture 20, 21, 64, 122, 124.
    See also Koolhaas, Rem; Ramus, Joshua
Oklahoma City National Memorial **207**, 207–11
Olmsted, Frederick Law 108
Olympics
    1992, Barcelona 216
    1996, Atlanta 190. *See also* World Athletes Monument
    2008, Beijing 8, 29, 32, 42, 42–47
    2012, planning for 46
    brief history 45
Olympic Tower 288
Onassis, Jacqueline 70, 146
Ove Arup & Partners 228

Paramount Building 130
500 Park Avenue 112, 114, 279
515 Park Avenue **278**, 279–80, 282, 290
740 Park Avenue 279, 284, 285
Pataki, George 171–72, 173
Paternoster Square 197
Paxton, Joseph 26

Peachtree Street, Atlanta 188, 190, 191
Pedersen, William 120
Pei, I. M. 70, 133, 238, 266, 296
Pelli, Cesar 158, 252, 253, 254
Pentagram 156, 158, 159
Philadelphia Museum of Art 88–90
Philharmonic Hall, New York 133, 134, 135
Phillips, Lisa 269, 270
Piano, Renzo
    Centre Pompidou, Paris 197, **227**, 227–31
    Morgan Library & Museum **256**, 257–59
    museum architecture, general 239
    New York Times Newsroom 156, 157–59
    Whitney Museum Expansion, New York 256, 258–59
Picasso 61, 71, 238, 254, 297
Piedmont Driving Club 188, 189, 190
Platt Byard Dovell 116, 118
Plaza 52, 57, 93, 159, 168, 178, 279, 288, 302
Polites, Peter 191, 192
Ponti, Gio 261
Porro, Ricardo 56
Port Authority 95, 120, 157, 171, 172, 173, 175
Port Authority Bus Terminal 120, 157
Potsdamer Platz, Berlin 170
Pottery Barn 166, 167, 308, 309, 310, 312, 313
Poundbury, Dorset **193**, 194, 195
Power Broker, The 91–96
Prada New York Epicenter 9, 23, **122**, 123–26
Predock, Antoine 63
Prefab housing. *See* LV Prefabricated House
Price Tower 249
Prince Charles monument. *See* World Athletes
    Monument
Prince of Wales's Institute of Architecture 195, 198
Pritzker Prize 28, 112, 240, 243
PTW Architects 42–47
Pulitzer, Joseph, Jr. 240, 241
Pulitzer, Emily Rauh 239, 240, 241
Pulitzer Foundation, St. Louis 237, 239–41, 243

Quadracci Pavilion 237, 238
Queens Museum of Art 92
Quintana, Nicolás 53, 54

Radburn, New Jersey 299, 300
Ramus, Joshua 21, 22, 23. *See also* Office for Metropolitan
    Architecture
Rapson, Ralph 80
Ratner, Bruce 162, 163
Reed & Stem 39
Reichstag, Berlin 150, 233
Reiser, Jesse 297
Related Companies 147, 302
Renfro, Charles 141. *See also* Diller Scofidio + Renfro
Rennert, Ira 297
Resolution: 4 Architecture 293
retail 21, 67, 77, 80, 110, 113, 122–26, 135, 145, 146, 165, 166,
    168, 173, 180, 221, 224, 239, 244, 265, 311–13
Rhinelander Mansion 310
Rice, Peter 228
Richardson, Henry Hobson 301
Riehl House **84**, 86–87
Riley, Terence 85, 254
Ritz Tower 280
Robertson, Rebecca 136
Roche, Kevin 79, 296
Rockefeller, John D., III 133, 134
Rockefeller, Nelson 92
Rockefeller Center 118, 129, 133, 165, 252

Rockefeller Plaza 168
Rockwell, David 139
2 Rodeo Drive 192, 219
Rodríguez, Eduardo Luis 51, 52, 53, 54, 56, 57, 58
Rodríguez, Patricia 58
Rodríguez, Raúl 53
Rogers, Richard 38, 39–41, 114, 194, 195, 197, 200, 227,
    228, 297
Romero, Rocio 291–95
Rose, Marshall 136, 162
Rosenthal, Richard 247
Rosenthal, Tony 302
Ross, Stephen 147, 302
Roth, Emery 280, 281, 282, 284, 290, 302
Royal Institute of British Architects 195
Roy, Lindy 297, 298
Rudolph, Paul 72, 248
Ruppert, Colonel Jacob 152, 153, 155

Saarinen, Eero 33–34, 39, 40, 72, 79, 80–81, 134, 238
Saarinen, Eliel 80
Safdie, Moshe 146
Sagaponack 297, 299
Salk, Jonas 71, 74
Salomon Brothers headquarters 146, 147
SANAA 268, 269, 270
Sasaki Associates 46, 47
Scharoun, Hans 18
Scheeren, Ole 65
Schraeger, Ian 131, 160
Schuman Lichtenstein Claman Efron 280, 281, 289
Sciame, Frank J. 36
Scofidio, Ric 136, 138, 141, 231. *See also* Diller and
    Scofidio; Diller Scofidio + Renfro
Scott Brown, Denise 60, 61, 62, 87, 125. *See also* Venturi
    and Scott Brown
Scully, Vincent 70, 72, 302
Seagram Building 36, 84, 85, 87, 149, 191, 199, 288, 289, 303
Sears Tower 37
Seattle Public Library **20**, 20–23
Sejima, Kazuyo 268, 269, 270. *See also* SANAA
Selldorf, Annabelle 289, 298
September 11, 2001 149, 171, 172, 173. *See also* Ground Zero
Serra, Richard 218, 241, 243, 248
Shanghai 6, 65, 178, 179, 180, 181, 200, 286
Shea Stadium 93, 153
Shui On 180, 181
Shutze, Philip Trammell 189, 190, 192
Siegel, Robert 303. *See also* Gwathmey Siegel
Signature Theatre Company 175
Sills, Beverly 136, 137
Silverstein, Larry 171, 172, 173, 175, 208
Silvetti, Jorge 224. *See also* Machado and Silvetti
Skidmore, Owings & Merrill 86, 112, 118, 120, 134, 144–47,
    150, 288, 297
Skyscraper Museum 119, 124
skyscrapers. *See under specific building names*
SLCE Architects. *See* Schuman Lichtenstein Claman
    Efron
Smirke, Robert 233, 234, 235, 236
Smirke, Sydney 233, 236
Snøhetta 174
Soane, John 82, 196
SOHO China 67
Solomon R. Guggenheim Foundation 216
Spear, Laurinda 128, 129, 130. *See also* Arquitectonica
Speer, Albert 85, 205
sports stadiums 28–32, 152–55
Spreiregen, Paul 209, 210

Standard Oil Headquarters 145
Starck, Philippe 309
Steinbrenner, George 153
Stein, Clarence 299
Stern, Robert A. M. 130, 279, 281, 282, 283, 284–86, 290
St. Florian, Friedrich 202, 203–6
Stirling, James 194, 200, 201, 269
Stone, Edward Durell 71, 133, 145, 251, 270, 272, 273, 274.
    See also Goodwin and Stone
Stonorov, Oscar 72
St. Pancras Station 193, 234
Studio Pei Zhu 42, 44
Studios Architecture 156, 158
Sullivan, Louis 99, 112, 118, 239, 301
Sulzberger, Arthur, Jr. 156, 157
Sussman, Deborah 81
Sydney Opera House 134, 215

Taft, William Howard 153
Taniguchi, Yoshio 251–55
Tate Modern 30, 233
Taverne, Suzanna 235
technology, effect of on daily life 305–7
Terry, Quinlan 194
Thompson, Ventulett, Stainback 25
Thorn, George 263
Three on the Bund 181
Tiananmen Square 43, 67
1 Times Square 120, 160
Times Square, New York
    atmosphere of 126, 130–31, 150, 165
    "Disneyfication" of 165
    new architecture in 9, 116–21, 123–25, 128, 129, 151, 157.
    See also 42nd Street Development Project
Time Warner Center **144**, 145, 146, 147, 151, 286, 289, 302
Tishman Realty & Construction 128
Tobin, Austin 95
Toledo Museum of Art 269
Toyoto, Yasuhisa 18
Toys 'R' Us 9, 122, 123–26, 166
Trump, Donald 172, 302
Trump Tower 168, 279, 288
Tschumi, Bernard 247, 252
Tucker, Marcia 269
Turning Torso Tower **33**, 34–37
Tyng, Alexandra 70, 73, 74
Tyng, Anne 70, 150

Umemoto, Nanako 297
United Nations General Assembly Building 131
United Nations Plaza 279, 288
Universal Studios, Los Angeles 192, 219
Urban Glass House 289
Urban, Joseph 149, 150
USS *Arizona* Memorial 202
Utzon, Jørn 134

van Berkel, Ben 98
Vanna Venturi House **84**, 88
Varnedoe, Kirk 252
Venturi and Scott Brown 88, 89, 90
Venturi, Robert 60, 61, 62, 84, 87, 88, 89, 125, 296–97. *See
    also* Venturi and Scott Brown
Vietnam Veterans Memorial 202, 205, 209, 210
Viñoly, Rafael 25, 88, 146
Vivian Beaumont Theater 133, 136, 137, 138

Wainwright Building 239, 240
Walker Art Center, Minneapolis 31, 248

Walker, Peter 174
Wallace, Mike 105–10
Wallach Art Gallery, Columbia 92
Wall Street 104, 118, 130, 173, 174, 189, 298
Wal-Mart 53, 310
Walt Disney Concert Hall **16**, 16–19, 162, 303
Warhol, Andy 78, 241, 245
Washington, George 95, 135, 183, 184, 185, 210
Washington, John Augustine, Jr. 184–85
Washington Monument 203, 204, 210
Water Cube. *See* National Aquatics Center, Beijing
Westin Hotel 9, 10, 127–31
White, Stanford 86
Whitney Museum 85, 87, 137–38, 139, 248, 256, 257,
    258–59
Williams, Frank 278, 280, 290
Williams-Sonoma 308, 311
Wilson, Colin St. John 194
Wilson, Marc 265
Wolfe, Tom 189, 192
Wood, Benjamin 178, 179–81
Woolworth Building 117, 118
World Athletes Monument 188, 190–92
World Trade Center 12, 95, 117, 135, 139, 145, 171, 172, 173,
    174, 207, 208, 261
World War II 45, 110, 170, 202, 203, 205, 206
Wright, Frank Lloyd 84, 85
    and Daniel Burnham 97–98, 99, 101
    Fallingwater 183
    Guggenheim Museum, New York 150, 217, 218, 229,
        238, 262
    Johnson Wax headquarters, Wisconsin 239
    Price Tower 249
    San Fransisco shop 122–23
    Taliesins 82
    Unity Temple 240
Wright, Henry 299

Xintiandi, Shanghai 178–81

Yale Center for British Art 69, 235, 244
Yankees 152, 153, 155
Yankee Stadium 152–55

Zeckendorf, Arthur and William Lie 279, 286
Zuckerman, Mortimer 146, 147
Zumthor, Peter 239

Philip Friedman

Paul Goldberger is the architecture critic for *The New Yorker*. He also holds the Joseph Urban Chair in Design and Architecture at the New School in New York City. He began his career at the *New York Times,* where his architecture criticism was awarded the Pulitzer Prize for Distinguished Criticism, the highest award in journalism.

Goldberger is the author of several books, including the recently published *Why Architecture Matters*. His chronicle of the process of rebuilding Ground Zero, *Up from Zero: Politics, Architecture, and the Rebuilding of New York,* was named one of the *New York Times* Notable Books for 2004. He has also written *The City Observed: New York, The Skyscraper, On the Rise: Architecture and Design in a Post-Modern Age, Above New York,* and *The World Trade Center Remembered.*